W9-AXA-688

MY COUNTRY
AND MY PEOPLE

by
Lin Yutang

© 2010 Oxford City Press.

Truth does not depart from human nature. If what is regarded as truth departs from human nature, it may not be regarded as truth.

—CONFUCIUS

INTRODUCTION

ONE of the most important movements in China to-day is the discovery of their own country by young Chinese intellectuals. A generation ago the most progressive of their fathers were beginning to feel a stirring discontent with their own country. They were conscious, indeed the consciousness was forced upon them, that China as she had been in the past was not able to meet the dangerous and aggressive modernity of the West. I do not mean the political modernity so much as the march of economic, educational and military events. These Chinese fathers, fathers of the present generation in China, were the real revolutionists. They forced out of existence the old dynastic rule, they changed with incredible speed the system of education, with indefatigable zeal they planned and set up a scheme of modern government. No ancient government under an emperor ever accomplished with more imperial speed such tremendous changes in so great a country.

In this atmosphere of change, the present intellectual youth of China has grown up. Where the fathers imbibed the doctrine of Confucius and learned the classics and revolted against them, these young people have been battered by many forces of the new times. They have been taught something of science, something of Christianity, something of atheism, something of free love, something of communism, something of Western philosophy, something of modern militarism, something, in fact, of everything. In the midst of the sturdy medievalism of the masses of their countrymen the young intellectuals have been taught the most extreme of every culture. Intellectually they have been forced to the same great omissions that China has made physically. They have skipped, figuratively speaking, from the period of the unimproved country road to the aeroplane era. The omission was too great. The mind could not compensate for it. The spirit was lost in the conflict.

The first result, therefore, of the hiatus was undoubtedly to produce a class of young Chinese, both men and women, but chiefly men, who frankly did not know how to live in their own country or in the age in which their country still was. They were for the most part educated abroad, where they forgot the realities of their own race. It was easy enough for various revolutionary leaders to persuade these alienated minds that China's so-called backwardness was due primarily to political and material interference by foreign powers. The world was made the scapegoat for China's medievalism. Instead of realizing that China was in her own way making her own steps, slowly, it is true, and somewhat ponderously, toward modernity, it was easy hue and cry to say that if it had not been for foreigners she would have been already on an equality, in material terms, with other nations.

The result of this was a fresh revolution of a sort. China practically rid herself of her two great grievances outside of Japan, extraterritoriality and the tariff. No great visible change appeared as a consequence. It became apparent that what had been weaknesses were still weaknesses, and that these were inherent in the ideology of the people. It was found, for instance, that when a revolutionary leader became secure and entrenched he became conservative and as corrupt, too often, as an old style official. The same has been true in other histories. There were too many honest and intelligent young minds in China not to observe and accept the truth, that the outside world had very little to do with China's condition, and what she had to do with it could have been prevented if China had been earlier less sluggish and her leaders less blind and selfish.

Then followed a period of despair and frenzy and increased idealistic worship of the West. The evident prosperity of foreign countries was felt to be a direct fruit of Western scientific development. It was a time when the inferiority complex was rampant in China, and the young patriots were divided between mortification at what their country was and desire to conceal it from foreigners. There was no truth to be found in them, so far as their own country was concerned. They at once hated and admired the foreigners.

What would have happened if the West had continued prosperous and at peace cannot be said. It is enough that the

West did not so continue. The Chinese have viewed with interest and sometimes with satisfaction the world war, the depression, the breakdown of prosperity, and the failure of scientific men to prevent these disasters. They have begun to say to themselves that after all China is not so bad. Evidently there is hunger everywhere, there are bandits everywhere, and one people is not better than another, and if this is so, then perhaps China was right in olden times, and perhaps it is just as well to go back and see what the old Chinese philosophy was. At least it taught people to live with contentment and with enjoyment of small things if they had not the great ones, and it regulated life and provided a certain amount of security and safety. The recent interest in China on the part of the West, the wistfulness of certain Western persons who envy the simplicity and security of China's pattern of life and admire her arts and philosophy have also helped to inspire the young Chinese with confidence in themselves.

The result to-day is simply a reiteration of the old Biblical adage that the fathers have eaten sour grapes and the children's teeth are set on edge. Young China, being wearied of the revolutionary ardours of its fathers, is going back to old China. It is almost amusing to see the often self-conscious determin-ation to be really Chinese, to eat Chinese food, to live in Chinese ways, to dress in Chinese clothes. It is as much of a fad and a pose to be entirely Chinese these days among certain young westernized Chinese as it was for their fathers to wear foreign clothes and eat with knives and forks and want to go to Harvard. These present young people have worn foreign clothes all their lives and eaten foreign food and they did go to Harvard, and they know English literature infinitely better than their own, and now they are sick of it all and want to go back to their grandfathers.

The trend is apparent everywhere, and not only in the ex-ternals of dress and customs. Far more importantly is it to be seen in art and literature. The subject of modern Chinese novels of a few years ago, for instance, dealt chiefly with modern love situations, with semi-foreign liaisons, with rebellion against home and parents, and the whole tone was somewhat sickly and certainly totally unrooted in the country. There is still more than enough of this in both art and literature, but health is beginning to creep in, the health of life from plain people living plain and sturdy lives upon their earth. The young intellectuals are beginning to discover their own masses. They are beginning to find that life in the countryside, in small towns and villages, is the real and native life of China, fortunately still fairly untouched with the mixed modernism which has made their own lives unhealthy. They are beginning to feel themselves happy that there is this great solid foundation in their nation, and to turn to it eagerly for fresh inspiration. It is new to them, it is delightful, it is humorous, it is worth having, and above all, it is purely Chinese.

They have been helped to this new viewpoint, too. They would not, I think, have achieved it so well alone, and it is the West which has helped them. We of the West have helped them not only negatively, by exhibiting a certain sort of breakdown in our own civilization, but we have helped them positively, by our own trend toward elemental life. The Western interest in all proletarian movements has set young China to thinking about her own proletariat, and to discovering the extraordinary quality of her country people, maintaining their life pure and incredibly undisturbed by the world's confusion. It is natural that such tranquillity should greatly appeal to intellectuals in their own confusion and sense of being lost in the twisted times.

Communism, too, has helped them. Communism has brought about class consciousness, it has made the common man articulate and demanding, and since modern education in China has been available to the children of common people, they have already been given a sort of voice, at least, wherewith to speak for themselves, however inadequately. In the art and literature of the young Leftists in China there is a rapidly spreading perception of the value of the common man and woman of their country. The expression is still crude and too much influenced by foreign art, but the notion is there. One sometimes sees these days a peasant woman upon a canvas instead of a bird upon a bamboo twig, and the straining figure of a man pushing a wheelbarrow instead of goldfish flashing in a lotus pool.

Yet if we of the West were to wait for the interpretation of China until these newly released ones could find adequate and articulate voice, it would be to wait long—longer, perhaps, than our generation. Happily there are a few others, a few spirits large enough not to be lost in the confusion of the times, humorous enough to see life as it is, with the fine old humour of generations of sophistication and learning, keen enough to understand their own civilization as well as others, and wise enough to choose what is native to them and therefore truly their own. For a long time I have hoped that one of these few would write for us all a book about his own China, a real book, permeated with the essential spirit of the people. Time after time I have opened a book, eagerly and with hope, and time after time I have closed it again in disappointment, because it was untrue, because it was bombastic, because it was too fervent in defence of that which was too great to need defence. It was written to impress the foreigner, and therefore it was unworthy of China.

A book about China, worthy to be about China, can be none of these things. It must be frank and unashamed, because the real Chinese have always been a proud people, proud enough to be frank and unashamed of themselves and their ways. It must be wise and penetrative in its understanding, for the Chinese have been above all peoples wise and penetrative in their understanding of the human heart. It must be humorous, because humour is an essential part of Chinese nature, deep, mellow, kindly humour, founded upon the tragic knowledge and acceptance of life. It must be expressed in flowing, exact, beautiful words, because the Chinese have always valued the beauty of the exact and the exquisite. None but a Chinese could write such a book, and I had begun to think that as yet even no Chinese could write it, because it seemed impossible to find a modern English-writing Chinese who was not so detached from his own people as to be alien to them, and yet detached enough to comprehend their meaning, the meaning of their age and the meaning of their youth.

But suddenly, as all great books appear, this book appears, fulfilling every demand made upon it. It is truthful and not ashamed of the truth: it is written proudly and humorously and with beauty, seriously and with gaiety, appreciative and understanding of both old and new. It is, I think, the truest, the most profound, the most complete, the most important book yet written about China. And, best of all, it is written by a Chinese, a modern, whose roots are firmly in the past, but whose rich flowering is in the present.

PEARL S. BUCK.

PREFACE

IN this book I have tried only to communicate my opinions, which I have arrived at after some long and painful thought and reading and introspection. I have not tried to enter into arguments or prove my different theses, but I will stand justified or condemned by this book, as Confucius once said of his *Spring and Autumn Annals*. China is too big a country, and her national life has too many facets, for her not to be open to the most diverse and contradictory interpretations. And I shall always be able to assist with very convenient material anyone who wishes to hold opposite theses. But truth is truth and will overcome clever human opinions. It is given to man only at rare moments to perceive the truth, and it is these moments of perception that will survive, and not individual opinions. Therefore, the most formidable marshalling of evidence can often lead one to conclusions which are mere learned nonsense. For the presentation of such perceptions, one needs a simpler, which is really a subtler, style. For truth can never be proved; it can only be hinted at.

It is also inevitable that I should offend many writers about China, especially my own countrymen and great patriots. These great patriots—I have nothing to do with them, for their god is not my god, and their patriotism is not my patriotism. Perhaps I too love my own country, but I take care to conceal it before them, for one may wear the cloak of patriotism to tatters, and in these tatters be paraded through the city streets to death, in China or the rest of the world.

I am able to confess because, unlike these patriots, I am not ashamed of my country. And I can lay bare her troubles because I have not lost hope. China is bigger than her little patriots, and does not require their whitewashing. She will, as she always did, right herself again.

Nor do I write for the patriots of the West. For I fear more their appreciative quotations from me than the misunderstandings of my countrymen. I write only for the men of simple common sense, that simple common sense for which ancient China was so distinguished, but which is so rare to-day. My book can only be understood from this simple point of view. To these people who have not lost their sense of ultimate human values, to them alone I speak. For they alone will understand me.

My thanks are due to Pearl S. Buck who, from the beginning to the end, gave me kind encouragement and who personally read through the entire manuscript before it was sent to the press and edited it, to Mr. Richard J. Walsh who offered valuable criticism while the book was in progress, and to Miss Lillian Peffer, who styled the manuscript, read the proofs and made the index. Acknowledgements are also due to Mrs. Selskar M. Gunn, Bernardine Szold Fritz and Baroness Ungern-Sternberg, who, sometimes singly and sometimes in chorus, nagged me into writing this book. Lastly, I am indebted to my wife who patiently went through with me the less pleasant aspects of authorship, which only an author's wife could appreciate.

THE AUTHOR.

June, 1935
Shanghai

CONTENTS

CONTENTS

CONTENTS

Appendices

ILLUSTRATIONS

PART ONE

BASES

WHEN one is in China, one is compelled to think about her, with compassion always, with despair sometimes, and with discrimination and understanding very rarely. For one either loves or hates China. Perhaps even when one does not live in China one sometimes thinks of her as an old, great big country which remains aloof from the world and does not quite belong to it. That aloofness has a certain fascination. But if one comes to China, one feels engulfed and soon stops thinking. One merely feels she is there, a tremendous existence somewhat too big for the human mind to encompass, a seemingly inconsequential chaos obeying its own laws of existence and enacting its own powerful life-drama, at times tragic, at times comical, but always intensely and boisterously real; then after a while, one begins to think again, with wonder and amazement.

This time, the reaction will be temperamental; it merely indicates whether one is a romantic cosmopolitan individual or a conceited, self-satisfied prig, one either likes or dislikes China, and then proceeds to justify one's likes or dislikes. That is just as well, for we must take some sort of attitude toward China to justify ourselves as intelligent beings. We grope for reasons, and begin to tell one another little anecdotes, trifles of everyday life, escaped or casual words of conversation, things of tremendous importance that make us philosophers and enable us to become, with great equanimity, either her implacable critics, allowing nothing good for her, or else her ardent, romantic admirers. Of course, these generalizations are rather silly. But that is how human opinions are formed all over the world, and it is unavoidable. Then we set about arguing with one another. Some always come out from the argument supremely satisfied of their rightness, self-assured that they have an opinion of China and of the Chinese people. They are the happy people who rule the world and import merchandise from one part of it to another, and who are always in the right. Others find themselves beset with doubts and perplexities, with a feeling of awe and bewilderment, perhaps of awe and mystification and they end where they began. But all of us feel China is there, a great mystical *Dasein*.

For China is the greatest mystifying and stupefying fact in the modern world, and that not only because of her age or her geographical greatness. She is the oldest living nation with a continuous culture; she has the largest population; once she was the greatest empire in the world, and she was a conqueror; she gave the world some of its most important inventions; she has a literature, a philosophy, a wisdom of life entirely her own; and in the realms of art, she soared where others merely made an effort to flap their wings. And yet, to-day she is undoubtedly the most chaotic, the most misruled nation on earth, the most pathetic and most helpless, the most unable to pull herself together and forge ahead. God—if there be a God—intended her to be a first-class nation among the peoples of the earth, and she has chosen to take a back seat with Guatemala at the League of Nations; and the entire League of Nations, with the best will in the world, cannot help her—cannot help her to pull her own house in order, cannot help her to stop her own civil wars, cannot help her to save herself from her own scholars and militarists, her own revolutionists and gentry politicians.

Meanwhile—and this is the most amazing fact—she is the least concerned about her own salvation. Like a good gambler, she took the loss of a slice of territory the size of Germany itself without a wince. And while General T'ang Yülin was beating a world record retreat and losing half a million square miles in eight days, two generals, an uncle and a nephew, were matching their strength in Szechuen. One begins to wonder whether God will win out in the end, whether God Himself can help China to become a first-class nation in spite of herself.

And another doubt arises in one's mind: What is China's destiny? Will she survive as she so successfully did in the past, and in a way that no other old nation was able to do? Did

God really intend her to be a first-class nation? Or is she merely "Mother Earth's miscarriage"?

Once she had a destiny. Once she was a conqueror. Now her greatest destiny seems to be merely to exist, to survive, and one cannot but have faith in her ability to do so, when one remembers how she has survived the ages, after the beauty that was Greece and the glory that was Rome are long vanished, remembers how she has ground and modelled foreign truths into her own likeness and absorbed foreign races into her own blood. This fact of her survival, of her great age, is evidently something worth pondering upon. There is something due an old nation, a respect for hoary old age that should be applied to nations as to individuals. Yes, even to mere old age, even to mere survival.

For whatever else is wrong, China has a sound instinct for life, a strange supernatural, extraordinary vitality. She has led a life of the instinct; she has adjusted herself to economic, political and social environments that might have spelled disaster to a less robust racial constitution; she has received her share of nature's bounty, has clung to her flowers and birds and hills and dales for her inspiration and moral support, which alone have kept her heart whole and pure and prevented the race from civic social degeneration. She has chosen to live much in the open, to bask in the sunlight, to watch the evening glow, to feel the touch of the morning dew and to smell the fragrance of hay and of the moist earth; through her poetry, through the poetry of habits of life as well as through the poetry of words, she has learned to refresh her, alas! too often wounded, soul. In other words, she has managed to reach grand old age in the same way as human individuals do by living much in the open and having a great deal of sunlight and fresh air. But she has also lived through hard times, through recurrent centuries of war and pestilence, and through natural calamities and human misrule. With a grim humour and somewhat coarse nerves, she has weathered them all, and somehow she has always righted herself. Yes, great age, even mere great age, is something to be wondered at.

Now that she has reached grand old age, she is beyond bodily and spiritual sorrows, and one would have thought, at times, beyond hope and beyond redemption. Is it the strength or the weakness of old age, one wonders? She has defied the world, and has taken a nonchalant attitude toward it, which her old age entitles her to do. Whatever happens, her placid life flows on unperturbed, insensible to pain and to misery, impervious to shame and to ambition—the little human emotions that agitate young breasts—and undaunted even by the threat of immediate ruin and collapse for the last two centuries. Success and failure have ceased to touch her; calamities and death have lost their sting; and the overshadowing of her national life for a period of a few centuries has ceased to have any meaning. Like the sea in the Nietzschean analogy, she is greater than all the fish and shell-fish and jelly-fish in her, greater than the mud and refuse thrown into her. She is greater than the lame propaganda and petulance of all her returned students, greater than the hypocrisy, shame and greed of all her petty officials and turncoat generals and fence-riding revolutionists, greater than her wars and pestilence, greater than her dirt and poverty and famines. For she has survived them all. Amidst wars and pestilence, surrounded by her poor children and grandchildren, Merry Old China quietly sips her tea and smiles on, and in her smile I see her real strength. She quietly sips her tea and smiles on, and in her smile I detect at times a mere laziness to change and at others a conservatism that savours of haughtiness. Laziness or haughtiness, which? I do not know. But somewhere in her soul lurks the cunning of an old dog, and it is a cunning that is strangely impressive. What a strange old soul! What a great old soul!

II

But what price greatness? Carlyle has said somewhere that the first impression of a really great work of art is always unnerving to the point of painfulness. It is the lot of the great to be misunderstood, and so it is China's lot. China has been greatly, magnificently misunderstood. Greatness is often the term we confer on what we do not understand and wish to have done with. Between being well understood, however, and being called great, China would have preferred the former, and it would have been better for everybody all round. But how is China to be understood? Who will be her interpreters? There is that long history of hers, covering a multitude of kings and emperors and sages and poets and scholars and brave mothers and talented women. There are her arts and philosophies, her paintings and her theatres, which provide the common people with all the moral notions of good and evil, and that tremendous mass of folk literature and folklore. The language alone constitutes an almost hopeless barrier. Can China be understood merely through pidgin English? Is the Old China Hand to pick up an understanding of the soul of China from his cook and amah? Or shall it be from his Number One Boy? Or shall it be from his compradore and shroff, or by reading the correspondence of the *North China Daily News?* The proposition is manifestly unfair.

Indeed, the business of trying to understand a foreign nation with a foreign culture, especially one so different from one's own as China's, is usually not for the mortal man. For this work there is need for broad, brotherly feeling, for the feeling of the common bond of humanity and the cheer of good fellowship. One must feel with the pulse of the heart as well as see with the eyes of the mind. There must be, too, a certain detachment, not from the country under examination, for that is always so, but from oneself and one's subconscious notions, and from the deeply imbedded notions of one's childhood and the equally tyrannous ideas of one's adult days, from those big words with capital letters like Democracy, Prosperity, Capital, and Success and Religion and Dividends. One needs a little detachment, and a little simplicity of mind, too, that simplicity of mind so well typified by Robert Burns, one of the most Scottish and yet most universal of all poets, who strips our souls bare and reveals our common humanity and the loves and sorrows that common humanity is heir to. Only with that detachment and that simplicity of mind can one understand a foreign nation.

Who will, then, be her interpreters? The problem is an almost insoluble one. Certainly not the sinologues and librarians abroad who see China only through the reflection of the Confucian classics. The true Europeans in China do not speak Chinese, and the true Chinese do not speak English. The Europeans who speak Chinese too well develop certain mental habits akin to the Chinese and are regarded by their compatriots as "queer." The Chinese who speak English too well and develop Western mental habits are "denationalized," or they may not even speak Chinese, or speak it with an English accent. So by a process of elimination, it would seem that we have to put up with the Old China Hand, and that we have largely to depend upon his understanding of pidgin.

The Old China Hand, or O.C.H.—let us stop to picture him, for he is important as your only authority on China. He has been well described by Mr. Arthur Ransome.[1] But to my mind, he is a vivid personality, and one can now easily picture him in the imagination. Let us make no mistake about him. He may be the son of a missionary, or a captain or a pilot, or a secretary in the consular service, or he may be a merchant to whom China is just a market for selling sardines and "sunkist" oranges. He is not always uneducated; in fact, he may be a brilliant journalist, with one eye to a political advisorship and the other to a loan commission. He may even be very well informed within his limits, the limits of a man who cannot talk three syllables of Chinese and depends on his English-speaking Chinese friends for his supplies of information. But he keeps on with his adventure and he plays golf and his golf helps to keep him fit. He drinks Lipton's tea and reads the *North China Daily News*, and his spirit revolts against the morning reports of banditry and kidnapping and recurrent civil wars, which spoil his breakfast for him. He is well shaved and dresses more neatly than his Chinese associates, and his boots are better shined than they would be in England, although this is no credit to him, for the Chinese boys are such good boot-blacks. He rides a distance of three or four miles from his home to his office every morning, and believes himself desired at Miss Smith's tea. He may have no aristocratic blood in his veins nor ancestral oil portraits in his halls, but he can always circumvent that by going further back in history and

[1] *The Chinese Puzzle*, especially the chapter on "The Shanghai Mind."

discovering that his forefathers in the primeval forests had the right blood in them, and that sets his mind at peace and relieves him of all anxiety to study things Chinese. But he is also uncomfortable every time his business takes him through Chinese streets where the heathen eyes all stare at him. He takes his handkerchief and vociferously blows his nose with it and bravely endures it, all the while in a blue funk. He broadly surveys the wave of blue-dressed humanity. It seems to him their eyes are not quite so slant as the shilling-shocker covers represent them to be. Can these people stab one in the back? It seems unbelievable in the beautiful sunlight, but one never knows, and the courage and sportsmanship which he learned at the cricket field all leave him. Why, he would rather be knocked in the head by a cricket bat than go through those crooked streets again! Yes, it was *fear*, primeval fear of the Unknown.

But to him, it is not just that. It is his *humanity* that cannot stand the sight of human misery and poverty, as understood in his own terms. He simply cannot stand being pulled by a human beast of burden in a rickshaw—he has to have a car. His car is not just a car, it is a moving covered corridor that leads from his home to his office and protects him from Chinese humanity. He will not leave his car and his civilization. He tells Miss Smith so at tea, saying that a car in China is not a luxury but a necessity. That three-mile ride of an enclosed mind in an enclosed glass case from the home to the office he takes every day of his twenty-five years in China, although he does not mention this fact when he goes home to England and signs himself "An Old Resident Twenty-Five Years in China" in correspondence to the London *Times*. It reads very impressively. Of course, he should know what he is talking about.

Meanwhile, that three-mile radius has seldom been exceeded, except when he goes on cross-country paper hunts over Chinese farm fields, but then he is out in the oepn and knows how to defend himself. But in this he is mistaken, for he never has to, and this he knows himself, for he merely says so, when he is out for sport. He has never been invited to Chinese homes, has sedulously avoided Chinese restaurants, and has never read a single line of Chinese newspapers. He goes to the longest bar in the world of an evening, sips his cocktail and picks up and imbibes and exchanges bits of sailors' tales on the China coast handed down from the Portuguese sailors, and is sorry to find that Shanghai is not Sussex, and generally behaves as he would in England.[1] He feels happy when he learns that the Chinese are beginning to observe Christmas and make progress, and feels amazed when he is not understood in English; he walks as if the whole lot of them did not exist for him, and does not say "sorry" even in English when he steps on a fellow-passenger's toes; yes, he has not even learned the Chinese equivalents of "*danke sehr*" and "*bitte schön*" and "*verzeihen Sie*," the minimum moral obligations of even a passing tourist, and complains of anti-foreignism and despairs because even the pillaging of the Pekin palaces after the Boxer Uprising has not taught the Chinese a lesson. There is your authority on China. Oh, for a common bond of humanity!

All this one can understand, and it is even quite natural, and should not be mentioned here were it not for the fact that it bears closely on the formation of opinions on China in the West. One needs only to think of the language difficulty, of the almost impossible learning of the Chinese writing, of the actual political, intellectual and artistic chaos in present-day China, and of the vast differences in customs between the Chinese and the Westerners. The plea here is essentially for a better understanding on a higher level of intelligence. Yet it is difficult to deny the Old China Hand the right to write books and articles about China, simply because he cannot read the Chinese newspapers. Nevertheless, such books and articles must necessarily remain on the level of the gossip along the world's longest bar.

There are exceptions, of course—a Sir Robert Hart or a Bertrand Russell, for example—who are able to see the meaning

---

[1] A writer signing himself "J. D." says in an article on "Englishmen in China" published in *The New Statesman*, London: "His life is spent between his office and the club. In the former, he is surrounded by foreigners as equals or superiors and by Chinese as inferiors—clerks and so forth. In the latter, except for the servants, he sees nothing but foreigners, from whom every night he hears complaints about Chinese dishonesty and stupidity, interspersed by stories of the day's work, and by discussions on sport, which is the one thing that saves the Englishman in China. It is the only alternative to abuse of the Chinese."

in a type of life so different from one's own, but for one Sir
Robert Hart there are ten thousand Rodney Gilberts, and for
one Bertrand Russell there are ten thousand H. G. W. Wood-
heads. The result is a constant, unintelligent elaboration of
the Chinaman as a stage fiction, which is as childish as it is
untrue and with which the West is so familiar, and a con-
tinuation of the early Portuguese sailors' tradition minus the
sailors' obscenity of language, but with essentially the same
sailors' obscenity of mind.   .

The Chinese sometimes wonder among themselves why
China attracts only sailors and adventurers to her coast.
To understand that, one would have to read H. B. Morse
and trace the continuity of that sailor tradition to the present
day, and observe the similarities between the early Portuguese
sailors and the modern O.C.H.s in their general outlook, their
interests and the natural process of selection and force of circumstances which have washed them ashore on this corner of the
earth, and the motives which drove, and are still driving, them
to this heathen country—gold and adventure. Gold and
adventure which in the first instance drove Columbus, the
greatest sailor-adventurer of them all, to seek a route to China.

Then one begins to understand that continuity, begins to
understand how that Columbus-sailor tradition has been so
solidly and equitably carried on, and one feels a sort of pity
for China; a pity that it is not our humanity but our gold and
our capacities as buying animals which have attracted the
Westerners to this Far Eastern shore. It is gold and success, Henry James's "bitch-goddess," which have bound the
Westerners and the Chinese together, and thrown them into this
whirlpool of obscenity, with not a single human, spiritual tie
among them. They do not admit this to themselves, the Chinese
and the English; so the Chinese asks the Englishman why he
does not leave the country if he hates it so, and the Englishman
asks in retort why the Chinese does not leave the foreign
settlements, and both of them do not know how to reply. As
it is, the Englishman does not bother to make himself understood to the Chinese, and the true Chinese bothers even less
to make himself understood to the Englishman.

III

But do the Chinese understand themselves? Will they be China's best interpreters? Self-knowledge is proverbially difficult, much more so in a circumstance where a great deal of wholesome, sane-minded criticism is required. Assuredly no language difficulty exists for the educated Chinese, but that long history of China is difficult for him also to master; her arts, philosophies, poetry, literature and the theatre are difficult for him to penetrate and illuminate with a clear and beautiful understanding; and his own fellow-men, the fellow-passenger in a street car or a former fellow-student now pretending to rule the destiny of a whole province, are for him, too, difficult to forgive.

For the mass of foreground details, which swamps the foreign observer, swamps the modern Chinese as well. Perhaps he has even less the cool detachment of the foreign observer. In his breast is concealed a formidable struggle, or several struggles. There is the conflict between his ideal and his real China, and a more formidable conflict between his primeval clan-pride and his moments of admiration for the stranger. His soul is torn by a conflict of loyalties belonging to opposite poles, a loyalty to old China, half romantic and half selfish, and a loyalty to open-eyed wisdom which craves for change and a ruthless clean-sweeping of all that is stale and putrid and dried up and mouldy. Sometimes it is a more elementary conflict between shame and pride, between sheer family loyalty and a critical ashamedness for the present state of things, instincts wholesome in themselves. But sometimes his clan-pride gets the better of him, and between proper pride and mere reactionism there is only a thin margin, and sometimes his instinct of shame gets the better of him, and between a sincere desire for reform and a mere shallow modernity and worship of the modern bitch-goddess, there is also only a very thin margin. To escape that is indeed a delicate task.

Where is that unity of understanding to be found? To combine real appreciation with critical appraisal, to see with the mind and feel with the heart, to make the mind and the heart at one, is no easy state of grace to attain to. For it involves no less than the salvaging of an old culture, like the sorting of family treasures, and even the connoisseur's eyes are sometimes deceived and his fingers sometimes falter. It requires courage and that rare thing, honesty, and that still rarer thing, a constant questioning activity of the mind.

But he has a distinct advantage over the foreign observer. For he is a Chinese, and as a Chinese, he not only sees with his mind but he also feels with his heart, and he knows tha⁺ the blood, surging in his veins in tides of pride and shame is Chinese blood, a mystery of mysteries which carries withii its bio-chemical constitution the past and the future of China bearer of all its pride and shame and of all its glories and it iniquities. The analogy of the family treasure is therefor(incomplete and inadequate, for that unconscious nationa. heritage is within him and is part of himself. He has perhap: learned to play English football but he does not love football; he has perhaps learned to admire American efficiency, but his soul revolts against efficiency; he has perhaps learned to use table napkins, but he hates table napkins, and all through Schubert's melodies and Brahms' songs, he hears, as an overtone, the echo of age-old folk songs and pastoral lyrics of the Orient, luring him back. He explores the beauties and glories of the West, but he comes back to the East, his Oriental blood overcoming him when he is approaching forty. He sees the portrait of his father wearing a Chinese silk cap, and he discards his Western dress and slips into Chinese gowns and slippers, oh, so comfortable, so peaceful and comfortable, for in his Chinese gowns and slippers his soul comes to rest. He cannot understand the Western dog-collar any more, and wonders how he ever stood it for so long. He does not play football any more, either, but begins to cultivate Chinese hygiene, and saunters along in the mulberry fields and bamboo groves and willow banks for his exercise, and even this is not a "country walk" as the English understand it, but just an Oriental saunter, good for the body and good for the soul. He hates the word "exercise." Exercise for what? It is a ridiculous Western notion. Why, even the sight of respectable grown-up men dashing about in a field for a ball now seems ridiculous, supremely ridiculous; and more ridiculous still, the wrapping oneself up in hot flannels and woollen sweaters after the game on a hot summer day. Why all the bother? He reflects. He remembers he used to enjoy it himself, but then he was young and immature and he was not himself. It was but a passing fancy, and he has not really the instinct for sport. No, he is born differently; he is born for kowtowing and for quiet and peace, and not for football and the dog-collar and table napkins and efficiency. He sometimes thinks of himself as a pig, and the Westerner as a dog, and the dog worries the pig, but the pig only grunts, and it may even be a grunt of satisfaction. Why, he even wants to be a pig, a real pig, for it is really so very comfortable, and he does not envy the dog for his collar and his dog-efficiency and his bitch-goddess success. All he wants is that the dog leave him alone.

That is how it is with the modern Chinese as he surveys Eastern and Western culture. It is the only way in which the Eastern culture should be surveyed and understood. For he has a Chinese father and a Chinese mother, and every time he talks of China, he thinks of his father and his mother or of the memories of them. It was a life, their lives, so full of courage and patience and suffering and happiness and fortitude, lives untouched by the modern influence, but lives no less grand and noble and humble and sincere. Then does he truly understand China. That seems to me to be the only way of looking at China, and of looking at any foreign nation, by searching, not for the exotic but for the common human values, by penetrating beneath the superficial quaintness of manners and looking for real courtesy, by seeing beneath the strange women's costumes and looking for real womanhood and motherhood, by observing the boys' naughtiness and studying the girls' day-dreams. This boys' naughtiness and these girls' day-dreams and the ring of children's laughter and the patter of children's feet and the weeping of women and the sorrows of men—they are all alike, and only through the sorrows of men and the weeping of women can we truly understand a nation. The differences are only in the forms of social behaviour. This is the basis of all sound international criticism.

Chapter One

THE CHINESE PEOPLE

I. NORTH AND SOUTH

IN the study of any period of literature or of any epoch of history, the final and highest effort is always an attempt to gain a close view of the man in that period or epoch, for behind the creations of literature and the events of history there is always the individual who is after all of prime interest to us. One thinks of a Marcus Aurelius or a Lucian in the times of decadent Rome, or of a François Villon in the medieval ages, and the times seem at once familiar and understandable to us. Names like "the age of Johnson" are more suggestive to us than a name like "the eighteenth century," for only by re-calling how Johnson lived, the inns he frequented, and the friends with whom he held conversations does the period become real to us. Perhaps the life of a lesser literary light or of an ordinary Londoner in Johnson's time would be just as instructive, but an ordinary Londoner could not be very interesting, because ordinary people throughout the ages are all alike. Whether ordinary people drink ale or Lipton's tea is entirely a matter of social accident, and can make no important difference because they are ordinary men.

That Johnson smoked and that he frequented eighteenth-century inns is, however, of great historical importance. Great souls react in a peculiar way to their social environment and make it of importance to us. They have that quality of genius which affects and is affected by the things they touch; they are influenced by the books they read and by the women with whom they come into contact, which make no impress on other lesser men. In them is lived to its full the life of their age or generation; they absorb all there is to absorb and respond with finest and most powerful sensitiveness.

Yet, in dealing with a country the common man cannot be ignored. Ancient Greece was not entirely peopled by Sophocleses and Elizabethan England was not strewn with Bacons and Shakespeares. To talk of Greece and only think of Sophocles and Pericles and Aspasia is to get a wrong picture of the Athenians. One has to supplement it with an occasional glimpse of the son of Sophocles who sued his father for incompetency in managing his family affairs, and with characters from Aristophanes, who were not all in love with beauty and occupied in the pursuit of truth, but who were often drunk, gluttonous, quarrelsome, venal and fickle, even as were common Athenians. Perhaps the fickle Athenians help us to understand the downfall of the Athenian republic as much as Pericles and Aspasia help us to understand its greatness. Individually they are naught, but taken in the aggregate they influence to a very large measure the course of national events. In the past epoch, it may be difficult to reconstruct them, but in a living country the common man is always with us.

But who is the common man, and what is he? The Chinaman exists only as a general abstraction in our minds. Apart from the cultural unity which binds the Chinese people as a nation, the southern Chinese differ probably as much from the northerners, in temperament, physique and habits, as the Mediterraneans differ from the Nordic peoples in Europe. Happily, within the orbit of the Chinese culture there has not been a rise of nationalism, but only of provincialism, which after all was what made peace within the empire possible for centuries. The common historical tradition, the written language, which has in a singular way solved the problem of Esperanto in China, and the cultural homogeneity achieved through centuries of slow, peaceful penetration of a civilization over comparatively docile aborigines, have achieved for China the basis of the common brotherhood so much desirable now in Europe. Even the spoken language presents no difficulty nearly so great as confronts Europe to-day. A native of Manchuria can, with some difficulty, make himself understood in south-west Yunnan, a linguistic feat made possible by a slow colonization process and helped greatly by the system of writing, the visible symbol of China's unity.

This cultural homogeneity sometimes makes us forget that racial differences, differences of blood, do exist within the country. At close range the abstract notion of a Chinaman disappears and breaks up into a picture of a variety of races, different in their stature, temperament and mental make-up. It is only when we try to put a southern commander over northern soldiers that we are abruptly reminded of the existing differences. For on the one hand we have the northern Chinese, acclimatized to simple thinking and hard living, tall and stalwart, hale, hearty and humorous, onion-eating and fun-loving, children of nature, who are in every way more Mongolic and more conservative than the conglomeration of peoples near Shanghai and who suggest nothing of their loss of racial vigour. They are the Honan boxers, the Shantung bandits and the imperial brigands who have furnished China with all the native imperial dynasties, the raw material from which the characters of Chinese novels of wars and adventure are drawn.

Down the south-east coast, south of the Yangtse, one meets a different type, inured to ease and culture and sophistication, mentally developed but physically retrograde, loving their poetry and their comforts, sleek undergrown men and slim neurasthenic women, fed on birds'-nest soup and lotus seeds, shrewd in business, gifted in *belles-lettres*, and cowardly in war, ready to roll on the ground and cry for mamma before the lifted fist descends, offsprings of the cultured Chinese families who crossed the Yangtse with their books and paintings during the end of the Ch'in Dynasty, when China was overrun by barbaric invaders.

South in Kwangtung, one meets again a different people, where racial vigour is again in evidence, where people eat like men and work like men, enterprising, carefree, spendthrift, pugnacious, adventurous, progressive and quick-tempered, where beneath the Chinese culture a snake-eating aborigines tradition persists, revealing a strong admixture of the blood of the ancient *Yüeh* inhabitants of southern China. North and south of Hankow, in the middle of China, the loud-swearing and intrigue-loving Hupeh people exist, who are compared by the people of other provinces to "nine-headed birds in heaven" because they never say die, and who think pepper not hot enough to eat until they have fried it in oil, while the Hunan people, noted for their soldiery and their dogged persistence, offer a pleasanter variety of these descendants of the ancient Ch'u warriors.

Movements of trade and the imperial rule of sending scholars to official posts outside their native provinces [1] have brought about some mixture of the peoples and have smoothed out these provincial differences, but as a whole they continue to exist. For the significant fact remains that the northerner is essentially a conqueror and the southerner is essentially a trader, and that of all the imperial brigands who have founded Chinese dynasties, none have come from south of the Yangtse. The tradition developed that no rice-eating southerners could mount the dragon throne, and only noodle-eating northerners could. In fact, with the exception of the founders of the T'ang and Chou Dynasties, who emerged from north-east Kansu and were therefore Turkish-suspect, all the founders of the great dynasties have come from a rather restricted mountainous area, somewhere around the Lunghai Railway, which includes eastern Honan, southern Hopei, western Shantung and northern Anhui. It should not be difficult to determine the mileage of the radius within which imperial babies were born with a point on the Lunghai Railway as the centre of the area. The founder of the Han Dynasty came from Peihsien in modern Hsuchow, that of the Ch'in Dynasty came from Honan, that of the Sung Dynasty came from Chohsien in southern Hopei, and Chu Hungwu of the Ming Dynasty came from Fengyang in Honan.

To this day, with the exception of Chiang Kaishek of Chekiang whose family history has not been made public, the generals for the most part come from Hopei, Shantung, Anhui and Honan, also with the Lunghai Railway as the central point. Shantung is responsible for Wu P'eifu, Chang Tsungch'ang, Sun Ch'üanfang and Lu Yunghsiang. Hopei gives us Ch'i Hsüehyüan, Li Chinglin, Chang Chihchiang and Lu Chunglin. Honan produced Yüan Shihk'ai and Anhui produced Feng Yühsiang and Tuan Ch'ijui. Kiangsu has produced no great generals, but has given us some very fine hotel

---

[1] Often the families of these officials settle down in their new homes.

boys. Over half a century ago, Hunan in the middle of China produced Tseng Kuofan, the exception that proves the rule; for although Tseng was a first-class scholar and general, being born south of the Yangtse and consequently a rice-eater instead of a noodle-eater, he was destined to end up by being a high-minded official and not by founding a new dynasty for China. For this latter task, one needed the rawness and ruggedness of the North, a touch of genuine lovable vagabondage, the gift of loving war and turmoil for its own sake—and a contempt for fair play, learning and Confucian ethics until one is sitting secure on the dragon throne, when Confucian monarchism can be of extreme usefulness.

The raw, rugged North and the soft, pliable South—one can see these differences in their language, music and poetry. Observe the contrast between the Shensi songs, on the one hand, sung to the metallic rhythm of hard wooden tablets and keyed to a high pitch like the Swiss mountain songs, suggestive of the howling winds on mountain tops and broad pastures and desert sand-dunes, and on the other, the indolent Soochow crooning, something that is between a sigh and a snore, throaty, nasal, and highly suggestive of a worn-out patient of asthma whose sighs and groans have by force of habit become swaying and rhythmic. In language, one sees the difference between the sonorous, clear-cut rhythm of Pekingese mandarin that pleases by its alternate light and shade, and the soft and sweet babbling of Soochow women, with round-lip vowels and circumflex tones, where force of emphasis is not expressed by a greater explosion but by long-drawn-out and finely nuanced syllables at the end of sentences.

The story is recounted of a northern colonel who, on reviewing a Soochow company, could not make the soldiers move by his explosive "Forward March!" The captain who had stayed a long time in Soochow and who understood the situation asked permission to give the command in his own way. The permission was granted. Instead of the usual clear-cut *"K'aipu chou!"* he gave a genuine persuasive Soochow *"kebu tser nyiaaaaaaaah!"* and lo and behold! the Soochow company moved.

In poetry, this difference is strikingly illustrated in the

poems of the North and the South during the fourth, fifth and sixth centuries, when northern China was for the first time submerged under a Tartar rule, and the cultured Chinese migrated southward. For it was a time when sentimental love lyrics flourished in the southern courts, and the southern rulers were many of them great lyric poets, while a peculiar form of love ditties, the *tzüyehko*, developed among the people. A contrast between this sentimental poetry and the fresh, naïve poetry of the North would be highly instructive. So sang the anonymous poet of the South in the popular ditties:

> Kill the ever-crowing cock!
> Shoot the early announcer of the dawn!
> That there might be an uninterrupted
> Rolling darkness till Next Year's morn!

Or again:

> The roads are muddy and forsaken,
> Despite the cold I came to thee.
> Go and look at the footprints in snow,
> If thou wilt not believe me.

During the Southern Sung Dynasty, we saw a peculiar development of a sentimental lyric in intricate metre, the *tz'u*, which invariably sang of the sad lady in her boudoir, and her tearful red candles at night and sweet-flavoured rouge and eyebrow pencils, and silk curtains and beaded window screens and painted rails and departed springs, and pining lovers and emaciated sweethearts. It was natural that a people given to this kind of sentimental poetry should be conquered by a northern people who had but short, naïve lines of poetry, taken, as it were, direct and without embellishment from the dreary northern landscape.

> Down by the Chehleh river,
> Beneath the Yin hills,
> Like an inverted cup is the sky
> That covers the wasteland.

Enormous is the earth,
And the sky is a deep blue;
The wind blows, the tall grass bends,
And the sheep and cattle come into view.

It was with this song that a northern general, after suffering a heavy defeat, rallied his soldiers and sent them again to battle. And in contrast to the southern songs of love, we have a general singing about a newly bought broadsword:

I have just bought me a five-foot knife,
I swing it with a gleaming cadence.
I fondle it three times a day,
I won't change it for fifteen maidens!

Another song handed down to us reads:

In the distance I descry the Mengchin river,
The willows and poplars stand in silent grace.
I am a Mongol's son,
And don't know Chinese lays.
A good rider requires a swift horse,
And a swift horse requires a good rider.
When it clatters off amidst a cloud of dust,
You know then who wins and who's the outsider.[1]

Lines like these open up a vista of speculation as to the differences of northern and southern blood that went into the make-up of the Chinese race, and seem to make it possible to understand how a nation subjected to two thousand years of kowtowing and indoor living and a civilization without popular sports could avoid the fate of civic racial degeneration that overtook Egypt, Greece and Rome and the other ancient civilizations. How has China done it?

---

[1] These songs are quoted by Dr. Hu Shih in support of the same thesis.

II. DEGENERATION

Degeneration is a highly misleading term, for it can only be relative in meaning. Since the invention of the flush toilet and the vacuum carpet cleaner, the modern man seems to judge a man's moral standards by his cleanliness, and thinks a dog the more highly civilized for having a weekly bath and a winter wrapper round his belly. I have heard sympathetic foreigners talking of Chinese farmers "living like beasts," whose first step of salvation would seem to lie in a generous disinfection of their huts and belongings.

Yet it is not dirt but the fear of dirt which is the sign of man's degeneration, and it is dangerous to judge a man's physical and moral sanity by outside standards. Actually, the European man living in overheated apartments and luxurious cars is less fitted to survive than the Chinese farmer living in his lowly and undisinfected hut. Nor is cruelty, natural in all children and savages, a sign of degeneration; rather the fear of pain and suffering is a sign of it. The dog which remembers only to bark and not to bite, and is led through the streets as a lady's pet, is only a degenerate wolf. Even physical prowess of the type of Jack Dempsey's can lay no claim to human glory outside the ring, but rather only the power to work and to live a happy life. Not even a more highly developed animal whose body is a more sensitized and complicated organism, with greater specialized powers and more refined desires, is necessarily a more robust or healthy animal, when life and survival and happiness come into the question. The real question of physical and moral health in man as well as in animals is how well he is able to do his work and enjoy his life, and how fit he is yet to survive.

If one takes merely the physical evidences, one can see clear traces of the effects of thousands of years of civilized life. Man in China has adapted himself to a social and cultural environment that demands stamina, resistance power and negative strength, and he has lost a great part of mental and physical powers of conquest and adventure which characterized his forebears in the primeval forests. The humour of the Chinese people in inventing gunpowder and finding its best use in making firecrackers for their grandfathers' birthdays is merely symbolical of their inventiveness along merely pacific lines. The preference for daintiness over power in art has a physical basis in man's lessened vitality and mellowed instincts, and the preference for reasonableness over aggressiveness in philosophy may be actually traceable to the rounded chin and the amorphous face.

So also have the contempt for physical prowess and sports and the general dislike of the strenuous life intimately to do with man's decreased bodily energy, especially in the city-living bourgeois class. This is easily observable in a street car crowd or a faculty meeting, where Europeans and Chinese are placed in a row side by side. Unhygienic forms of living and the general overeating on the part of the bourgeois Chinese account, in many cases, for the drooping ·shoulders and the listless eye. The constitutional differences between European and Chinese children at school age are unmistakable. On the athletic field, it is invariably found that boys who have a European father or mother distinguish themselves by their greater swiftness, agility and general exuberance of energy, while they seldom excel in tests of endurance and never in scholastic attainments. The much vaunted bossing of the Hankow Nationalist Government in 1927 by a man called Borodin is due to the simple fact that the energetic Russian, who is taking merely a second-rate place at home, did three times the work of a Chinese official, and could talk the Chinese leaders to sleep until the latter had to give in in order to be let alone.

Many Europeans in Shanghai wonder why they are dropped by their Chinese friends without realizing the simple reason that the latter are not able to stand the strain of a long and exciting conversation, especially when it is in a foreign language. Many a Sino-European partnership, matrimonial or commercial, has been wrecked on the European's impatience with Chinese stodgy smugness and the Chinaman's impatience with the European's inability to keep still. The way in which American jazz-band conductors shake their knees and European passengers pace a steamship deck is, to the Chinese, highly ridiculous.

With the exception of Chiang Kaishek and T. V. Soong, the Chinese leaders do not "work like a horse"; they simply work like civilized human beings, where life is regarded as not worth the bother of too much human effort, and eventually if Chiang Kaishek and T. V. Soong come out on top, it will be just on account of their greater stamina and capacity for drudgery. It was T. V. Soong who, using a Chinese idiom, announced that he was "as strong as an ox" when he resigned, and failed to give diabetes or hardened liver or tired nerves for his political resignation, which all the rest of the Chinese officials unashamedly do. A list of the physical and mental ailments, from wrecked stomachs and overworked kidneys to shattered nerves and muddled heads, publicly announced by the officials during their political sicknesses, most of which are genuine, would cover all the departments and wards of a modern hospital.

With the exception of the late Sun Yatsen, the Chinese leaders, first-rate scholars all, do not keep up their reading and do not write. A work like Trotzky's autobiography by a Chinese leader is simply unimaginable, and even a manifestly lucrative first-class biography of Sun Yatsen has not yet been written by a Chinese, almost a decade after the great leader's death, nor are there adequate biographies of Tseng Kuofan or Li Hungchang or Yüan Shihkai.

It seems the sipping of tea in the yamen and the interminable talking and eating of melon seeds at home have consumed all our scholars' time. Facts like these explain why gem-like verses, dainty essays, short prefaces to friends' works, funeral sketches of friends' lives and brief descriptions of travels comprise the works of ninety-five per cent of the famous Chinese authors. When one cannot be powerful, one must choose to be dainty, and when one cannot be aggressive, one has to make a virtue of reasonableness. Only once in a while do we meet a Ssŭma Ch'ien or a Cheng Ch'iao or a Ku Yenwu, whose prodigious labours suggest to us the indefatigable bodily energy of a Balzac or a Victor Hugo. That is what two thousand years of kowtowing could do to a nation.

A study of the hair and skin of the people also seems to indicate what must be considered results of millenniums of civilized indoor living. The general lack or extreme paucity of beard on man's face is one instance of such effect, a fact which makes it possible for most Chinese men not to know the use of a personal razor. Hair on men's chests is unknown, and a moustache on a woman's face, not so rare in Europe, is out of the question in China. On good authority from medical doctors, and from references in writing, one knows that a perfectly bare *mons veneris* is not uncommon in Chinese women. The pores of the skin are finer than those of the Europeans, with the result that Chinese ladies, on the whole, have more delicate complexions than have European ladies, and their muscles are considerably more flabby, an ideal consciously cultivated through the institution of footbinding, which has other sex appeals. The Chinese are evidently aware of this effect, for in Hsinfeng, Kwangtung, keepers of poultry yards keep their chickens shut up for life in a dark coop, without room for movement, giving us the Hsinfeng chicken, noted for its extreme tenderness. Glandular secretions from the skin must have correspondingly decreased, for the Chinese explain the foreigners' habit of taking their (imagined) daily baths by their comparatively stronger bodily odour. Perhaps the most marked difference is in the loss of the full, rich resonant quality in the Chinese voice, compared with that of the Europeans.

While facts regarding the senses are not to my knowledge available, there is no reason to suppose a deterioration in the fine use of the ears and the eyes. The refined olfactory sense is reflected in the Chinese *cuisine* and in the fact that, in Peking, one speaks of kissing a baby as "smelling" a baby, which is what is done actually. The Chinese literary language has also many equivalents of the French *odeur de femme*, like "flesh odour" and "fragrance from marble (a woman's body)." On the other hand, sensitiveness to cold and heat and pain and general noise seems to be much more blunt in the Chinese than in the white man. One is well trained for such hardness in the Chinese family communal living. Perhaps the one thing that compels admiration from Westerners is our nerves. While sensitiveness is often very refined along specialized lines—the obvious proof of this is the great beauty of Chinese handicraft products in general—there seems to be a corresponding coarseness as regards response to pain and general suffering.[1] The Chinese capacity for endurance in suffering is enormous.

III. INFUSION OF NEW BLOOD

But the Chinese people, as a race, did not survive merely on the strength of coarse nerves or of capacity for suffering. Actually, they survived on the sinolization[2] of Mongolian peoples. A kind of phylogenetic monkey-gland grafting took place, for one observes a new bloom of culture after each introduction of new blood. The brief sketch of the general constitution and physical condition of the Chinese people shows, not that they have entirely escaped the effects of long civilized living, but that they have developed traits which render them helpless at the hands of a fresher and more war-like race. Life with the Chinese seems to move on a slower, quieter level, the level of sedate living, not the level of action and adventure, with corresponding mental and moral habits of a peaceful and negative character. This makes it easily understandable why periodic conquests from the North were inevitable. Politically, the nation has perished several times at the hands of these conquerors. The problem is then how, in the midst of this political subjugation, the nation remained as a nation; not how the nation warded off these military disasters, as Christendom stopped the advance of the Moslems at the battle of Tours, but how it survived these disasters and, in fact, profited from them by the infusion of new blood, without losing its racial individuality or cultural continuity. The national life, it seems, was organised on such a pattern that the loss of the pristine vigour did not mean the loss of racial stamina and power for resistance. The key to this racial stamina and power for resistence is the key to China's survival.

---

[1] Arthur Smith's renowned *Chinese Characteristics* has a chapter on "The Absence of Comfort and Convenience," recounting his experience and observations of Chinese dress, houses, pillows and beds, which all European readers find amusing. I wager it is ten times more amusing to Chinese readers to learn of Arthur Smith's account of his sufferings and discomforts. The white man's nerves are undoubtedly degenerate.

[2] This word, though here used for the first time, is preferable to the atrocious "Sinification."

The infusion of new blood must explain to a large extent the racial vigour that the Chinese people possess to-day. Historically, this occurs with such striking regularity, at the interval of every eight hundred years, as to lead one to suppose that actually a periodic regeneration of the race was necessary, and that it was the internal degeneration of the moral fibre of the people that brought about these periodic upheavals, rather than vice versa. Dr. J. S. Lee, in a striking paper on "The Periodic Recurrence of Internecine Wars in China,"[1] has made a statistical study of these occurrences, which reveal an exact parallelism in these cycles of peace and disorder which "far exceeds the limit of probability" and is "perhaps too exact to be expected from the proceedings of human affairs."

For the striking fact is that Chinese history can be conveniently divided into cycles of eight hundred years. Each cycle begins with a short-lived and militarily strong dynasty, which unified China after centuries of internal strife. Then follow four or five hundred years of peace, with one change of dynasty, succeeded by successive waves of wars, resulting soon in the removal of the capital from the North to the South. Then came secession and rivalry between North and South with increasing intensity, followed by subjugation under a foreign rule, which ended the cycle. History then repeats itself and with the unification of China again under Chinese rule there is a new bloom of culture.

The parallelism of events within each cycle unfolded itself with an unreasonable mechanical exactness as to time and sequence. Dr. Lee mentions, for instance, the undertaking of a great engineering feat which was repeated with fatal regularity and at the exact stage in each cycle, namely, immediately at the beginning of a new bloom of culture: for the first cycle, the building of the Great Wall under the Ch'in Dynasty and the colossal palaces, the *Ofangkung*, which were soon subjected to a conflagration lasting three months; for the second cycle, the building of the Grand Canal under the Sui Emperor, who had also magnificent palaces, noted for their grandeur and luxury; and for the third cycle, the rebuilding of the Great Wall, in which form it has survived to the present day, the opening up

[1] *The China Journal of Science and Arts*, March and April, 1931.

of several new canals and dams, and the building of the city of Peking under the Emperor Yunglo of the Ming Dynasty, who was also famous for his great Yunglo Library.

These cycles comprise: (1) from the Ch'in Dynasty to the end of the Six Dynasties and the Tartar invasion (221 B.C.–A.D. 588) covering about 830 years; (2) from the Sui Dynasty to the Mongol invasion (589–1367), covering about 780 years; and (3) the modern cycle from the Ming Dynasty to the present time, a cycle which is yet uncompleted, but which has so far unfolded itself in the last six hundred years with amazing fidelity to the previous pattern. The peace of five hundred years which was granted us under the Ming and Manchu Dynasties seems to have run its due course, and with the Taiping Rebellion in the 1850's, which marked the first big wave of internecine wars, we are on the crescendo of disorder and of internecine strife, which so far has lived up to its tradition in the removal of the capital from Peking to Nanking in 1927.

It is almost prophetic to note that a division between North and South and the subjugation of Northern China by a foreign race for the outstanding two hundred years have not yet come.[1]

The following diagrams are reproduced here partly for their intrinsic interest, and partly because they are the best short summary of China's political history of over two thousand years within the scope of a printed page. The curves represent the frequency of wars in China proper.

Dr. Lee also mentions the fact that the same parallelism may be observed in the Chou Period preceding the first cycle in the diagram. The Chou Dynasty, which represented the first bloom of Chinese culture, lasted officially 900 years, beginning in the year 1122 B.C. After the first four hundred and fifty years of comparative peace and expansion inside China, the capital was moved east owing to pressure from the north-west in 770 B.C., from which date on we see increasing wars and strifes among the kingdoms, with the central government steadily

[1] A mixture of Chinese and Japanese blood, though very rare, has already produced two rather noteworthy Chinese, Koxinga, a good general, carrying on a losing campaign against the Manchus, and Su Manshu, a delicate poet in the beginning of the present century.

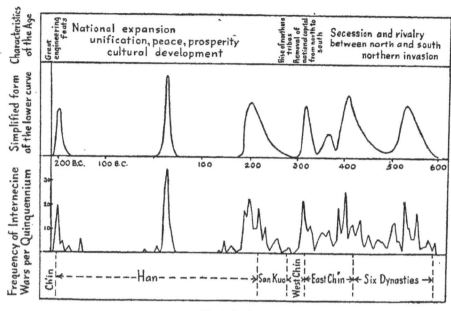

First Cycle
(221 B.C.–A.D. 588)
c. 830 years

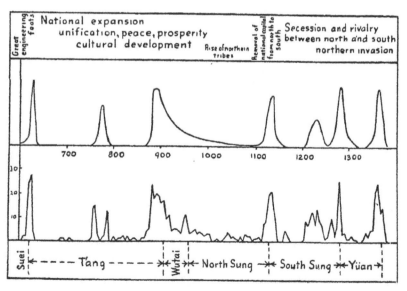

Second Cycle
(589–1367)
c. 780 years

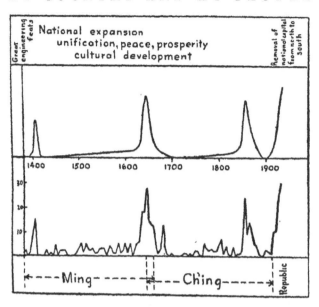

Modern Cycle
(1368 to the present)

losing its control over the feudal lords, giving us the *Ch'unch'iu* Period of Confucius' Annals (722–481 B.C.) and the later *Chankuo* Period or the Period of the "Warring Kingdoms" (402–221 B.C.) with Ch'u constantly extending its territory to virtually the whole southern part of the then civilized China. The cycle was then closed with the conquest and reunification of the whole of China by a tribe with a strong mixture of barbarian blood and foreign customs, led by the great Ch'in Emperor.

Facts like these call for an explanation, ethnological, economic or climatic. Over-population, which in its nature can be regularly reached in four or five hundred years of peace, seems to be an important factor. Peace and culture in any country in the world for over five hundred years are unknown to history, and there is no reason why China should be an exception. Yet the review of China's literary history seems to offer another obvious explanation. There was a decadence of moral fibre reflected in poetry and literature during these periods of northern and southern secession and rivalry, as already seen in the poems quoted above in this chapter. The period of northern invasion in the first cycle, the so-called

Six Dynasties, from Eastern Chin to the unification of China under Sui, during which North China was overrun with barbaric conquerors, and the period of northern invasion in the second cycle, from the Southern Sung Dynasty to the Mongol Dynasty inclusive, seem to have corresponded with periods of effeminacy of living and decadence of literary style, the first period noted for its artificial and flowery *ssŭliu* euphuistic prose, and the second for its effeminate sentimental poetry. One observes, in fact, not a paucity but an over-abundance of words, played out to their finest nuances, with no more the smell of the soil, but the decadent, cultivated, super-refined flavour of court perfume. The Chinese showed a certain *fin-de-siècle* delight in the sounds of words, and an extreme refinement in literary and artistic criticism, and in aristocratic habits of living.

For it was in these periods that painting and calligraphy flourished, and aristocratic families rose and established themselves to carry on the artistic tradition. Chinese literary criticism first became conscious of itself in the Six Dynasties, and Wang Hsichih, the first and greatest calligraphist, who was born of a great aristocratic family, lived in this period. Political weakness and disgrace somehow coincided with artistic refinement, and southern China was ruled in these periods by kings who could not keep their thrones secure but could write exquisite verse. Such ruler-poets were Liang Wuti, Nant'ang Houchu, and Ch'en Houchu, all of them kings of extremely short-lived dynasties and writers of tender love lyrics. The Emperor Huichung of the Southern Sung Dynasty was also a noted painter.

Yet it was in these periods that the germ for the racial revival was laid. For the northern conquerors remained conquerors only in official power, the substrata remaining Chinese. The great Northern Wei Dynasty, whose rulers were of the Sienpei race, not only adopted Chinese culture but also freely intermarried with the Chinese. So were the so-called Kin (Manchu) kingdoms in the Sung Dynasty largely Chinese. A fermenting process was at work. Even culturally, these periods were periods of penetration of foreign influence, notably that of Buddhism and Indian sculpture in the end of the first cycle, and of Mongol drama and music in that of the second cycle. The clearest effect of this ethnological mixture is perhaps to be found in the linguistic and physical traits of the modern northern Chinese, with altered tones and hardened consonants in the language, and a taller stature and a gay rustic humour in the people. It was this amalgamation of foreign blood that accounted for, to a large extent, the race's long survival.

IV. CULTURAL STABILITY

Yet this does not explain all. The question remains how it was possible for the nation to survive these periodic political disasters and not be submerged by them, as old Rome was submerged under the Lombards. Wherein does that racial stamina and capacity for absorbing foreign blood consist? Only by going deeper into these problems can one gain a real understanding of the situation as it stands to-day.

The so-called racial stamina and racial vitality, which in spite of the retrograde character of the Chinese bourgeois class enabled the Chinese people to survive political disasters and regenerate itself through foreign blood, is partly constitutional and partly cultural. Among the cultural forces making for racial stability must be counted first of all the Chinese family system, which was so well-defined and organized as to make it impossible for a man to forget where his lineage belonged. This form of social immortality, which the Chinese prize above all earthly possessions, has something of the character of a religion, which is enhanced by the ritual of ancestor worship, and the consciousness of it has penetrated deep into the Chinese soul.

Such a well-organized and religiously conceived family system was of tremendous force when the Chinese race was thrown into contact with a foreign people with a less well-defined family consciousness. Barbaric tribes or children of mixed parentage were all too anxious to join the family and claim part of the family immortality, indulging in the luxurious feeling that when one dies, one does not die, but one's self lives on in the great stream of the family life. The family system also acted as a direct incentive to quantitative reproduction, for in order that the Lin branch should survive, it is necessary that many Lin babies should come into this world.

Perhaps it was due entirely to the family system that the Chinese were able to absorb the Jews of Honan, who to-day are so thoroughly sinolized that their Jewish tradition of not eating pork has become a mere memory. The race consciousness of the Jews can be shamed into oblivion only by the greater race consciousness of the family-minded Chinese, and it was no mean accomplishment in the ethnological field. With a less race-conscious and race-proud people than the Jews, like the northern Tartars, for instance, it is easy to see that the Chinese native inhabitants were placed in a great advantage over their foreign invaders. It is in this sense that Manchuria will remain Chinese in spite of all Japanese machinations; the political order may be changed, and rulers may come and rulers may go, but the Chinese families will remain Chinese families.

Another cultural force making for social stability was the complete absence of established classes in China, and the opportunity open for all to rise in the social scale through the imperial examination system. While the family system accounted for their survival through fecundity, the imperial examination system effected a qualitative selection, and enabled talent to reproduce and propagate itself. This system, which was started in the T'ang Dynasty and based on the ultimate Chinese belief that no man is born noble,[1] had its rudiments in the system of civil service and official recommendations in the Han Dynasty. After the Wei and Ch'in Dynasties (third and fourth centuries A.D.) a change in the control of selection for office brought about a system favouring influential families, so much so that it was stated that "there were no poor scholars in the higher classes and no sons of official families in the lower classes."[2] This favoured the growth of aristocratic families in the Ch'in Dynasty.

With the imperial examination system in the T'ang Dynasty (seventh to ninth centuries inclusive) a system was put into

[1] The Chinese for this is, "There is no blood in premiers and generals."
[2] These refer to the "nine classes" of scholars in the Ch'in Dynasty.

effect which, however it was modified in the following dynasties, maintained down to 1905 an open door for all to rise from poverty to power and fame. While the tests were necessarily somewhat mechanical in nature, and were not devised to attract real genius, they were suitable for selecting talent, and might be regarded as intelligence tests. Such a system made possible a constant infiltration of talent from the country to the cities, thereby making up for the loss of racial vigour in the upper classes and maintaining a cycle of internal regeneration so much needed for social health. Viewed across the centuries, it must have had a selective effect on the quality of the ruling class that made for social stability.

What seems still more important is the fact that the ruling class not only came from the country but also returned to the country, as the rural mode of life was always regarded as the ideal. This rural ideal in art, philosophy and life, so deeply imbedded in the Chinese general consciousness, must account in a large measure for the racial health to-day. Did the creators of the Chinese pattern of life do more wisely than they knew in maintaining a level between civilization and the primitive habits of living? Was it their sound instinct which guided them to choose the agricultural civilization, to hate mechanical ingenuity and love the simple ways of life, to invent the comforts of life without being enslaved by them, and to preach from generation to generation in their poetry, painting and literature the "return to the farm"?

For to be close to nature is to have physical and moral health. Man in the country does not degenerate; only man in the cities does. To scholars and well-to-do families in the cities, persistently the call of the good earth comes. The family letters and instructions of well-known scholars abound in such counsel, and reveal an important aspect of the Chinese civilization, an aspect which subtly but profoundly accounts for its long survival. I select at random from the extremely precious family letters of Cheng Panch'iao to his younger brother, letters that should be counted among the greatest in the world:

The house you bought is well-enclosed and indeed suitable for residence, only I feel the courtyard is too small, and when you look at the sky, it is not big enough. With my unfettered nature, I do not like it. Only a hundred steps north from this house, there is the Parrot Bridge, and another thirty steps from the Bridge is the Plum Tower, with vacant spaces all around. When I was drinking in this Tower in my young days, I used to look out and see the willow banks and the little wooden bridge with decrepit huts and wild flowers against a background of old city walls, and was quite fascinated by it. If you could get fifty thousand cash, you could buy a big lot for me to build my cottage there for my latter days. My intention is to build an earthen wall around it, and plant lots of bamboos and flowers and trees. I am going to have a garden path of paved pebbles leading from the gate to the house door. There will be two rooms, one for the parlour, one for the study, where I can keep books, paintings, brushes, ink-slabs, wine-kettle and tea service, and where I can discuss poetry and literature with some good friends and the younger generation. Behind this will be the family living-rooms, with three main rooms, two kitchens and one servants' room. Altogether there will be eight rooms, all covered with grass-sheds, and I shall be quite content. Early in the morning before sunrise, I could look east and see the red glow of the morning clouds, and at sunset, the sun will shine from behind the trees. When one stands upon a high place in the court-yard, one can already see the bridge and the clouds and waters in the distance, and when giving a party at night, one can see the lights of the neighbours outside the wall. This will be only thirty steps to your house on the south, and will be separated from the little garden on the east by a small creek. So it is quite ideal. Some may say, "This is indeed very comfortable, only there may be burglars." They do not know that burglars are also but poor people. I would open the door and invite them to come in, and discuss with them what they may share. Whatever there is, they can take away, and if nothing will really suit them, they may even take away the great Wang Hsienchih's old capret to pawn it for a hundred cash. Please, my younger brother, bear this in mind, for this is your stupid brother's provision for spending a happy old age. I wonder whether I may have what I so desire.

This is typical of the sentiment in Chinese literature. This rural ideal of Cheng Panch'iao's is as much based on his poetic feeling of common brotherhood with the poor peasant, which comes natural to a Taoistic soul, as the rural ideal of Tseng Kuofan's is based on the desire for the preservation for the family, and closely connected with the Confucian family system. For the rural ideal of life is part of the social system which makes the family the unit and part of the politico-cultural system which makes the village the unit. It may be amusing to learn that Tseng Kuofan, the great general and first minister of his times, in his family letters to his children and nephews continually warned them against extravagant habits and advised them to plant vegetables, rear pigs and manure their own farms, yet such advice on frugality and industry was expressly given with the aim that the family prosperity might be prolonged.

If simplicity can keep a family integrity long, it should do the same for the national integrity. For to Tseng Kuofan, it was plain that "the official families whose children learn expensive habits of living, prosper only for a generation or two: the merchant families who are industrious and frugal may prosper for three or four generations, the families who till the ground and study books and have simple and careful habits prosper for five or six generations, while the families who have the virtues of filial piety and friendliness prosper for eight or ten generations."

It is therefore entirely easy to understand why Tseng regards "the keeping of fish, the keeping of pigs, the planting of bamboos and the planting of vegetables" as "the four things which should not be neglected. On the one hand, we may thus keep up the tradition of our forefathers, and, on the other hand, one will feel a sense of life and growth when looking in over our walls, and a sense of prosperity when entering our court. Even if you should have to spend a little more money and hire a few more helpers, the money spent on these four things will be well spent. . . . From these four things, you can see whether a family is prospering or is going down."

And somehow from the family instructions of Yen Chiht'ui (531–591), Fan Chungyen (989–1052), Chu Hsi (1130–1200), down to those of Ch'en Hungmu (1696–1771) and Tseng

Kuofan (1811–1872), this family ideal of industry and frugality and living the simple life persisted and was recognized as the soundest moral heritage of the nation. The family system somehow wove itself into the rural pattern of life and could not be separated from it. Simplicity was a great word among the Greeks, and simplicity, *shunp'o*, was a great word among the Chinese. It was as if man knew the benefits of civilization and knew also the dangers of it. Man knew the happiness of the joys of life, but also was aware of its ephemeral nature, fearful of the jealousy of the gods, and was willing to take the joys that were simpler but would last longer. For to enjoy too many good things of life was, according to the Chinese, to *chehfo*, or decrease one's lot of happiness in this life. Therefore "one should be just as careful in choosing one's pleasures as in avoiding calamities." "Choose the lighter happiness," said a scholar at the end of the Ming Dynasties, and somehow there was an echo of consent in the Chinese breasts. For human happiness is so precarious that the retreat to nature and simplicity is the best safeguard for it. It must be so, and the Chinese knew it by instinct. They wanted survival for their families, and they achieved it for their nation.

V. RACIAL YOUTH

It would seem, therefore, that the Chinese, as a people, avoided the dangers of civic deterioration by a natural distrust of civilization and by keeping close to primitive habits of life. This might suggest that the so-called Chinese civilization must be understood in a greatly modified sense, that it was a civilization in love with primitivism itself and was not quite ready to say good-bye to it. Certainly it was not a civilization that had guaranteed the people peace without intermittent periods of bloodshed and disorder, or that had made wars and famines and floods impossible.

That a country after two thousand years of comparatively civilized living could furnish living material for such a story as *All Men Are Brothers*, when the eating of human flesh, though rare, was still possible, certainly reveals in a measure the mystery of this enigma of social continuity against the havoc of civilization. Sung Chiang, Li Kuei and the host of robust robbers on the top of Liangshanpo, although coming almost fifteen centuries after Confucius, do not suggest to us representatives of an outworn civilization, but rather happy children of a people in the twilight of a dawning culture, when security of life was yet unknown. It seems as if the race, instead of reaching full maturity with Confucius, was really enjoying a prolonged childhood.

This brings us to the extremely interesting question of the racial constitution of the Chinese race: whether, as an ethnological entity, it reveals not so much the characteristics of an old people as those of a people in many respects still in its racial youth and far from reaching racial maturity. A distinction may be made by saying that the Chinese are culturally old but racially young, a theory which has found support among some of the modern anthropologists. Griffith Taylor[1] thus classifies the Chinese among the youngest strata in the evolution of the human race, according to his migration-zone scheme. Havelock Ellis also characterizes the Asiatics as being racially infantile, in the sense of retaining some of the adaptability, flexibility and pristine all-round *shunp'o* nature of childhood before reaching specialized development. Perhaps "a prolonged childhood" is the better term, for infantilism and arrested development or stagnation are misleading terms.

Cultural stagnation of the Chinese is only a misconception of one looking at China from the outside, without knowledge of her inner life. One needs only to think of the late development of the Chinese porcelain, which did not come, as many foreigners imagine, from the time of Confucius, but from as late as the tenth century, and was then only slowly developed until it reached its perfection under K'anghsi and Ch'ienlung in the seventeenth century, almost before our eyes. Progress in lacquer, printing, and painting was slow, but each dynasty brought it a step forward.[2] The renowned Chinese style of painting did not come into being until the last thousand years

---

[1] *Environment and Race*, Oxford University Press, 1927.
[2] See the enlightening article by V. K. Ting: "How China Acquired Her Civilization," in *A Chinese Symposium* (published by the Institute of Pacific Relations).

of the Chinese national life, a late period for an old civilization. And in literature, one needs only to think of the lateness of the prose epic and tale of wonder, for the *Shuihu* (*All Men Are Brothers*) and *Hsiyuchi* must be considered such, and they were certainly perfected after the fourteenth century, almost two thousand years after Confucius and Laotse had lived and died.

The epic was strangely unknown in ancient China, or it was irretrievably lost without any existing trace in literature. The narrative poem came only in the Han Dynasty, and there were not many of them. The drama came into popularity only with the Mongol Dynasty in the eleventh century. Tales of imagination like the *Hsiyuchi* came about the same time, when the Chinese imagination was stimulated by Buddhism. The novel as such really had a humble beginning only in the ninth century, had its mature development late in the fourteenth and fifteenth centuries (Ming) and reached its climax in the beginning of the Manchu Dynasty with the *Red Chamber Dream*, a contemporary and Oriental counterpart of *Clarissa Harlowe*. Had China's cultural life flowered and then ended a few centuries after Confucius as the Greek genius did, there would have been only some fine moral maxims and folk lyrics, and certainly none of China's great paintings, novels and architecture to offer to the world. This sounds as if we are not watching the arrested development of a nation that reached its full bloom in its young Golden Age like Greece and Rome, but that we are watching the prolonged childhood of a race that took millenniums to reach full development, and then is perhaps still courageous enough for further spiritual adventure.

Chapter Two

THE CHINESE CHARACTER

I. MELLOWNESS

"CHARACTER" is a typically English word. Apart from the English, few nations have laid such stress on character in their ideal of education and manhood as the Chinese. The Chinese seem to be so preoccupied with it that in their whole philosophy they have not been able to think of anything else. Totally devoid of any extra-mundane interests, and without getting involved in any religious claptrap, this ideal of building of character has, through the influence of their literature, the theatre, and proverbs, permeated to the lowliest peasant, and provided him with a philosophy of life. But while the English word "character" suggests strength, courage, "guts," and looking merely glum in moments of anger or disappointment, the Chinese word for "character" brings to us the vision of a mature man of mellow temperament, retaining an equanimity of mind under all circumstances, with a complete understanding not only of himself but of his fellow-men.

The Sung philosophy has a tremendous confidence in the power and supremacy of the mind over emotions, and an overweening assurance that the human mind, through its understanding of oneself and of one's fellow-men, is able to adjust itself to the most unfavourable circumstances and triumph over them. *The Great Learning*, the Confucian primer with which Chinese schoolboys used to begin their first lesson at school, defines the "great learning" as consisting of the attainment of a "*clear* character," which is almost an impossible English expression, but by which is meant the illumination of understanding, developed and cultivated through knowledge. A mellow understanding of life and of human nature is, and always has been, the Chinese ideal of character, and from that understanding other qualities are derived, such as pacifism, contentment, calm and strength of endurance which distinguish the Chinese character. Strength of character is really strength of the mind, according to the Confucianists. When a man has cultivated these virtues through mental discipline, we say he has developed his character.

Very often these virtues are attained also through the help of Confucian fatalism. For contrary to the general belief, fatalism is a great source of peace and contentment. A beautiful and talented girl may rebel against an unsuitable marriage, but if the peculiar circumstances of her meeting with her fiancé can convince her that it is the gods who have decreed the match, she can at once, through an act of understanding, become a happy and contented wife. For the husband has in her eyes become a "predestined enemy," and the Chinese proverb says "predestined enemies will always meet in a narrow alleyway." With that understanding, they can love and fight each other furiously ever after, knowing all the time that the gods are looking on and causing them all this trouble.

If we review the Chinese race and try to picture their national characteristics, we shall probably find the following traits of character: (1) sanity, (2) simplicity, (3) love of nature, (4) patience, (5) indifference, (6) old roguery, (7) fecundity, (8) industry, (9) frugality, (10) love of family life, (11) pacifism, (12) contentment, (13) humour, (14) conservatism, and (15) sensuality. They are, on the whole, simple great qualities that would adorn any nation.[1] Some of these characteristics are vices rather than virtues, and others are neutral qualities; they are the weakness as well as the strength of the Chinese nation. Too much mental sanity often clips imagination of its wings and deprives the race of its moments of blissful madness; pacifism can become a vice of cowardice; patience, again, may bring about a morbid tolerance of evil; conservatism

---

[1] I have not put down honesty, because all over the world farming people are honest, and the reputation of the Chinese merchant for honesty is only a concomitant of his provincial method of doing business, and a mere result of the predominance of the rural pattern and ideal of life. When Chinese are put in a seaport, they lose to a marked extent that pristine honesty and can be as dishonest as any Wall Street stock-jobber.

may at times be a mere synonym for sloth and laziness, and fecundity may be a racial virtue but an individual vice.

But all these qualities may be summed up in the word *mellowness*. They are passive qualities, suggestive of calm and passive strength rather than as youthful vigour and romance. They suggest the qualities of a civilization built for strength and endurance rather than for progress and conquest. For it is a civilization which enables man to find peace under any circumstance, and when a man is at peace with himself, he cannot understand the youthful enthusiasm for progress and reform. It is the old culture of an old people who know life for what it is worth and do not strive for the unattainable. The supremacy of the Chinese mind flays its own hopes and desires, and by making the supreme realization that happiness is an unattainable bluebird and giving up the quest for it—"taking a step backwards," as the Chinese expression goes—it finds happiness nestling in its own hand, almost strangled to death during the hot pursuit of an imagined shadow. As a Ming scholar puts it, "by losing that pawn, one wins the whole game."

This so-called mellowness is the result of a certain type of environment. In fact, all national qualities have an organic unity, which finds its explanation in the kind of social and political soil that nourishes them. For mellowness somehow grows naturally out of the Chinese environment as a peculiar variety of pear grows out of its natural soil. There are American-born Chinese, brought up in a different environment, who are totally devoid of the characteristics of the common Chinese, and who can break up a faculty meeting by the sheer force of their uncouth nasal twang and their direct forceful speech, a speech which knows no fine modulations. They lack that supreme, unique mellowness peculiar to the sons of Cathay. On the other hand, Chinese college youths are considerably more mature than American students of the same age, for even young Chinese freshmen in American universities cannot get interested in football and motor-cars. They have already other and more mature interests.[1] Most probably they are

[1] It is extremely dangerous, therefore, to send fresh American college graduates out to China as missionaries and put them over Chinese teachers or preachers twice as mature as themselves. Many of them have not even tasted the agony of first love.

already married. They have wives and families to think about, their parents to remember, and perhaps some cousins to help through school. Responsibility makes men sober, and a national cultural tradition helps them to think sanely about life at a period earlier than they could arrive at individually.

But their mellowness does not come from books; it comes from a society which is apt to laugh young enthusiasm out of court. The Chinese have a certain contempt for young enthusiasm and for new brooms that will sweep this universe clean. By laughing at that enthusiasm and at the belief that everything is possible in the world, Chinese society early teaches the young to hold their tongues while their elders are speaking. Very soon the Chinese youth learns this, and instead of being foolish enough to support any proposed scheme or socialistic venture, he learns to comment unfavourably upon it, pointing out all the possible difficulties, and in that way gets his pass into mature society. Then, after coming back from Europe or America, he begins to manufacture tooth-paste and calls it "saving the country by industrialization" or he translates some American free verse and calls it "introduction of the Western culture." And since he has usually a big family to support and some cousins for whom to secure positions, he cannot remain a school teacher if he is in the teaching profession, but must think of ways and means to rise higher, perhaps become a dean, and in that way become a *good* member of his family. That process of trying to rise higher teaches him some memorable lessons of life and human nature, and if he escapes all that experience and remains a round-eyed, innocent hot-headed young man at thirty, still enthusiastic for progress and reform, he is either an inspired idiot or a confounded genius.

II. PATIENCE

Let us take the three worst and most striking characteristics, patience, indifference and old roguery, and see how they arose. I believe that these are effects of culture and environment and hence are not necessarily a part of the Chinese mental make-up. They are here to-day because for thousands of years we have been living under certain cultural and social influences. The natural inference is that when these influences are removed, the qualities will also correspondingly diminish or disappear. The quality of patience is the result of racial adjustment to a condition where over-population and economic pressure leave very little elbow-room for people to move about, and is, in particular, a result of the family system, which is a miniature of Chinese society. Indifference is largely due to the lack of legal protection and constitutional guarantee for personal liberty. Old roguery is due, for lack of a better word, to the Taoistic view of life. Of course, all these qualities are products of the same environment, and it is only for the sake of clearness that one assigns any single cause for any resulting quality.

That patience is a noble virtue of the Chinese people no one who knows them will gainsay. There is so much of this virtue that it has almost become a vice with them. The Chinese people have put up with more tyranny, anarchy and misrule than any Western people will ever put up with, and seem to have regarded them as part of the laws of nature. In certain parts of Szechuen, the people have been taxed thirty years in advance without showing more energetic protest than a half-audible curse in the privacy of the household. Christian patience would seem like petulance compared with Chinese patience, which is as unique as Chinese blue porcelain is unique. The world tourists would do well to bring home with them some of this Chinese patience along with Chinese blue porcelain, for true individuality cannot be copied. We submit to tyranny and extortion as small fish swim into the mouth of a big fish. Perhaps had our capacity for sufferance been smaller, our sufferings would also be less. As it is, this capacity for putting up with insults has been ennobled by the name of patience, and deliberately inculcated as a cardinal virtue by Confucian ethics. I am not saying that this patience is not a great quality of the Chinese people. Jesus said, "Blessed are the meek, for they shall inherit the earth," and I am not sure but that Chinese patience has enabled us to inherit half a continent and keep it. The Chinese also inculcate it consciously as a high moral virtue. As our saying goes, "A man who cannot tolerate small ills can never accomplish great things."

The training school for developing this virtue is, however, the big family, where a large number of daughters-in-law, brothers-in-law, fathers and sons daily learn this virtue by trying to endure one another. In the big family, where a closed door is an offence, and where there is very little elbow-room for the individuals, one learns by necessity and by parental instruction from early childhood the need for mutual toleration and adjustments in human relationships. The deep, slow, everyday wearing effect on character can scarcely be over-estimated.

There was once a prime minister, Chang Kungni, who was much envied for his earthly blessedness of having nine generations living together under the same roof. Once the emperor, T'ang Kaochung, asked him the secret of his success, and the minister asked for a brush and paper, on which he wrote a hundred times the character "patience" or "endurance." Instead of taking that as a sad commentary on the family system, the Chinese people have ever after envied his example, and the phrase "hundred patience" (po-jen) has passed into current moral proverbs which are written on red paper and pasted on all house-doors on New Year's Day: "*peaceableness brings good luck*"; "*patience is the best family heritage,*" etc. But so long as the family system exists and so long as society is built on the principle that a man is not an individual but attains his full being only in living in harmonious social relationships, it is easy to see how patience must be regarded as a supreme virtue and must grow naturally out of the social system. For in such a society, patience has a reason for existence.

III. INDIFFERENCE

But if the Chinese people are unique in their patience, they are still more justly famous for their indifference. This, again, I believe, is a product of social environment. There is no more significant contrast than that between the parting instruction

x

of Tom Brown's mother in the English classic *Tom Brown's School Days* to "hold his head high and answer straight" and the traditional parting instruction of the Chinese mother that her son should "not meddle with public affairs." This is so because, in a society where legal protection is not given to personal rights, indifference is always safe and has an attractive side to it difficult for Westerners to appreciate.

I think this indifference is not a natural characteristic of the people, but is a conscious product of our culture, deliberately inculcated by our old-world wisdom under the special circumstances. Taine once said that vice and virtue are products like sugar and vitriol. Without taking such an absolute view, one can nevertheless subscribe to the general statement that any virtue will be more generally encouraged in a society where that virtue is easily seen to be "good," and is more likely to be generally accepted as part of life.

The Chinese people take to indifference as Englishmen take to umbrellas, because the political weather always looks a little ominous for the individual who ventures a little too far out alone. In other words, indifference has a distinct "survival-value" in China. Chinese youths are as public-spirited as foreign youths, and Chinese hot-heads show as much desire to "meddle with public affairs" as those in any other country. But somewhere between their twenty-fifth and their thirtieth years, they all become wise (*"hsüeh kuai liao,"* as we say), and acquire this indifference which contributes a lot to their mellowness and culture. Some learn it by native intelligence, and others by getting their fingers burned once or twice. All old people play safely because all old rogues have learned the benefits of indifference in a society where personal rights are not guaranteed and where getting one's fingers burned once is bad enough.

The "survival-value" of indifference consists, therefore, in the fact that in the absence of protection of personal rights, it is highly unsafe for a man to take too much interest in public affairs, or "idle affairs," as we call them. When Shao P'iao-p'ing and Lin Poshui, two of our most daring journalists, got shot by a Manchurian war-lord in Peiping in 1926 without even a trial, the other journalists naturally learned the virtue of this indifference in no time, and "became wise." The most successful journalists in China are those who have no opinion of their own. Like all Chinese gentlemen, and like the Western diplomats, they are proud of committing themselves to no opinion on life in general, and on the crying question of the hour in particular.[1] What else can they do? One can be public-spirited when there is a guarantee for personal rights, and one's only look-out is the libel law. When these rights are not protected, however, our instinct of self-preservation tells us that indifference is our best constitutional guarantee for personal liberty.

In other words, indifference is not a high moral virtue but a social attitude made necessary by the absence of legal protection. It is a form of self-protection, developed in the same manner as the tortoise develops its shell. The famous Chinese apathetic gaze is only a self-protective gaze, acquired by a lot of culture and self-discipline. This is borne out by the fact that Chinese robbers and bandits, who do not depend upon legal protection, do not develop this indifference, but are the most chivalrous and public-spirited class of people we know in China. Chinese chivalry, under the name of "haohsieh," is invariably associated with the robbers as in Shuihu. The vicarious pleasure derived in reading the life and adventures of such heroes accounts for the popularity of such novels, in the same way that Elinor Glyn's popularity was to be accounted for by the large number of old maids in the United States. The strong, therefore, are public-spirited because they can afford to be so, and the meek who constitute the majority of the people are indifferent because they need to protect themselves.

Historically, this could be strikingly proved in the history of the Wei and Ch'in Dynasties, when scholars became admired for their indifference to national affairs, resulting soon in the sapping of national strength and the conquest of North China by barbarians. It was the fashion for scholars of the Wei and Ch'in Dynasties to give themselves up to drinking, "light

[1] The oldest and biggest daily paper in China, Shun Pao, formerly enjoyed the reputation of editorially handling (1) foreign and not domestic questions; (2) distant and not immediate topics, and (3) general and not specific subjects, like "The Importance of Diligence," "The Value of Truth," etc.

conversation" (*ch'ingt'an*), and dreaming about Taoist fairies and discovering the pill of immortality. This period seemed to be politically the lowest period of the Chinese race since the Chou and Han times, representing the end of a progressive degeneration of the race until, for the first time in its history, China was submerged under barbarian rule. Was this cult of indifference natural, and if not, how was it brought about? History reveals this to us in no uncertain terms.

Toward the end of the Han Dynasty, the Chinese scholars were not indifferent. In fact, political criticism was at its height during this period. Leading scholars and "university" students, numbering over thirty thousand, were often embroiled over questions of current politics, and dared the wrath of the eunuchs and the Emperor in their intrepid attacks on government policies or the conduct of members of the imperial household. Yet, because of the absence of constitutional protection, this movement ended in complete suppression at the hands of the eunuchs. Two or three hundred scholars and sometimes their whole families were sentenced to death, exile or imprisonment. This occurred in the years A.D. 166–169, and was known as the *tangku*, or "party cases." This was carried out in such a thorough fashion and on such a grand scale that the whole movement was cut short, and its remaining effects were felt for over a century afterward. Then came the reaction and the cult of indifference and the developing crazes for wine, women, poetry and Taoistic occultism. Some of the scholars went into the mountains and built themselves mudhouses without a door, receiving their food through a window till their death. Others disguised themselves as woodcutters and begged their relatives to save them from recognition by refraining from making calls.

Immediately after that came the seven poets, or the "Pléiade of the Bamboo Grove." Liu Ling, a great poet, could go on a drunken fit for months. He used to travel on a cart with a jug of wine, a shovel and a grave-digger, giving the latter the order as they started: "*Bury me when I am dead!—anywhere, any time.*" People admired him and called him "clever." All scholars affected either extreme rusticity or extreme sensuality and extreme superficiality. Another great poet, Yüan Hsien, had illicit relations with his maid. When he learned at a public feast that his wife had sent the maid away, he immediately borrowed a horse from a friend and galloped off after the maid until he overtook her and carried her back on horseback in the presence of all the guests. These were the people who became admired for their cleverness. People admired them as a small tortoise admires the thick shell of a big tortoise.

Here we seem to have laid our finger on the fatal disease of the body politic, and to see the origin of that indifference which explains the proverbial inability of the Chinese people to organize themselves. It would seem that the curing of the disease is simple, by having constitutional protection for the people's civil rights. Yet no one has seen the far-reaching consequences of this. No one desires it. No one sincerely wants it.

IV. Old Roguery

Perhaps the most striking quality of the Chinese people is what, for want of a better term, must be termed its "old roguery." It is the most difficult characteristic to explain to a Westerner, and yet at the same time it is most profound, in that it goes back directly to a different philosophy of life. Compared with this view of life, the whole fabric of Western civilization seems extremely raw and immature. When a young man tries to drag his old grandfather from his fireside for a sea bath on a September morning and fails to do so, the young man will perhaps show angered astonishment, while the old man will merely show a smile of amusement. That smile is the smile of the old rogue, and it is difficult to say which one is right. All this bustle and restlessness of the spirit of the young man—where will it all lead to? And all this enthusiasm and self-assertion and struggle and war and hot-headed nationalism —where will it all end, and what is it all for? Perhaps it will be futile to find an answer to the question, and equally futile to force one party to accept the view of the other, since it is all a matter of age.

An old rogue is a man who has seen a lot of life, and who is materialistic, nonchalant, and sceptical of progress. At its best, this old roguery gives us mellowness and good temper, which in old men make many girls prefer them for husbands. For if life is worth anything, it is that it teaches a lesson of kindliness. The Chinese people have arrived at this point of view, not by having found any religious sanction for it, but from a profound observation and a knowledge of the vicissitudes of life. Typical of this extremely shrewd philosophy is the following famous dialogue of two poet-monks of the T'ang Dynasty:

> Once Hanshan asked Shihteh: "If one slanders me, insults me, sneers at me, despises me, injures me, hates me, and deceives me, what should I do?" Shihteh replied: "Only bear with him, yield to him, let him, avoid him, endure him, respect him, and ignore him. *And after a few years, you just look at him.*"

In myriad other forms, this spirit of Laotse finds expression in our literature, poetry and proverbs. Whether the expression be "By losing that pawn, one wins the whole game," or "Of all the thirty-six alternatives, running away is the best," or "A true hero never incurs present risk," or "Taking a step backwards in your thought," this attitude toward life's problems has permeated the whole fibre of Chinese thought. Life is then full of second-thoughts and of "the thirty-sixth alternatives"; its angularities are smoothed off, and one achieves that true mellowness which is the mark of Chinese culture.

At its worst, this old roguery, which is the highest product of Chinese intelligence, works against idealism and action. It shatters all desire for reform, laughs at the futility of human effort and renders the Chinese people incapable of idealism and action. It has a strange way of reducing all human activities to the level of the alimentary canal and other simple biologic needs. Mencius was a great rogue when he declared the chief desires of mankind to be food and women, or alimentation and reproduction. The late President Li Yüanhung was also a great rogue when he pronounced the heartily accepted dictum of Chinese political philosophy and formula for solving all Chinese party differences by saying *"When there is rice, let everybody share it."* President Li was a grim realist without knowing it, and he spoke wiser than he knew when he was thus giving an economic interpretation of current Chinese history. The economic interpretation of history is not new to the Chinese people, nor is the biologic interpretation of human life of the Émile Zola school. With Zola, it is an intellectual fad, but with us it is a matter of national consciousness. In China one does not have to learn to become a realist: here one is born a realist. President Li Yüanhung was never noted for power of cerebration, but, as a Chinese, he instinctively felt that all political problems are not, and should not be, anything but problems of the rice-bowl. As a Chinese, he gave thus the profoundest explanation of Chinese politics of which I know.

This nonchalant and materialistic attitude is based on the very shrewd view of life to which only old people and old nations can attain. It would be futile for young men under thirty to understand it, as it is futile for young nations of the West to try to appreciate it. Perhaps it was no mere accident that the very name of Laotse, the author of *Taotehking*, the Bible of Taoism, means an "old man."[1] Someone has said that every man past forty is a crook. Anyway, it is undeniable that the older we grow, the more shameless we become. Young girls of twenty seldom marry for money; women of forty seldom marry for anything else—"security" is perhaps the word they call it. It is by no mere whim that, in Greek mythology, young Icarus was made to fly too high until the wax of his wings melted and he fell into the sea, while Daedalus, the old father, flew low, but flew safely home. When a man grows old, he develops a genius for flying low, and idealism is tempered with cool, level-headed common sense, as well as with a sense for dollars and pennies. Realism is, then, characteristic of old age, as idealism is characteristic of youth. When a man is past forty and does not become a crook, he is either feeble-minded or a genius. To the latter class belong the "big children,"

[1] This old man, around the sixth century B.C., was riding a donkey through the Hankukuan Pass, and saying good-bye to the world, when he was begged to leave the five thousand words of *Taotehking* for the enlightenment of his fellow-men.

like Tolstoy, Robert Louis Stevenson and Sir James Barrie, who have in them so much native childishness, which, combined with experience of fact, gives them that capacity for eternal youth which we call immortality.

All this is, however, pure Taoism, in theory and practice, for there is no profounder collection of a concentrated roguish philosophy of life than that contained in the five thousand words of Laotse's *Taotehking*. Taoism, in theory and practice, means a certain roguish nonchalance, a confounded and devastating scepticism, a mocking laughter at the futility of all human interference and the failure of all human institutions, laws, government and marriage, and a certain disbelief in idealism, not so much because of lack of energy as because of a lack of faith. It is a philosophy which counteracts the positivism of Confucius, and serves as a safety-valve for the imperfections of a Confucian society. For the Confucian outlook on life is positive, while the Taoistic outlook is negative, and out of the alchemy of these two strange elements emerges the immortal thing we call Chinese character.[1]

Hence all Chinese are Confucianists when successful, and Taoists when they are failures. The Confucianist in us builds and strives, while the Taoist in us watches and smiles. Therefore when a Chinese scholar is in office he moralizes, and when he is out of office he versifies, and usually it is good Taoistic poetry. That explains why almost all Chinese scholars write poetry, and why in *almost all* collected works of Chinese writers, poetry occupies the better and greater half.

For Taoism, like morphia, is strangely benumbing and therefore strangely soothing. It relieves Chinese headaches and heartaches. Its romanticism, its poetry and its worship of nature serve the Chinese as handsomely in times of trouble and disorder as Confucianism serves them in times of peace and national integration. In that way it provides a safe retreat for the Chinese human heart and a balm for the Chinese soul, when the flesh is submitted to trials and tribulations. The poetry of Taoism alone has made the rigoristic life on the Confucian pattern endurable, and its romanticism has saved

[1] So far as this negative attitude toward life is concerned, Buddhism is merely Taoism a little touched in its wits.

Chinese literature from becoming a mere collection of eulogies on the imperial virtues and a rehash of moral exhortations. All good Chinese literature, all Chinese literature that is worth while, that is readable, and that pleases the human mind and soothes the human heart is essentially imbued with this Taoistic spirit. Taoism and Confucianism are the negative and positive poles of Chinese thought which make life possible in China.

The Chinese are by nature greater Taoists than they are by culture Confucianists. As a people, we are great enough to draw up an imperial code, based on the conception of essential justice, but we are also great enough to distrust lawyers and law courts. Ninety-five per cent of legal troubles are settled out of court. We are great enough to make elaborate rules of ceremony, but we are also great enough to treat them as part of the great joke of life, which explains the great feasting and merry-making at Chinese funerals. We are great enough to denounce vice, but we are also great enough not to be surprised or disturbed by it. We are great enough to start successive waves of revolutions, but we are also great enough to compromise and go back to the previous patterns of government. We are great enough to elaborate a perfect system of official impeachment, and civil service, and traffic regulations, and library reading-room rules, but we are also great enough to break all systems, to ignore them, circumvent them, play with them, and become superior to them. We do not teach our young in the colleges a course of political science, showing how a government is supposed to be run, but we teach them by daily example how our municipal, provincial and central governments are actually run. We have no use for impracticable idealism, as we have no patience for doctrinaire theology. We do not teach our young to become like the sons of God, but we teach them to behave like sane, normal human beings. That is why I believe that the Chinese are essentially humanists and Christianity must fail in China, or it must be altered beyond recognition before it can be accepted. The only part of Christian teachings which will be truly accepted by the Chinese people is Christ's injunction to be "harmless as doves" but "wise as serpents." For these two virtues, dove-like gentleness and serpent-like wisdom, are attributes of the old rogue.

In one word we recognize the necessity of human effort, but we also admit the futility of it. This general attitude of mind has a tendency to develop passive defence tactics. "Great things can be reduced into small things, and small things can be reduced into nothing." On this general principle all Chinese disputes are patched up, all Chinese schemes are readjusted, and all reform programmes are discounted until there are peace and rice for everybody. "One bid is not so good as one pass," so runs another of our proverbs, which means the same thing as "Let well enough alone," and "Let sleeping dogs lie."

Human life moves on, therefore, on the line of least struggle and least resistance. This develops a certain calmness of mind, which enables one to swallow insults and to find oneself in harmony with the universe. It develops also certain defence tactics which can be more terrible than any tactics of aggression. When one goes to a restaurant and feels hungry, but the food does not come, one can repeat the order to the boy. If the boy is rude, one can complain to the management and do something about it. But if the boy replies in the most elegant manner, "Coming! coming!" and does not move a step, one can do absolutely nothing except pray or curse in the most elegant manner also. Such, in brief, is the passive strength of the Chinese people, a strength which those who are made to feel most will appreciate best. It is the strength of the old rogue.

V. Pacifism

So far we have been dealing with three of the worst characteristics that paralyse the Chinese people for organized action. These characteristics are seen to spring from a general view of life, as shrewd as it is mellow, distinguished by a certain tolerant nonchalance. It is evident that such a view of life is not without its virtues, and they are the virtues of an old people, not ambitious nor keen to sit on top of the world, but a people whose eyes have seen much of life, who are prepared to accept life for what it is worth, but who insist nevertheless that this life shall be lived decently and happily within one's lot.

For the Chinese are a hard-boiled lot. There is no nonsense about them: they do not live in order to die, as the Christians pretend to do, nor do they seek for a Utopia on earth, as many seers of the West do. They just want to order this life on earth, which they know to be full of pain and sorrow, so that they may work peaceably, endure nobly, and live happily. Of the noble virtues of the West, of nobility, ambition, zeal for reform, public spirit, sense for adventure and heroic courage, the Chinese are devoid. They cannot be interested in climbing Mont Blanc or in exploring the North Pole. But they are tremendously interested in this commonplace world, and they have an indomitable patience, an indefatigable industry, a sense of duty, a level-headed common sense, cheerfulness, humour, tolerance, pacifism, and that unequalled genius for finding happiness in hard environments which we call contentment—qualities that make this commonplace life enjoyable to them. And chief of these are pacifism and tolerance, which are the mark of a mellow culture, and which seem to be lacking in modern Europe.

Indeed it seems at times, on watching the spectacle of present-day Europe, that she is suffering less from a lack of "smartness" or intellectual brilliance than from the lack of a little mellow wisdom. It seems at times barely possible that Europe will outgrow its hot-headed youthfulness and its intellectual brilliance, and that after another century of scientific progress, the world will be brought so closely together that the Europeans will learn to take a more tolerant view of life and of each other, at the risk of total annihilation. They will perhaps learn to be a little less brilliant, and a little more mature. I have confidence that the change of view will be brought about, not by brilliant theories but by an instinct for self-preservation. Perhaps then the West will learn to believe less in self-assertion and more in tolerance, for tolerance will be direly needed when the world is closely knit together. They will be a little less desirous to make progress, and a little more anxious to understand life. And the voice of the Old Man of Hankukuan Pass will be listened to more widely.

From the Chinese point of view, pacifism is not "noble"; it is simply "good" because it is common sense. If this earthly life is all the life we can have, we must try to live in peace if we want to live happily. From this point of view, the self-assertion and the restlessness of the spirit of the West are signs of its youthful rawness. The Chinese, steeped in his Oriental philosophy, can see that that rawness will gradually wear off at Europe's coming of age. For, strange as it may seem, out of the extremely shrewd philosophy of Taoism there always emerges the word "tolerance." Tolerance has been, I think, the greatest quality of Chinese culture, and tolerance will also become the greatest quality of modern culture, when that culture matures. To learn tolerance, one needs a little sorrow and a little cynicism of the Taoist type. True cynics are often the kindest people, for they see the hollowness of life, and from the realization of that hollowness is generated a kind of cosmic pity.

Pacifism, too, is a matter of high human understanding. If man could learn to be a little more cynical, he would also be less inclined toward warfare. That is perhaps why all intelligent men are cowards. The Chinese are the world's worst fighters because they are an intelligent race, backed and nurtured by Taoistic cynicism and the Confucian emphasis on harmony as the ideal of life. They do not fight because they are the most calculating and self-interested of peoples. An average Chinese child knows what the European grey-haired statesmen do not know, that by fighting one gets killed or maimed, whether it be an individual or a nation. Chinese parties to a dispute are the easiest to bring to their senses. That calculating philosophy teaches them to be slow to quarrel and quick to patch up. That mellow, old roguish philosophy which teaches the Chinese patience and passive resistance in times of trouble, also warns them against momentary pride and assertion at the moment of success. The Chinese counsel for moderation says: "When fortune comes, do not enjoy all of it; when advantage comes, do not take all of it." To be over-assertive and to take full advantage of one's position is called "showing too much edge," a mark of vulgarity and an omen of downfall. Whereas the English believe in "not striking a man when he is down" out of respect for fair play, the Chinese equivalent expression "do not push a fellow to the wall" is merely a matter of culture, or *hanyang*, as we call it.

To the Chinese, the Versailles Treaty is not only unfair, it is merely vulgar or lacking in *hanyang*. If the Frenchman had been inbued a little with the spirit of Taoism at the moment of his victory, he would not have imposed the Versailles Treaty, and his head would rest more easily on his pillow to-day. But France was young, and Germany would certainly have done the same thing, and no one realizes the extreme silliness of two nations like France and Germany each trying to keep the other permanently under its iron heels. But Clemenceau had not read Laotse. Nor has Hitler. So let them fight, while the Taoist watches and smiles.

Chinese pacifism is also largely a matter of temperament as well as of human understanding. Chinese boys fight much less in the street than Western boys. As a people, we fight much less than we ought to, in spite of our interminable civil wars. Put the American people under the same misrule and there would have been thirty revolutions, not three, in the last twenty years. Ireland is now at peace because the Irish fought hard, and we are still fighting to-day because we do not fight hard enough.

Nor are Chinese civil wars fighting in the real sense of the word. Until recently, civil wars were never glorified. Conscription for service is unknown, and the soldiers who do the fighting are poor people who do not know how to make a living otherwise. These soldiers do not relish a good fight, and the generals relish the fight because they do not do the fighting. In any major campaign silver bullets have always won, in spite of the fact that the conquering hero may make a majestic triumphal return to the capital to the accompaniment of the boom of guns. Those guns—they suggest so much the sound of battle, and they are typical, for in Chinese private quarrels and civil warfare, it is the sound and noise that make up the essence of the battle. One does not see fighting in China; one merely hears it. I heard two such battles, one in Peking, and one in Amoy. Aurally, it was satisfying. Usually a superior army merely awes the inferior enemy into defeat, and what would be a protracted campaign in a Western country is finished in a month. The defeated general, according to the Chinese idea of fair play, is then given a hundred thousand dollars travelling expenses and sent on a "tour of industrial investigation to Europe," with the full knowledge that in the next war his services may be needed by the present conqueror. With the next turn of events, the most probable thing is that you will find the victor and the vanquished riding in the same car like two sworn brothers. That is the beauty of Chinese *hanyang*. Meanwhile, the people have nothing to do with it. They hate war, and will always hate war. Good people never fight in China. For "good iron is not made into nails, and good men are not made soldiers."

VI. CONTENTMENT

Travellers in China, especially those wayward travellers who go through the seldom visited parts of the Chinese inland, are equally amazed at the low standard of living of the Chinese toiling masses and at their cheerfulness and contentment under such conditions. Even in the famine-stricken provinces, like Shensi, this spirit of contentment generally prevails in all except extreme cases, and some Shensi farmers probably can still smile.

Now a lot of the so-called misery of the Chinese people is due undoubtedly to the application of a warped European standard, the standard which cannot conceive of any man being happy unless he is living in an overheated apartment and owns a radio. If this standard were correct, there should have been no happy person in the world before 1850, and there should be more happy people in the United States than in *gemütliches* Bavaria, where there are very few rotating, adjustable collapsible and reversible barber chairs, and certainly very few switches and buttons. There are still fewer switches and buttons in the Chinese countryside, although in progressive Shanghai the old-fashioned barber chair that is a real chair, and that one can still find on Kingsway in London or in Montmartre in Paris to-day, has completely disappeared. For myself, I am inclined to think that the man who sits on a chair that is a real chair, and sleeps on a bed that is a real bed (and not a daytime sofa) is a happier man. The standard that measures a man's civilization by the number of mechanical buttons he presses in a day must, therefore, be a false standard, and a lot of this so-called mystery of Chinese contentment is of the Westerner's own making.

It is true, however, that Chinese people are perhaps more contented than Western people, class for class, when living under the same conditions. This spirit of cheerfulness and contentment is found in both the literate and illiterate classes, for such is the penetration of the Chinese racial tradition. It may be seen in the gay, babbling rickshaw boy of Peking, for ever laughing and joking all the way and ready to laugh at a fellow-man's discomforts, or it may be seen in the panting and perspiring sedan-chair coolies who carry you up to the top of Kuling, or it may be seen in the boat-trackers who pull your boat up the Szechuen rapids and who earn for their living a bare pittance beyond two simple but hearty meals a day. A simple but hearty meal eaten without much worry is, however, a great deal of luck, according to the Chinese theory of contentment, for as a Chinese scholar has put it, "a well-filled stomach is indeed a great thing: all else is luxury of life."[1]

For contentment is another of those words, like "kindliness" and "peaceableness," which are written on red paper and pasted on all doors on New Year's Day. It is part of the counsel for moderation, part of that human wisdom which says, "When good fortune comes, do not enjoy all of it," and of that advice of a Ming scholar "to choose the lighter happiness." Among the epigrams of Laotse which have passed into current phraseology is the maxim that "one who is contented will not meet with disgrace." Another form of this maxim is, "One who is contented is always happy." In literature, it emerges as a praise of the rural life and of the man who has few worries, a sentiment which is found in all poems and private letters. I

[1] The Chinese description of this happy state of going to bed with a filled stomach is: "soft, well-filled, dark and sweet"—the last two adjectives referring to sweet slumber. This expression is positively voluptuous in the Chinese language.

pick at random from a collection of letters of Ming scholars.
Thus wrote Lu Shen to his friend:

> To-night we are going to have a full moon. How about
> getting a painted houseboat and bringing along a few
> musicians? . . . Can you come and spend a night with me
> in this early autumn? I am going to have a recluse's gown
> made, and when my resignation is accepted, I shall be indeed
> a carefree old man of the mountains.

It is this sort of sentiment which, when passing into the current
thoughts and feelings of the Chinese scholar, enables him to
find happiness in his lowly hut.

Human happiness is a frail thing, for the gods are evidently
jealous of it. The problem of happiness is therefore the most
elusive problem of life, but after all is said and done about
culture and progress, it should remain the primary concern of
mankind's highest wisdom to solve it. The Chinese, with their
usual common sense, have bent their highest efforts toward
the finding of this happiness, and like the utilitarians that they
are, have always been more interested in the problem of
happiness than in the problem of progress.

Mrs. Bertrand Russell wisely pointed out that "the right to
be happy" was, and still is, a forgotten right that nobody in
the West is interested in, Westerners being preoccupied with the
more secondary rights to vote, to pass upon the King's expenditure, to declare war, and to be tried when arrested. The
Chinese have never even thought of the right to be tried when
arrested, but they have always been supremely jealous of their
right to happiness, which neither poverty nor disgrace is
allowed to take away from them. The Western approach to
the problem of happiness is positive, while the Chinese approach is negative. The question of happiness is always
reduced, in the last analysis, to the question of a man's wants.

The fact is, we are very much in confusion as to what we
really want. For this reason, the story of Diogenes who pro-
claimed to the world that he was a happy man because he did
not want anything, and who threw away his bowl on seeing a
boy drinking from his hands, always provokes some laughter

and a certain amount of real envy from the modern man. The modern man finds himself in continual perplexity in regard to many problems, and most of all in problems that affect closely his personal life. He cannot spare himself a certain luxurious envy for that ascetic ideal of Diogenes, and is at the same time far from willing to miss a really good show or movie. That gives us the so-called "restlessness" of the modern spirit.

The Chinese, without going so far as Diogenes, for the Chinese never go far in anything, take the negative approach to happiness through their philosophy of contentment. Unlike Diogenes, however, a Chinese man wants quite a few things. But he wants only the things that make for happiness, and at the same time does not insist on having them if they are out of his reach. He wants at least a pair of clean shirts, for Diogenes in the story book may exhale a certain spiritual fragrance, but Diogenes as a bedfellow would be a different story. But if he is extremely poor and can have only one shirt, he will not mind, either. And unlike Diogenes, he wants also a good show, and he would give himself up to the full enjoyment of it. But if he must go without that, he will not be too sorry. He wants some tall old trees in his neighbourhood, but if he cannot have them, a date-tree in his yard will give him just as much happiness. He wants many children, and a wife who personally prepares his favourite dishes; and if he is wealthy, then a good cook, too, and a pretty maidservant in red pyjamas to tend the incense while he is reading or painting. He wants some good friends, and a woman who understands, preferably to be found in the person of his wife; if not, then in one of the sing-song girls. If he is not born with such "voluptuous luck," then he will not be sorry, either. He wants a filled stomach, but *congee* and pickled carrots are not so costly in China; and he wants a good jug of wine, but rice-wine is often home-brewed, or he can pay only a few cash for a bowl at the good old wine-shops. He wants leisure, and leisure he can have in China, and he is as happy as a bird if he

Has met a monk in a bamboo-covered yard
And enjoyed another of life's leisurely half-days.

He wants a secluded hut, if he cannot have an entire pleasure garden, situated among the mountains with a mountain rill running past his hut, or in a valley where of an afternoon he can saunter along the river bank and watch cormorants catching fish for the fisher. But if he cannot have that luck and must live in the city, he will not be sorry, either. For he would have, in any case, a cage bird and a few potted flowers and the moon, for he can always have the moon. So did Su Tungp'o the poet write about the moon in a perfect gem-like little essay, called "A Night Promenade at Ch'engt'ien":

On the twelfth night of the tenth moon of the sixth year of Yüanfeng, I had undressed and was going to bed, when the moonlight entered my door, and I got up, happy of heart. I thought there was no one to share this happiness with me. So I walked over to the Ch'engt'ien Temple to look for Huaimin. He, too, had not yet gone to bed. So we paced about in the yard. The yard looked like a transparent pool with the shadows of water-grass in it, but they were really the shadows of bamboos and pine-trees cast by the moonlight. Isn't there a moon on every night? And aren't there bamboos and pine-trees everywhere? Only there are few carefree people like the two of us.

A strong determination to get the best out of life, a keen desire to enjoy what one has, and no regrets if one fails: this is the secret of the Chinese genius for contentment.

VII. HUMOUR

Humour is a state of mind. More than that, it is a point of view, a way of looking at life. The flower of humour blooms whenever in the course of development of a nation there is an exuberance of intellect able to flay its own ideals, for humour is nothing but intellect slashing at itself. In any period of history, when mankind was able to perceive its own futility, its own smallness, and its own follies and inconsistencies, a humorist appeared, like Chuangtse of China, Omar Khayyám

THE CHINESE CHARACTER 63

of Persia, and Aristophanes of Greece. Athens would be infinitely poorer had there been no Aristophanes, and the Chinese intellectual heritage would be infinitely less rich had there been no Chuangtse.

Since Chuangtse lived and wrote, however, all Chinese politicians and bandits have become great humorists, because they have been imbued, directly or indirectly, with the Chuang-tsean view of life. Laotse had laughed before him, a thin, shrill yet cataclysmic laughter. He must have been a bachelor all his life, or he could not have laughed so roguishly. Anyway there is no record that he ever married or had any progeny. The last coughs of Laotse's laughter were caught up by Chuangtse and he, being a younger man, had a richer voice, and the ring of his laughter has reverberated throughout the ages. We still cannot resist a chance to laugh, yet sometimes I feel we are carrying the joke too far, and laugh a little out of season.

The abysmal ignorance of the foreigner about China and the Chinese cannot be more impressive than when he asks the question: Do the Chinese have a sense of humour? It is really as surprising as if an Arab caravan were to ask: Are there sands in the Sahara desert? It is strange, however, how little a person may see in a country. Theoretically, at least, the Chinese people should have humour, for humour is born of realism; and the Chinese are an unusually realistic people. Humour is born of common sense, and the Chinese have an overdose of common sense. Humour, especially Asiatic humour, is the product of contentment and leisure, and the Chinese have contentment and leisure to a supreme degree. A humorist is often a defeatist, and delights in recounting his own failures and embarrassments, and the Chinese are often sane, cool-minded defeatists. Humour often takes a tolerant view of vice and evil and instead of condemning them, laughs at them, and the Chinese have always been characterized by the capacity to tolerate evil. Toleration has, then, a good and a bad side, and the Chinese have both of them. If the characteristics of the Chinese race we have discussed above—common sense, toleration, contentment and old roguery—are true, then humour is inevitable in China.

Chinese humour, however, is more in deeds than in words. The Chinese have their words for the various types of humour, but the commonest type, called *huach'i*, in which sometimes the Confucian scholars indulge under pseudonyms, really means to me only "trying to be funny." Such writings are only literary relaxations of a too rigoristic classical tradition, but humour as such had no proper place in literature. At least there was no open acknowledgement of the rôle and value of humour in literature. Humour, indeed, abounds in Chinese novels, but novels were never accepted as "literature" by the classicists.

There is very first-class humour in *Shiking* (Book of Poetry), in the Confucian *Analects* and in *Hanfeitse*, but the Confucian gentleman, brought up in his puritan view of life, could not see any fun in Confucius, just as he failed to see the wonderful tender love lyrics in *Shiking*, giving them fantastic interpretations, as the Western theologians give of the *Song of Songs*. There is a very fine humour in T'ao Yüanming's writings, too, a sort of quiet leisurely content and a refined luxury of self-abnegation, the best example of which is his poem on his unworthy sons:

My temples are grey, my muscles no longer full.
Five sons have I, and none of them likes school.
Ah-shu is sixteen and as lazy as lazy can be.
Ah-hsüan is fifteen and no taste for reading has he.
Thirteen are Yung and Tuan, yet they can't tell six from
    seven.
A-t'ung wants only pears and chestnuts—in two years he'll
    be eleven.
Then, come! let me empty this cup, if such be the will of
    Heaven.

Humour there is, too, in Tu Fu's and Li Po's poetry, Tu Fu who often produces in his readers a bitter smile, and Li Po who pleases by his romanticist nonchalance, but we do not call it "humour." The unholy awe in which Confucianism was held as the national religion also restricted the free expression of ideas and made the presentation of novel points of view and ideas taboo, and humour only lives on novel and original points of view. It is clear that such a conventional environment is not conducive to the production of humorous literature. If anyone were to make a collection of Chinese humour, he would have to cull it from the folk-songs and the Yüan dramas and the Ming novels, all outside the pale of the classical "literature," and in the private notes and letters of scholars (especially those of the Sung and Ming Dynasties), when they are a little off their guard.

But the Chinese have nevertheless a humour all their own, for they always love a good joke. It is humour of a grimmer sort, and is based on the farcical view of life. In spite of the extremely serious style in their editorial and political writings, which are seldom relieved by humour, they often surprise the foreigners by the extremely light manner in which they take important reform programmes and movements, like the Kuomintang agrarian programme, the Sanmin Doctrine, the flood and famine relief, the New Life Movement, and the Anti-Opium Bureaux. An American professor, recently visiting Shanghai and lecturing in the Chinese colleges, was completely surprised by the burst of laughter among the student audience whenever he made a perfectly sincere reference to the New Life Movement. If he had made a serious reference to the Anti-Opium Bureaux, he would have been met by still louder volleys of silvery laughter.

For humour is, as I have said, a point of view, a way of looking at life. With that view of life we are more or less familiar. Life is a huge farce, and we human beings are mere puppets in it. The man who takes life too seriously, who obeys library reading-room rules too honestly, who actually keeps off the lawn because merely a signboard says so, always makes a fool of himself and is usually subjected to laughter from his older colleagues, and since laughter is contagious, very soon he becomes a humorist, too.

This humorist farcicality then results in the inability of the Chinese to take anything seriously, from the most serious political reform movement to a dog's funeral. The farcical element in Chinese funerals is typical. In the grandiloquent funeral processions of Chinese upper and middle classes, you can see street urchins with dirty faces wearing embroidered and multi-coloured robes, accompanied, in modern China, by brass bands playing "Onward, Christian Soldiers," which facts are often adduced by Europeans as proofs of the Chinese lack of humour. A Chinese funeral procession, however, is a perfect symbol of Chinese humour, for Europeans alone take a funeral procession seriously and try to make it solemn. A solemn funeral is inconceivable to the Chinese mind. Where the Europeans err is that, with their preconceived notions, they think *a priori* that a funeral should be a solemn affair. A funeral, like a wedding, should be noisy and should be expensive, but there is no reason why it should be solemn. Solemnity is already provided for in the grandiloquent gowns, and the rest is form, and form is farce. To this day, I cannot distinguish between a funeral and a wedding procession until I see a coffin or a wedding-chair.

Chinese humour, then, as symbolized by the highly farcical funeral procession, consists in compliance with outward form as such and the total disregard of the substance in actuality. One who appreciates the humour of a Chinese funeral should be able to read and interpret Chinese political programmes properly also. Political programmes and official statements are issued as matters of form, being drafted by clerks who specialize in a kind of specious, bombastic phraseology, just as there are special shops keeping funeral procession gowns and paraphernalia for hire, and no intelligent Chinese ever takes them seriously. If foreign newspaper correspondents would bear this symbol of the funeral gown in mind, they would be less likely to be misled by them and then later give up the Chinese as a unique people that they fail to understand.

This farcical view of life and this formula regarding form and substance can be illustrated in a myriad different ways. Some years ago, a government order, originating in a request from the Central Kuomintang, prohibited the Chinese government ministries from keeping Shanghai offices in the foreign concessions. The actual carrying out of this order would mean a great inconvenience to the ministers who have their homes in Shanghai, and throw a number of people out of jobs. The Nanking ministers neither defied the Nanking order nor petitioned for its repeal on honest grounds of inconvenience and impracticability. No professional clerk could be clever enough to draft any such petition and make it accord with good form, since it meant the desire of Chinese officials to reside in foreign settlements, which would be unpatriotic. They did an infinitely cleverer thing by changing the door-plates of their Shanghai offices and calling them trade inspection bureaux. The door-plates probably cost twenty dollars apiece, no man was thrown out of a job, and no "face" was lost. The school trick pleased not only the Nanking ministers but also Nanking itself, where the original order was issued. Our Nanking ministers are great humorists. So are our bandits. So are our war-lords. The humour of Chinese civil wars has already been pointed out.

In contrast with this, we might take the case of mission schools as showing the Western lack of humour. The missions were put into a scare a few years ago when their registration was required, which involved the crossing out of religious instruction from the school curricula, the hanging of Sun Yatsen's picture in the assembly hall, and the holding of Monday memorial meetings. The Chinese authorities could not see why the mission schools could not comply with these simple regulations, while the missionaries could not see their way clear to accepting them, and there was a deadlock. Some missionaries actually had visions of closing up their schools, and in one instance, everything would have gone on smoothly except for the stupid honesty of the Western principal who refused to cancel one sentence from their school catalogue avowing religious instruction to be one of their aims. The principal wanted to be able to say honestly and openly that religious instruction was indeed the principal aim of their institution, and to this day that school is not registered. There was absolutely no lightness of touch. What this mission school should have done was to imitate the example of the Nanking ministers, comply with every official regulation, hang a picture of Sun Yatsen—and proceed *à la chinoise* as regards the rest. But I cannot help thinking that a school run with such stupid honesty must be an honest-to-goodness school.

Such is the Chinese farcical view of life. The Chinese language abounds in metaphors regarding the drama of human life. Chinese officials assuming and leaving their posts are spoken of as "entering the stage" and "making their exit," and a man coming with a high-sounding programme is referred to as "singing high opera." We really look upon life as a stage, and the kind of theatrical show we like best is always high comedy, whether that comedy be a new constitution, or a bill of rights, or an anti-opium bureau, or a disbandment conference. We always enjoy it, but I wish our people would sometimes be serious. Humour, above everything else, is ruining China. One can have too much of that silvery laughter, for it is again the laughter of the old rogue, at the touch of whose breath every flower of enthusiasm and idealism must wither and die.

VIII. CONSERVATISM

No portrait of the Chinese character would be complete without a mention of its conservatism. Conservatism in itself should not be a word of reproach. Conservatism is but a form of pride and rests on a feeling of satisfaction with the present. Since there is usually so little one can be proud of and so little satisfaction in the arrangement of human life in this world, conservatism is really a sign of inward richness, a gift rather to be envied.

The Chinese are by nature a proud race—excusably so, when one considers the whole course of their history except the last hundred years. For, though politically they were at times humiliated, culturally they were the centre of a vast humanist civilization that was conscious of itself and lacked no well-reasoned apologetics. China's only cultural rival of any importance that represented a different point of view was Indian Buddhism, and for Buddhism, the true Confucianist had always some measure of sneering contempt. For the Confucianist was immeasurably proud of Confucius, and in being proud of Confucius, he was proud of the nation, proud of the Chinese having understood life in its moral essence proud of their knowledge of human nature, and proud of their having solved the problems of life in all its ethical and political relationships.

In a way, he was justified. For Confucianism not only asked about the meaning of life but also answered it in a way that left people satisfied with having found the meaning of human existence. The answer was solid, clear and sensible, so that it left people with no desire to speculate about the future life or to change the present one. Man naturally becomes conservative when he realizes he has got something that works and therefore something that is true. The Confucianist saw no other way of life, thought no other way possible. The fact that Westerners, too, have a well-organized social life and that a London policeman would help an old woman across the street without any knowledge of the Confucian doctrine of respect for old age comes to the Chinese always more or less as a shock.

When the realization came that Westerners possess all the Confucian virtues of courtesy, orderliness, honour, kindliness, courage, and honesty of government, and that Confucius would have personally approved of the London policeman and tube conductor, that racial pride was badly shaken. There were things that displeased the Chinese and struck him as raw, uncouth and barbarian, like husband and wife walking hand in hand together, father and daughter kissing each other, kissing on the screen, kissing on the stage, kissing on the railway platform, and kissing everywhere. These things confirmed him in the belief that the Chinese civilization was really superior. But there were other things, like the common people being able to read, women being able to write letters, general cleanliness (which he imagined was a heritage from the Middle Ages instead of a nineteenth-century invention), students' respect for teachers, and English boys always saying "Yes, sir," to their superiors and the like which were immeasurably impressive. These, together with good roads, the railway, the steamship, good leather boots, Parisian perfume, the wonderfully sweet white children, the X-ray pictures, the camera, the phonograph, the telephone, and many similar things, have completely shattered the native pride.

Helped by the extraterritorial rights and the generous use of European boots against Chinese coolies, for which there is no legal redress, the loss of pride became an instinctive fear of the foreigner. The old celestial pride is now no more. The hullabaloo raised by foreign merchants against possible Chinese attacks on the settlements is only a negative testimony of their courage and of their knowledge of modern China. Some inward indignation against those European boots and their liberal use against Chinese coolies there must always be, but if the foreigner thinks that the Chinese will ever show their indignation by reprisal with inferior leather boots, he is grossly mistaken. If they did, they would not be Chinese, but Christians. Practically speaking, admiration for the Europeans and fear of their aggressiveness are now universal.

Some such bad shock must have been responsible for the ultra-radicalism that brought about the Republic of China. No one could think China would become a republic. It was a change so vast and gigantic that it could appeal to none except the idiotic or the inspired. It was like building a bridge of rainbow across to heaven and then walking on it. But the Chinese revolutionists of 1911 were inspired. Following upon the Chinese defeat in the Sino-Japanese War of 1895, there was an active propaganda for modernization of China. There were two schools, the constitutionalists who stood for a modernized limited monarchy, and the revolutionists who were for a republic. The left wing was led by Sun Yatsen, while the right wing was led by K'ang Yuwei, and his disciple Liang Ch'ich'ao, who later forsook his master and turned left. For a long time, the adherents of these parties were fighting literary battles in Japan, but the question was finally settled, not by any argument but by the apparent hopelessness of the Manchu régime and by the intrinsic appeal to racial pride. The political radicalism of 1911 was followed by the literary radicalism of 1916, when the Chinese Renaissance movement was started by Hu Shih, and succeeded by the ideological radicalism of 1926, with the result that Communism is to-day colouring the thought of practically all primary schoolteachers of the country.

The consequence is that, to-day, China is divided into two

armed camps of Communism and reaction. There is a deep chasm separating the younger generation from the older generation, which is an extremely regrettable state of affairs. While the thinking younger generation are decidedly for a cataclysmic upheaval of the whole ideological and political system, a movement of conservative reaction has set in among the ruling authorities. The conservative reaction is unfortunately unconvincing, owing to the fact that its champions are mostly war-lords and politicians whose personal lives are far from being models of Confucian conduct. Actually, such conservatism is only a cloak of hypocrisy and a sadistic reprisal giving outlet to their hatred of the young. For Confucianism teaches respect for old age and authority. The shining political light who utters large mouthfuls of Confucianism happens also to initiate Thibetan-lama-Buddhist prayers for divine succour against Japanese aggression. The jumble of Confucian platitudes mixed with Sanscrit *om mani padme hum* and Thibetan prayer-wheels creates an extremely weird effect unlikely to arouse the interest of the young Chinese.

This is the surface struggle between conservatism and radicalism in China. Its outcome will depend largely upon Japanese and European politics, for no mere argument will settle the question. China may yet be driven to Communism, if the champions of conservatism cannot prove themselves worthy to find a way out for China. As regards the true temperament of the Chinese race and the large mass of people who either read Chinese only or read nothing at all, conservatism will always remain.

Most important, however, is the fact that Chinese do not want to change. Behind all the outward changes of custom and women's dress and habits of locomotion, the Chinese retains a sneering smile for the hot-headed young man who wears a foreign coat or who speaks English too well. That young man always looks immature and is often shamed out of his progressiveness. The strange thing is that the man who no longer looks immature veers towards conservatism in China. The returned student arrives at maturity by putting on a Chinese gown and accepting the Chinese way of life. He loves its mellowness, its leisure, its comforts, and its commonplace contentment. In his Chinese gown, his soul has come to rest. The strange fascination of Chinese surroundings which keeps many "queer" Europeans in China for life comes over him toward middle age.

Meanwhile, the large majority of the people will keep in their old ruts, not by any conscious conviction but by a kind of racial instinct. I feel the racial tradition is so strong that its fundamental pattern of life will always remain. Even if a cataclysmic upheaval like a communistic régime should come, the old tradition of individuality, toleration, moderation and common sense will break Communism and change it beyond recognition, rather than Communism with its socialistic, impersonal and rigoristic outlook break the old tradition. It must be so.

Chapter Three

THE CHINESE MIND

I. INTELLIGENCE

IF the preceding chapter on the Chinese character has any general conclusion, it is that of the supremacy of the human mind over material surroundings. Supremacy of the mind has more than one meaning. It means not only the application of human cunning to convert a world known to be full of pain and misery into a habitable place for human beings, but it implies also a certain contempt for mere physical courage and strength as such. Confucius long ago condemned the Jack Dempsey type of physical courage in his disciple Tzŭlu, and I am sure he would have preferred a Gene Tunney who could be at home in circles of educated friends as well. Mencius, too, distinguished between mental labour and manual labour, and did not hesitate to put the former above the latter. For the Chinese had no nonsense about equality, and respect for the mental labourers or the educated class has been an outstanding characteristic of the Chinese civilization.

This respect for learning must be taken in a different sense from that usually understood in the West, for, devoted as some Chinese scholars are to their learning, the devotion of some Western professors to their special subjects, sometimes amounting to a morbid pride and professional jealousy, seems to me much more impressive. The Chinese respect for the scholar is based on a different conception, for they respect that type of education which increases his practical wisdom, his knowledge of world affairs, and his judgment in times of crisis. It is a respect which, in theory at least, must be earned by actual worth. In local as in national troubles, the people look to him for cool judgment, for far-sightedness, for a better envisagement of the manifold consequences of an act or decision, and therefore for natural guidance and leadership, and real leadership is conceived as a leadership of the mind. With the majority of people illiterate, it is easy to maintain that leadership, sometimes by a mere jumble of unusual phrases that the illiterate only half understand, or by a reference to history, of which the common people have only such knowledge as they can pick up from the theatre. The reference to history generally settles the question, and it is characteristic, because the Chinese mind thinks in terms of concrete analogy, which somehow puts the situation in a form that the common people can grasp in its entirety.

I have already suggested that the Chinese suffer from an overdose of intelligence, as shown in their old roguery, their indifference, and in their pacifism, which so often borders on cowardice. But all intelligent men are cowards, because intelligent men want to save their skins. There can be nothing more silly, if we keep our minds clear enough to see it, than a man popping his head "over the top," with gin-manufactured courage, in order to meet a lead bullet and die for a newspaper-manufactured "cause." If he can use his head in reading newspapers, he will not be at the front, and if he can abstain from gin and keep a cool head, he will logically and humanly be in a blue funk. The last war has taught us that many gentle souls who shine at school or college undergo a mental torture of which the more robust and less intelligent have no inkling of an idea. And it is not the novice but the man in service for four years who begins to realize that desertion is often a virtue one owes to oneself and the only sane course open to a sensible and honest man.

But the general mental intelligence of the Chinese race can be proved from other sources than cowardice. Chinese students in America and European colleges often distinguish themselves academically, and I think this is hardly due to a process of selection. The Chinese mind is long used to academic discussions at home. The Japanese have sarcastically dubbed the Chinese "a literary nation," and justifiably so. An example of this is the enormous output of current Chinese magazines which seems to crop up wherever a group of four or five friends get together in a city, and the tremendous number of writers who keep the magazine editors overwhelmed with their articles. The old imperial examinations which, as I have pointed out, were a kind of intelligence test, long ago sharpened the Chinese scholar's mind in the fine use of words and in subtle literary distinctions, and the cultivation of poetry has trained them in the higher spheres of literary expression, and in taste and finesse. The Chinese art of painting has reached a height yet unreached by the West, and in calligraphy they have forged a way alone and reached what I believe to be the maximun variety and refinement in the conception of rhythmic beauty.

The Chinese mind therefore cannot be accused of lacking originality or creativeness. Its inventiveness has been equal to the handicraft stage in which Chinese industries have always remained. Because of the failure to develop a scientific method and because of the peculiar qualities of Chinese thinking, China has been backward in natural science. I have confidence, however, that with the importation of the scientific method, and with adequate research facilities, China will be able to produce great scientists and make important contributions to the scientific world in the next century.

Nor is such native intelligence confined to the educated class. Chinese servants are greatly welcomed on account of their general intelligence and human understanding, and must be put at least on a par with European servants. Chinese merchants have prospered in the Malay States, in the East Indies and in the Philippines chiefly because their intelligence has been greater than that of the natives and because of those virtues that come from intelligence, such as thrift, steady industry and far-sightedness. The respect for scholarship has brought about a general desire for refinement even among the lower middle class, of which the foreigner is seldom aware. Foreign residents in Shanghai sometimes offend the department-store salesmen by talking down to them in "pidgin," not knowing that many of them are particular about a split infinitive. Chinese labourers are easily trained to be skilled mechanics where precision is required. One rarely sees in the slums and factory districts that type of big, husky animal of a similar class in the West, distinguished only by his big jaw, low forehead and brute strength. One meets a different type, with intelligent eyes and cheerful appearance and an eminently reasonable temperament. Perhaps the variability of intelligence is decidedly lower among the Chinese than among many Western races, the same lower variability that we see in the mental powers of women as compared with variability in men.

II. Femininity

Indeed, the Chinese mind is akin to the feminine mind in many respects. Femininity, in fact, is the only word that can summarize its various aspects. The qualities of the feminine intelligence and feminine logic are exactly the qualities of the Chinese mind. The Chinese head, like the feminine head, is full of common sense. It is shy of abstract terms, like women's speech. The Chinese way of thinking is synthetic, concrete and revels in proverbs, like women's conversation. They never have had higher mathematics of their own, and seldom have gone beyond the level of arithmetic, like many women, with the exception of those masculine women prize-winners at college.[1] Women have a surer instinct of life than men, and the Chinese have it more than other people. The Chinese depend largely upon their intuition for solving all nature's mysteries, that same "intuition" or "sixth sense" which makes many women believe a thing is so because it is so. And finally Chinese logic is highly personal, like women's logic. A woman would not introduce a professor of ichthyology as professor of ichthyology, but as the brother-in-law of Colonel Harrison who died in India while she was undergoing an operation for appendicitis in New York by that lovable old Doctor Cabot you should look at his handsome forehead. In the same way, a Chinese judge cannot think of law as an abstract entity, but as a flexible quantity as it should be personally applied to Colonel Huang or Major Li. Accordingly, any law which is not personal enough to respond to the personality of Colonel

[1] This refers, of course, to general womanhood as brought about by the present social system.

Huang or Major Li is inhuman and therefore no law at all. Chinese justice is an art, not a science.

Jespersen, in his well-known book, *The Growth and Structure of English*, once referred to the masculine qualities of the English language by pointing to its love of economy, common sense and forcefulness. Without wishing to contradict so great an authority on the English language, I beg to differ on a point which concerns the sexes. Common sense and the practical mind are characteristics of women rather than of men, who are more liable to take their feet off the ground and soar to impossible heights. The Chinese language and grammar show this femininity exactly because the language, in its form, syntax and vocabulary, reveals an extreme simplicity of thinking, concreteness of imagery and economy of syntactical relationships.

This simplicity is best illustrated from pidgin, which is English meat with Chinese bones, as we say in China. There is no reason why a sentence like "He come, you no come; you come, he no come" should not be considered as clear as the more roundabout "You needn't come, if he comes, and he needn't come, if you come." In fact, this simplicity makes for clarity of expression. Moon, in *Dean's English*, quotes an English Somerset farmer as testifying before the judge: "He'd a stick, and he'd a stick, and he licked he, and he licked he; if he licked he as hard as he licked he, he'd a killed he, and not he he," and this seems to me a much more sensible way of talking than one with the Germanic case-distinctions. For according to the Chinese, the difference between "I lick he" and "he lick I" is perfectly clear without the subjective-accusative complex, and the adding of the third person singular ending "s" is as superfluous as is already proved to be in the past tense (I had, he had; I went, he went). Actually lots of people are saying "us girls" and "them things" without ever being misunderstood or losing anything except a meaningless "class" which has nothing to do with the beauty of expression. I have great hope that English and American professors will one day bravely and respectably pronounce a "he don't" in the classrooms and that the English language may one day become as sensible and clear as the Chinese, through the influence of pidgin.

G

A certain feminine practical instinct has already guided the English to abbreviate all their subordinate clauses as much as possible, like "weather permitting," "God willing," "if possible," "whenever necessary," "as expected," "if I don't (*not* shall not) come back to-night," and "if war breaks out (*not* shall break out) next week." Jespersen already mentions such examples of Chinese simplicity in English as "first come, first served," "no cure, no pay," "once bitten, twice shy," which are all standard pidgin. They are beginning to drop the "whom," too ("Who are you speaking to?"). English grammar is therefore not far from salvation. The Chinese love of simplicity is, however, far ahead, as in the expression "Sit eat mountain empty" which to the Chinese clearly means that "if you only sit and eat and do nothing, even a fortune as big as a mountain will vanish." Therefore it will be some time before the English can catch up with us.

The Chinese concrete way of thinking can also be illustrated by the nature of its abstract terms and prevalence of proverbs and metaphoric expressions. An abstract notion is often expressed by the combination of two concrete qualities, as "big-small" for "size," "long-short" for "length," "broad-narrow" for "breadth" ("What is the big-small of your shoes?"). "Long" and "short" also refer to the right and wrong of parties in dispute, as the Chinese expression is whether "one's argument is long (or short)" and therefore we have expressions like "I don't care for its long-short" (similar to the English "the long and the short of it is. . . .") and "that man has no right-wrong" meaning he is a good man because he preserves a God-like indifference toward all questions, and does not get involved in private disputes. Abstract endings like "-ness" are also unknown in Chinese, and the Chinese simply say, with Mencius, that "the white of a white horse is not the same as the white of a white jade." This has a bearing on their lack of analytic thinking.

Women, so far as I know, avoid using abstract terms. This, I think, has been proved by an analytical study of the vocabulary of women authors. (The analytical, statistical method is in itself a habit of the Western mind, for the Chinese has far too much common sense to go to the trouble of counting word to prove it. When he feels the truth directly that women's vocabulary in speech and writing is decidedly less abstract, that is sufficient for him.) With the Chinese as with women, concrete imagery always takes the place of abstract terminology. The highly academic sentence: "There is no difference but difference of degree between different degrees of difference and no difference," cannot be exactly reproduced in Chinese, and a Chinese translator would probably substitute for it the Mencian question: "What is the difference between running away fifty steps and running away a hundred steps [in battle]?" Such a substitute expression loses in definition and exactness, but gains in intelligibility. To say, "How could I perceive his inner mental processes?" is not so intelligible as "How could I know what is going on in his mind?", and this in turn is decidedly less affective than the Chinese "Am I a tapeworm in his belly?"

Chinese thought, therefore, always remains on the periphery of the visible world, and this helps a sense of fact which is the foundation of experience and wisdom. This dislike of abstract terms is further seen in the Chinese names for classifications which usually require sharply defined terms. Instead, the Chinese always seek the most expressive names for different categories. Thus in Chinese literary criticism there are different methods of writing called "the method of watching a fire across the river" (detachment of style), "the method of dragon-flies skimming the water surface" (lightness of touch), "the method of painting a dragon and dotting its eyes" (bringing out the salient points), the method of releasing a captive before capturing him" (playing about a subject), "the method of showing the dragon's head without its tail" (freedom of movement and waywardness of thought), "the method of a sharp precipice overhanging a ten-thousand-feet ravine" (abruptness of ending), "the method of letting blood by one needle-prick" (direct, epigrammatic gibe), "the method of going straight into the fray with one knife" (direct opening), "the method of announcing a campaign on the east and marching to the west" (surprise attack), "the method of side-stabs and flanking attacks" (light raillery), "the method of a light mist hanging over a grey lake" (mellow and toned-down style), "the method of layers of clouds and hilltops" (accumulation), "the method of throwing lighted firecrackers at a horse's buttocks" (final stab toward conclusion) etc., etc. Such names suggest picturesque terms like the "bow-wow," "pooh-pooh" and "sing-song theories" of the origin of speech.

This profuseness of imagery and paucity of abstract terminology has an influence on the style of writing and, consequently, on the style of thought. On the one hand, it makes for vividness; on the other, it may easily degenerate into a senseless decorativeness without exact content, which has been the besetting sin of many periods of Chinese literature, and against which Han Yü in the T'ang Dynasty set up a revolt. Such a style suffers from lack of exactness of expression, but at its best it brings about, as in the best "non-classical" novels, a sauntering prose, racy, idiomatic and smelling of the soil, like the prose of Swift and Defoe, "in the best English tradition," as we say. It also avoids the pitfalls of a type of academic jargon which is rapidly growing in American university circles, especially among the psychologists and sociologists, who talk of human life only in terms of "factors," "processes," "individualization," "departmentalization," "quotas of ambition," "standardization of anger" and "coefficients of happiness." Such a style is practically untranslatable into Chinese, although some ludicrous efforts have been made in it under the slogan of "Europeanization of Chinese," which is rapidly dying out of vogue. Translation from English into Chinese is hardest in scientific treatises, while translation from Chinese into English is hardest in poetry and decorative prose, where every word contains an image.

III. LACK OF SCIENCE

Sufficient discussion of the characteristics of Chinese thinking has been made to enable us to appreciate the cause of their failure to develop natural science. The Greeks laid the foundation of natural science because the Greek mind was essentially an analytical mind, a fact which is proved by the striking modernity of Aristotle. The Egyptians developed geometry and astronomy, sciences which required an analytical mind: and the Hindus developed a grammar of their own. The Chinese, with all their native intelligence, never developed a science of grammar, and their mathematics and astronomical knowledge have all been imported. For the Chinese mind delights only in moral platitudes, and their abstract terms like "benevolence," "kindliness," "propriety" and "loyalty" are so general that in such discussions they are naturally lost in vague generalities.

Of all the ancient philosophers of the Chou Dynasty, only Motse and Hanfeitse developed a style akin to cogent reasoning. Mencius, who was undoubtedly a great sophist, cared only for such big words as "utility" and "righteousness." All the rest of them, like Chuangtse, Liehtse and Huainantse, delighted in graceful metaphors. The disciples of Motse, Huei Shih and Kungsun Lung, who were great sophists, were interested in spinning scholastic conundrums, and in endeavouring to prove such propositions as "eggs have hair on them," "horses lay eggs," "a dog may be a lamb," "a chicken has three legs," "fire is not warm," "the wheel never touches the ground," "a tortoise is longer than a snake," etc. The scholars of the Han Dynasty, which soon followed, were interested only in making Alexandrian commentaries on the classics of the preceding period. The Ch'in scholars after them revived Taoism and depended on their "intuition" for the solving of the mysteries of their own bodies and the universe. Experimentation was never thought of, and no scientific method had been developed. The Sung philosophers reinterpreted Confucianism in the light of Buddhism, and transformed it into a system of mental discipline and moral hygiene. They developed a reputation for grasping the general content of a book "without wanting to know it thoroughly." The Sung scholars had therefore the most unscientific philology, or no philology at all. Only as late as the Ch'ing (Manchu) Dynasty was there developed a *comparative* method, which at once put the Ch'ing philology on a height unattained before. Ch'ing philology was the nearest approach to a scientific method in China.

It is easy to see why the Chinese mind cannot develop a scientific method; for the scientific method, besides being analytical, always involves an amount of stupid drudgery, while the Chinese believe in flashes of common sense and insight. And inductive reasoning, carried over to human relationships (in which the Chinese are primarily interested), often results in a form of stupidity not so rare in American universities. There are to-day doctorate dissertations in the inductive method which would make Bacon turn in his grave. No Chinese could possibly be stupid enough to write a dissertation on ice-cream, and after a series of careful observations, announce the staggering conclusion that "the primary function of sugar [in the manufacture of ice-cream] is to sweeten it,"[1] or after a methodical study in "Time and Motion Comparison on Four Methods of Dish-washing" happily perceive that "stooping and lifting are fatiguing";[2] or that, in "A Study of the Bacterial Content of Cotton Undershirts," "the number of bacteria tends to increase with the length of time garments are worn."[3]   A newspaper report several years ago stated that a University of Chicago student, after making a "comparative study" of the impressional power of various types of lettering, found that *the blacker the lines, the more striking they are to the eye*.

This sort of stupidity, although useful to business advertisement, could really be arrived at, I think, just as correctly by a moment of Chinese common sense and "intuition." The best cartoon I have ever seen in *Punch* is that of a congress of behaviourists who, after passing a number of pig "subjects" through a test, with a thermometer in the snout and a pearl necklace dangling in front, unanimously resolve that pigs do not respond to the sight of jewellery. These things cannot be merely prostitution of the scientific method, for we find that Professor Cason of Rochester University read a paper at the Ninth Annual International Conference of Psychologists on the "Origin and Nature of Common Annoyances," in which he had noted 21,000 kinds of annoyances, which, after deducting duplications and "spurious annoyances," were later reduced

[1] *Teachers' College Record*, Columbia University, Feb., 1930, p. 472, quoted by Abraham Flexner: *Universities, American, English and German.*
[2] Flexner, *ibid.* "A dissertation submitted to the Graduate Faculty in candidacy for degree of Master of Arts," University of Chicago.
[3] Flexner, *ibid.* "A dissertation submitted in partial fulfilment of the requirements of Kansas State Agricultural College for Degree of Doctor of Science."

to 507 (!), and in which he succeeded in grading these "annoyances," like 26 marks for "hair in food," 2 for "the sight of a bald head" and 24 for "cockroaches."

A certain amount of stupid drudgery is of course part and parcel of true scientific work. Only true scientific discipline can enable a scientist to take delight in the discovery that an earthworm has a certain protective covering, for it is on the accumulation of such minutely observed facts that science grew from generation to generation to its present magnificent attainments. Without that scientific outlook, and with a large share of humour and common sense, the Chinese must necessarily consider the study and observation of the life of an earthworm or of a gold-fish as beneath the dignity of a scholar.

IV. LOGIC

This brings us to the problem of Chinese logic, which is based on the Chinese conception of truth. Truth, according to Chinese, can never be proved: it can only be suggested. Chuangtse long ago pointed out the subjectivity of knowledge in his *Ch'iwulun:*

> In an argument between you and me, you think you have got the better of me, and I will not admit your superiority. Then are you really right, and I really wrong? I think I have got the better of you and you will not admit my superiority—then am I really right and you really wrong? Or perhaps are we both right, or perhaps are we both wrong? This you and I cannot know. Thus we are encircled in darkness, and who is going to establish the truth? If we let a man who agrees with you establish it, then he already agrees with you, so how could he establish it? If we let one who agrees with me establish the truth, then he already agrees with me, so how could he establish it? If we let one who disagrees with both of us establish the truth, then he already disagrees with both of us, so how could he establish it? If we let one who agrees with both of us establish the truth, then he already agrees with both of us, so how could he establish it? Thus you and I and other people cannot know the truth, and how can we wait for the other one?

According to this theory of knowledge, truth cannot be proved, although it may be grasped by the mind in a "dialectic without words" (Chuangtse). One "knows it is so without knowing why it is so." "*Tao*, or truth, is that which we know not the manner of." It can therefore be felt only by a sort of intuitive perception. The Chinese, without all consciously accepting this Chuangtsean epistemology, essentially agree with it. Instead of relying on logic, which is never developed as a science, they rely on the perhaps healthier common sense. Anything like cogent reasoning is unknown in Chinese literature, for the Chinese inherently disbelieve in it. Consequently no diale ctic has been evolved, and the scientific treatise as a literary form is unknown.

Bernhard Karlgren recently wrote a paper showing the fallacies of many arguments used by Chinese "higher critics" in proving the genuineness or spuriousness of ancient works. Some of the mistakes really seem childish, but they only seem so after the application of the Western method. A Chinese never writes a treatise of ten thousand, or even five thousand, words to establish a point. He puts down only a note about it, leaving it to be sustained or disproved by posterity on its intrinsic merit. That is why Chinese scholars always bequeath to us so many collections of "notebooks," called *shuipi* or *pichi*, consisting of unclassified paragraphs, in which opinions on the authorship of literary works and corrections of errors in historical records are mixed up with accounts of Siamese twins, fox spirits and sketches of a red-bearded hero or a centipede-eating recluse.

A Chinese author presents you with one or two arguments and then states his conclusions: in reading him, you seldom see him arriving at the conclusion, for the arguments and evidences are never long, but you see in a flash that he already has it. The best of such notebooks, like the *Jih-chih-lu* of Ku Yenwu (beginning of the seventeenth century), establish their reputation, not by their logic but by the essential correctness of their statements, which can only be proved or disproved by posterity. The writing of two or three lines in Ku's *Notebook* was sometimes the result of years of research and investigation which was scientific enough, and the determination of a single point of historic fact might have involved repeated trips and an encyclopædic erudition, but his errors are difficult to check and the fact that he is correct is not immediately visible, and can only be appreciated because no writer in the three centuries after him has been able to establish a point against him.

Thus we see an opposition of "logic" versus common sense, which takes the place of inductive and deductive reasoning in China. Common sense is often saner because the analytic reasoning looks at truth by cutting it up into various aspects, thus throwing them out of their natural bearings, while common sense seizes the situation as a living whole. Women have a more robust common sense than men, and in times of any emergency, I always depend on the judgment of a woman rather than that of a man. They have a way of sizing up a situation in its totality without being distracted by its individual aspects. In the best Chinese novels, like the *Red Chamber Dream* and the *Yehsao Paoyen (An Uncouth Old Man's Chats)*, the women are pictured as the soundest judges of situations, and their speech has a way of putting it as a rounded whole which is extremely fascinating. Logic without such common sense is dangerous, because when a man holds an opinion it is easy enough for him, with his academic brain, to evolve arguments "a," "b" and "c" to his own satisfaction, and yet he may be like the scholar, Mr. Casaubon, in *Middlemarch* who fails to perceive what every man could perceive in the life of his own wife.

This religion of common sense has a philosophic basis. It is interesting to note that the Chinese do not judge the correctness of a proposition by the appeal to reason alone, but by the double appeal to reason *and* to human nature. The Chinese word for "reasonableness" is *ch'ingli*, which is composed of two elements, *ch'ing (jench'ing)*, or human nature, and *li (t'ienli)*, or eternal reason. *Ch'ing* represents the flexible, human element, while *li* represents the immutable law of the universe. Out of the combination of these two factors comes the standard of judgment for a course of action or an historical thesis.

Something of this distinction may be seen in the English contrast between "reason" and "reasonableness." It was Aristotle, I believe, who said that man is a reasoning, but not a reasonable, being. Chinese philosophy admits this, but adds that man should try to be a reasonable, and not a merely reasoning, being. By the Chinese, reasonableness is placed on a higher level than reason. For while reason is abstract, analytical, idealistic and inclined toward logical extremes, the spirit of reasonableness is always more realistic, more human, in closer touch with reality, and more truly understanding and appreciative of the correct situation.

For a Westerner it is usually sufficient for a proposition to be logically sound. For a Chinese it is not sufficient that a proposition be logically correct, but it must be at the same time in accord with human nature. In fact, to be "in accord with human nature," to be *chinch'ing*, is a greater consideration than to be logical. For a theory could be so logical as to be totally devoid of common sense. The Chinese are willing to do anything against reason, but they will not accept anything that is not plausible in the light of human nature. This spirit of reasonableness and this religion of common sense have a most important bearing on the Chinese ideal of life, and result in the Doctrine of the Golden Mean, which I shall discuss in the following chapter.

V. INTUITION

Nevertheless, this type of thinking has its limitations, too for the logic of common sense can only be applied to human affairs and actions; it cannot be applied to the solution of the riddles of the universe. One can use reasonableness to settle a dispute but not to locate the relative positions of the heart and liver or determine the function of the pancreatic juice Hence in divining nature's mysteries and the secrets of the human body, the Chinese have to resort largely to intuition Strangely enough, they have intuitively felt the heart to be on the right and the liver to be on the left side of the human chest. An erudite Chinese scholar, whose voluminous *Note books*[1] are widely read, came across a copy of *Human Anatomy* translated by the Jesuits Jacobus Rho, James Terrence, and

Nicolaus Longobardi, and finding that in the book the heart
is placed on the left and the liver on the right, decided that
Westerners have different internal organs from the Chinese,
and deduced therefrom the important conclusion that since
their internal organs are different, therefore their religion
must be also different—this deduction is in itself a perfect
example of intuitive reasoning—and hence only Chinese whose
internal organs are imperfect could possibly become Christian
converts. The erudite scholar slyly remarked that if the Jesuits
only knew this fact they would not be interested in preaching
Christianity in China and in making converts of half-normal
beings.

Such assertions are made in perfect seriousness and in fact
are typical of Chinese "intuition" in the realms of natural
science and human physiology. One begins to believe that
there is something after all in the scientific method, for with
this method, though one might be seriously concerned in the
findings that the "primary function of sugar [in the manufacture of ice-cream] is to sweeten it," yet one could be
saved from the other sort of puerile thinking represented by
the author of the above *Notebooks*. He could at least have felt
the palpitation of his heart by his own hand, but evidently
the Chinese scholar never descended to manual labour.

Free thus from stupid drudgery in the use of his eyes and
his hands, and having a naïve faith in the power of his "intuition," the Chinese scholar goes about explaining the mysteries
of the human body and the universe to his own satisfaction.
The whole science of Chinese medicine and physiology is
based on the Taoistic philosophy of the Five Elements—
Gold, Wood, Water, Fire and Earth. The human body is in
itself a symbol of the universe in its composition. The kidneys
represent the water element, the stomach represents the earth
element, the liver represents the fire element, the lungs represent the gold element and the heart represents the wood
element. Not that this medicine does not work in practice. A
man suffering from high blood-pressure is considered to have
too warm a "liver-fire," while a man suffering from indigestion
may be referred to as having too much earth, and a laxative
is used to encourage the function of the kidneys by way of

helping the "water element," and the indigestion is *usually* cured. If a man is suffering from nervous trouble, he should drink a lot of water and use palliatives, so that the "kidney-water" will go up and dampen a little of the "liver-fire" and thus help maintain in him a more equable temper. There is no doubt that Chinese medicine works: the quarrel is only with its diagnosis.

Here enter the survivals of savage traits in Chinese thinking. Unchecked by a scientific method, "intuition" has free room and often borders on a naïve imagination. Some kinds of Chinese medicine are based on a mere play of words or on some fantastic association of thought. The toad who has a wrinkled skin is used in the cure of skin troubles, and a peculiar kind of frog that lives in cool, deep ponds on hillsides is supposed to have a "cooling" effect on the bodily system. For the last two years the local papers in Shanghai have been full of advertisements of a certain "lung-shaped plant" which is produced in Szechuen and recommended as the best cure for tuberculosis. And this goes on in an uninterrupted series until we come to the popular belief that a schoolboy should not eat chicken's claws lest he develop the habit of scratching the pages of his book.

The superstitious belief in the power of words may be traced in all departments of life, for here we are dealing neither with logic nor with common sense, but with a survival of the savage state of mind which does not distinguish, and is not interested in distinguishing playful fancy from serious truth. The bat and the deer are popular motives for embroidery work because the word "bat" (*fu*) is a homonym for "luck" and the word "deer" (*lu*) is a homonym for "official power." The Chinese bride and bridegroom have, after the wedding ceremony, a dinner à *deux* consisting of a pig's heart, because they are thus going to have "the same heart," which is the word for "harmony."

It is difficult to say how much of it is serious belief and how much of it mere light playful fancy. Certain taboos are evidently taken quite seriously, for the boatman will look troubled when you turn over the fish at dinner in the boat, which suggests the "overturning" of the boat itself. He does not quite know

whether it is true or not, but "so people say," and he is not
interested in undertaking a research to verify it. It is a state
of mind that belongs to the borderland of truth and fiction,
where truth and fiction are pleasurably and poetically mixed,
as in a dreamer's tale.

VI. IMAGINATION

This *naïveté* we must try to understand, for it brings us to the
world of the Chinese imagination and Chinese religion. By
religion, I mean a good heaven and a hot hell and real, living
spirits, and not the "kingdom . . . within you" of the Boston
Unitarians, or the belief in the impersonal and amorphous
"Power in and around us, which makes for righteousness" of
Matthew Arnold.

This world of the imagination is not confined to the illiterate.
Confucius himself exhibited a certain *naïveté* regarding the
spirits when he said, "If one were to try to please the god of
the south-west corner of the house, it would be preferable to
try to please the god of the kitchen stove." He spoke of the
spirits with an ease of mind which was truly charming: "Offer
sacrifices to the spirits *as if* the spirits were present," and
"Respect the spirits, but keep them at a distance." He was
willing to let the spirits exist if they would let him go his own
way.

Han Yü, the great Confucianist of the T'ang Dynasty,
continued this naïve attitude. He was officially reprimanded
and compelled to go to the neighbourhood of modern Swatow
to serve as a magistrate, and when this district was suffering
from an invasion of crocodiles, he wrote a high-flown sacrificial
appeal to the crocodiles. The crocodiles seemed to appreciate his literary style (for he was one of the best writers in
China's history), and, according to his own testimony, they
disappeared from the district. It would be futile to ask if he
sincerely believed in it or not. To ask that question is completely to misunderstand the situation, for his reply would
most probably be: How can I know it is true, but how can
you know it is untrue? It was an agnosticism which openly

admitted the impossibility of settling the question with our mental powers, and therefore brushed it aside. Han Yü's was a powerful mind, and he was not superstitious, for he was the man who wrote the famous essay dissuading the Emperor from sending a delegation to bring back the "Buddha's bones" from India. I am sure he was half laughing when he composed that sacrificial appeal to the crocodiles. There have been other powerful minds, more rationalistic in temperament, like that of Ssŭma Wenkung of the following dynasty, who tried to disprove the Buddhistic hell by asking why the Chinese people never dreamed of hell until they heard of Buddhism. But such rationalism is not typical of the Chinese mind.

To me the most characteristic creatures of the Chinese imagination are the lovely female ghosts that the Chinese scholar spins out of his imagination, such as those told in the *Strange Stories From a Chinese Studio*.[1] The stories are about the female ghosts and spirits of wronged and disgraced women who possess the body of some maid-servant and thus communicate their complaints to the living, and the dead sweetheart who returns to her lover and bears him children. It is these stories with their human touch which are most loved by the Chinese people. For the Chinese ghosts are wonderfully human, and the female ghosts are wonderfully lovely, too: they love and become jealous and take part in the ordinary human life.

It is not the kind of ghosts that scholars need fear when they are alone at night in their studies. For when the lamp is burning low and the scholar has fallen asleep, he hears the noise of a silken dress and opens his eyes to see a demure maiden of sixteen or seventeen, with a wistful look and a serene air, looking and smiling at him. She is usually a passionate creature, for I have no doubt these stories are the wish-fulfilment of the solitary scholars. But she can bring him money and help him through poverty, by all sorts of cunning wiles. She can nurse him through sickness with more gentleness than an average modern nurse. What is stranger still, she will sometimes try to save money for him, and will wait patiently for him during his months or years of absence. She can therefore be chaste as well. The period of this cohabitation may

---

[1] Translated by Professor H. A. Giles.

last a few days or weeks or it may extend to a generation until she has borne him children, who, after their success in examinations, come back for their mother and then find that the gorgeous mansion has disappeared and in its place is an old, old grave, with a hole underground, where lies a dead old mother fox. For she is only one of those fox spirits the Chinese delight to tell about. Sometimes she leaves behind a note saying that she was sorry to leave them, but that she was a fox and only wanted to enjoy human life, and now, since she has seen them prosper, she is grateful and hopes they will forgive her.

This is typical of the Chinese imagination which, without soaring aloft to God-like heights, invests the creatures of its mind with human passions and human sorrows. It has the pagan virtue of accepting the imaginary with the real, and has no desire for a world perfectly rationalized and completely explained. This quality of the Chinese imagination is so little known that I will give here a translation of a tale, *The Tale of Ch'ienniang*, handed down from the T'ang Dynasty. I don't know whether the story is true or not, but the affair happened in the years around A.D. 690, during the reign of the Empress Wuhou. Our novels, dramas and scholars' works are full of this type of story, in which the supernatural is made believable because it is made human.

Ch'ienniang was the daughter of Mr. Chang Yi, an official in Hunan. She had a cousin by the name of Wang Chou, who was a brilliant and handsome young man. They had grown up together from childhood, and as her father was very fond of the young boy, he had said that he would take Wang Chou as his son-in-law. This promise they had both heard, and as she was the only child, and they were very close together, their love grew from day to day. They were now grown-up young people, and even had intimate relationships with each other. Unfortunately, her father was the only man who failed to perceive this. One day a young official came to beg for her hand from her father, and, ignoring or forgetting his early promise, he consented. Ch'ienniang, torn between love and filial piety, was ready to die with grief, while the young man was so disgusted that he decided he would go abroad rather than stay and see his sweetheart become the bride of another person. So he made up a pretext and informed his uncle that he had to go away to the capital. As the uncle could not persuade him to stay, he gave him money and presents and prepared a farewell feast for him. Wang Chou, sad to take leave of his lover, was thinking it all over while he partook of the feast, and he told himself that it was best to go, rather than remain to carry on a hopeless romance.

So Wang Chou set out on a boat of an afternoon, and before he had gone a few miles it was already dark and he told the boatman to tie up the boat along shore and rest for the night. That night he could not sleep, and toward midnight he heard the sound of quick footsteps approaching. In a few minutes the sound had drawn near the boat. He got up and inquired, " Who is there at this hour of the night?" "It is I, even Ch'ienniang," was the reply. Surprised and delighted beyond his expectations, he led her down to the boat, and there she told him that she had hoped to be his wife, that her father had been unfair to him, and that she could not bear parting from him. She was afraid, too, that he, lonely and travelling in strange parts, might be driven to take his own life. So she had braved the censure of society and the anger of her parents and come to follow him wherever he should go. Thus they were happy together and continued their journey to Szechuen.

Five years passed happily and she bore him two sons. But they had no news from the family, and she was daily thinking of her parents. It was the only thing that marred their happiness. She did not know whether her parents were living and well or not, and one night she began telling Wang Chou how unhappy she was and that since she was the only child, she felt guilty of great filial impiety to leave the old parents thus. "This is your filial piety," said her husband. "I am with you in thinking this way. But it seems that now after five years have passed, surely they are not still angry with us. Why not go home?" Ch'ienniang was overjoyed to hear this, and so they made preparations to go home with their two children.

When the boat had reached her home town, Wang Chou
said to Ch'ienniang, "I do not know what state of mind
your parents are in. So let me go alone first to find out."
His heart was palpitating as he drew near his father-in-law's
house. On seeing his father-in-law, Wang Chou knelt down
and kowtowed, and begged for forgiveness. On hearing
this, Chang Yi was greatly surprised, and said, "What are
you talking about? Ch'ienniang has been lying unconscious
in bed for these last five years since you left. She has never
even left her bed." "I am not lying," said Wang Chou.
"She is well and waiting in the boat."

Chang Yi did not know what to think, so he sent two maid-
servants to see Ch'ienniang. They saw her sitting, well-
dressed and happy, in the boat, and she even told the servants
to convey her love to her parents. Bewildered, the two
maid-servants ran home to make their report, and Chang Yi
was still more greatly puzzled. Meanwhile, she who was
lying in bed in her chamber had heard of the news, and it
seemed her illness was gone, and there was light in her eyes.
She rose up from her bed and dressed herself before her
mirror. Smiling and without saying a word, she came
straight to the boat. She who was in the boat was starting
for home, and they met on the river-bank. When the two
came close together, their bodies melted into one shape, and
their dresses were double, and there appeared the old
Ch'ienniang, as young and as lovely as ever.

Both her parents were overjoyed, but they bade their
servants keep the secret and not tell the neighbours about
it, in order to avoid gossip. So no one, except the close
relatives of the Chang family, ever knew of this strange
happening.

Wang Chou and Ch'ienniang lived on as husband and
wife for over forty years before they died.

It is perhaps well that the world is not completely explained
and that there is some room for this type of imagination. The
proper use of imagination is to give beauty to the world. For
as in the moral life human intelligence is used to convert the
world into a place of contentment for human existence, so in

the artistic life the gift of imagination is used to cast over the commonplace workaday world a veil of beauty to make it throb with our æsthetic enjoyment. In China, the art of living is one with the arts of painting and poetry. As Li Liweng at the end of the seventeenth century expressed it in a dramatic passage,

> First we look at the hills in the painting,
> Then we look at the painting in the hills.

The imagination, by its contemplation of sorrow and poverty, turns sorrow and poverty into beauty, as we see so clearly in Tu Fu's poetry. For beauty resides in the huts, in the grasshoppers, in the cicada's wings, and, strangest of all, in the rocks, too. The Chinese alone in the world would paint a piece of jagged rock and hang it on the wall for daily contemplation and enjoyment. These rocks—they are not the carved stones of Venice or of Florence, but the rugged and untamed works of nature, still retaining the rough rhythm of their natural appearance, from which our æsthetic enjoyment is drawn. I think the enjoyment of the rhythm of a common clock is the last refinement of the Chinese mind. Indeed the Chinese mind is as keen to detect the beauty in a common pebble as it is anxious to squeeze the last ounce of happiness from an insecure and fate-ruled world. That painting of a solitary rugged rock or of a cat watching a grasshopper he would hang on his wall and contemplate, although a civil war might be raging outside his very doors. To find beauty in common life, that is the value of the Wordsworthian and the Chinese imagination, for Wordsworth is the most Chinese in spirit of all English poets. "If you do not run away from the raindrops, you will find them most beautiful," said Hsiao Shihwei at the end of the Ming Dynasty. He was speaking of the familiar style of writing diaries. But it was not only a literary doctrine. It was a doctrine of life.

Chapter Four

IDEALS OF LIFE

I. CHINESE HUMANISM

TO understand the Chinese ideal of life one must try to understand Chinese humanism. The term "humanism" is ambiguous. Chinese humanism, however, has a very definite meaning. It implies, first a just conception of the ends of human life; secondly, a complete devotion to these ends; and thirdly, the attainment of these ends by the spirit of human reasonableness or the Doctrine of the Golden Mean, which may also be called the Religion of Common Sense.

The question of the meaning of life has perplexed Western philosophers, and it has never been solved—naturally, when one starts out from the teleological point of view, according to which all things, including mosquitoes and typhoid germs, are created for the good of this cocksure humanity. As there is usually too much pain and misery in this life to allow a perfect answer to satisfy man's pride, teleology is therefore carried over to the next life, and this earthly life is then looked upon as a preparation for the life hereafter, in conformity with the logic of Socrates, which looked upon a ferocious wife as a natural provision for the training of the husband's character. This way of dodging the horns of the dilemma sometimes gives peace of mind for a moment, but then the eternal question, "What is the meaning of life?" comes back. Others, like Nietzsche, take the bull by the horns, and refuse to assume that life *must* have a meaning and believe that progress is in a circle, and human achievements are a savage dance, instead of a trip to the market. But still the question comes back eternally, like the sea-waves lapping upon the shore: "What is the meaning of life?"

The Chinese humanists believe they have found the true

end of life and are conscious of it. For the Chinese the end
of life lies not in life after death, for the idea that we live in
order to die, as taught by Christianity, is incomprehensible;
nor in Nirvana, for that is too metaphysical; nor in the satisfaction of accomplishment, for that is too vainglorious; nor
yet in progress for progress' sake, for that is meaningless. The
true end, the Chinese have decided in a singularly clear manner,
lies in the enjoyment of a simple life, especially the family life,
and in harmonious social relationships. The first poem that a
child learns in school runs:

> While soft clouds by warm breezes are wafted in the morn,
> Lured by flowers, past the river I roam on and on.
> They'll say, "Look at that old man on a spree!"
> And know not that my spirit's on happiness borne.

That represents to the Chinese, not just a pleasant poetic
mood but the *summum bonum* of life. The Chinese ideal of life
is drunk through with this sentiment. It is an ideal of life
that is neither particularly ambitious nor metaphysical, but
nevertheless immensely real. It is, I must say, a brilliantly
simple ideal, so brilliantly simple that only the matter-of-
fact Chinese mind could have conceived it, and yet one often
wonders how the West could have failed to see that the meaning of life lies in the sane and healthy enjoyment of it. The
difference between China and the West seems to be that the
Westerners have a greater capacity for getting and making
more things and a lesser ability to enjoy them, while the
Chinese have a greater determination and capacity to enjoy
the few things they have. This trait, our concentration on
earthly happiness, is as much a result as a cause of the absence
of religion. For if one cannot believe in the life hereafter as
the consummation of the present life, one is forced to make the
most of this life before the farce is over. The absence of religion
makes this concentration possible.

From this a humanism has developed which frankly pro-
claims a man-centred universe, and lays down the rule that
the end of all knowledge is to serve human happiness. The
humanizing of knowledge is not an easy thing, for the moment

man swerves, he is carried away by his logic and becomes a tool of his own knowledge. Only by a sharp and steadfast holding to the true end of human life as one sees it can humanism maintain itself. Humanism occupies, for instance, a mean position between the other-worldliness of religion and the materialism of the modern world. Buddhism may have captured popular fancy in China, but against its influence the true Confucianist was always inwardly resentful, for it was, in the eyes of humanism, only an escape from life, or a negation of the truly human life.

On the other hand, the modern world, with its over-development of machinery, has not taken time to ensure that man enjoys what he makes. The glorification of the plumber in America has made the man forget that one can live a very happy life without hot and cold running water, and that in France and Germany many men have lived to comfortable old age and made important scientific discoveries and written masterpieces with their water jug and old-fashioned basin. There needs to be a religion which will transcribe Jesus' famous dictum about the Sabbath and constantly preach that the machine is made for man and not man made for the machine. For after all, the sum of all human wisdom and the problem of all human knowledge is how man shall remain a man and how he shall best enjoy his life.

II. RELIGION

Nothing is more striking than the Chinese humanist devotion to the true end of life as they conceive it, and the complete ignoring of all theological or metaphysical phantasies extraneous to it. When our great humanist Confucius was asked about the important question of death, his famous reply was, "Don't know life—how know death?"[1] An American Presbyterian minister once tried to drive home to me the importance of the question of immortality by referring to the alleged astronomical theory that the sun is gradually losing

[1] I am using pidgin English here in order to retain the terseness and force of the original.

its energy and that perhaps, after millions of years, life is sure to become extinct on this planet. "Do you not realize, therefore," asked the minister, "that after all, the question of immortality is important?" I told him frankly I was unperturbed. If human life has yet half a million years, that is enough for all practical purposes, and the rest is unnecessary metaphysical worry. That anybody's soul should want to live for more than half a million years and not be perfectly content is a kind of preposterousness that an Oriental mind cannot understand. The Presbyterian minister's worry is as characteristically Teutonic as my unconcern is characteristically Chinese. The Chinese, therefore, make rather poor Christian converts, and if they are to be converted they should all become Quakers, for that is the only sort of Christianity that the Chinese can understand. Christianity as a way of life can impress the Chinese, but Christian creeds and dogmas will be crushed, not by a superior Confucian logic but by ordinary Confucian common sense. Buddhism itself, when absorbed by the educated Chinese, became nothing but a system of mental hygiene, which is the essence of Sung philosophy.

For a certain hard-headedness characterizes the Chinese ideal of life. There may be imagination in Chinese paintings and poetry, but there is no imagination in Chinese ethics. Even in painting and poetry there is a sheer, whole-hearted, instinctive delight in commonplace life, and imagination is used to throw a veil of charm and beauty over this earthly life, rather than to escape from it. There is no doubt that the Chinese are in love with life, in love with this earth, and will not forsake it for an invisible heaven. They are in love with life, which is so sad and yet so beautiful, and in which moments of happiness are so precious because they are so transient. They are in love with life, with its kings and beggars, robbers and monks, funerals and weddings and childbirths and sicknesses and glowing sunsets and rainy nights and feasting days and wine-shop fracas.

It is these details of life upon which the Chinese novelists fondly and untiringly dwell, details which are so real and human and significant because we humans are affected by them. Was it a sultry afternoon when the whole household from mistress to servants had gone to sleep and Taiyü, sitting behind the beaded screen, heard the parrot calling the master's name? Was it a mid-autumn day, that memorable mid-autumn day of a certain year, when all the sisters and Paoyü were gathered to write poems and mix in light raillery and bantering laughter over the feast of crabs, in a happiness so perfect that it could hardly last, like the full moon, as the Chinese saying goes? Or was it a pair of innocent newlyweds on their first reunion on a moonlit night, when they sat alone near a pond and prayed to the gods that their married life might last till death, but dark clouds came over the moon, and in the distance they heard a mysterious noise as if a wandering duck had splashed into the water, pursued by a prowling fox, and the young wife shivered and ran up a high fever the next day? Yes, life which is so poignantly beautiful is worth recording, down to its lowliest details. It seems nothing of this earthly life can be too material or too vulgar to enter literature. A characteristic of all Chinese novels is the incessant and never-tiring enumeration of the names of dishes served at a family feast or a traveller's supper at an inn, followed frequently by. stomach aches and trips to the vacant lot which is the natural man's toilet. So the Chinese novelists write and so the Chinese men and women live, and it is a life too full to be occupied with thoughts of immortality.

This realism and this attached-to-the-earth quality of the Chinese ideal of life has a basis in Confucianism, which, unlike Christianity, is of the earth, earth-born. For Jesus was a romanticist, Confucius a realist; Jesus was a mystic, Confucius a positivist; Jesus was a humanitarian, Confucius a humanist. In these two personalities we see typified the contrast between Hebrew religion and poetry and Chinese realism and common sense. Confucianism, strictly speaking, was not a religion: it had certain feelings toward life and the universe that bordered on the religious feeling, but it was not a religion. There are such great souls in the world who cannot get interested in the life hereafter or in the question of immortality or in the world of spirits in general. That type of philosophy could never satisfy the Germanic races, and certainly not the Hebrews, but it satisfied the Chinese race—in general. We shall see below how it really never quite satisfied even the Chinese, and how that deficiency was made up for by a Taoist or Buddhist supernaturalism. But this supernaturalism seems in China to be separated in general from the question of the ideal of life: it represents rather the spiritual by-plays and outlets that merely help to make life endurable.

So true was Confucianism to the humanist instinct that neither Confucius nor any of his disciples was ever made a god, although many lesser literary and military figures in Chinese history were duly canonized or deified. A common woman, who suffered wrongs and faced death to uphold her chastity, might in an amazingly short time become a popular local goddess, prayed to by all the villagers. Typical of the humanist temperament is the fact that although idols were made of Kuan Yü, a brave and loyal general in the time of the Three Kingdoms, idols were not made of Confucius, nor of the ancestors in the halls of ancestral worship. Iconoclasts have really nothing to do when they enter a Confucian temple. In the Confucian and ancestral temples there are merely oblong wooden tablets, inscribed with characters bearing the names of the spirits they represent, having as little resemblance to idols as a calendar block. And in any case, these ancestral spirits are not gods, but merely human beings who have departed but who continue to take an interest in their progeny as they did in their lifetime. They can perhaps, if they are great souls, protect their descendants, but they themselves need their progeny's protection and succour through offerings of food for their hunger and burnt paper money for their sundry expenses in hell, from which place it is the duty of their children to save them by a Buddhist mass. In a word, they are to be cared for and served as they have been cared for and served by their children in their old age. That is about as close as Confucianism comes to religion in the matter of worship.

I have often observed with interest the differences between a religious culture like that of Christendom and a frankly agnostic culture like that of the Chinese, and how these differences are adapted to man's inner needs, which I assume are essentially the same for all human races. These differences correspond to the threefold actual functions of religion, as commonly understood. First, religion as an embodiment of priestcraft, with its dogmas, its apostolic succession, its appeal to miracles, its patent cures for sins and selling of pardons, its salvation "made easy" and its good solid heaven and hell. This religion, so eminently saleable, is common to all peoples, the Chinese included, and may be regarded as satisfying man's needs in certain stages of human culture. Because there is need for these things among the people, Taoism and Buddhism have furnished them to the Chinese, since Confucianism refused to furnish them.

Secondly, there is religion as a sanction for moral conduct: here the Chinese and the Christian points of view differ widely. Humanist ethics is a man-centred, not a God-centred ethics. To the West, it seems hardly imaginable that the relationship between man and man (which is morality) could be maintained without reference to a Supreme Being, while to the Chinese it is equally amazing that men should not, or could not, behave toward one another as decent beings without thinking of their indirect relationship through a third party. It should seem possible to conceive that man should try to do good, simply because it is the human, decent thing to do. I have wondered what the development of European ethics would have been if it had not been overshadowed by Pauline theology. It would have developed, I think, by sheer necessity along the lines of Marcus Aurelius's meditations. Pauline theology has brought in the Hebrew notion of sin, which has clouded the entire field of Christian ethics, and from which there seems no escape except by religion, such as is provided in the Doctrine of Redemption. As it is, a European ethics divorced from religion seems such a strange notion that it has seldom occurred to people's minds.

And thirdly, there is religion as an inspiration and living emotion, a feeling for the grim grandeur and mystery of the universe and a quest for security in life, satisfying man's deepest spiritual instincts. There are moments in our lives, perhaps during the loss of our dear ones or during the period of convalescence from a great illness, or perhaps on a chilly autumn morning as we look at the falling leaves and a sense of death and futility overcomes us, when we live more than the life of the senses and we look over the visible world to the Great Beyond.

These moments come to the Chinese as to the Europeans, but the reactions are decidedly different. It has seemed to me, formerly a Christian and now a pagan, that though religion gives peace by having a ready-made answer to all these problems, it decidedly detracts from the sense of the unfathomable mystery and the poignant sadness of this life, which we call poetry. Christian optimism kills all poetry. A pagan, who has not these ready-made answers to his problems and whose sense of mystery is for ever unquenched and whose craving for security is for ever unanswered and unanswerable, is driven inevitably to a kind of pantheistic poetry. Actually, poetry has taken over the function of religion as an inspiration and a living emotion in the Chinese scheme of life, as we shall see in the discussion on Chinese poetry. To the West, unused to this type of sheer pantheistic abandon to nature, religion seems the natural escape. But to the pagan, this religion seems to be based on the fear that there is not enough poetry and imagination in this present life to satisfy the human being emotionally, the fear that there is not enough power and beauty in the beech forests of Denmark or the cool sands of the Mediterranean shore to comfort the wounded human soul, and the supernatural is then found necessary.

But Confucian common sense, which dismisses supernaturalism as the realm of the unknowable and expends extremely little time over it, is equally emphatic in the assertion of the superiority of the human mind over nature and in the denial of nature's way of life, or naturalism, as the human way, an attitude clearest in Mencius. The Confucian conception of man's place in nature is that "Heaven, earth and man" are regarded as "the three geniuses of the universe." This is a distinction somewhat corresponding to the Babbittian threefold distinction of supernaturalism, humanism and naturalism. Heaven is seen as consisting of the clouds, the stars, and all those unknowable forces which Western legal phraseology sums up as "acts of God," while the earth is seen as consisting of mountains and rivers and all those forces ascribed in Greek mythology to Demeter, and man occupies an all-important place between the two. Man knows where he belongs in the scheme of things and is proud of his position. Like the Chinese roof, and unlike the Gothic spires, his spirit does not aspire to heaven but broods over the earth. Its greatest achievement is to attain a measure of harmony and happiness in this earthly life.

The Chinese roof suggests, therefore, that happiness is first to be found in the home. Indeed, the home stands for me as a symbol of Chinese humanism. A masterpiece remains to be painted of an improved version of "Sacred and Profane Love." There should be three women instead of two, a wan-faced nun (or a missionary lady with an umbrella), a voluptuous prostitute, and a radiant mother in her third month of pregnancy. Of the three, the housewife should be the commonest, simplest, and yet most truly satisfying figure. They would thus stand for religion, humanism and naturalism, typifying the three ways of life.

Such simplicity is difficult, for simplicity is the quality of great minds. The Chinese have achieved this simple ideal, not by mere laziness of effort but by a positive worship of simplicity, or the Religion of Common Sense. How this was achieved we shall now see.

III. The Doctrine of the Golden Mean

The religion of common sense or the spirit of reasonableness is part and parcel of Confucian humanism. It is this spirit of reasonableness which has given birth to the Doctrine of the Golden Mean, the central doctrine of Confucianism. Reference has already been made in the preceding chapter to the spirit of reasonableness, as contrasted with logic or reason itself. It has been shown there that the spirit of reasonableness is largely intuitive and practically identical with English common sense. It has been further shown that for a Chinese it is not enough that a proposition be "logically correct"; it is much more important that it be "in accord with human nature."

The aim of the Chinese classical education has always been the cultivation of the reasonable man as the model of culture.

An educated man should, above all, be a reasonable being, who is always characterized by his common sense, his love of moderation and restraint, and his hatred of abstract theories and logical extremes. Common sense is possessed by all common people. The academic scholar is in constant danger of losing this common sense. He is apt to indulge in excesses of theory; the reasonable man, or the Chinese man of culture, should avoid all excesses of theory and conduct. You have, for instance, the historian Froude saying that the divorce of Henry VIII from Catherine of Aragon was for purely political reasons, and you have Bishop Creighton claiming, on the other hand, that it was entirely dictated by animal lust,[1] whereas the common-sense attitude should be that both considerations were effective, which is probably nearer the truth. In the West one scientist is infatuated by the idea of heredity and another is obsessed by the notion of environment, and each one goes about doggedly to prove his theory with great learning and stupidity, whereas the Oriental, without much cerebration, would allow something for both. A typically Chinese judgment is: "*A* is right, and *B* is not wrong either."

Such self-sufficiency is sometimes infuriating to a logical mind, but what of it? The reasonable mind keeps a balance when the logical mind has lost it. The idea that a Chinese painter could, like Picasso, take the perfectly logical remark that the world of objects could be reduced to cones, planes and angular lines and then proceed logically to carry that theory into painting is obviously impossible in China. We have a natural distrust of arguments that are too perfect and theories that are too logical. Against such logical freaks of theories, common sense is the best and most effective antidote. Bertrand Russell has acutely pointed out that "In art, they [the Chinese] aim at being exquisite, and in life at being reasonable."

The result of this worship of common sense is therefore a dislike of all extravagances of theory in thought and all excesses of conduct in morals. The natural consequence of this is the Doctrine of the Golden Mean, which is really the same as the "nothing too much" ideal of the Greeks. The Chinese word for

[1] See the extremely illuminating little book, *The Magic of Common Sense*, by George Frederick Wates (John Murray, London).

moderation is *chungho*, meaning "not extreme and harmonious," and the Chinese word for restraint is *chieh*, which means "control to proper degree." In the *Shuking (Book of History)*, supposed to contain the earliest Chinese political documents, the advice of Emperor Yao, on his abdication, to Emperor Shun was "Hold the mean!" Mencius said of another ideal emperor, T'ang, that he "held the mean." It is said that this emperor used to "listen to both extremes of counsel and then apply the mean to the people," which means that he would listen to two contradictory propositions, and give a fifty-per-cent discount of each. So important is the Doctrine of the Golden Mean to the Chinese that they have called their own country the "Middle Kingdom." It is more than a geographical notion: it signifies a way of life which, by holding on to the mean, the normal and the essentially human, claims, as the old scholars did, that they have discovered all the essential truths of all schools of philosophy.

The Doctrine of the Golden Mean covers all and envelops all. It dilutes all theories and destroys all religions. In an argument with a Buddhist priest who is probably able to spin out an absolute proof of the non-existence of matter and the futility of life, a Confucianist would simply say, in his matter-of-fact and illogical way, "What would become of the world, the state and the human race if everybody left his home and entered a monastery like you?" That illogical but supremely sensible appeal to life has a clinching force of its own. Not only against Buddhism, but against all religions and all theories, the test of life holds. We cannot afford to be logical. In fact, all theories have become theories only by certain ideas developing into a psychosis in the minds of their founders. The Freudian complex is Freud himself, and the Buddhist complex is Buddha. All such theories, whether of Freud or of Buddha, seem to be based on an exaggerated illusion. The sufferings of mankind, the troubles of married life, the sight of a sore-ridden beggar or the pains and groanings of a sick man, which to us common men are no sooner felt than healthily forgotten, must have struck Buddha's hyper-sensitive nerves with a force which gave him the vision of a Nirvana. Confucianism, on the other hand, is the religion of the common man, who cannot afford to be hyper-sensitive or the world will go to pieces.

The working out of the Doctrine of the Golden Mean may be illustrated in all spheres of life and knowledge. Logically no man should get married, but practically all men should, so Confucianism advises marriage. Logically all men should be equal, but practically all men aren't, so Confucianism teaches authority and obedience. Logically men and women should not be different, but practically they are, so Confucianism teaches the differentiation of the sexes. One philosopher, Motse, taught the love of all men, and another, Yang Chu, taught the love of oneself, and Mencius condemned them both, merely saying: "Love your own parents." It was such a sensible thing to say. One philosopher believes in repression of the passions, and another believes in naturalistic abandon, but Tzŭssŭ counselled moderation in all things.

Take the question of sexual passion in particular. There are two opposite views of sexual ethics, one represented by Buddhism and Calvinism, which regard sex as the culmination of sin, the natural consequence of which is asceticism. The other extreme is naturalism which glorifies virility, of which many a modern man is a secret follower. The conflict between these points of view gives the modern man his so-called restlessness of spirit. The man who tries to take a sane and healthy view of sex as a normal human passion, like Havelock Ellis, inevitably veers toward the Greek view, which is the humanist view. The Confucian position with regard to sex is that it is a perfectly normal function, and more than that, it is connected with the perpetuation of the family and the race. The sanest view of sex I have encountered is that in *Yehsao Paoyen*, an out-and-out Confucianist novel, which takes special delight in exposing the libertinism of the monks, and whose hero, a Confucian superman, goes about persuading his bachelor bandits and bandit girls to marry and bear children for the glory of their ancestors. Unlike *Chinp'inmei*, which is devoted to libertinism, the men and women in *Yehsao Paoyen* are decent people, who make ideal husbands and wives. The only reason why this novel is considered obscene is that the author makes its men and women go through extremely compromising situations. Yet the total effect is a convincing argument for marriage and the home, and a glorification of motherhood. This view of sex is but one manifestation of the entire Confucian theory about passions, as stated by Tzŭssŭ, Confucius's grandson, in *Chung Yung* (*The Golden Mean*), which emphasizes moderation with regard to all the seven passions.

That such an attitude is a difficult thing is well demonstrated by what an Oriental calls the excesses of Western theories. It is all too easy for man to be enslaved by nationalism, fascism, socialism or communism, which are all consequences of the excesses of industrialism, and forget that the state exists for the individual and not the individual for the state. A communist state in which the human individual is regarded but as a member of a class or a state organism would at once lose its attractiveness by the Confucian appeal to the true end of human life. Against all systems as such, the human individual asserts his right to exist and seek happiness. For more important than all the political rights is man's right to happiness. A fascist China would have a hard time persuading the Chinese gentleman that the strength of the nation is more important than the welfare of the individual. Close observers of the communist state when it was set up in Kiangse offer as the greatest reason why Communism must fail in China, in spite of its great superiority over the feudalism of other parts, the fact that life was too systematized and too inhuman there.

An equally undesirable effect of the Chinese spirit of reasonableness and its consequent hatred of logical extremes has been that the Chinese, as a race, are unable to have any faith in a system. For a system, a machine, is always inhuman, and the Chinese hate anything inhuman. The hatred of any mechanistic view of the law and government is so great that it has made government by law impossible in China. A rigorous, harshly legalistic régime, or a really impersonal administration of the law, has always failed among us. It has failed because it was not liked by the people. The conception of a government by law was propounded and developed by thinkers in the third century B.C. It was tried by Shang Yang, a wonderfully efficient administrator, who helped to build the power of the Ch'in state, but eventually Shang Yang had to pay for his efficiency with his life. It had worked in Shang Yang's country,

Ch'in, a country with suspicious barbarian elements in Kansu, had enabled that country to develop a devilishly efficient war machine and conquer the whole of China, and had then died out miserably in two decades when the same type of régime was applied to the Chinese people *en masse*. The building of the Great Wall was so efficient but so inhuman that it cost Ch'in Shih Huang his empire.

On the other hand, the Chinese humanists preached, and the Chinese people have always been under, a personal government, according to which the deficiencies of a system, the principle of *ching*, can always be remedied by "expediency," the principle of *ch'üan*. Instead of a government by law, they have always accepted a government by "gentlemen," which is more personal, more flexible and more human. An audacious idea this—it assumes that there are enough gentlemen to go round ruling the country! Just as audacious is the assumption of democracy that one can find out truth by a mechanical count of an odd jumble of opinions of common unthinking men. Both systems are admittedly imperfect, but the personal system seems always to have better suited the Chinese humanist temper, Chinese individualism and the Chinese love of freedom.

This trait, the lack of system, characterizes all our social organizations, our civil service, our colleges, our clubs, our railways, our steamship companies—everything except the foreign-controlled Post Office and Maritime Customs—and the failure invariably goes back to the intrusion of the personal element, like nepotism and favouritism. For only an inhuman 'mind, 'an unemotional iron face" can brush aside personal considerations and maintain a rigid system, and such "iron faces" are not in too great public favour in China, for they are all bad Confucianists. Thus has been brought about the lack of social discipline, the most fatal of Chinese characteristics.

The Chinese err, therefore, rather on the side of being too human. For to be reasonable is synonymous with making allowance for human nature. In English, to say to a man, "Do be reasonable," is the same as making an appeal to human nature as such. When Doolittle, the father of the flower-girl in *Pygmalion*, wants to touch Professor Higgins for a five-pound note, his appeal is, "Is this reasonable . . . ? The girl belongs to me. You got her. Where do I come in?" Doolittle further typifies the Chinese humanist spirit by asking for five pounds and refusing Professor Higgins's ten pounds, for too much money would make him unhappy, and a true humanist wants money only to be happy and buy a little drink. In other words, Doolittle was a Confucianist and knew how to be happy and wanted only to be happy. Through this constant appeal to reasonableness, the Chinese have developed a capacity for compromise, which is the perfectly natural consequence of the Doctrine of the Golden Mean. When an English father is unable to decide whether to send his son to Cambridge or Oxford, he may end up by sending him to Birmingham. So when the son, starting out from London and arriving at Bletchley, changes neither to the east for Cambridge, nor to the west for Oxford, but goes straight north to Birmingham, he is merely carrying out the Doctrine of the Golden Mean. That road to Birmingham has certain merits. By going straight north he succeeds in offending neither Cambridge nor Oxford. If one understands this application of the Doctrine of the Golden Mean, one can understand the whole game of Chinese politics in the last thirty years, and prophesy the outcome of any Chinese declaration of policy blindfold. One ceases to be frightened by its literary fireworks.

IV. TAOISM

But has Confucian humanism been sufficient for the Chinese people? It has and it has not. If it had completely satisfied man's instincts, there would have been no room for Taoism or Buddhism. The middle-class morality of Confucianism has worked wonderfully for the common people, both those who wear official buttons and those who kowtow to them.

But there are people who do not wear or kowtow to the official buttons. Man has a deeper nature in him which Confucianism does not quite touch. Confucianism, in the strict sense of the word, is too decorous, too reasonable, too correct. Man has a hidden desire to go about with dishevelled hair, which Confucianism does not quite permit. The man who enjoys slightly rebellious hair and bare feet goes to Taoism. It has been pointed out that the Confucian outlook on life is positive, while the Taoistic outlook is negative. Taoism is the Great Negation, as Confucianism is the Great Affirmation. Confucianism, through its doctrine of propriety and social status, stands for human culture and restraint, while Taoism, with its emphasis on going back to nature, disbelieves in human restraint and culture.

Of the two cardinal Confucian virtues, benevolence and righteousness, Laotse contemptuously said: "No character, then benevolence; no benevolence, then righteousness." Confucianism is essentially an urban philosophy, while Taoism is essentially rural. A modern Confucianist would take city-licensed pasteurized Grade A milk, while a Taoist would take fresh milk from the milkman's pail in the country fashion. For Laotse would have been sceptical of the city licence and pasteurization and the so-called Grade A, which smells not of the natural cream flavour, but of the city councillors' ledgers and bankbooks. And who, after tasting the peasant's milk, can doubt that Laotse was perhaps right? For while your health officers can protect your milk from typhoid germs, they cannot protect it from the rats of civilization.

There are other deficiencies in Confucianism also. It has too much realism and too little room for fancy and imagination. And the Chinese are childishly imaginative. Something of that youthful wonder which we call magic and superstition remains in the Chinese breast. Confucianism provides for the existence of spirits, but takes care to keep them at a distance. It recognizes the spirits of the mountains and the rivers, and even symbolically those of human ancestors, but it has no heaven and hell, no hierarchy of gods and no cosmogony, and its rationalism shows little interest in magic and the pill of immortality. Even the realistic Chinese, apart from their rationalistic scholars, always have a secret desire for immortality. Confucianism has no fairies, while Taoism has. In short, Taoism stands for the childish world of wonder and mystery for which Confucianism fails to provide.

Taoism, therefore, accounts for a side of the Chinese character which Confucianism cannot satisfy. There is a natural romanticism and a natural classicism in a nation, as in an individual. Taoism is the romantic school of Chinese thought, as Confucianism is the classic school. Actually, Taoism is romantic throughout. Firstly, it stands for the return to nature and the romantic escape from the world, and revolts against the artificiality and responsibilities of Confucian culture. Secondly, it stands for the rural ideal of life, art and literature, and the worship of primitive simplicity. And thirdly, it stands for the world of fancy and wonder, coupled with a childishly naïve cosmogony.

The Chinese have been adjudged a matter-of-fact people. Yet there is a romantic side to their character which is even deeper, and which shows itself in their intense individuality, in their love of freedom and their happy-go-lucky view of life, which so often completely mystifies the foreign observers. For myself, I think the Chinese people are immeasurably greater for it. In every Chinese there is a hidden vagabond, with his love of vagabondage. Life under the Confucian code of decorum would be unbearable without this emotional relief. For Taoism is the playing mood of the Chinese people, as Confucianism is their working mood. That accounts for the fact that every Chinese is a Confucianist when he is successful and a Taoist when he is a failure. The naturalism of Taoism is the balm that soothes the wounded Chinese soul.

It is interesting to note how Taoism is more the creation of the Chinese people even than Confucianism and to see how the naturalistic philosophy of Laotse became allied, through the working of the folk-mind, with the Chinese interpretation of the world of spirits. Laotse himself had nothing to do with the pill of immortality or with Taoistic magic. His was a philosophy of *laissez faire* in government and naturalism in ethics. For he believed in a "government which does nothing" as the ideal government. What man needed was to be let alone in his state of primitive freedom. Laotse regarded civilization as the beginning of man's degeneration, and considered the sages of the Confucian type as the worst corrupters of the people, as Nietzsche regarded Socrates as the first corrupter of Europe. With his mordant wit, he said, "Sages no dead, robbers no end."[1] His great follower Chuangtse followed up with brilliant satires against Confucian hypocrisy and futility.

It was all so easy. For Confucianism, with its emphasis on ceremonialism and anxiety over the distinctions of mourning periods and the thickness of coffin panels, and with the intense desire of its followers to seek official positions and save the world, lent itself easily to caricature. The hatred of the Taoist against the Confucianist was the natural hatred of the romanticist against the classicist. Perhaps it was not hatred; it was merely an irresistible, mocking laughter.

From this thorough-going scepticism it was but a step to romantic escape from the world and return to nature. Laotse left his post, according to legend, in his old age and disappeared outside the Hankukuan Pass. Chuangtse was offered a high post by the King of Ch'u, but replied by asking whether it was wise to be kept and fed like a pig and then be slaughtered and offered up on the sacrificial altar. From that moment on Taoism has always been associated with the recluse, the retirement to the mountains, the worship of the rural life, the cultivation of the spirit and the prolongation of man's life, and the banishment of all worldly cares and worries. And from this we derive the most characteristic charm of Chinese culture, the rural ideal of life, art and literature.

The question may be asked: How much was Laotse responsible for this recluse ideal? The *Taotehking*, ascribed to him, is a lesser literary accomplishment than the books of Chuangtse, the Chinese Nietzsche, but it is a more concentrated essence of old-roguish wisdom. It is, to my mind, the most brilliantly wicked philosophy of self-protection in world literature. Besides teaching *laissez faire* and passive resistance, it taught also the wisdom of stupidity, the strength of weakness, the advantage of lying low, and the importance of camouflage. One of its maxims was, "Never be the first of the world," for the simple reason that thus one could never be exposed to attack, and consequently never fall. It was, so far as I know, the only known theory of ignorance and stupidity as the best camouflage

---

[1] English readers will kindly excuse my grammar, as it is found impossible to convey the forceful terseness of the original except by recourse to pidgin. Any grammatical improvement will spoil it.

in life's battle, in spite of the fact that the theory itself was the result of the highest human intelligence.

Human intelligence in Laotse had seen its own dangers and began to preach "Be stupid!" as its greatest message. It had seen the futility of human effort, and therefore advised the doctrine of "doing nothing" as a saving of energy and a method of prolonging life. From this point on the positive outlook on life became negative, and its influence has coloured the whole Oriental culture. As may be seen in the novel *Yehsao Paoyen* and in all lives of great Chinese, the conversion of a bandit or a recluse into a man of the world with responsibilities toward one's fellow-beings, was always represented by a Confucian argument, while the romantic escape from the world was always represented by the Taoistic or Buddhistic point of view. In Chinese, these two opposite attitudes are called "entering the world" and "leaving the world." Sometimes these two points of view struggle for supremacy in the same man and at different periods in his life, as may be seen in the life of Yüan Chunglang. A living example is that of Professor Liang Suming, who was a Buddhist living in the mountains, but who was reconverted to Confucianism, married and is now conducting a rural middle school in Shantung.

The rural ideal of life, art and literature, which is such an important feature of the Chinese civilization, owes a large measure to this Taoistic feeling for nature. In Chinese paintings on scrolls and porcelain there are two favourite themes, one being the happiness of family life with pictures of women and children in their leisure, the other being the happiness of the rural life, with pictures of a fisherman, or a woodcutter, or a recluse sitting on the ground under a group of pine-trees. These two themes may represent respectively the Confucianist and the Taoistic ideal of life. The woodcutter, the herb-gatherer, and the recluse are more closely associated with Taoism than the average foreigner would suspect. The Taoistic feeling is well expressed by this favourite poem:

> I asked the boy beneath the pines.
> He said, "The Master's gone alone
> Herb-picking somewhere on the mount.
> Cloud-hidden, whereabouts unknown."

This feeling for nature practically overflows in all Chinese poetry, and forms an important part of the Chinese spiritual heritage. Yet here, Confucianism plays an equally important part. The worship of primitive simplicity was consciously a part of the Confucian tradition. The agricultural basis of Chinese national life was partly built on the family system, which identified itself with ownership of land in the country, and partly on the Confucian dream of the Golden Age. Confucianism always harked back to the early period of the Emperors Yao and Shun, as the Golden Age when life was at its simplest and the needs of man were fewest. It was spoken of as a period when the people squatted on the earth and sang to the rhythm of sticks beaten on the ground, so happy and innocent that the burden of their song was:

> We go to work at sunrise.
> And come back to rest at sunset.
> We know nothing and learn nothing.
> What has the emperor's virtue to do with us?

The worship of the ancients then became identical with the worship of simplicity, for in Chinese the two notions are closely related, as in the word *kup'o,* or "ancient and simple." The Confucian ideal of the family has always been that the men partly study and partly till the ground, while the women spin and weave. As against the Taoistic poem quoted, and essentially supporting it in the praise of the simple life, we have, for instance, the poem which Ch'en Chiju, a scholar at the end of the sixteenth century, handed to his children as his family heritage:

> Life is complete
> With children at your feet;
> Just a handful of hay hides your cot.
> If land is sterile,
> To make it fertile,
> A young calf will surely help a lot.
> Teach thy sons to read, too, in spare hours,
> Not for fame nor for Mandarin collars.
> Brew your wine, plant bamboos, water flowers,
> Thus a house for generations of scholars.

The Chinese ideal of happiness was, then, not the "exercise of one's powers along the lines of their excellence," as was that of the Greeks, but the enjoyment of this simple rural life, together with the harmony of social relationships.

The real force of Taoism, especially among the people, however, consists largely in supplying a world of unknowables, which Confucian good sense banished from its province of ideas. It is recorded in the *Analects* that Confucius seldom talked about the supernatural and the spirits. Confucianism offered no hell and no heaven, nor any formula for immortality of the soul. It solved the problems of human nature, but left out of consideration the riddle of the universe. It was at a loss to know even the workings of the human body. In this way, it left a large loophole in its philosophy, and allowed the popular mind to disentangle, with the help of Taoistic mysticism, the mysteries of nature.

The workings of this mind were soon apparent in Huainantse (178-122 B.C.), who mixed philosophy with a wonderland of spirits and legends. Starting out with the dualistic notion of *yin* (female) and *yang* (male) principles, already current in the period of the Warring Kingdoms, Taoism soon added to its territory the fairies of the ancient Shantung barbarians, who dreamed of a fairyland out on the high seas, to which place the first emperor of Ch'in actually started out with five hundred boys and virgins to seek his immortality. The hold on the imagination then became irresistible, and from that time till the present Taoism has always maintained a firm foothold on the Chinese people, especially in the T'ang Dynasty, when it became for a long period the state religion, known as the Mystic Religion (because the T'ang imperial house had the same surname as Laotse, Li). In the Wei and Ch'in Dynasties its vogue was so great as to completely overshadow Confucianism, and the fashion for Taoism became connected with the first romantic movement of Chinese literature and with the reaction against Confucian decorum, as it had been transformed by the late Han scholars. One of the famous poets compared the Confucian gentleman walking in his narrow path of righteousness to a bug creeping along the seams of a man's trousers. Man's nature had rebelled against Confucian restraint and its ceremonialism.

In the meanwhile, Taoism widened its sphere, and included under its arts medicine (or secret knowledge of the herbs), physiology and cosmogony (all more or less symbolically explained on the basis of the *yin* and *yang* principles and the Five Elements), magic, witchcraft, aphrodisiacs, incantations, astrology, a good hierarchy of gods, some beautiful legends, a priesthood and a pope—all those paraphernalia that go to make up a good, solid popular religion. It took care, too, of Chinese athletics, by specializing in boxing, and the combination of boxing and witchcraft produced the Huangchin Rebellion at the end of the Han Dynasty. Last of all, it offered a formula for bodily hygiene, chiefly by deep-breathing, leading up to immortality by ascent to heaven on the back of a stork. Its most useful word was *ch'i* (air? breath? spirit?) which, being invisible, was most susceptible of "mystic" handling. The application of this *ch'i* was practically universal, from the rays of a comet to boxing, deep-breathing and sexual union, which was sedulously practised as an art (with preference for virgins), in the cause of prolongation of life. Taoism was, in short, the Chinese attempt to discover the mysteries of nature.

V. BUDDHISM

Buddhism is the only important foreign influence that has become part and parcel of Chinese life. The influence is so deep that we now speak of children's dolls, and sometimes the children themselves, as "little buddhisatvas" (*hsiao p'usa*), and the Empress Dowager herself was addressed as "Old Buddha." The Goddess of Mercy and the smiling Buddha have become Chinese household words. Buddhism has affected our language, our food, our arts, our sculpture and directly inspired the characteristic pagoda. It has stimulated our literature and our whole world of imagination. The little monkish figure, with his bald head and his grey robes, forms an intimate part of any panorama of society, and Buddhist temples, rather than those of Confucius, are the centre of the town and village life, where the elders gather to decide on village matters and annual celebrations. Its monks and nuns penetrate the privacies of Chinese households, on all occasions of births, deaths and weddings, as no other persons are allowed to do, and hardly a widow or virgin can be seduced, according to the Chinese novels, without the help of these religious figures.

Buddhism, in short, means to the Chinese people what religion means to people in other countries, namely, something that comes to the rescue when human reason falters or fails. In modern China Buddhist monks are more popular than Taoist monks and for every Taoist temple (*kuan*) there are ten Buddhist temples (*miao*) to be found. As late as 1933-4 the Panchen Lama of Thibet sprinkled holy water over tens of thousands of people in Peiping and Nanking, including high government personages like Tuan Ch'ijui and Tai Chit'ao, and was royally entertained by the Central and local governments in Nanking, Shanghai, Hangchow and Canton. As late as May, 1934, Nola Kotuhutu, another Thibetan lama, as official guest of the Canton Government, publicly declared his ability to protect people against poison gas by incantations, and actually was able to influence a certain general to change the position of his guns at this fort through his superior knowledge of astrology and necromancy. Their influence would not be so great if the Chinese could see a clear way to repel Japanese attacks by modern military science. The Chinese reason here falters, and therefore turns to religion. Since the Chinese army cannot help the Chinese, they are willing to be helped by Buddha.

Buddhism has conquered China as a philosophy and as a religion, as a philosophy for the scholars and as a religion for the common people. Whereas Confucianism has only a philosophy of moral conduct, Buddhism possesses a logical method, a metaphysics, and a theory of knowledge. Besides, it is fortunate in having a high tradition of scholarship in the translations of Buddhist classics, and the language of these translations, so succinct and often so distinguished by a beautiful lucidity of language and reasoning, cannot but attract scholars with a philosophical bias. Hence Buddhism has always enjoyed a prestige among the Chinese scholars, which so far Christianity has failed to achieve.

Buddhist influence has been so great as to transform Confucianism itself. Confucian scholarship since the Chou Dynasty was confined to textual emendations and philologic commentaries. The fashion for the study of Buddhism, believed to be introduced to China in the first Christian century, rose steadily throughout the Northern Wei and Ch'in Dynasties, and produced a change of emphasis from textual commentaries to the inner philosophic meaning (*yili*). In the Sung Dynasty there arose directly under its influence a new Confucian school, or several schools, which called themselves *lihsüeh*, or "philosophy." The preoccupation was still with moral problems, but terms like *hsing* (nature), *li* (reason), *ming* (predestination), *hsin* (mind), *wu* (matter), and *chih* (knowledge) were brought into the foreground. There was a reawakened interest in the Confucian *Yiking* (*Book of Changes*), which studies the mutations of human events. These Sung Confucianists, one and all, especially the Ch'eng brothers, had delved deep into Buddhism and came back to Confucianism with a newly-won perspective. The realization of truth was spoken of, as by Lu Chiuyen, as an "awakening" in the Buddhistic sense, following a long meditation. Buddhism did not convert these scholars, but it changed the tenor of Confucianism itself.

Equally great was its influence over writers like Su Tungp'o, who were in an armed camp against these scholars, but who played with Buddhism in their own light, dilettante way. Su Tungp'o styled himself a *chüssü*, which means a Confucian scholar living in Buddhistic retirement without becoming a monk, a most peculiarly Chinese invention which allowed a follower of Buddhism to live in married life and become a vegetarian for periods at leisure. One of Su's best friends was a learned monk, Foyin, and the difference between these two friends was only a difference of degree of conversion. This was the time when Buddhism prospered under imperial protection, with a Government Bureau for the translation of Buddhist classics, and counting at one time almost half a million monks and nuns. Since Su Tungp'o's time, and largely due to his great literary influence, many a scholar of high standing has played with Buddhism and become a *chüssü* of Su's type, if not actually entering a monastery as a monk. In times of national disorder, as during the change of dynasties, a great number of scholars shaved their heads and took monastic orders, as much for personal protection as out of feeling for the helpless chaos of the world.

There is justification enough in a chaotic country for the popularity of a religion which declares the vanity of the world and offers a refuge from the pains and vicissitudes of this earthly life. We have to-day an extant copy of the life of Lu Liching by his daughter. Lu Liching, at the end of the Ming Dynasty and the beginning of the Manchu Dynasty, disappeared from the world in his old age, and after long years of separation from his wife and children, once entered the city of Hangchow to cure the sickness of his brother, but refused to see his own family living next door. What disillusionment a man must have perceived of the phenomena of this life to do such a thing!

And yet it is not impossible to understand it after reading his daughter's *Life*. The depth of disillusionment was equal only to the depth of his personal sufferings. Accused of having a hand in the publication of a work by another author, which was considered disrespectful to the new Manchu régime, this man, after bidding farewell to his ancestors in a sacrificial prayer, started out with his whole family to Peking, in chains and under guard, with the constant expectation that his wife and children and close relatives would be slaughtered wholesale. He had said in his prayer that if he came back alive he would become a monk, and he did. In this sense Buddhism was an unconscious gesture of man in his battle with life, a form of revenge somewhat similar in psychology to suicide, when life proved too cruelly superior. Many beautiful and talented girls at the end of the Ming Dynasty took the monastic vow through disappointment in love caused by those catastrophic changes, and the first emperor of the Manchu Dynasty became a monk for the same reason.

But apart from this negative protest against life, there is an aspect of Buddhism which has an evangelical influence on the common people, and works for general kindness. The most vivid and direct influence it exercises over the people is through its doctrine of transmigration. Buddhism has not taught the

Chinese to befriend the animals, but it has largely restrained the consumption of beef. The Chinese Doctrine of the Golden Mean has encouraged the people in the consumption of pork as an inevitable evil and on the plea that the pig is a less useful animal than the cow except as food. But it has driven home to the Chinese consciousness the idea that butchery is inhuman and displeasing to the gods. During the flood in 1933 the Hankow local government forbade butchery for three days as an atonement toward the river god, and this practice is practically universal whenever there is a drought or famine. Vegetarianism can hardly be defended on biologic grounds, since man is born with natural carnivorous, as well as herbivorous, teeth, but it can be defended on humane grounds. Mencius was conscious of this cruelty, but being unwilling to forgo meat entirely, he fought his way out by giving the formula that "a gentleman kept away from the kitchen." The fact that one does not see what happens in the kitchen eases the Confucian conscience. This solution of the dietetic difficulty was typical of the Doctrine of the Golden Mean. Many a Chinese grandmother, wishing to please Buddha and not willing to forgo meat entirely, would apply the Doctrine of the Golden Mean in a different fashion by turning vegetarian for a definite period from a single day to three years.

But, on the whole, Buddhism forces the Chinese people to admit butchery as an inhuman act. This is but one consequence of the doctrine of transmigration, which works for general humaneness toward animals and one's fellow-beings. For the consequent doctrine of retribution and the possible soul survival in the form of a sore-ridden beggar or a flea-ridden dog may be a more effective object-lesson for good behaviour than a hell of pointed knives learned by hearsay. Actually, the true Buddhist follower is a kinder person, more pacific, more patient, and more philanthropic, than others. His philanthropy may not be ethically worth much, since every cent given and every cup of tea offered to the passing stranger is an investment in personal future happiness, and therefore essentially selfish, but what religion does not use the same bait? William James has wisely said that religion is the most colossal chapter in the history of human selfishness. Man, outside the sincere humanist, seems to need this selfish bait. Nevertheless, Buddhism has given rise to the great institution of well-to-do families providing big earthen jars of cold tea for passing wayfarers on hot summer days. It is, in common phraseology, a good thing, irrespective of motive.

Many Chinese novels, like the tales of Boccaccio, have accused the monks and nuns of immorality. This is based on the universal human delight taken in exposing all forms of hypocrisy. It is natural and easy therefore to make Casanovas of Chinese monks, provided with witchcraft and secret aphrodisiacs. There are actually cases, in certain parts of Chekiang, for example, where a nunnery is but a house of prostitution. But on the whole, the charge is unfair, and most monks are good, retiring, polite and well-behaved people, and any Don Juan exploits are limited to transgressing individuals, and are grossly exaggerated in novels for effect. From my personal observation, most monks are underfed, anæmic and incapable of such exploits. Besides, this misjudgment is due to the failure to see the connection between sex and religion in China. The monks have a greater chance to see beautifully dressed women than any other class of people in China. The practice of their religion, whether in private homes or in their temples, brings them in daily contact with women who are otherwise shut away from the public. Thanks to the Confucian seclusion of women, the only unimpeachable pretext for women to appear in public is to go to the temples and "burn incense." On the first and fifteenth of every month, and on every festive occasion, the Buddhist temple is the rendezvous of all the local beauties, married or otherwise, dressed in their "Sunday best." If any monk eats pork on the sly, he may also be expected to indulge in occasional irregularities. Add to this the fact that many monasteries are exceptionally well endowed, and many monks have plenty of money to spend, which is the cause of mischief in many cases that have come to light in recent years. In 1934 a nun actually had the audacity to sue a monk for infidelity in a Shanghai court. Anything may happen in China.

I give here a refined example of the literary handling of the sexual problems of the monks. The poem is called a "Young

Nun's Worldly Desires," which is a favourite topic and has many versions. It is taken from a popular Chinese drama, *The White Fur-Coat*, and in Chinese is incidentally first-class poetry, in the form of the young nun's soliloquy.

> A young nun am I, sixteen years of age;
> My head is shaven in my young maidenhood.
>
> For my father, he loves the Buddhist sutras,
> And my mother, she loves the Buddhist priests.
>
> Morning and night, morning and night,
> I burn incense and I pray. For I
> Was born a sickly child, full of ills.
> So they decided to send me here
> Into this monastery.
>
> Amitabha! Amitabha!
> Unceasingly I pray.
> Oh, tired am I of the humming of the drums and the
>   tinkling of the bells;
> Tired am I of the droning of the prayers and the crooning
>   of the priors;
> The chatter and the clatter of unintelligible charms,
> The clamour and the clangour of interminable chants,
> The mumbling and the murmuring of monotonous psalms.
> Panjnaparamita, Mayura-sutra,
>   Saddharamapundarika—
>   Oh, how I hate them all!
>
> While I say mitabha,
>   I sigh for my beau.
> While I chant saparah,
>   My heart cries, "Oh!"
> While I sing tarata,
>   My heart palpitates so!
>
> Ah, let me take a little stroll,
> Let me take a little stroll,

*(She comes to the Hall of the Five Hundred Lohan, which are
known for their distinctive facial expressions.)*

Ah, here are the Lohan,
What a bunch of silly, amorous souls!
    Every one a bearded man!
How each his eyes at me rolls!

Look at the one hugging his knees!
    His lips are mumbling my name so!
And the one with his cheek in his hand.
    As though thinking of me so!
That one has a pair of dreamy eyes,
    Dreaming dreams of me so!

    But the Lohan in sackcloth!
What is he after,
    With his hellish, heathenish laughter?
With his roaring, rollicking laughter,
    Laughing at me so!
                    ——Laughing at me, for
When beauty is past and youth is lost,
    Who will marry an old crone?
When beauty is faded and youth is jaded,
    Who will marry an old, shrivelled cocoon?

The one holding a dragon,
    He is cynical;
The one riding a tiger,   -
    He looks quizzical;
And that long-browed handsome giant,
    He seems pitiful,
For what will become of me when my beauty is gone?

These candles of the altar,
    They are not for my bridal chamber.
These long incense-containers,
    They are not for my bridal parlour.
And the straw prayer cushions,
    They cannot serve as quilt or cover.
            Oh, God!

Whence comes this burning, suffocating ardour?
   Whence comes this strange, infernal, unearthly ardour?
   I'll tear these monkish robes!
   I'll bury all the Buddhist sutras;
   I'll drown the wooden fish,
   And leave all the monastic putras!
I'll leave the drums,
   I'll leave the bells,
       And the chants,
           And the yells,
And all the interminable, exasperating, religious chatter!
I'll go downhill, and find me a young and handsome lover—
Let him scold me, beat me!
   Kick or ill-treat me!
I will *not* become a buddha!
I will *not* mumble mita, panjra, para!

This brings us to the topic of the actual service of the Buddhistic religion as an emotional outlet for the Chinese people. First, it makes the seclusion of women not so complete and more endurable. The desire of women to go to the temple, as against the lesser desire of men to do the same, is as much due to their emotional need for going outdoors as to the usual greater "religiosity" of women. The first and fifteenth days of a month and the festive occasions are days actually anticipated for weeks ahead by women in their secluded chambers.

Secondly, its spring pilgrimages provide legitimate outlet for the very much atrophied Chinese *Wanderlust*. These pilgrimages come in early spring, and coincide with Easter. Those who cannot go far away at least may go to weep on the relatives' graves on *ch'ingming* day, which has the same emotional basis. Those who can, put on sandals or go in sedan chairs to the famous temples. Some people in Amoy still persist in sailing about five hundred miles on old sailing junks to the Pootoo Islands off the coast of Ningpo every spring. In the North, the annual pilgrimage to Miaofengshan is still a prevailing custom. Thousands of pilgrims, old and young, men and women, may be seen on the trail carrying sticks and yellow bags, travelling nights and days to the sacred temple. Among them the spirit of jollity prevails as it did in Chaucer's times, and tales are told on the way like those Chaucer recorded.

Hence, thirdly, it provides the Chinese with a chance to enjoy mountain scenery, for most Buddhist temples are situated on high mountains at scenic spots. It is the one little pleasure the Chinese allow themselves in their usual humdrum everyday life. They arrive and put up in what seem to be superior hotel rooms, and drink tea and gossip with the monks. The monks are polite conversationalists, they offer good vegetarian dinners and reap an enormous sum in their coffers. The pilgrims then go home with freshened spirits and renewed energy for their exacting daily routine. Who can deny that Buddhism has an important place in the scheme of Chinese life?

PART TWO

LIFE

PROLOGUE TO PART TWO

WE have now surveyed the mental and moral constitution of the Chinese people, and the ideals of life which influence the fundamental pattern of Chinese life. It remains to make a study of Chinese life itself in its sexual, social, political, literary and artistic aspects. Stated briefly, these will cover Chinese women, society, governments, literature and art, together with a special chapter devoted to the art of living as the Chinese have conceived and practised it. These arrange themselves again into two groups. The first three are necessarily connected, for an understanding of the life of women and the home will lead to a consideration of the Chinese social life, and only from a true understanding of the Chinese social life will it be possible to understand the administration of justice and government in China. The study of these visible aspects of Chinese life will naturally lead to an inquiry into the subtler and less known problems of Chinese culture, especially in the field of art, with an outlook and a history of development peculiar to the Chinese people and totally different from the West. The Chinese culture is one of the truly indigenous cultures of the world, and as such will be found to offer many interesting points of comparison with Western culture.

For culture is a product of leisure, and the Chinese have had the immense leisure of three thousand years to develop it. In these three thousand years they have had plenty of time to drink tea and look at life quietly over their teacups, and from the gossip over the teacups they have boiled life down to its essence. They have had plenty of time, too, to discuss their forefathers, to ponder over their achievements and to review the successive changes of the modes of art and of life, and to see their own in the light of the long past. And from this gossiping and pondering history came to have a great meaning: it came to be spoken of as the "mirror" which reflects human experience for the benefit of the present and which is like a gathering stream, uninterrupted, continuous. The writing of history then became the most serious form of literature and the writing of poetry became its highest and most refined emotional outlet.

Sometimes, when the "wine was fragrant and the tea well-brewed," amidst the singing of the kettle and the gurgling of the spring, a happy thought came to the Chinese, and at intervals of about five hundred years, or under the forces of changed circumstances, their minds became creative and a new discovery was made either in the metre of poetry or in the improvement of porcelain, or in the art of grafting pear-trees, and the nation moved on. They gave up speculation about immortality as something for ever unknowable but for ever to be conjectured and gossiped about, half seriously and half playfully. Equally they gave up the mysteries of nature, thunderstorms and lightning and hail and snow, and the mysteries of their own bodily functions, such as the connection between salival flow and hunger. They did not use the test-tube or the scalpel. So sometimes it seemed to them as if the whole sphere of the knowable had been exhausted by their ancient forefathers, and the last word on human philosophy said, and the last rhythm in calligraphy discovered.

So they fell more seriously to the business of living than to the business of making progress. They took infinite pains and spent sleepness nights over the planning of their private gardens or the cooking of sharks' fins, and fell to eating with the seriousness and gusto of an Omar Khayyám, who trailed the dust of philosophy in vain and took again the vine for his spouse. In this, they crossed the threshold of all the arts, and entered the hall of the art of life itself, and art and life became one. They achieved that crown of Chinese culture, the art of living, which is the end of all human wisdom.

Chapter Five

WOMAN'S LIFE

I. THE SUBJECTION OF WOMEN

SOMETHING in the Chinese blood never quite gave woman her due from primeval times. The fundamental dualistic outlook, with the differentiation of the *yang* (male) and the *yin* (female) principles, went back to the *Book of Changes*, which was later formulated by Confucius. The respect for women, a certain tenderness toward the female sex, which was characteristic of the Teutonic races already in their barbaric days, was absent in the early pages of Chinese History. As early as the time of the folk-songs, collected in the *Book of Poems*, there was a sexual inequality, for "when a baby boy was born he was laid on the bed and given jade to play with, and when a baby girl was born she was laid on the floor and given a tile to play with." (This song must have been centuries older than Confucius.) But woman was not subjected until she was civilized. The progressive subjection of women followed pace by pace the increasing development of Confucianism.

The original social system was a matriarchal system, and this is important, for something of this spirit still survives in Chinese womanhood to the present day. The Chinese woman is, on the whole, a constitutionally sounder animal than her male companion, and we still have plenty of matriarchs even in the Confucian households. Traces of this matriarchy were still clearly visible in the Chou Dynasty, when the family name, or *hsing*, was the woman's name, and man had only a personal name, or *shih*, after his place of birth or his official position. Throughout the folk-songs of the *Book of Poems* we fail to see any traces of the seclusion of women. Something of the freedom in the choice of mates, like what still prevails among the southern aborigines of Kwangsi, must have prevailed in the

ancient times. It was raw and it was free. One folk-song from
the *Book of Poems* runs thus:

> If thou thinkest of me,
> I will lift my petticoat
>   And cross the river Ts'en.[1]
> If thou thinkest not of me,
> Why, are there not other men?
>   —Oh, thou silly boy!

> If thou thinkest of me,
> I will lift my petticoat
>   And cross the River Wo.
> If thou thinkest not of me,
> Why, are there not other beaux?
>   —Oh, thou silly boy!

The *Book of Poems* also has many examples of songs of women
who ran away with their lovers. The marriage system had
not yet become the severe bondage of women that it was in
later days. The sexual relations of men in the times of Confucius, especially those prevailing in the upper classes, had
something analogous to those in the days of decadent Rome,
with numerous cases of incest with stepmothers, with daughters-
in-law, with sisters-in-law, the presentation of one's wife to a
neighbouring ruler, the marrying of a son's wife for one's own
benefit, illicit relations between the queen and the prime
minister, etc., with which the *Chochüan* abounds. Woman, who
is always powerful in China, was powerful then. The Queen of
Wei made the King summon the handsomest man in the country
to her boudoir. Divorce was still easy and divorcées could
remarry. The cult of feminine chastity had not yet become an
obsession with men.

Then came Confucianism with its seclusion of women. The
separation of men and women was soon pushed by the Confucianists to such extremes that married sisters could not eat
at the same table with their brothers, according to the *Book of*

---

[1] The spellings of these river names have been slightly altered to suit the
rhyme.

Rites. To what extent such ceremonial "rites" in the books were observed in practice it is impossible to ascertain. It is easy to understand this seclusion from the viewpoint of the whole Confucian social philosophy. It stood for a society with emphasis on distinction between superiority and inferiority. It stood for obedience, for recognition of authority in a family as in a state, and for the division of labour between man's duties outside and women's duties in the home. It encouraged the womanly woman, and naturally taught such feminine virtues as quietness, obedience, good manners, personal neatness, industry, ability in cooking and spinning, respect for the husband's parents, kindness to the husband's brothers, courtesy to the husband's friends, and all those virtues desirable from the male point of view. Nothing was radically wrong in these moral instructions, and with their economic dependence and their love of conventions, women accepted them. Perhaps the women desired to be good, or perhaps they desired to please the men.

Confucianism saw that this sexual differentiation was necessary for social harmony, and perhaps Confucianism was quite near the truth. Then Confucianism also gave the wife an "equal" position with the husband, somewhat below the husband, but still an equal helpmate, like the two fish in the Taoist symbol of *yin* and *yang*, necessarily complementing each other. It also gave the mother an honoured position in the home. In the best spirit of Confucianism, this differentiation was interpreted, not as a subjection but as a harmony of relationships. Women who could rule their husbands knew that dependence on this sexual arrangement was their best and most effective weapon for power, and women who could not were too dull to raise feminist problems.

This was the Confucian attitude toward women and women's position in society before it came under the influence of the later men scholars. It had not yet developed that curiously and perversely selfish aspect characteristic of the later attitudes, but the basic notions of woman's inferiority were there. One flagrant instance was the rule that while the husband's mourning period for the wife was only one year, the wife's mourning period for the husband was three years, and while the normal mourning period for one's parents was three years, that of the wife for her own father was only one year, if the husband's father was still living. Typically feminine virtues, like obedience and loyalty, were codified by Liu Hsiang in the Han Dynasty, into something like a feminine ethics, quite distinct from that for the men, and Pan Ch'ao, the woman author of *Women's Guide*, was the great exponent of the "three obediences and four virtues" of women. The three obediences were: when a woman is in her maiden home she obeys her father; when married she obeys her husband; and when her husband dies she obeys her son." The last was of course never carried out, owing to the superior position of the mother in the Confucian scheme. In this Dynasty women who died for their chastity were already officially honoured with stone *pailou* or with official titles from the court. But women could still marry a second time.

In tracing the development of the theory of chaste widowhood, it would be dangerous to lend too much weight to academic theory, for the Chinese are always a realistic people and have a way of withering theories with a laugh. Practice must have lagged behind theory, and even as late as the Manchu times chaste widowhood was expected of the wife of a scholar with official titles but not of the common women. Even in the T'ang Dynasty the daughter of the great scholar Han Yü married a second time. Of the T'ang princesses, twenty-three married a second time and four of them married a third time. But the tradition started in the Han Dynasty centuries before was there at work, reinforcing the early tradition that men could remarry but women could not.

After this came the Sung scholars, who imposed a secluded life on women and made the remarrying of widows a moral crime. Worship of chastity, which they so highly prized in women, became something of a psychological obsession and women were henceforth to be responsible for social morals, from which the men were exempt. More than that, women were to be responsible for courage and strength of character also, which curiously the men so admired in the gentle sex, for the emphasis had shifted from women's ordinary routine domestic virtues to female heroism and self-sacrifice. Already

in the ninth century a widow was greatly praised by the
Confucian males for cutting off her arm because a hotel-keeper
had dragged her by it, when she was refused entrance on her
way home accompanying her husband's coffin. In the Mongol
Dynasty another widow was greatly honoured for refusing to
show her ulcered breast to the doctor and heroically dying of
it.[1]

In the Ming Dynasty this doctrine of chaste widowhood
became an official institution. Women who kept their widowhood from any age under thirty to the age of fifty were officially
honoured with *pailou*, and their families were exempt from
official labour service. It became then not only highly moral
to admire purity of character in women, but also highly convenient for the male relatives to do so. Chaste widowhood
became not only popular with the men and the widows'
relatives, but also became one of the easiest ways for women to
distinguish themselves. They lent honour, not only to their
own families but to their whole village or clan. In this sense
it had truly become a popular obsession, with just a few
occasional protests from independent minds. It was this
doctrine of chaste widowhood that caused Confucianism to be
denounced during the "Renaissance" of 1917 as a "man-
eating religion."

Along with the development of Confucian theory a stream of
real life was going on, based on social conventions, and still
more on economic pressure. More important than the influence of Confucianism was the fact that men controlled the
purse. For while Confucianism had erected chaste widowhood
into a religion, jewels and pearl necklaces, which had nothing
to do with Confucianism, turned women into concubines and
cocottes. The accumulation of wealth and the rise of great
houses during the Wei and Ch'in Dynasties, coupled with the
general political disorder, encouraged concubinage on the
one hand and forced the drowning of baby girls on the other,
owing to the fact that poor parents could not provide for the

[1] Most of these stories can be found in the official histories of the different
dynasties, where special sections are devoted to lives of great women, along
with those of men. A woman who distinguished herself by committing suicide
to guard her chastity had a fair chance of leaving her name in literature in one
form or another.

expensive wedding ceremonies of their daughters. In these times many rulers and rich families had dancing girls in their private households by the tens and hundreds, and the life of licentious luxury and female entertainment was something that would have satisfied a roué's dreams. Women, in short, had become the playthings of men. Shih Ts'ung, who had dozens of concubines, used to make them tread on a bed spread with rare incense powder and those who were light enough to leave no footprint on it would be rewarded with strings of pearl necklaces, while those who did would be "put on the diet" and instructed to reduce. Those pearl necklaces, rather than Confucianism, were the cause of women's downfall in China as in ancient Rome or modern New York. The situation was therefore ripe for the institution of footbinding, which was the last sophistication of male fancy.

Paradoxically, it was in this period that Chinese women were known throughout for their jealousy, and henpecked officials often appeared at court with bruised faces, resulting in punishment of their jealous wives by royal decree. A certain Liu Poyü used to recite the *Ode to the Goddess of River Lo*, and once remarked with a sigh in his wife's hearing, "What a beauty for a wife!" His wife said, "Why do you praise the Goddess of River Lo and insult me? When I die, I will become a water spirit." That night she drowned herself in the river. Seven days afterwards the wife appeared before Poyü in a dream and said, "You wanted to marry a goddess, now I am a goddess." For the rest of his life Liu Poyü never dared cross a stream. Whenever women passed the river at this ferry, called the "Ferry of the Jealous Woman" (in Shantung), they had to hide or crumple their beautiful dresses and disfigure themselves, otherwise a storm would come up. But if the women were ugly the goddess was not jealous. And women who passed the ferry without raising a storm thought they must be ugly themselves.

It is easy to see how women's jealousy grew with the system of concubinage. It was their only weapon of defence. A jealous wife could, by the sheer force of this instinct, prevent her husband from having concubines, modern instances of which can still be found. If man had sense enough to see that marriage is woman's best and only profession he would be able

to excuse in her such professional ethics, whether with concubines or not. Our scholar, Yü Chenghsieh, discovered as
early as 1833 that "jealousy is no vice in women." Women who
lose their husbands' favour have about the same feeling as a
professional clerk who loses the good favour of his employer,
and unmarried girls have about the same feeling as a man out
of employment. Man's professional jealousy in commercial
competition is just as merciless as woman's in the field of love,
and a small trader has just as much liking for being put out of
business as a shopkeeper's wife has in seeing her husband take
to another woman. Such is the logic of the economic dependence of women. The failure to see this is responsible for the
jokes about gold-diggers, for gold-diggers are merely the female
counterpart of successful business men: they are more clear-
minded than their sisters, sell their goods to the highest bidders
in a professional spirit, and get what they want. Successful
business men and gold-diggers want the same thing, money,
and they ought to respect each other for his or her clear-
mindedness.

II. HOME AND MARRIAGE

Anything is possible in China, however. I have been carried
in a sedan chair by women up the mountains in the outskirts
of Soochow. The women sedan-bearers insisted on carrying
me, a man, up those hills. Somewhat shamefacedly, I let them,
for, I thought, these are the descendants of the ancient Chinese
matriarchs, and sisters of the women in southern Fukien, with
glorious breasts and an erect bearing, who carry coal and till
the field, who rise early in the morning, dress and wash and do
their hair neatly and go to work and come back to nurse their
children with their own milk. They are the sisters, too, of those
women in rich families who rule the household and their husbands as well.

Have women really been suppressed in China, I often
wonder? The powerful figure of the Empress Dowager
immediately comes to my mind. Chinese women are not the
type to be easily suppressed. Women have suffered many

disadvantages, have been prevented from holding stenographic positions or judicial posts, but women have ruled nevertheless in the home, apart from those debauchee households where women have become toys. Even in these homes some of the concubines manage to rule their lords. And what is still more important, women have been deprived of every right, but they have never been deprived of the right to marry. To every girl born in China a home of her own is provided. Society insists that even slave-girls should be married off at proper age. Marriage is women's only inalienable right in China, and with the enjoyment of that right they have the best weapon for power, as wife and as mother.

There are two sides to this picture. Man has undoubtedly been unfair to woman, yet it is interesting to see how sometimes woman has her revenge. The total effect of the subjection of women consists in the general recognition of the inferiority of women, in women's self-abasement, in their deprivation of the social advantages of the men, in their lesser education and knowledge, in their cheaper, harder and less free lives, and in the double sex standard. The oppression of women is more the invisible sort, resulting from the general recognition of their inferiority. Where there is no love between husband and wife the husband may be very autocratic, and in such cases the wife has no other recourse but submission. The women merely endure family autocracy as the Chinese people endure political autocracy. But no one dare say there are more autocratic husbands or less happy marriages in China, for reasons we shall soon see. The women are expected not to be garrulous, not to gad about from family to family, and not to look at men in the streets. But many of them are extremely garrulous, many of them gad about from family to family, and many of them look at men in the streets. They are expected to be virtuous, while men are not, but this is not such a great hardship, since most women are naturally chaste. They are deprived of the consideration and social advantages which Western women enjoy, but once they get used to it, they don't care about going to mixed parties, for they have their social occasions and home parties as well, and just as little do they care for the privileges of policing the streets or peddling iron wares. In fact, all the rest is unimportant compared with their position in the home, in which they live and move and have their being.

In the home the woman rules. No modern man can still believe with Shakespeare that "Frailty, thy name is woman!" Shakespeare disproved this himself with his Cleopatra, and with King Lear's daughters. Close observation of Chinese life seems to disprove the prevalent notion of woman's dependence. The Chinese Empress Dowager ruled the nation, whether Emperor Hsienfeng was living or not. There are many Empress Dowagers in China still, politically or in common households. The home is the throne from which she makes appointments for mayors or decides the professions of her grandsons.

The more one knows Chinese life, the more one realizes that the so-called suppression of women is an Occidental criticism that somehow is not borne out by a closer knowledge of Chinese life. That phrase certainly cannot apply to the Chinese mother and supreme arbiter of the household. Anyone who doubts this should read the *Red Chamber Dream*, a monument of Chinese home life. Study the position of the grandmother Chiamu, the relationship between Fengchieh and her husband, or that of any other couple (that of the father Chia Cheng and his wife is perhaps most normal and typical) and see whether it is the man or the woman who rules in the family. Some Western women readers might envy the position of the old grandmother, who was the most honoured person in the whole household, who was treated with decency and respect, and to whose chamber the daughters-in-law repaired almost every morning to pay their respects and decide the most important family affairs. What if Chiamu had a pair of bound feet and was secluded? The doorkeepers and men servants had to use their feet more than she. Or study the character of Madame Water, the mother of the Confucian hero in *Yehsao Paoyen*, who was well educated and a model of Confucian wisdom, and who was undoubtedly the highest character in the whole novel. One word from her could bring her son the prime minister to his knees, and she watched over the welfare of the big family with infinite wisdom as a mother hen guards over her chicken-yard. She ruled with a wise and benign rulership, and all the daughters-in-law were her willing slaves. The character is perhaps overdrawn, but it is not mere fiction. Yes, woman rules in the family, while man rules outside it, for Confucius has set this sharp division of labour.

The women know it, too. To-day the salesgirls in the department stores of Shanghai still look with eyes of envy on the married women with their fat handbags, and wish they were buying instead of selling. Sometimes they wish they were knitting sweaters for their babies instead of counting the change, and standing for a stretch of eight hours is long and tiring in high-heeled shoes. Most of them know instinctively which is the better thing. Some of them prefer their independence, but the so-called independence in a man-ruled society does not amount to much. The cynical ones laugh a little at this "independence." The primeval urge of motherhood—formless, wordless and vague and strong—fills their whole beings. The maternal urge causes the cosmetic urge, all so innocent, so natural and so instinctive, and they count the savings from their starvation wages which hardly suffice to buy them the mesh stockings they are selling themselves. They wish they had a boy friend to buy them presents, and they would perhaps ask him to, indirectly, shyly, in an effort to keep their self-respect. Chinese girls are essentially decent, but why shouldn't they ask men to buy them presents? How else may they purchase mesh stockings, which their instinct tells them they must have? Life is such a mix-up! All too clearly the idea dawns upon them that they want one man to buy them presents for life. They want to marry. Their instinct is right. What is wrong in marriage? What is wrong in protected motherhood?

In the home they have arrived. They knit and they sew, although now in the middle-class families in Kiangsu and Chekiang they do not even cook or sew. For men have beat them on their own ground, and the best tailors and cooks are men and not women. Men will continue to beat them in every profession except marriage. For men have every advantage over women outside marriage, while inside marriage women have every advantage over men, and they know it. In every nation the happiness of women does not depend on how many social advantages they enjoy, but on the quality of the men they live with. Women suffer more from male tyranny and

coarseness than from the disqualification to vote. When men
are naturally reasonable and good-tempered and considerate,
women do not suffer. Besides, women have always the weapon
of sex, which they can use to great advantage. It is nature's
guarantee for their equality. Somehow every man, from
emperor to butcher, baker and candlestick-maker, has scolded
his wife and been scolded by her, because nature has ordained
that man and woman should meet in their intimacies as equals.
Certain fundamental relations, like that between husband and
wife, differ much less in the different countries than one would
imagine from travellers' descriptions. Westerners are apt to
imagine Chinese wives as mute slaves of their husbands,
although actually Chinese husbands, on the average, are
fairly reasonable and considerate beings; while Chinese are
apt to think that, because the Westerners have never heard of
Confucius, therefore Western wives don't look after their
husbands' laundry and stomachs, but simply go to the beach
in pyjama suits or live in a continuous round of dancing-parties.
The unique and the exotic make such interesting after-dinner
stories, while the central and common truths of humanity are
forgotten.

In real life, then, women have not really been oppressed by
men. Many men who marry concubines and make cats' nests
of their homes and dodge from one woman's chamber to another
are the real sufferers. There is, moreover, that curious sexual
attraction which makes it impossible for relatives of any
degree, of different sex, to dislike each other strongly. Women,
therefore, are not oppressed by their husbands or by their
fathers-in-law, nor can sisters-in-law oppress one another,
since they are of equal rank, although they never like each
other. The only remaining possibility is that daughters-in-law
may be oppressed by the mothers-in-law and this is often what
actually happens. The life of the daughter-in-law in a big
Chinese family with its manifold responsibilities is often a very
hard one. For it must be remembered that a marriage in
China is not an individual affair but a family affair; a man
does not marry a wife but "marries a daughter-in-law," as
the idiomatic expression goes, and when a son is born, the
idiomatic expression is "a grandson has been born." A

daughter-in-law, therefore, has more severe obligations toward her parents than toward her husband. A poem of the T'ang Dynasty by Wang Chien recorded a sympathetic sentiment for the "New Bride":

> On the third day, washing her hands,
> She goes to make a soup of special savour.
> She knows not how the parents like it,
> And makes her husband's sister taste its flavour.

For a woman to please a man is a noble effort, but for her to please another woman is heroic, and many of them fail. The son, torn between loyalty to parents and love for his wife, never quite dares stand up for her. Practically all tales of cruelty to women could be traced to an oppressor of the same sex. But then, the daughter-in-law bides her time to be mother-in-law in turn. If she does arrive at that much-desired old age, it is truly a position of honour and power, well earned by a life of service.

III. Ideal of Womanhood

The seclusion of women has, however, a very definite influence over our ideal of beauty, our ideal of womanhood, the education of our daughters, and the forms of love and courtship in China.

The Chinese and the Western conceptions of the feminine differ. While both conceptions envelop the feminine with a sense of charm and mystery, yet the point of view is essentially different. This is clearest in the field of art. While in Western art the feminine body is taken as the source of inspiration and the highest perfection of pure rhythm, in Chinese art the feminine body itself borrows its beauty from the rhythms of nature. To a Chinese, nothing is more striking than that the statue of a woman should be placed high up in the harbour of New York, to be looked at by all people coming into the country. The idea of feminine exposure is indecorous to the extreme. And when he learns that the woman there does not represent the feminine but the idea of liberty, he is still more shocked. Why should Liberty be represented by a woman? And why should Victory and Justice and Peace be represented by women? The Greek ideal to him is new. For in the West man's imagination has somehow deified woman and conferred on her a spiritual, ethereal quality, representing all that is pure, noble, beautiful and unearthly.

To a Chinese, a woman is a woman, who does not know how to enjoy herself. A Chinese boy is told that he cannot grow up if he passes under a woman's trousers on the washing-line. The idea of worship of a woman on a pedestal and the exposure of woman's body are therefore manifestly impossible. With the seclusion of women, the exposure of the female form, both in art and in everyday life, seems indecorous to the extreme, and some of the masterpieces of Western painting in the Dresden Gallery are definitely classed under the category of pornography. The fashionable modern Chinese artists who are aping the West dare not say so, but there are Continental artists who frankly admit the sensuous origin of all art and make no secret of it.

But the Chinese libido is there, only dressed in a different expression. Women's dress is not designed to reveal the body of the human form but to simulate nature. A Western artist may see, through the use of his sensuous imagination, a female nude form in the rising sea waves, while a Chinese sees in the draperies of the Goddess of Mercy the sea waves themselves. The whole rhythm of a woman's form is modelled after the graceful rhythm of the weeping willows, which accounts for her intentionally drooping shoulders. Her eyes suggest the apricot, her eyebrows the crescent moon, the light of her eyes the silent waters of an autumn lake, her teeth are like the seeds of pomegranate, her waist like the weeping willows, her fingers like the spring bamboo-shoots and her bound feet again like the crescent moon. Such poetic expressions are by no means absent in the West, but the whole spirit of Chinese art, and the pattern of Chinese women's dress in particular, justify the taking of such expressions seriously. For woman's body, as body, the Chinese have no appreciation. We see very little of it in art. Chinese artists fail dismally in the portrayal of the human form, and even an artist like Ch'iu Shihchou (Ming Period), famous for his paintings of female life, shows the upper part of the female nude form very much like a potato. Few Chinese, unversed in Western art, can tell the beauty of a woman's neck or of a woman's back. The *Tsashih Pishin*, a work ascribed to the Han Dynasty but really belonging to the Ming Period, gave a fairly good account of the perfect female nude body, showing a real delight in its form as such, but it is almost the only exception. This is one result of the seclusion of women.

As a matter of fact, these changes of fashion do not matter. Women's costumes will change, and men will admire them as long as they are worn by women, and women will wear them as long as men think them beautiful. The change from the Victorian crinoline and farthingale to the slim boyish figure of the early twentieth century and on to the Mae West craze of 1935 is actually more striking than the difference between the Chinese and foreign women's dress. As long as women wear it, it is always divine for men. An international pageant of women's dress ought to make this point sufficiently clear. Only a decade ago Chinese women paraded the streets in trousers and to-day they are floating in long gowns covering the ankles, while women in the West are wearing skirts, but the trousered pyjama has every possibility of coming into fashion. The only effect such changes give is that it engenders in men a broad mind.

What is of far more importance is the connection between women's seclusion and the ideal of womanhood. That ideal is the ideal of a "helpful wife and wise mother," a phrase very much held up to ridicule in modern China, especially by those modern women who desire above all "equality," "independence," "self-expression" and who regard wives and mothers as dependent upon men, representing thus a typical confusion of ideas.

Let us get the sexual relationships straight. It seems that a woman, when she becomes a mother, never thinks of her position as "dependent" on the pleasure of her husband. It is only when she ceases to be a mother that she feels her utter dependence. There was a time even in the West when motherhood and bearing and rearing children were not despised by society or by the women themselves. A mother seems to fit in with her position, a very highly honoured position, in the family. To bring a child into the world and lead him and guide him with her mother's wisdom into manhood is enough work for any human being in a sane-minded society. Why she should be regarded as "dependent" on man, either socially or economically, because she can do this noble work, and do it better than man, is a notion that is difficult to grasp. There are talented women, as there are talented men, but their number is actually less than democracy would have us believe. For these women, self-expression has a more important meaning than just bearing children. But for the common people, whose number is legion, let the men earn bread to feed the family, and let the women bear children. As for their self-expression, I have seen selfish, mean little wights blossom forth into gentle, all-loving and self-sacrificing mothers, who are models of perfection and virtue in their children's eyes. I have also seen beautiful girls who do not marry and who shrivel up in their thirties and never reach that second period of woman's beauty, glorious like the autumn forest, more mature, more human, and more radiant, best seen in a happy wife three months after her confinement.

Of all the rights of women, the greatest is to be a mother. Confucius spoke of the ideal society as the one in which there were "no unmarried men or women," and this, in China, has been achieved through a different conception of romance and marriage. In Chinese eyes the great sin of Western society is the large number of unmarried women, who, through no fault of their own except the foolish belief in such a real being as Prince Charming, are unable to express themselves. Many of them are great as teachers or actresses, but they would be still greater as mothers. By falling in love and marrying perhaps an unworthy husband, a woman may fall into nature's trap, whose sole concern is for her to propagate the race, but she also may be rewarded by nature with a curly-headed child, her triumph and her delight, more surprising than the greatest book she has ever written and saturating her with more real happiness than the moment of her greatest triumph on the stage. Isadora Duncan was honest enough to confess this. If nature is cruel, nature is fair. To the common women, as to the talented ones, she gives this comfort. For the joys of motherhood are enjoyed by the clever women and the common ones. So nature has ordained, and so let men and women live.

IV. EDUCATION OF OUR DAUGHTERS

The different ideal of womanhood in China involved a different training for our daughters. The training for girls differs, or used to differ, radically from that for boys. It was much more severe for girls than for boys, and, coupled with the general earlier maturity of women, girls learned this family discipline earlier and were consequently soberer and better behaved than boys of the same age. The girl in any case had less of a childhood than the boy, and from the age of fourteen she began to seclude herself and learn the manners of womanliness, for the Chinese conception emphasizes the womanly woman: She rises earlier than her brothers, dresses more neatly than they, helps in the kitchen and often helps to feed her younger brothers. She plays with fewer toys, does more work, talks more quietly, walks about more delicately, and sits more properly, with her legs close together. She learns, above all, demureness, at the cost of sprightliness. Something of the childish fun and tomfoolery goes out of her, and she does not laugh but only smiles. She is conscious of her virginity, and virginity in old China was a possession more precious than all the learning of the world. She does not easily let strangers see her, although she often peeps from behind the partitions. She cultivates the charm of mystery and distance, and the more she is secluded the more she is worth. Actually, in a man's mind, a lady shut up in a medieval castle is more enchanting than a girl you daily see face to face across the lunch counter. She learns embroidery, and with her young eyes and adroit fingers she does excellent work and gets along much faster than she would in trigonometry. The embroidery is pleasant because it gives her time to dream, and youth always dreams. Thus she is prepared for the responsibilities of wifehood and mother-hood.

In educated families the girls learned also to read and to write. There have always been talented women in China, and to-day there are over half a dozen women authors who have achieved a more or less national reputation. Many celebrated educated women were known in the Han Dynasty, and later in the Wei and Ch'in Dynasties. One of these women was Hsieh Taoyün, who, as a conversationalist, often saved her brother-in-law from the verbal attacks of his guests. Literacy was limited in China, for men and for women, but scholars' families always taught their daughters to read and to write. The content of this literary education was necessarily limited to literature, poetry, history and human wisdom, as absorbed from the Confucian classics. The girls stopped there, but really the men did not advance very much further. Literature, history, philosophy and the wisdom of life, together with some special knowledge of medicine or the rules of government, were the sum of human knowledge. The education of women was still more definitely humanistic. The difference was in intensiveness rather than in scope.

For, reversing Pope's dictum, the Chinese held that "too much learning was a dangerous thing for women's virtue." In painting and in poetry they often played a hand, for the writing of short lyrics seemed especially suitable to women's genius. These poems were short, dainty and exquisite, not powerful. Li Ch'ingchao (1081–1141?), the greatest poetess of China, left a handful of immortal, imperishable verse, full of the sentiment of rainy nights and recaptured happiness. The tradition of woman's poetry has been practically unbroken, until in Manchu times we can count almost a thousand women who left poetry in print in this dynasty alone. Under the influence of Yüan Mei, the man who was against footbinding, a mode was set up for women to write poetry, which was greatly deprecated by another outstanding scholar, Chang Shihtsai, as being detrimental to the sound ideal of womanhood. But writing poetry did not really interfere with women's duties as wife and mother, and Li Ch'ingchao was an ideal wife. She was no Sappho.

The Chinese girl in ancient times was actually less socially accomplished than the Western girl, but under a good family breeding she had a better chance of succeeding as wife and mother and she had no career except the career of wife and mother. The Chinese men are now faced with the dilemma of choosing between the modern girl and the conservative girl for a wife. The ideal wife has been described as one "with new knowledge but old character." The conflict of ideals (the new one being the wife who is an independent being and who looks down upon the expression "helpful wife and wise mother") calls for a ruthless application of common sense. While I regard the increased knowledge and education as an improvement and approaching the ideal of womanhood, I wager that we are not going to find, as we have not yet found, a world-renowned lady pianist or lady painter. I feel confident that her soup will still be better than her poetry and that her real masterpiece will be her chubby-faced boy. The ideal woman remains for me the wise, gentle and firm mother.

V. Love and Courtship

The question may arise: How with the seclusion of women was romance and courtship possible in China? Or rather in what way was the natural love between young people influenced by this classical tradition? In youth and romance and love, the world is pretty much the same, only the psychological reactions differ as a result of different social traditions. For secluded as women may be, no classical teaching has yet succeeded in shutting out love. Its tenor and complexion may be altered, for love, which is a gushing, overwhelming feeling in nature, can become a small voice of the heart and thoughts. Civilization may transform love but it never stifles it. Love is there, only somehow receiving a different tenor and expression accidentally borrowed, as it were, from a different social and cultural background. It peeps in at the beaded curtains, it fills the air of the back garden, and it tugs at the maiden's heart. Perhaps she has no lover, and she does not quite know what ails her. Perhaps she is not interested in any particular man, but she is in love with man, and being in love with man she is in love with life. That makes her work a little more neatly at her embroidery and imagine she is in love with the rainbow-coloured embroidery itself, as symbolizing life, which seems to her so beautiful. Very probably she is embroidering the design of a pair of mandarin ducks for someone's pillow, those mandarin ducks which always go together, swim together, nest together in pairs, one male, the other female. If she stretches her imagination too much, she is liable to forget herself and make a wrong stitch. She tries again, but it goes wrong again. She pulls hard at the silken thread, a little too hard, and it slips out of the needle. She bites her lips and feels annoyed. She is in love.

That feeling of annoyance at a vague unknown something, perhaps at spring and the flowers, that sudden overwhelming sense of loneliness in the world, is nature's sign of a girl's maturity for love and marriage. With the repressions of society and social conventions, a girl did her best to cover up this vague and strong yearning, but subconsciously youth dreamed on. Yet pre-marital love was a forbidden fruit in old China, open courtship was impossible, and she knew that to love was to suffer. For that reason, she dared not let her thoughts dwell too fondly on the spring and the flowers and the butterflies, which are symbols of love in ancient poetry, and if she were educated, she would not allow herself to spend too much time on poetry, lest her emotions be touched too profoundly. She kept herself busy with her home duties and guarded her feelings as sacredly as a delicate flower preserves itself from premature contact with the butterflies. She wished to wait until the time should come when love would be lawful and sanctified by marriage, and happy was she who escaped all entanglements of passion. Yet nature sometimes conquered in spite of all human restraints. For like all forbidden fruits, the keenness of sexual attraction was enhanced by its rarity. It was nature's law of compensation. Once a girl's heart was distracted, according to the Chinese theory, love stopped at nothing. That was actually the common belief back of the careful seclusion of women.

Even in her deepest seclusion every girl generally learned

about all the marriageable young men of her class in town, and secretly distributed her approval and disapproval in her heart. If by casual chance she met one of the approved young men, even though it was only an exchange of glances, more than likely she succumbed, and had no more of the peace of mind of which she had been so proud. Then a period of secret, stolen courtship began. In spite of the fact that an exposure would mean shame and often suicide and in spite of the full consciousness that by so doing she was defying all codes of moral conduct and braving social censure, she would meet her young man. And love always found a way.

In the mad, mutual attraction of sex it was impossible to say who was wooing and who was being wooed. A girl had many ingenious ways of making her presence felt. The most innocent form was showing one's small red shoes beneath the wooden partitions. Another was standing on the verandah at sunset. Another was accidentally showing one's face amidst peach blossoms. Another was going to the lantern festivals of January and June at night. Another was playing on the *ch'in*, a stringed instrument, and letting the young man in the next house hear it. Another was asking the teacher of her younger brother to correct her poetry, with the younger brother as the messenger boy. The teacher, if he were young and romantic, might send a verse in reply. Still another means of communication was the maid-servant, or the sympathetic sister-in-law, or the cook's wife next door, or the nun. If both parties were attracted to each other, a secret meeting could always be arranged. Such meetings were extremely unhealthy; the young girl did not know how to protect herself, and love, which had been denied its gay flirtations, came back with a revenge, as all Chinese love stories portray, or wish to portray. She might come to expect a child. A real period of ardent courtship and love-making followed, overpowering and yet tender, precious because it was stolen, and generally too happy to last.

In this situation anything might happen. The young man or the young lady might become betrothed to others by no consent of their own, and the girl regret having lost her chastity. Or the young man might go away and, becoming successful in his official examinations, might have a wife forced upon him by a more distinguished family. Or one of the families might move to another city and they might never see each other again. Or even if the young man sojourning abroad should remain faithful, yet a war might come between, and there might be interminable waiting and delay. For the young maiden waiting in the secluded chamber there was only sadness and longing. If the girl were a real and passionate lover she became seriously lovesick (which is amazingly common in Chinese love stories), with all light and gladness gone from her eyes, and her parents, alarmed at the situation, would then begin to make inquiries and save her life by arranging the desired marriage, and so after all they might live happily ever after.

Love then was mixed with tears and sadness and longing in Chinese thought, and the effect of this seclusion of women was to introduce a plaintive, languorous tone in all Chinese love poetry. Any Chinese love song after the T'ang Dynasty is invariably one of longing, resignation and infinite sadness. Often it is the song of the secluded maiden pining for her lover, or *kweiyüan*, or that of the forsaken wife, *ch'i fu*, both of which were, strange to say, extremely favourite topics with the male poets.

Consonant with the general negative attitude toward life, Chinese songs of love are songs of absence, of departure, of frustrated hopes and unquenchable longing, of rain and the twilight and the empty chamber and the "cold bed," of solitary regret and hatred against man's inconstancy and the castaway fan in autumn, of departing spring and faded blossoms and fading beauty, of the flickering candlelight and winter nights and general emaciation, of self-pity and approaching death. This mood finds its typical expression in Taiyü's poem before her approaching death, after she knew that her cousin was going to become Paoyü's wife, lines that are memorable for their infinite sadness:

> This year I am burying the dropped blossoms,
> Next year who is going to bury me?

But sometimes the girl may be lucky and may become a

"helpful wife and wise mother." The Chinese drama usually ends up happily with the refrain, "May all the lovers of the world become united in wedlock!"

VI. The Courtesan and Concubinage

This is all very nice so far as woman goes. Woman is "helpful wife and wise mother." She is loyal, she is obedient, she is always a good mother, and she is instinctively chaste. The trouble is with man. Man sins, and he must sin, but every time he sins there is a woman in it.

Eros, who rules the world, rules China also. Some Western travellers have ventured the opinion that in China we find comparatively less sex repression than in the West, owing to a more frank acceptance of sex in human life. Havelock Ellis has noted that modern civilization has surrounded man with the greatest sexual stimulation coupled with the greatest sexual repression. To an extent, sexual stimulation and sexual repression are less in China. But this is only half the truth. The more frank acceptance of sex applies to man and not to woman, whose sexual life is often repressed. The clearest instance is that of Feng Hsiaoch'ing, who lived when Shakespeare was doing his best work (1595–1612), and who, as concubine, was forbidden to see her husband and was shut up in a villa in the West Lake by the jealous wife, and who consequently developed the most singular case of narcissism. She showed inclinations to look at her own image in the water, and shortly before her death she had three successive portraits of herself made, to which she burned incense and offered sacrifice in self-pity. Accidentally she left some verse in an amah's hands which showed poetic genius.

On the other hand, there is no sexual repression for men, especially those of the richer class. Most well-known respectable scholars, like the poets Su Tungp'o, Ch'in Shaoyü, Tu Mu and Po Chüyi, went to courtesans' houses, or had courtesans for their concubines, and frankly said so. In fact, to be an official and avoid dinners with female entertainers was impossible. There was no opprobrium attached to it. Through the Ming and Manchu Periods, Ch'inhuaiho, the dirty creek in front of the Confucian Temple at Nanking, was the scene of many a love romance. The proximity to the Confucian Temple was appropriate and logical, because it was the place of the official examinations where scholars gathered for the examinations and celebrated their successes or consoled their failures in the company of women. To this day some editors of small papers still frankly detail their adventures in sing-song houses, and poets and scholars have written so profusely about the sing-song tradition that the name of Ch'inhuaiho has been intimately associated with Chinese literary history.

It is impossible to exaggerate the romantic, literary, musical, and political importance of the courtesan in China. Because men thought it improper for decent family girls to handle musical instruments, which were dangerous to their virtue, or to have too much literary learning, which was equally subversive of their morality, and but rarely encouraged painting and poetry for them, they did not, on that account, cease to desire female company of the artistic and literary type. The sing-song girls cultivated these things because they did not need ignorance as a bulwark of their virtue. So the scholars all went to Ch'inhuaiho. There in the summer night, when darkness had transformed the dirty creek into a Venetian canal, they would sit in a house-boat and listen to the singing of love ditties by girls in the neighbouring "lantern boats" passing up and down.

In this atmosphere scholars sought for those *hetaeras* who could distinguish themselves from the rest either in poetry, music, painting or witty repartee. Of such accomplished and well-known *hetaeras* who flourished especially at the end of the Ming Period, perhaps the one best loved by all was Tung Hsiaowan, who became the mistress of Mao Pichiang. To the T'ang Dynasty belonged Su Hsiaohsiao, whose tomb by the side of the West Lake has become the object of pilgrimage of every scholar tourist for ages. Not a few were closely connected with the political destinies of the nation, as in the case of Ch'en Yüanyüan, the beloved mistress of General Wu Sankwei. Her capture by Li Tzŭch'eng during the latter's conquest of Peking led Wu Sankwei to enter Peking with the assistance of Manchu troops for her recovery, and in this way directly contributed to the founding of the Manchu Dynasty. It is noteworthy that after Wu had thus brought about the downfall of the Chinese Ming empire, Ch'en Yüanyüan separated from him and chose to live as a nun in a specially built monastery on Shangshan. We have also the case of Li Hsiangchün, who was reputed for her constancy and whose political inclinations and courage put many a man to shame by comparison. She had more political chastity than many men revolutionists of to-day. After her lover had been hounded out of Nanking she shut herself up, and when she was forcibly brought to the home of the official in power and commanded to sing at a wine-feast, she improvised songs of satire in the presence of her captors, who were her political enemies, calling them "adopted sons of the eunuch." Poems and songs written by these ladies have been handed down to the present. The history of Chinese intellectual women will have to be sought partly in the lives of such accomplished courtesans as Hsüeh T'ao, Ma Hsianglan, Liu Jushih and others.

The courtesan supplied the need for courtship and romance which many men missed in their youth before marriage. I speak of "courtship" advisedly, because the sing-song girl, differing from the common prostitutes, had to be courted. Such was the respect for ladies in China that, as we are told in the novel *Chiuweikuei* (*Nine-Tailed Tortoise*) describing modern times, many a man had to court a lady of supposedly easy virtue for months and spend three or four thousand dollars before he was permitted to pass a night in her boudoir. Such a preposterous situation was possible only with the seclusion of women, but when men could not find female company and romance elsewhere, it was also perfectly natural. The man, inexperienced in female company and tired of his wife-cook-and-sock-darner, began to experience what Western men call romance before their marriage. He saw a lady who took his fancy, desired her, and began to have a feeling analogous to falling in love. The lady, being so much more experienced and accomplished, had an easy game, and the man sometimes had a feeling almost of worship. It was, in fact, the one kind of court-ship legitimate and proper in China.

Sometimes an actual romance developed, as with Western men and their mistresses. The story of Tung Hsiaowan and Mao Pichiang, from the difficulties of their first meeting to their short-lived, blissful wedded life, reads in no way differently from any other romance. There were romances with happy and unhappy endings. While Li Hsiangchün ended up in a monastery, Ku Hengp'o and Liu Jushih ended up as *grandes dames* in rich official families, to the envy and admiration of their generation.

The courtesan, therefore, taught many Chinese romantic love, as the Chinese wife taught them a more earthly, real love. Sometimes the situation was actually confusing, and Tu Mu, who led a wild life for ten years, came back to his old wife after an awakening. Sometimes, too, the chastity of the courtesan was amazing, as in the case of Tu Shihniang. Besides, she carried on the musical tradition of the country, which without her would have died off. She was more cultivated, more independent, and more at home in men's society than were the family women; in fact, she was the emancipated lady in ancient China. Her influence over high officials often gave her a measure of political influence, for sometimes it was in her house that political appointments were interceded for and decided upon.

A really deserving courtesan often became a concubine or mistress, as did practically all the above-mentioned women. Concubinage is as old as China itself, and the problem behind concubinage is as old as monogamy. When the marriage is unhappy the Oriental solves it by going to the sing-song girl or taking a concubine, while the Occidental solves it by keeping a mistress or having occasional escapades. The modes of social behaviour are different, while the fundamental problems are curiously the same. What makes a difference is the social attitude, especially that of women, toward such behaviour. Chinese take mistresses with public consent, while Westerners have the decency not to talk about it.

The insistence on male progeny also greatly encouraged concubinage. Some Chinese wives actually pleaded with their husbands to take concubines, when they themselves had failed to produce a son. The laws of the Ming Dynasty officially sanctioned the marrying of concubines in the case of a man reaching forty without male progeny.

Moreover, concubinage in a way takes the place of divorce in Western countries. Marriage and divorce are the most complicated social problems, and no one has yet solved them. No perfect solution has yet been invented by the human mind, except that Roman Catholic solution which ignores the existence of such problems altogether. The only thing sure is that marriage is the safest protection for women, and whenever men's morals relax it is the women who suffer, whether it be through divorce, concubinage, companionate marriage or free love. There is by nature something eternally unequal and unfair in the sexual arrangement. For sexual equality is an unknown word in nature, whose sole concern is the propagation of the race. The so-called modern marriages on a fifty-fifty basis have always become a seventy-five and twenty-five arrangement in favour of the men with the advent of children, and if the woman is sporting enough to release the husband "when love ceases" the man of forty enjoys advantages which the divorced woman of forty and mother of three children cannot have. No true equality is possible.

It is in this sense that some defence may be made in favour of concubinage. The Chinese regard marriage as a family affair, and when marriage fails they accept concubinage, which at least keeps the family intact as a social unit. The West, in turn, regards marriage as an individual, romantic and senti-mental affair, and therefore accepts divorce, which breaks up the social unit. In the East, when a man gets too rich, has nothing to do, degenerates and neglects his wife for his favourite, the wife suppresses her libido but keeps her established position, still very highly honoured as head of the family and sur-rounded by her own children. In the West, the modern wife sues for divorce, gets her alimony and goes away, perhaps to remarry. Whether the wife who remains neglected by her husband but honoured by the household and holding at least a theoretic supremacy over the concubines, or the wife who gets her alimony and lives apart is happier is a question that is perplexing in the highest degree. In China, where the women have not the spirit of independence of their Western sisters, the castaway wife often seems an infinitely pathetic spectacle, with her social position lost and her home broken. Always there is one happy woman, and one who cannot be made happy by any human arrangement. Even real economic independence of women will not solve it.

In China such cases are happening every day before our eyes, and it has sometimes seemed to me that the modern woman who drives out the old wife with her feminine ferocity approximates very nearly the state of barbarism of our fore-fathers, in spite of the fact that she is modern enough not to tolerate living under the same roof with another woman as her equal. In the past a really good woman, who was caught in circumstances that involved her with a married man and who truly loved him, was willing to go to his family as concubine and serve the wife with humility and respect. Now driving one another out and taking one another's place by turn in the name of monogamy seems to the women to be the better way. It is the modern, emancipated, so-called civilized way. If women prefer it that way, let them have it, since it is they who are primarily affected by it. The young and beautiful ones, however, will win in the battle against their own sex at the expense of the older women. The problem is really so new and yet so old. The marriage system will be imperfect as long as human nature is imperfect. Let us therefore agree to leave the problem unsolved. Perhaps only an innate sense of equity and fair-play and an increased sense of parental responsibility will ever reduce the number of such cases.

Of course, it is useless to defend concubinage, unless one is ready to defend polyandry at the same time. Ku Hungming, the Edinburgh M.A. and profuse quoter of Thomas Carlyle and Matthew Arnold, once defended concubinage by saying: "You have seen a tea-pot with four tea-cups, but did you ever see a tea-cup with four tea-pots?" The best reply to this are the words of P'an Chinlien, concubine of Hsimen Ch'ing in *Chinp'inmei:* "Do you ever see two spoons in the same bowl that do not knock against each other?" She knew what she was talking about.

VII. Footbinding

The nature and origin of footbinding has been greatly misunderstood. Somehow it has stood as a symbol of the seclusion and suppression of women, and very suitably so. The great Confucian scholar Chu Hsi of the Sung Dynasty was also enthusiastic in introducing footbinding in southern Fukien as a means of spreading Chinese culture and teaching the separation of men and women. But if it had been regarded only as a symbol of the suppression of women, mothers would not have been so enthusiastic in binding the feet of their young daughters. Actually, footbinding was sexual in its nature throughout. Its origin was undoubtedly in the courts of licentious kings, its popularity with men was based on the worship of women's feet and shoes as a love-fetish and on the feminine gait which naturally followed, and its popularity with women was based on their desire to curry men's favour.

The time of origin of this institution is subject to debate, which is somewhat unnecessary, since it would be more proper to speak of its "evolution." The only proper definition of footbinding is the binding of the feet by long yards of binding cloth and the discarding of the socks, and this seemed to be first definitely mentioned in connection with Nant'ang Houchu, in the first part of the tenth century, or before the Sung Dynasty. Yang Kweifei (T'ang Dynasty) still wore socks, for one of her socks was picked up by her amah and shown to the public after her death, at the admission rate of a hundred cash a person. Rapturous praise of women's small feet and their "bow-shoes" had become a fashion in the T'ang Dynasty. The "bow-shoes," with upturned heads like the bow of a Roman galley, were the beginnings or rudimentary forms of footbinding. These were used by the dancing girls of the court, and in this luxurious atmosphere of female dancing and court perfume and beaded curtains and rare incense, it was natural that a creative mind should have appeared and put the last finishing touch to this sensual sophistication. This creative mind belonged to the ruler of Nant'ang (Southern T'ang, a short-lived dynasty), who was an exquisite poet besides. One of his girls with bound feet was made to dance with light tiptoe steps on a golden lily six feet high, hung all over with jewels and pearls and golden threads. Thereafter, the fashion was set and imitated by the public, and the bound feet were euphuistically called "golden lilies" or "fragrant lilies," which enabled them to pass into poetry. The word "fragrant" is significant, for it suggests the voluptuous atmosphere of the rich Chinese, whose chambers were filled with rare and fine perfume on which whole volumes have been written.

That women were not only willing but actually glad to be fashionable and *à la mode* at the expense of bodily comfort is nothing peculiarly Chinese. As late as 1824, English girls were willing to lie on the floor while their mothers by foot and hand were helping to squeeze their bodies inside the whale-bones.[1] These whale-bones must have greatly assisted the eighteenth-century and early nineteenth-century European women in fainting at the proper moment. Women may be frail in China, but it has never been the fashion to faint. The tiptoe dancing of the Russian ballet is but another example of the beauty of human torture which may be honoured with the name of an art.

The small feet of Chinese women are not only pleasing in men's eyes but in a strange and subtle way they influence the whole carriage and walking gait of the women, throwing the hips backward, somewhat like the modern high-heeled shoes, and effecting an extremely gingerly gait, the body "shimmying" all over and ready to fall at the slightest touch. Looking at a woman with bound feet walking is like looking at a rope-dancer, tantalizing to the highest degree. The bound foot is indeed the highest sophistication of the Chinese sensual imagination.

Then, entirely apart from the feminine gait, men had come to worship and play with and admire and sing about the small feet as a love-fetish. From now on, night shoes were to occupy an important place in all sensual poetry. The cult of the "golden lily" belonged undoubtedly to the realm of sexual

---

[1] A fashion journal of the time says: "When lacing the new stays, the young lady should lie face downwards on her bedroom floor, and her mother should place her foot in the small of her daughter's back in order to obtain good purchase. There should be then no difficulty in making the stays meet."

psychopathology. As much artistic finesse was exercised in the appreciation of different types of bound feet as was ever expended over the criticism of T'ang poetry. When one remembers that really small and well-shaped feet were rare, perhaps less than ten in a city, it is easy to understand how men could be moved by them as they might be moved by exquisite poetry. Fang Hsien of the Manchu Dynasty wrote an entire book devoted to this art, classifying the bound feet into five main divisions and eighteen types. Moreover, a bound foot should be (A) *Fat*, (B) *Soft* and (C) *Elegant;* so says Fang:

> Thin feet are cold, and muscular feet are hard. Such feet are incurably vulgar. Hence fat feet are full and smooth to the touch, soft feet are gentle and pleasing to the eye, and elegant feet are refined and beautiful. But fatness does not depend on the flesh, softness does not depend on the binding, and elegance does not depend on the shoes. Moreover, you may judge its fatness and softness by its form, *but you may appreciate its elegance only by the eye of the mind.*

All those who understand the power of fashion over women will understand the persistence of this institution. It is curious to note that the decree of the Manchu Emperor K'anghsi to stop footbinding among the Chinese was rescinded within a few years, and Manchu girls were soon imitating Chinese girls in this fashion until Emperor Ch'ienlung issued an edict and forbade them. Mothers who wanted their girls to grow up into ladies and marry into good homes had to bind their feet young as a measure of parental foresight, and a bride who was praised for her small feet had a feeling analogous to filial gratitude. For next to a good face, a woman was immeasurably proud of her small feet, as modern women are proud of their small ankles, for these feet gave her an immediate distinction in any social gathering. Her bound feet were painful, unmercifully painful, during the time of growing youth, but if she had a well-shaped pair, it was her pride for life.

This monstrous and perverse institution was condemned by at least three scholars, Li Juchen (author of a feminist novel, *Chinghuayüan*, written in 1825), Yüan Mei (1716–1799), and

Yü Chenghsieh (1775–1840), all scholars of independent minds and considerable influence. But the custom was not abolished until the Christian missionaries led the crusade, a debt for which Chinese women ought to be grateful. But in this the missionaries have been fortunately helped by the force of circumstances, for Chinese women have found in the modern high-heeled shoes a tolerable substitute. They enhance the women's figures, develop a mincing gait and create the illusion that the feet are smaller than they really are. Li Liweng's profound observation in his essays on the art of living is still true: "I have seen feet of three inches without heeled shoes and feet of four or five inches on heeled shoes stand on the same place, and felt that the three-inch feet are bigger than the four- or five-inch feet. Because with heels, the toes point downwards, the flat feet seem pointed, while without heels, the jade bamboo-shoots [the toes] rise toward heaven, and pointed feet look flat." Such profound observation on the details of an idle life is always characteristic of the Chinese genius.

VIII. EMANCIPATION

The seclusion of women has now gone. It has gone so fast that people who left China ten years ago find, on coming back, a change in the whole physical and mental outlook of Chinese girls so vast as to shake their most profound convictions. The girls of the present generation differ in temperament, grace, bearing and spirit of independence from the "modern" girls of ten or twelve years ago. Myriad influences are at work, causing this change. In general, they may be called the Western influences.

Specifically they are: the change from monarchy to republic in 1911, admitting sexual equality; the Renaissance started in 1916–17, headed by Dr. Hu Shih and Ch'en Tuhsiu, denouncing the "chaste widowhood" of the "man-eating religion" (Confucianism) and the double sex standard; the May Fourth Movement or Student Movement of 1919, brought about by the secret selling of China by the Allies at the Versailles Conference, and precipitating the active part taken in politics by boy and girl students; the first admittance of girl students to the Peking National University in the autumn of 1919, followed by co-education in almost all colleges; the continued interest taken in national politics by boy and girl students, leading to the National Revolution of 1926–7, which was largely the work of the students, under the combined leadership and encouragement of the Kuomintang and the Communist Party, and in which Chinese girls figured prominently as party workers and nurses and even as soldiers; the continued position of girl Kuomintang members in the party headquarters after the founding of the government of Nanking; the sudden prominence of girl civil service servants in all official bureaux of the government after 1927; the promulgation by the Nanking Government of the law entitling daughters and sons to equal inheritance; the progressive disappearance of concubinage; the prevalence of girls' schools; the great popularity of athletics for girls after 1930, and in particular swimming for girls in 1934; the vogue for nude pictures, to be seen every day in newspapers and magazines; the coming of Margaret Sanger to China in 1922, and the general spread of birth-control and sex education; the introduction of contraceptive appliances (which alone must precipitate a revolution in ethics); the publication of weekly "women's supplements" in most big papers, devoted to the discussion of women's problems; the publication of *Sex Histories* (rather degenerating) by Chang Chingsheng, a French-returned student; the influence of Greta Garbo, Norma Shearer, Mae West, and Chinese movie stars, and the popularity of movie magazines, of which there are several; the great spread of dancing cabarets which came over China about 1928, and in which the Chinese girls gave everybody a surprise by their ready adaptability; the permanent wave, English high-heeled shoes, Parisian perfumes and American silk stockings, the new high-slit flowing gowns, the brassière (in place of the former chest-binding jacket), and the one-piece female bathing suit.

From bound feet to one-piece bathing suit is indeed a far cry, and these changes, superficial as they seem, are nevertheless profound. For life is made up of such superficialities, and by altering them we alter the whole outlook of life.

Modern girls are subjected to current ridicule in Chinese magazines for their superficialities, their love of luxury, and their loss of industry and other domestic virtues. For apparently the influence of Mae West is greater than that of Mary Wollstonecraft. The fact is, there are two types of girls: those who figure so prominently in city life, and the more serious-minded and intellectual ones who are not in such prominence and who disappear into good homes. Some of the politically prominent women who court publicity are the worst scoundrels of their sex; they therefore do not represent modern Chinese womanhood. On the whole, these modern influences must be taken as liberalizing influences working for the good of Chinese womanhood and therefore of the race. The first important effect is on the girl's physique. The exposure of female thighs in athletic contests, so much regretted by the older generation, must in the end work for the good of the nation. With the development of physique comes a more naturally graceful movement than the boudoir-cultivated movements of the bound feet.

Consequent upon this physical change is a change in the ideal of female beauty, from the repressed quietness of former days to the more natural sprightliness of a human being, approaching that of European ladies. For it does one good to hear women laugh a hearty laugh, and it is better than to hear them giggle. The artificial restraint and over-sexualization of women under Confucianism must give place to a more human view, and can no longer come back. The danger is rather of desexualization and of the total loss of the womanly woman. The idea of women trying to ape men in their manners is in itself a sign of women's bondage. Let women be proud of their own sex, for only in the fulfilment of their sex and its grave responsibilities will they be truly great. Compared with the Western women, the modern mature Chinese women are still perhaps more poised and dignified, but they lack, on the other hand, the spontaneity and spirit of independence of their Western sisters. Perhaps it is in their blood, but if so, let it be as it is, for only by being true to their race can they be great also.

Chapter Six

SOCIAL AND POLITICAL LIFE

I. ABSENCE OF THE SOCIAL MIND

THE Chinese are a nation of individualists. They are family-minded, not social-minded, and the family mind is only a form of magnified selfishness. It is curious that the word "society" does not exist as an idea in Chinese thought. In the Confucian social and political philosophy we see a direct transition from the family, *chia*, to the state, *kuo*, as successive stages of human organization, as in such sayings as "When the family is orderly, then the state is peaceful," or "Put the family in order and rule the state in peace." The nearest equivalent to the notion of society is, then, a compound of the two words, *kuochia*, or "state-family," in accordance with the rule for forming Chinese abstract terms.

"Public spirit" is a new term, so is "civic consciousness," and so is "social service." There are no such commodities in China. To be sure, there are "social affairs," such as weddings, funerals, and birthday celebrations and Buddhistic processions and annual festivals. But the things which make up English and American social life, viz., sport, politics and religion, are conspicuously absent. There is no church and no church community. The Chinese religiously abstain from talking politics; they do not cast votes, and they have no club-house debates on politics. They do not indulge in sport, which binds human beings together, and which is the essence of the English and American social life. They play games, to be sure, but these games are characteristic of Chinese individualism. Chinese games do not divide the players into two parties, as in cricket, with one team playing against the other. Team work is unknown. In Chinese card games, each man plays for himself. The Chinese like poker, and do not like bridge. They have always played *mahjong*, which is nearer to poker than to bridge. In this philosophy of *mahjong* may be seen the essence of Chinese individualism.

An illustration of Chinese individualism may be seen in the organization of a Chinese newspaper. The Chinese run their papers as they play their *mahjong*. I have seen Chinese daily papers so edited as to require an editor-in-chief whose only business is to write editorials. The man in charge of domestic news has his page, the man in charge of international cables has his, and the man in charge of city news again has his own ground. These four men handle their respective departments like the four hands at a *mahjong* table, each trying to guess what the others have got. Each tries to make up his set and throws out the unwanted bamboo to the next man. If there is too much domestic news, it can conveniently flow over (without warning, as far as the reader is concerned) to the page for city news, and if this again has too much copy, it can conveniently flow over to the murders and conflagrations. There is no necessity for front-page make-up, no selection, no co-ordination, no subordination. Each editor can retire at his own good time. The scheme is simplicity itself. Moreover, both the editors and the readers are born individualists. It is the editor's business to publish the news, and the reader's business to look for it. They do not interfere with one another. This is the journalistic technique of some of the oldest, largest and most popular daily papers in China to this day.

If you ask why there is no co-ordination, the answer is, there's no social mind. For if the editor-in-chief tries to initiate reforms and fire the city editor for obstruction, he will run up against the family system. What does he mean by interfering with other people's business? Does he mean to throw the city editor out and break his rice-bowl, starving all the people dependent upon him? And if the city editor's wife is the proprietor's niece, can he throw him out? If the editor-in-chief has any Chinese social consciousness, he will not attempt such a thing, and if he is a raw American-returned graduate of the Missouri School of Journalism, he will soon have to get out. Another man who knows Chinese social ways will get in, the old scheme will go on working, the readers will go on hunting for their news and the paper will go on increasing its circulation and making money.

Some such psychology is hidden behind all Chinese social intercourse, and it would be easy to multiply examples showing a lack of the social mind truly bewildering to the twentieth-century Western man. I say "twentieth-century man" because he has received the benefits of nineteenth-century humanitarianism, with a broadened social outlook. As a typically bewildering example, which is yet truly representative of Chinese thought regarding social work, I quote verbally from the *Analects Fortnightly* (a magazine devoted to unconscious Chinese humour) reporting the speech of a native war-lord regarding the movement for mass education. The young people caught with the modern American enthusiasm for social service organized a movement for "annihilating literary blindness." So saith the General, therefore, in a speech: "Students ought to work at their books and not meddle with public affairs. *The people do their own business and eat their own rice, and you want to annihilate the people!*" The persuasive argument is this: the illiterate are not interfering with you, why must you interfere with them? Those words, so short, so forceful, are yet so true because they come direct and undisguised from the speaker's heart. To a Chinese, social work always looks like "meddling with other people's business." A man enthusiastic for social reform or, in fact, for any kind of public work always looks a little bit ridiculous. We discount his sincerity. We cannot understand him. What does he mean by going out of his way to do all this work? Is he courting publicity? Why is he not loyal to his family and why does he not get official promotion and help his family first? We decide he is young, or else he is a deviation from the normal human type.

There were always such deviations from type, the *haohsieh* or "chivalrous men," but they were invariably of the bandit or vagabond class, unmarried, bachelors with good vagabond souls, willing to jump into the water to save an unknown drowning child. (Married men in China do not do that.) Or else they were married men who died penniless and made their wives and children suffer. We admire them, we love them, but we do not like to have them in the family. When we see a boy who has too much public spirit getting himself into all sorts of scrapes, we confidently predict that boy will be the death of his parents. If we can break him early enough, well and good; if not, he will go to jail and ruin the family fortune besides. But it isn't always as bad as that. If we cannot break him, he will probably run away from home and join the public-spirited brigands. That is why they are "deviations."

How is such a state of things possible? The Chinese are not such heathens, deep-drowned in their sins, as the Christian missionaries would imagine, although here the word "heathen," with all the force of Christian contempt and condemnation, seems eminently applicable. It would be better if the missionaries tried to understand them and attack the evil from its source, for back of it is a social philosophy different from theirs. The difference is a difference of point of view. The best modern educated Chinese still cannot understand why Western women should organize a "Society for the Prevention of Cruelty to Animals." Why bother about the dogs, and why do they not stay at home and nurse their babies? We decide that these women have no children and therefore have nothing better to do, which is probably often true. The conflict is between the family mind and the social mind. If one scratches deep enough, one always finds the family mind at work.

For the family system is the root of Chinese society, from which all Chinese social characteristics derive. The family system and the village system, which is the family raised to a higher exponent, account for all there is to explain in the Chinese social life. Face, favour, privilege, gratitude, courtesy, official corruption, public institutions, the school, the guild, philanthropy, hospitality, justice, and finally the whole government of China—all spring from the family and village system, all borrow from it their peculiar tenor and complexion, and all find in it enlightening explanations for their peculiar characteristics. For from the family system there arises the family mind, and from the family mind there arise certain laws of social behaviour. It will be interesting to study these and see how man behaves as a social being in the absence of a social mind.

II. THE FAMILY SYSTEM

There were formerly no such words as "family system" as a sociological term; we knew the family only as "the basis of the state," or rather as the basis of human society. The system colours all our social life. It is personal, as our conception of government is personal. It teaches our children the first lessons in social obligations between man and man, the necessity of mutual adjustment, self-control, courtesy, a sense of duty, which is very well defined, a sense of obligation and gratitude toward parents, and respect for elders. It very nearly takes the place of religion by giving man a sense of social survival and family continuity, thus satisfying man's craving for immortality, and through the ancestral worship it makes the sense of immortality very vivid. It breeds a sense of family honour, for which it is so easy to find parallels in the West.

It touches us even in very personal ways. It takes the right of contracting marriage from our hands and gives it to those of our parents; it makes us marry, not wives but "daughters-in-law," and it makes our wives give birth, not to children but to "grandchildren." It multiplies the obligations of the bride a hundredfold. It makes it rude for a young couple to close the door of their room in the family house in the daytime, and makes privacy an unknown word in China. Like the radio, it accustoms us to noisy weddings, noisy funerals, noisy suppers and noisy sleep. And like the radio, it benumbs our nerves and develops our good temper. The Western man is like a maiden who has only herself to look after, and who consequently manages to look neat and tidy, while the Chinese man is like the daughter-in-law of a big family who has a thousand and one household obligations to attend to. It therefore breeds in us soberness at an early age. It keeps our young in their places. It overprotects our child.ren, and it is strange how few children rebel and run away Where the parents are too self-centred and autocratic, it often deprives the young man of enterprise and initiative, and I consider this the most disastrous effect of the family system on Chinese character. A parent's funeral interferes with a scholar's chances at the official examinations for three years, and is good ground for the resignation of a cabinet minister.

Family ethics interferes even with our travel and sport, for the theory was developed in the *Hsiaoking*, or *Classic of Filial Piety* (which every schoolboy used to memorize), that "the body, the hair and the skin are received from the parents and may not be injured." Tsengtse, the great disciple of Confucius, said on his deathbed, "Examine my hands, examine my feet," which had been kept intact to return to his forefathers. This already borders on a religious feeling. It limits our travels, for Confucius said, "A man does not travel to distant places when his parents are living, and if he does he must have a definite destination." The best form of travel, i.e., travel without destination and without hoping to arrive anywhere, is therefore theoretically impossible. The filial son "does not climb high, and does not tread on dangerous places." There is therefore not a single filial son in the Alpine Club.

In short, the family system is the negation of individualism itself, and it holds a man back, as the reins of the jockey hold back the dashing Arabian horse. Sometimes the jockey is good, and then he helps the horse to win the race, but sometimes he is not so good. Sometimes it is not a jockey that is holding the horse back but merely a refuse cart. But then, Chinese society has no use for fine Arabian thoroughbreds, the best proof of which is that we have not produced them. We murder them, assassinate them, hound them into the mountains, or send them into the asylum. We want only steady, plodding draught horses. And we get plenty of them.

The Doctrine of Social Status, as Confucianism has been popularly called, is the social philosophy behind the family system. It is the doctrine that makes for social order in China. It is the principle of social structure and social control at the same time. The principal idea is status, or *mingfen*, which gives every man and woman a definite place in society. In conformity with the humanist ideal of "everything in its place," the social ideal is also that of "every man in his place." *Ming* means "name," and *fen* means "duty." Confucianism is actually known as *mingchiao*, or "religion of names." A name is a title that gives a man his definite status in any society and defines his relationships with others. Without a name, or a definition of the social relationship, a man would not know his *fen*, or duties in that relationship, and hence would not know how to behave. The Confucian idea is that if every man knows his place and acts in accordance with his position, social order will be ensured. Of the "five cardinal human relationships," four are occupied with the family. They are the relationships between king and subject, between father and son, between husband and wife, and those between brothers and between friends. The last relationship between friends may be identified with the family, because friends are those who can be included in the family circle—"family friends." The family then becomes the starting-point for all moral conduct.

It is only fair to mention that Confucius never intended family consciousness to take the place of social or national consciousness and develop into a form of magnified selfishness —consequences which, with all his practical wisdom, he had not foreseen. The evils of the family system were already. apparent in the times of Hanfeitse (end of the third century B.C.), in my opinion the greatest of China's political thinkers of that period. Pictures of the political practices of his times contained in Hanfeitse's works fit in perfectly for present-day China, such as the breaking down of the civil service system through nepotism and favouritism, robbing the nation to enrich the family, the erection of rich villas by politicians, the absence of any punishment for offending officials, the consequent absence of "public citizenship" (in Hanfeitse's own words) and general lack of social consciousness. These were all pointed out by Hanfeitse, who advocated a government by law as the way out, and who had to drink hemlock, like Socrates.

But, in theory at least, Confucius did not mean family consciousness to degenerate into a form of magnified selfishness at the cost of social integrity. He did, in his moral system, also allow for a certain amount of ultra-domestic kindness. He meant the moral training in the family as the basis for general moral training, and he planned that from the general moral training a society should emerge which would live happily and harmoniously together. Only in this sense can one under-

stand the tremendous emphasis placed on "filial piety," which
is regarded as the "first of all virtues." The Chinese word for
"culture" or "religion," *chiao*, is even derived from the word
for "filial piety," *hsiao*, being written with the sign for "filial
piety" plus a causative radical (meaning "making filial"). So
explains the *Hsiaoking* (*Classic of Filial Piety*):

> Confucius said: "The reason why the gentleman teaches
> filial piety is not because it is to be seen in the home and
> everyday life. He teaches filial piety in order that man may
> respect all those who are fathers in the world. He teaches
> brotherliness in the younger brother, in order that man may
> respect all those who are elder brothers in the world. He
> teaches the duty of the subject, in order that man may respect
> all who are rulers in the world."

Again, Confucius said:

> "Those who love their parents dare not show hatred to
> others. Those who respect their parents, dare not show
> rudeness to others."

In this sense he could say to Tsengtse, his disciple:

> "Filial piety is the basis of virtue, and the origin of culture.
> Sit down again, and let me tell you. The body and hair and
> skin are received from the parents, and may not be injured:
> this is the beginning of filial piety. To do the right thing and
> walk according to the right morals, thus leaving a good name
> in posterity, in order to glorify one's ancestors: this is the
> culmination of filial piety. Filial piety begins with serving
> one's parents, leads to serving one's king, and ends in
> establishing one's character. . . ."

The whole moral philosophy was based on the theory of
imitation in society and the theory of habit in education. The
method of social education was by *establishing the right mental
attitude* from childhood, beginning naturally at home. There
is nothing wrong in this. Its only weakness was the mixing of

politics with morals. The consequences are fairly satisfactory for the family, but disastrous for the state.

Seen as a social system, it was consistent. It firmly believed that a nation of good brothers and good friends should make a good nation. Yet, seen in modern eyes, Confucianism omitted out of the social relationships man's social obligations toward the stranger, and great and catastrophic was the omission. Samaritan virtue was unknown and practically discouraged. Theoretically, it was provided for in the "doctrine of reciprocity." Confucius said of the gentleman: "Wanting to be successful himself, he helps others to be successful; wanting to stand on his own feet, he helps others to stand on their feet." But this relationship toward the "others" was not one of the five cardinal relationships, and not so clearly defined. The family, with its friends, became a walled castle, with the greatest communistic co-operation and mutual help within, but coldly indifferent toward, and fortified against, the world without. In the end, as it worked out, the family became a walled castle outside which everything is legitimate loot.

III. NEPOTISM, CORRUPTION AND MANNERS

Every family in China is really a communistic unit, with the principle of "do what you can and take what you need" guiding its functions. Mutual helpfulness is developed to a very high degree, encouraged by a sense of moral obligation and family honour. Sometimes a brother will cross the sea thousands of miles away to redeem the honour of a bankrupt brother. A well-placed and comparatively successful man generally contributes the greater, if not the entire, share of the expenses of the whole household, and it is common practice, worthy of no special merit, for a man to send his nephews to school. A successful man, if he is an official, always gives the best jobs to his relatives, and if there are not ready jobs he can create sinecure ones. Thus sinecurism and nepotism developed, which, coupled with economic pressure, became an irresistible force, undermining, rather than being undermined, by any political reform movement. The force is so great that repeated efforts at reform, with the best of intentions, have proved unsuccessful.

To look at it kindly, nepotism is no worse than favouritism of other sorts. A minister does not place only his nephews in the ministry, but he also has to place the nephews of other high officials, if they are high enough, who write him letters of recommendation. Where is he going to place them, except in sinecure posts and "advisorships"? The economic pressure and the pressure of overpopulation are so keen, and there are so many educated men who can write literary essays but who cannot repair a carburettor or set up a radio, that every new public organ or every official assuming a new post is daily flooded with, literally, hundreds of letters of recommendation. It is quite natural, therefore, that charity should begin at home. For the family system must be taken as the Chinese traditional system of insurance against unemployment. Every family takes care of its own unemployed, and having taken care of its unemployed, its next best work is to find employment for them. It is better than charity because it teaches in the less lucky members a sense of independence, and the members so helped in turn help other members of the family. Besides, the minister who robs the nation to feed the family, either for the present or for the next three or four generations, by amassing half a million to ten million or more dollars,[1] is only trying to glorify his ancestors and be a "good" man of the family. Graft, or "squeeze," may be a public vice, but is always a family virtue. As all Chinese are fairly "good" men, so, as Ku Hungming says, the commonest conjugation in Chinese grammar is that of the verb "to squeeze": "*I squeeze, you squeeze, he squeezes; we squeeze, you squeeze, they squeeze.*" It is a regular verb.

And so, strange as it may seem, Chinese communism breeds Chinese individualism, and family-defined co-operation results in general kleptomania with an altruistic tinge to it. Klepto-mania can go safely with the greatest personal honesty and

[1] I allow myself to mention only the dead as examples. General Wang Chanyüan, Governor of Hupeh, was worth about thirty millions; General Wu Chünsheng, Governor of Heilungkiang, was even richer, holding vast tracts of realty that would be difficult to estimate. God alone knows how much T'ang Yülin of Jehol fame was worth. He is still alive.

even with philanthropy, which is nothing strange even in the West. The pillars of society, who in China are the most photographed men in the daily papers and who easily donate a hundred thousand dollars to a university or a civic hospital, are but returning the money they robbed from the people back to the people. In this, the East and the West are strangely alike. The difference is that in the West there is always the fear of exposure, whereas in the East it is taken for granted. The rampant corruption of the Harding administration did, after all, end up in one official being brought to justice. However unfair that was on him, it did seem to say that graft is wrong.

In China, though a man may be arrested for stealing a purse, he is not arrested for stealing the national treasury, not even when our priceless national treasures in the National Museum of Peiping are stolen by the responsible authorities and publicly exposed. For we have such a thing as the *necessity* of political corruption, which follows as a logical corollary of the theory of "government by gentlemen" (see page 196). Confucius told us to be governed by gentlemen, and we actually treat them like gentlemen, without budgets, reports of expenditures, legislative consent of the people or prison cells for official convicts. And the consequence is that their moral endowments do not quite equal the temptations put in their way, and thus many of them steal.

The beauty of our democracy is that the money thus robbed or stolen always seeps back to the people, if not through a university, then through all the people who depend upon the official and serve him, down to the house servant. The servant who squeezes his master is but helping him to return the money to the people, and he does it with a clear conscience. The house servant has a domestic problem behind him, differing in magnitude but not in nature from the domestic problem of his master.

Certain social characteristics arise from the family system, apart from nepotism and official corruption already mentioned. They may be summed up as the lack of social discipline. It defeats any form of social organization, as it defeats the civil service system through nepotism. It makes a man "sweep the snow in front of his door, and not bother about the frost on his neighbour's roof." This is not so bad. What is worse is that it makes a man throw his refuse outside his neighbour's door.

The best illustration is the so-called Chinese courtesy, a very misunderstood topic. Chinese courtesy cannot be defined, as Emerson has defined it, as "the happy way of doing things." So much depends on who it is you are doing things with. Is he of your family or a friend of your family? The Chinese have just as much good manners toward people outside their families and friends as the Englishmen in the colonies have toward people outside their race. One Englishman told me that "the good thing is that we are not proud toward ourselves." This seems quite sufficient for the Englishmen, since "ourselves" make the universe. The Chinese are not bad-mannered toward their friends and acquaintances, but beyond that limit the Chinese as a social being is positively hostile toward his neighbour, be he a fellow-passenger in a street car or a neighbour at the theatre-ticket office.

I have seen on a rainy day at a bus station in the inland a fellow-passenger who, in the mad scramble for seats, found himself occupying the driver's seat, and who steadfastly refused to give it up against the entreaty of the station officials. A bit of "social consciousness" might have told him that without the driver no one in the bus could get home, but this spark of social consciousness was lacking. If one analyses still further, was he to blame? Why was there only one bus for about eighty passengers? The local militarist had commandeered the others for transportation purposes. Where, then, was the social consciousness of the militarist? Where system fails, and where men are forced into a mad scramble, all stranded on the road thirty miles away from home on a rainy day and all anxious to get home, what was the occupant of the driver's seat to expect if he gave it up? The case is therefore typical: it shows the maladjustment between the natural rural courtesy of the farmers and the age of speed, the political chaos which hastens individual scramble, and the lack of a tradition, based on a new social consciousness, which must take time to grow up.

This lack of social consciousness explains why all bus companies are losing money and why all mining companies have closed up. It goes on in an uninterrupted series from the library regulations to the law of the land. The great officials break the great laws, the small officials break the small laws, and the result is a total lack of social discipline and general disregard for social rules and regulations.

The fact is, the family system stands midway between extreme individualism and the new sense of social consciousness which, in the West, includes the whole society. Chinese society is cut up into little family units, inside which exists the the greatest communistic co-operation, but between the units no real bond of unity exists, except the state. As China has stood practically alone and unchallenged, even this sense of state, or nationalism, has not been greatly developed. So family consciousness has taken the place of the social consciousness and national consciousness in the West. Some form of nationalism is developing, but no one need be alarmed. The "yellow peril" can come from Japan but not from China. Deep down in our instincts we want to die for our family, but we do not want to die for our state. None of us ever want to die for the world. The propaganda of the Japanese militarist clique that says a nation should aggrandize itself in order to bring "peace and harmony" to Asia, or even to the world, can have no appeal to the Chinese. To such appeals we are strangely, superlatively, heathenishly callous. To such appeals, our only answer is, "What do you mean?" We will not save the world. Enough provocation there is in modern Chinese international relations to goad us and weld us into a national unity, but the surprising thing is how well we resist such influences and provocations.

Viewing the nation as a whole, it may really seem as if we mean to carry along as we were before. Travellers in 1935 in Japan and China can observe the greatest possible contrast in this respect. Compare the Japanese, busy and bustling, reading a newspaper in the tram or in the train, with a dogged face and determined chin and a cloud of imminent national disaster hanging over his brow, determined that Japan must either smash the world or be smashed in the next great conflict, and preparing for its coming—and the Chinese in his long gown, as placid, as contented, as happy-go-lucky, as if nothing

could ever shake him out of his dreams. You cannot go into
Chinese homes, eat in Chinese restaurants and walk about in
Chinese streets, and believe that a national or world disaster
is coming. The Chinese always say of themselves that their
nation is like "a tray of loose sands," each grain being, not an
individual but a family. On the other hand, the Japanese
nation is (grammatically one says the Chinese nation *are*,
but the Japanese nation *is*) welded together like a piece of
granite. Perhaps this is a good thing. The next world explosion may blow up the granite, but can at best but disperse
the sands. The sands will remain sands.

IV. PRIVILEGE AND EQUALITY

The Doctrine of Social Status, or the ideal of "every man in
his place," cuts through the idea of equality in a curious way,
and it is important to see this point in order to understand the
whole spirit of Chinese social behaviour, both good and bad.
The humanist temper is one emphasizing distinctions of all
kinds, distinctions between men and women (resulting in the
seclusion of women, as we have seen), between ruling authority
and subjects, and between the old and the young. Confucianism
always imagined itself as a civilizing influence going about
preaching these distinctions and establishing social order. It
hoped to bind society together by a moral force, by teaching
benevolence in the rulers and submission in the ruled, kindliness
in the elders and respect for old age in the young, "friendliness"
in the elder brother, and humility in the younger brother.
Instead of social equality, the emphasis is rather on sharply
defined differentiation, or stratified equality. For the Chinese
word for the five cardinal relationships, *lun*, means equality
within its class.

Such a society is not without its charms and graces. The
respect for old age, for instance, is always something touching,
and Professor A. E. Ross has noted that the old man in China
is a most imposing figure, more dignified and good to look at
than the old men in the West, who are made to feel in every
way that they have passed the period of their usefulness and

are now gratuitously fed by their children, as if they had not done their bit in bringing up the young in their prime of life! Or else, these old men of the West are continually shouting to people that they are still young in spirit, which of course makes them look ridiculous. No well-bred Chinese would gratuitously offend an old man, just as no well-bred Western gentleman would intentionally offend a lady. Some of that fine feeling is now gone, but a great part of it still remains in most Chinese families. That accounts for the poise and serenity of old age. China is the one country in which the old man is made to feel at ease. I am sure this general respect for old age is a thousand times better than all the old-age pensions in the world.

On the other hand, this theory of differentiated status has brought about privilege, always charming to the privileged classes and, until recently, also to their admirers. While the respect for old age is unquestionably good, the respect for scholars and officialdom is both good and bad. The social acclaim of the "literary wrangler," the first man in the imperial examinations, was something to touch a mother's heart, and many a maiden's, too. There he was, mounted on a white horse, personally decorated by the Emperor, parading the streets as the first and cleverest scholar of the land, a veritable Prince Charming, for it was important, too, that the first scholar should look handsome. Such was the glory of being a distinguished scholar, and such was the glory of being a mandarin official. Whenever he went out, a gong sounded announcing his coming, and yamen[1] servants cleared the way, brushing the passers-by away like so much dirt. The yamen servants had always been invested with part of their master's power and glory. What though they accidentally maimed or killed a man or two!

One cannot read old Chinese novels without coming upon such a scene. We do not call it power and glory; we call it "glowing fire and lapping flames," glorious as a conflagration. The yamen servants' only worry was that they might come across another train belonging to an official of higher rank (for so works the Doctrine of Status), which would dampen

[1] Yamen is the headquarters of an official.

their "fire" a little, or that they might unknowingly kill or maim a man who belonged to that higher official's household. Then they would cry, "I ought to die! I ought to die!" and actually they might be handed over to the higher official for whatever punishment that official deemed fit, including flogging and imprisonment, law or no law.

Privilege of this sort was always inspiring and fascinating, and it is no wonder that modern officials, deprived of such outward glory, are unwilling to give it up. No one enjoying a privilege is not flattered by it or highly pleased with it. What a democratic come-down to call these modern officials "public servants!" They may use the phrase themselves in circular telegrams, but in their hearts they hate it. In 1934 there still occurred a case in which the chauffeur of a high government official disobeyed the traffic signal, crossed the road at a busy corner, and pulling out a revolver, shot off the thumb of the policeman who tried to stop him. Such was the glowing flame of his official fire. Yes, privilege was a good thing, and it is still glowing to-day. .

Privilege is therefore the antithesis of equality and the officials are the natural enemies of democracy. Whenever the officials are willing to curtail their class privilege, enjoy less freedom of action and answer an impeachment by appearing at a law court, China can be transformed overnight into a true democracy. But not until then. For if the people are free, where will be the freedom of the officials and militarists? If the people have the inviolability of person, where will be the freedom of the militarists to arrest editors, close down the press and chop off men's heads to cure their headache?[1] Whenever the people are disrespectful to their officials or the young speak against their parents, we exclaim *"Fan liao! Fan liao!"* meaning that heaven and earth are overturned and the world has come to an end.

The notion is very deep-rooted in the Chinese mind, and the evil is not confined to the officials, but spreads like the roots of a banyan tree miles off. Like the banyan tree, too, it spreads its cool shade over all who come under it. We Chinese

[1] As did General Chang Yi in my native town, Changchow, Fukien. I can give his name because he is dead.

do not fight the banyan tree; we try to come under its shade. We do not impeach officials, like the Americans, or burn down the houses of the rich, like the Bolsheviks. We try to become their doorkeepers and enjoy their official umbrage.

V. SOCIAL CLASSES

It seems clear, then, that actually there are only two social classes in China, the yamen class who enjoyed extraterritorial rights without consular jurisdiction long before the Europeans came to China, and the non-yamen class who pay the taxes and obey the law. To put it a little more cruelly, there are only two classes in China, the top-dog and the under-dog, who take turns. With their cheerful fatalism, the Chinese bear this scheme of things quite nobly and well. There are no established social classes in China, but only different families, which go up and down according to the vicissitudes of fortune. There are the lucky yamen families, and there are the less lucky families, whose sons do not preside in the yamens or whose daughters do not marry into the yamendom. And no families stand quite alone. Through marriage, or through acquaintance, there is hardly a family in China that cannot find a distant cousin who knows the teacher of the third son of Mr. Chang whose sister-in-law is the sister of a certain bureaucrat's wife, which relationship is of extreme value when it comes to lawsuits.

Yamen families may indeed well be compared again to banyan trees whose roots cross and recross each other and spread fanwise, and Chinese society to a banyan tree on a hill. Through a process of adjustment, they all struggle for a place in the sun, and they live at peace with each other. Some stand at a better vantage point than others, and they all protect each other—"officials protect officials," as the current Chinese saying goes. The common people are the soil which nourishes these trees and gives them sustenance and makes them grow. As Mencius said, when he was defending the distinction between the gentleman and the common man, "Without the gentleman there would be no one to rule the common people, and without the common people there would be no one to *feed* the gentleman." Once the King of Ch'i asked Confucius about government, and on being told of the Doctrine of Social Status, the King exclaimed, "Well said, sir! If the king is not kingly, and the subjects do not fulfil their duties as subjects . . . *how can I be fed, though there be plenty of rice in the country?"* So between the sunshine from above and the sap of the earth from below, the trees prosper. Some trees are more vigorous than others and draw more sap from the earth, and people who sit under their shade and admire their green leaves do not know that it is the sap that does it.

The officials know it, however. Candidates for magistracy sitting and awaiting their chances in Peking know by heart and constant conversation which district is "fat" and which district is "thin." They, too, with a literary flourish, speak of the national revenue as "the people's fat and the people's marrow." The process of extraction of human fat and human marrow is a science comparable in diversity and ingenuity to organic chemistry. A good chemist can convert beetroot into sugar, and a really good one can draw nitrogen and make fertilizer out of air. The Chinese officialdom have nothing to lose by comparison.

The redeeming feature is the absence of caste or aristocracy in China. The yamen class is not a permanent hereditary institution, like the landed aristocracy in Europe, and it is impossible to identify it permanently with any group of individuals. There has been no family in China which can boast that its ancestors have never worked for the last five hundred years, like some aristocrats in France or the Habsburgs in Austria, except Confucius's family, which has not worked for the last two thousand years. The descendants of the Manchu army, which conquered China in 1644, may be truly said not to have worked for the last three hundred years, and now with the fall of the Manchu Dynasty they still refuse to work—that is, most of them. They are a most interesting case for socialists to study, as showing what can happen to a class of people fed by the nation for three centuries, for they are the true "leisure class" in China. But they are the exception.

There is no hard-and-fast line of distinction between the yamen and the non-yamen class.

The family, rather than any hereditary class, is the social unit. These families go up and down kaleidoscopically. Every man past forty has seen with his own eyes how some families rise and others go down. Social democracy is maintained in the West or in China, not by any constitution but, as someone has pointed out, by our prodigal sons. Of these prodigal sons, there are plenty in China who, through their prodigality, make the rise of a permanent rich class impossible, standing thus, as it were, as the bulwark of democracy. The civil examinations made it possible always for ambitious and able men to rise from the bottom of the scale. From such examinations none were excluded except the sons of beggars or prostitutes. And education was not so costly that only sons of the higher classes could afford it. While learning was a privilege of the talented, it was never the privilege of the rich. No one was known to be seriously handicapped in his academic career by his poverty. In this sense, it may be said that there was equality of opportunity for all.

The Chinese divide society into four classes, in the following order of importance: the scholars, the farmers, the artisans and the merchants. In a primitive agricultural society in which China always remained, the spirit was essentially democratic. There was no class antagonism, as there was no need. The intercourse between these classes, except, as we have mentioned, the yamen class, was not marred by "class feeling" and snobbery. In the best social tradition of China, a rich merchant or a high official may ask a woodcutter to have a cup of tea and chat quite sociably with him, perhaps with less condescension than the inmates of an English manor house speak to the farm-hand.[1] The farmers, the artisans and the merchants, being all part of the sap of the earth, are humble, quiet, self-respecting citizens. The farmers are placed, by Confucian theory, at the head of these three classes, for the rice-conscious Chinese always know where every grain comes from, and they are grateful. They, together with the merchants and artisans, all look up to the

[1] A striking example of this is contained in the sketch called "Democracy" in Somerset Maugham's *On a Chinese Screen*.

scholars as a class entitled to privilege and extra courtesy, and with the difficulty of acquiring a knowledge of the Chinese written characters, this respect comes from the bottom of their hearts.

VI. The Male Triad

But do the scholars deserve this respect? Mental labour is decidedly higher than manual labour, and the inequality really seems quite natural. The conquest of the animal kingdom by mankind was based on man's greater cerebral development. Through his mental development, he justified his supremacy over the animal world. But, of course, one can ask the question whether, *from the animals' point of view*, man has the right to take away the mountain forests from the lions and tigers and rob the buffalo of the prairie. The dog might agree, but the wolf might think otherwise. Man justified it merely by his greater cunning, and the scholar in China did the same. He alone knew the treasure of knowledge, he alone knew history and the law, and he alone knew how to murder a man by the dexterous use of one word in a legal brief. Learning is so complicated that respect for it is natural. He and his kind form the so-called "gentry" class in China. To continue the forest analogy, the gentry are the parasites, which have a way of reaching the top of the highest tree without great effort, and all Chinese banyans are surrounded by such parasites. In other words, they can reach the trees and whisper a kind word for the sap of the earth, incidentally pocketing a commission. More than that, they often undertake from the tree the duty of draining the sap of the earth.

This is the so-called "tax monopoly system" which is ruining both the financial condition of the people and the national revenue itself. These tax monopolies are the feeding ground of the local gentry, an evil which has been greatly aggravated since the establishment of the Republic. Actually, a tax monopoly which is bought out from the city government at thirty thousand dollars a year yields two to three times its price. The sap goes to nourish the parasites. The pity of it is that the people are duped without any benefit to the government or to society, except the fattening of the parasites' own families.

But the parasites are so thickly entrenched in their local ground that any new régime almost has to work with them and through them. They parcel out the butchery tax, the prostitution tax and the gambling tax, and from what they invest in, they naturally expect to get the greatest returns. This idea of the "greatest returns" proves ruinous to the people. There is no limit to their rapacity, for no definition of "the greatest" is possible. And with their professional knowledge, they can invent new taxes. Every new official has a few of these gentry friends officially or unofficially connected with his yamen. They may come for a visit, and between the sippings of tea may often utter a sigh: "Ah! come to think of it, there are at least 15,000 troughs for feeding pigs in every *hsien*, and 150,000 troughs in every district of ten *hsien*. A dollar per trough would net in a very handsome sum, very handsome indeed." Down goes another gulp of fine *lungching* tea. When there are many such sighs and flashes of insight, the official really begins to learn the art of extracting human fat and human marrow. The official is profoundly grateful and feels half ashamed of his own ignorance. He is maturing in "the ways of the world." Soon after the pig-trough tax, the gentry scholar discovers the coffin tax, and after that the wedding-sedan tax. . . .

I have always connected these scholar gentry in my thoughts with the divinely beautiful white cranes in Chinese paintings. They are so pure, so white, so unearthly. That is why they stand for the symbol of the Taoist recluse, and fairies go up to heaven on their backs. One would think they were fed on ether. But they are fed on frogs and earthworms. What if their plumes *are* so white and smooth and their steps so stately! The trouble is they must feed on something. The gentry, who know all the good things of life, must live, and in order to live, they must have money.

Their love of money forces them to work with the rich, and here we come to the real inequality in China, economic inequality. In Chinese towns there was always a male Triad: the magistrate, the gentry and the local rich, besides the female

Triad of Face, Fate and Favour. The male Triad more or less always worked together. A good magistrate had to fight his way out and directly reach the people over the shoulders of the other two. There were many such magistrates. But they had a hard time, and these people had always to attend to the administration personally themselves without the usual paraphernalia of the whole yamendom. Such a one, for instance, was Yüan Mei, and there were many others. They were good, but gratuitously good, to the people.

In modern times a fourth potentate has come into being in the countryside, and instead of a Triad we have in some parts of the country four monsters working hand in hand together: the magistrate, the gentry, the local rich and the bandit. Sometimes the local rich get out, and there remain only three. No wonder the fat of the land is running thin. No wonder that Communism grows. Communism, without Russian doctrine, could not find a more ideal growing ground. The movement of Communism, with its ruthless stand against the gentry and the local rich, and constantly growing and feeding upon the dislocated population, now homeless, fatless, and marrowless and being called "bandits," must be looked upon as an economic rebellion of the people, quite apart from the accident of Russian theories. And all this because Confucius, in outlining his social scheme of five human relationships, forgot to define the relationship between man and the stranger.

Communism has so changed the scheme of social life that a peasant may go directly to the magistrate and, resting his bamboo pole on the yamen wall, talk to the magistrate as man to man. This has become so deep-rooted that in territories recovered from the communistic area, the officials can no longer keep to their yamen style, but must speak to the peasant, as the communist officials used to speak to him. Certain things are still wrong, grievously wrong. The Kuomintang had on its literary programme the lightening of the tenants' contribution of crops to the landlords, the establishment of rural banks, and the forbidding of usury, etc., etc. And some day it is going to be forced to do all this. The Shanghai pawnshops still proclaim their generosity with the words in big characters outside their doors: "MONTHLY INTEREST EIGHTEEN PER CENT!"

VII. THE FEMALE TRIAD

With the Doctrine of Social Status and the conception of stratified equality, certain laws of Chinese social behaviour arise as a result. They are the three immutable laws of the Chinese universe, more eternal than a Roman Catholic dogma, and more authoritative than the Constitution of the United States. They are, in fact, the three Muses ruling over China, rather than General Chiang Kaishek or Wang Chingwei. Their names are Face, Fate and Favour. These three sisters have always ruled China, and are ruling China still. The only revolution that is real and that is worth while is a revolution against this female triad. The trouble is that these three women are so human and so charming. They corrupt our priests, flatter our rulers, protect the powerful, seduce the rich, hypnotize the poor, bribe the ambitious and demoralize the revolutionary camp. They paralyse justice, render ineffective all paper constitutions, scorn at democracy, contemn the law, make a laughing stock of the people's rights, violate all traffic rules and club regulations, and ride roughshod over the people's home gardens. If they were tyrants, or if they were ugly, like the Furies, their reign might not endure so long; but their voices are soft, their ways are gentle, their feet tread noiselessly over the law courts, and their fingers move silently, expertly, putting the machinery of justice out of order while they caress the judge's cheeks. Yes, it is immeasurably comfortable to worship in the shrine of these pagan women. For that reason, their reign will last in China for some time yet.

In order to understand the conception of favour, it is necessary to know the beautiful simplicity of life in which the Chinese have lived. The Chinese ideal of society has always been one in which the "administration is simple and the punishments are light." A personal, human touch always colours the Chinese conception of law and government. The Chinese are invariably suspicious of laws and lawyers, and of a highly mechanized society. Their ideal is one in which people living in the heyday of peace and leisure retain a good measure of primitive simplicity. In this atmosphere emerged favour, and in this atmosphere emerged that most beautiful of ancient Chinese characteristics, gratitude, the counterpart of favour. Of this gratitude, the common people of China, especially the agricultural population, have still a large "bellyful." A farmer who has been recipient of an act of favour remembers it for life and will probably worship you for life in the form of an inscribed wooden tablet in his private household, or serve you loyally "through fire and water." True, the people are left without constitutional protection at the mercy of the district magistrate. But if the magistrate is kind, kindness is all the more keenly appreciated because it is something gratuitous. There have been thousands of cases in which the village people surrounded the departing magistrate's sedan-chair, kneeling on the ground with tears of gratitude in their eyes. This is the best demonstration of Chinese gratitude, and of Chinese official favour. For the people know it as favour and not as justice.

In such an atmosphere originated favour, which came from a personal relationship between the man in power and the man in need of protection. It can, however, take the place of justice, and it often does so. When a Chinese is arrested, perhaps wrongly, the natural tendency of his relatives is not to seek legal protection and fight it out in a law court, but to find someone who knows the magistrate personally and intercede for his "favour." With the high regard for personal relationships and the importance attached to "face" in China, the man who intercedes is always successful if his "face" is "big" enough. It is always easy, and infinitely less costly than a protracted lawsuit. In this way, a social inequality arises between the powerful, the rich and the well-connected, and the poor who are not so fortunately circumstanced.

Some years ago there occurred in Anhui the arrest and imprisonment of two college professors for the ludicrously insignificant offence of some incautious remarks, and the relatives had no better way than to go to the provincial capital and plead with the military chief of the province for "favour." On the other hand, certain young men in the same province, connected with a powerful political party, were arrested in *flagrante delicto* for gambling, and after being released, went to the capital and demanded the dismissal of the offending police. An opium house in a city on the Yangtse was searched by the police and its store of opium confiscated two years ago, but on the telephone message of an influential local person, the Bureau of Public Safety not only had to apologize for the slip in manners, but had to send the opium back with police guards. A certain dentist who had taken out a tooth for a powerful general and was therefore invested for life with part of the latter's personal glory, was once asked for on the phone by the operator of a certain ministry by his personal name and surname and not by surname and official title. He went to the ministry, asked for the operator and slapped his face in the presence of the ministry staff. In July, 1934, a woman in Wuchang was arrested for sleeping outdoors with short trousers, because of the heat, and died consequently in imprisonment a few days afterwards. The woman, it turned out, was the wife of an official, and the offending policeman was shot. And so on, *ad infinitum*. Revenge is sweet. But as there are women who are not wives of officials but who may nevertheless be arrested, the consequence is not always sweet revenge. Confucianism stands for this, because as early as the *Book of Rites* there occurred the phrase, "Courtesy is not extended to the commoners, and punishment is not served up to the lords."

Favour was then part and parcel of the Doctrine of Social Status, and the logical consequence of the Confucian ideal of a "personal," "parental" government by "gentlemen." And was Laotse not right in saying: "Sages no dead, robbers no end"? Confucius was childishly naïve in thinking there were enough gentlemen in a country to go round ruling the people, and apparently he miscalculated. In an idyllically simple stage of life this might work, but in the modern age of aeroplanes and motor cars it must fail, and it has failed miserably.

The redeeming feature, as has been said, is the absence of caste and aristocracy in China. And this brings us to Fate. The feature that makes such apparent social inequality endurable is that no people are trodden down permanently, and the oppressor and oppressed take turns. We Chinese believe that every dog has his day, and "heaven's way always goes round." If a man has ability, steadiness and ambition, he can always rise and climb high. Who can tell? A bean-curd seller's daughter may suddenly catch the eyes of a powerful official or a colonel, or his son may by a strange accident become the doorkeeper of a city magistrate. Or a butcher's son-in-law, who may be a poor middle-aged village school-master, may suddenly pass the official examinations and, as we are told in the novel *Julinwaishih*, one gentry scholar from the city asks him to come and stay in his mansion, another comes to "exchange certificates" of sworn brotherhood with him, a third rich merchant presents him with rolls of silk and bags of silver, and the city magistrate himself sends him two maid-servants and a cook to relieve his peasant wife of her kitchen labour. The butcher moves into the new mansion in the city, happy of heart, forgetting how he had always bullied his son-in-law, says he has always believed in him, and is now ready to lay down the butcher's knife and be fed by him for life. When this happens, his day has come. We envy him but we do not call it unfair. For we call it fate, or his luck.

Fatalism is not only a Chinese mental habit, it is part of the conscious Confucian tradition. So closely related is this belief in fate connected with the Doctrine of Social Status that we have such current phrases as "keep your own status and resign your-self to heaven's will," and "let heaven and fate have their way." Confucius, in relating his own spiritual progress, said that at fifty he "knew heaven's will." At sixty "nothing he heard could disturb him." This doctrine of fatalism is a great source of personal strength and contentment, and accounts for the placidity of Chinese souls. As no one has all the luck all the time, and as good luck cannot apparently come to all, one is willing to submit to this inequality as something perfectly natural. There is always a chance for ambitious and able men to rise through the imperial examinations. And if, through luck or through ability, a man rises from the unprivileged to the privileged class, then it is his turn. Once in the privileged class, he is in love with it; a change of psychology takes place along with the change in elevation. He begins to love social inequality and all its privileges, and falls in love with it, as Ramsay MacDonald fell in love with Downing Street. The latter went up the steps of No. 10, sniffed its air and felt happy. Practically, this turn-about-face has been noticed in every modern successful Chinese revolutionist. He clamps down his iron heel on the freedom of the press more energetically than the militarist he denounced while in his revolutionary apprenticeship.

For he has now got a "big face." He stands above the law and the constitution, not to speak of traffic rules and museum regulations. That face is psychological and not physiological. Interesting as the Chinese physiological face is, the psychological face makes a still more fascinating study. It is not a face that can be washed or shaved, but a face that can be "granted" and "lost" and "fought for" and "presented as a gift." Here we arrive at the most curious point of Chinese social psychology. Abstract and intangible, it is yet the most delicate standard by which Chinese social intercourse is regulated.

But it is easier to give an example of Chinese face than to define it. The official in the metropolis, for instance, who can drive at sixty miles an hour, while the traffic regulations allow only thirty-five, is gaining a lot of face. If his car hits a man, and when the policeman comes round he silently draws a card from his pocket-book, smiles graciously and sails away, then he is gaining greater face still. If, however, the policeman is unwilling to give him face and pretends not to know him, the official will begin "talking mandarin" by asking the policeman "if he knows his father" and signalling to the chauffeur to go off, and thus his face waxes still greater. And if the incorrigible policeman insists on taking the chauffeur to the station, but the official telephones to the chief of police, who immediately releases the chauffeur and orders the dismissal of the little policeman who did not "know his father," then the face of the official becomes truly beatific.

Face cannot be translated or defined. It is like honour and is not honour. It cannot be purchased with money, and gives a man or a woman a material pride. It is hollow and is what men fight for and what many women die for. It is invisible and yet by definition exists by being shown to the public. It exists in the ether and yet can be heard, and sounds eminently respectable and solid. It is amenable, not to reason but to social convention. It protracts lawsuits, breaks up family fortunes, causes murders and suicides, and yet it often makes a man out of a renegade who has been insulted by his fellow-townsmen, and it is prized above all earthly possessions. It is more powerful than fate and favour, and more respected than the constitution. It often decides a military victory or defeat, and can demolish a whole government ministry. It is that hollow thing which men in China live by.

To confuse face with Western "honour" is to make a grievous error. Chinese girls used to die for face, if their bodies had been accidentally exposed to a man, as some Western women were once willing to drown themselves for having an illegitimate child. And yet in the West, the man who is slapped on the cheek and does not offer a challenge for a duel is losing "honour" but not losing face. On the other hand, the ugly son of a *taot'ai*, who goes to a sing-song girl's house, is insulted and returns with a company of police to order the arrest of the sing-song girl and the closing of the house, is getting "face," but we would hardly say he is guarding his "honour."

Battles have been lost and empires have been sacrificed because the generals were bargaining for some honorific titles or some inoffensive way of accepting defeat rather than proceeding according to military tactics. Hot controversies have raged and protracted legal battles have been fought, in which the wise arbiter knows that all the time nothing really prevents the parties from coming together except a nice way of getting out of it, or probably the proper wording of an apology. A general split a political party and changed the whole course of a revolution because he was publicly insulted by a fellow-worker. Men and women are willing to drudge all the summer in order to keep going a funeral celebration appropriate to the standing or face of the family, and old families on the decline are willing to go bankrupt and live in debt for life for the same reason.

Not to give a man face is the utmost height of rudeness and is like throwing down a gauntlet to him in the West. Many officials attend between three and four dinners in a night and injure all their chances of a normal digestive system rather than make one of their intended hosts lose face. Many defeated generals who ought to be beheaded or rot in prison are sent on tours of "industrial" or "educational inspection" to Europe as a price for their surrender, which saves their face and which explains the periodic recrudescence of civil wars in China. A whole government ministry was abolished four or five years ago in order to avoid the word "dismissal" and save the face of the minister who ought to have been told in plain terms to get out and perhaps get a jail sentence besides. (A dismissal would make the minister lose face, because there was no change of cabinet at the time.) Human, all too human, this face of ours. And yet, it is the goad of ambition and can overcome the Chinese love of money. It has caused a schoolteacher infinite misery because the foreign principal insisted on increasing his salary from eighteen dollars to nineteen dollars. He would rather take eighteen dollars or twenty or die than be called a nineteen-dollar man. A father-in-law, by refusing to ask his unworthy son-in-law to stay for supper and thus making him lose face, is probably only wanting to make a man out of him, and very possibly that solitary walk on his way back home may be the beginning of his making good.

It is safer on the whole, however, to travel with people who have no face than with people who have too much of it. Two soldiers on a Yangtse steamer insisted on having the face to go into a forbidden room containing cases of sulphur and sit on these cases and throw cigarette ends about, against the entreaty of the compradore. Eventually, the steamer was blown up, and the soldiers succeeded in saving their face but not their charred carcasses. This had nothing to do with ignorance or education. An educated Chinese general about five years ago thought his face entitled him to overweight baggage when going up in an aeroplane at Shanghai, despite the remonstrations and pleadings of the pilot. Moreover, he wanted to have extra face before his friends who came to see him off, and ordered the pilot to circle round. As he was a powerful militarist the extra face was "granted." But the pilot became nervous, the plane refused to go up evenly, it hit against a tree, and eventually the general paid for his face by losing one of his legs. Anybody who thinks face is good enough to compensate for overweight luggage in an aeroplane ought to lose his leg and be thankful for it.

So it seems that while it is impossible to define face, it is nevertheless certain that until everybody loses his face in this country, China will not become a truly democratic country. The people have not much face, anyway. The question is, when will the officials be willing to lose theirs? When face is lost at the public courts, then we will have safe traffic. When face is lost at the law courts, then we will have justice. And when face is lost in the ministries, and the government by face gives way to a government by law, then we will have a true republic.

VIII. The Village System

In the absence of the social mind, how is philanthropy possible in China, and what forms have collective enterprises for public good taken? The answer is to be found in the village system, which is the family raised to a higher exponent. The pastoral background which developed the personal system of running National Museums also developed a village consciousness, similar to the growing civic consciousness of a New Yorker or a Chicagoan. From the love of the family there grew a love for the clan, and from the love for the clan there developed an attachment for the land where one was born. Thus a sentiment arose which may be called "provincialism," in Chinese called *t'unghsiang kuannien*, or "the idea of being from the same native place." This provincialism binds the people of the same village, or the same district, or the same province together, and is responsible for the existence of district schools, public grainage, merchant guilds, orphanages, and other public foundations. Fundamentally, they spring from the family psychology and do not depart from the family pattern. It is the family mind enlarged so as to make some measure of civic co-operation possible.

In every big city on the coast or inland there are inevitably a number of provincial or district guilds, like the *Anhui Guild*, the *Ningpo Guild*, etc. Whenever there are rich merchants, these guilds are always liberally endowed. The *Changch'üan Guild* of my native town has in Shanghai a property valued at over a million dollars. It keeps a school in which our native children may study free of tuition. The guilds may always serve as hotels, like the Western club-houses, being very inexpensive, and sometimes have a peculiar system of paying for board, besides providing the travelling merchant with all the facilities of local guidance. In the Manchu days, when scholars from all over the country had to go to Peking for the triennial examinations, there was not a province or district that did not have its own guild-house in the capital. If one could not find one's district guild, one could always find a provincial guild. In these guilds the scholars and candidates for magistracies stayed, sometimes with their families, as in permanent hotels. Certain provinces, like Shansi and Anhui, spread a network of such guilds to enable their merchants to carry on trade all over the country.

Back at home, this village spirit enables the people to develop a system of communal government, the only real government in China, the "central government" being known only by its harassing yamen tax-collectors and its soldiers who always raise a hullabaloo on their official descents into the country. The central government really taxed the people very little in the good old imperial days, and from the villager's point of view, "the heaven was high and the emperor far away." Conscription for military service was unknown. When the country was at peace there was neither war nor banditry, and only the riffraff of society ever thought of becoming soldiers. When the country was not at peace, it was in any case difficult to distinguish between the soldiers of the government and the bandits of the country, a distinction which is totally unnecessary. In fact, no such distinction is logically tenable. As regards law and justice, the people always fought shy of the law court, ninety-five per cent of village disputes being settled by the village elders. To be involved in a lawsuit was *ipso facto* ignominious. Good old people often boasted that they had never entered an official yamen or law court in their lifetimes. So of the three most important functions of the central government, tax collection, maintaining peace and keeping justice, very little came to bother the people. According to the Chinese political philosophy, that government governs best which governs least. It was even so always. The real government of China may be described as a village socialism. And what applies to the village holds true in the general spirit for the town also.

The so-called village or town local government is invisible. It has no visible body of authority like the mayor or councillors. It is governed really morally by the elders by virtue of their great age, and by the gentry by virtue of their knowledge of law and history. Fundamentally, it is governed by custom and usage, the unwritten law. In case of disputes, the elders or patriarchs are invited to decide the right and wrong of the matter, according, as we have pointed out, not to reason alone but to "human nature and eternal reason" combined. When there are no lawyers it is always easy to find out, especially among parties well known to each other and living under the same social tradition, who is right and who is wrong. The absence of lawyers makes justice possible, and when there is justice there is peace in the human heart. The village gentry are as a class whiter than the town gentry, although their parasitic nature is economically determined. There are good and upright scholars who do not make it their profession to handle lawsuits, and who by their reputation for character and learning share the general respect of the villagers with the elders. Under these elders and scholars the people carry on. When disputes cannot be settled in this manner, as in cases of crime and division of property, or when two parties are determined to fight for face, then they go to the yamen. But it is only when both parties are prepared to ruin themselves, for they avoid the yamen like a plague.

The Chinese people can always govern themselves, have always governed themselves. If the thing called "government" can leave them alone, they are always willing to let the government alone. Give the people ten years of anarchy, when the word "government" will never be heard, and they will live peacefully together, they will prosper, they will cultivate deserts and turn them into orchards, they will make wares and sell them all over the country, and they will open up the hidden treasures of the earth on their own enterprise and initiative. Opium will cease to be grown because no one forces them to, and will become extinct automatically. And they will have saved enough to provide against all temporary floods and famines. Let there be no tax bureau with the sign-board, "Enriching the nation and fattening the people," and the nation will grow rich and the people will grow fat.

IX. "GOVERNMENT BY GENTLEMEN"

The most striking characteristic in our political life as a nation is the absence of a constitution and of the idea of civil rights. This is possible only because of a different social and political philosophy, which mixes morals with politics and is a philosophy of moral harmony rather than a philosophy of force. A "constitution" presupposes that our rulers might be crooks who might abuse their power and violate our "rights," which we use the constitution as a weapon to defend. The Chinese conception of government is the direct opposite of this supposition. It is known as a "parental government" or "government by gentlemen," who are supposed to look after the people's interests as parents look after their children's interests, and to whom we give a free hand and in whom we place an unbounded confidence. In these people's hands we place millions without asking for a report of expenditure and to these people we give unlimited official power without the thought of safeguarding ourselves. We treat them like gentle-men.

There could be no finer, juster and more acute criticism of this government by gentlemen than what was written twenty-one hundred years ago by Hanfeitse, a philosopher of the "legalist school" (*fachia*) who lived about three centuries after Confucius. As the last and also the greatest of this school, he stood for a government by law, instead of a government by persons. His analysis of the evils of this personal government is so acute, and his pictures of Chinese political life of his day are so strikingly appropriate for modern China, that he would not alter a word of it if he were speaking to us to-day.

According to Hanfeitse, the beginning of political wisdom lies in rejecting all moral platitudes and in shunning all efforts at moral reforms. I believe the sooner we stop talking about moral reforms of the people, the sooner shall we be able to give China a clean government. The fact that so many people persist in talking of moral reforms as a solution for political evils is a sign of the puerility of their thinking and their inability to grasp the political problems as political problems. They should see that we have been talking moral platitudes continuously for the last two thousand years without improving the country morally or giving it a cleaner and better government. They should see that, if moralizations would do any good, China should be a paradise of saints and angels to-day. I suspect that the reason why moral reform talks are so popular, especially with our officials, is because they know that such talks do nobody any harm. Probably all our moral uplifters have a bad conscience. I find that General Chang Tsungch'ang and others who want to restore Confucianism and uplift others' morals generally keep from five to fifteen wives and were adepts at seducing young girls. We say, "Benevolence is a good thing," and they echo, "True, benevolence is a good thing," and no harm is done anybody. On the other hand, I do not hear any of our officials talking about government by law, because the people would reply, "All right, we will prosecute you by law and send you to prison." The earlier, therefore, we stop talking about morality and switch over to the subject of the strict enforcement of law, the sooner we make it impossible for these officials to dodge the issue and pretend to read the Confucian classics in the foreign settlements.

Briefly, we may say, therefore, that there were two opposing conceptions of government in Hanfeitse's times, as well as in our own times: the Confucian conception of government by gentlemen and the legalist conception of government by law rather than by persons. The Confucian system assumes every ruler to be a gentleman and proceeds to treat him like a gentleman. The legalist system assumes every ruler to be a crook and proceeds to make provisions in the political system to prevent him from carrying out his crooked intentions. Obviously the first is the traditional view, and the second the Western view, and also the view of Hanfeitse. As Hanfeitse says, we should not expect people to be good, but we should make it impossible for them to be bad. That is the moral basis of the legalist philosophy. In other words, instead of expecting our rulers to be gentlemen and to walk in the path of righteousness, we should assume them to be potential prison-inmates and devise ways and means to prevent these potential convicts from robbing the people and selling the country. One can readily see that the latter system is more likely to be effective as a check for political corruption than waiting for a change of hearts in these gentlemen.

In China, however, we have been doing the reverse. Instead of assuming them to be potential crooks, as we should have done long ago, we assume them to be gentlemen. In the good old Confucian way, we expect them to be benevolent rulers and to love the people as their own sons. We expect them to be honest, and we say, "Go ahead, spend what you like out of the public funds, and we will not demand a public budget or a rendering of public accounts." We say to our militarists, "Go ahead, we trust you will love the people so much that we will let you tax us according to your conscience." And we say to our diplomats, "Go ahead, we have implicit faith in your patriotism, and will allow you to contract any and every sort of international treaty without having to submit it to us for approval." And to all our officials we say, "In case you turn out to be gentlemen, we will erect stone *pailou* in your honour, but in case you turn out to be crooks, we will not put you in prison." Never in other countries was there such a gentlemanly treatment of officials. Now Hanfeitse says this is all wrong: it is taking too many chances with their moral endowments. If Hanfeitse were living to-day he would advise us to assume them to be crooks and say to them, "We will not exhort you to the path of righteousness and we will not erect stone *pailou* in your honour in case you turn out to be gentlemen, but in case you turn out to be crooks, we will send you to prison." That seems to be a sounder and speedier way of putting an end to our political corruption.

I quote here a passage from Hanfeitse, in a rather free

rendering. He says: "You can expect generally about ten honest men in a country (which is a pretty good average). But there are, on the other hand, probably a hundred offices. As a result, you have more official positions than honest men to fill them, so that you have ten honest men and ninety crooks to fill all of the positions. Hence there will be more likelihood of a general misrule rather than a good government. Therefore, the wise king believes in a system and not in personal talents, in a method and not in personal honesty." Hanfeitse denied that a "parental government" would ever work, because, he pointed out, even parents do not always succeed in governing their children, and it would be unreasonable to expect rulers to love the people more than parents love their children. Hanfeitse coldly and humorously asked how many disciples Confucius got with all his tremendous benevolence and righteousness, and was not the fact that even Confucius could obtain only seventy disciples among hundreds and thousands of people a clear proof of the futility of virtue? Was it not unreasonable to expect all rulers to walk in virtue like Confucius and all their subjects to love virtue like his seventy disciples? There is a kind of pleasing cynicism, dry humour, and sound sense in those words.

Hanfeitse's description of the ills of his country agrees to a fault with those of present-day China. So similar was the character of the officials and people of those days that, in reading him, we might easily forget that he was not depicting modern China. He traced the corruption of the officials and the apathy of the people of his day to the lack of legal protection, to the fault of the system. Instead of moralizing about it, he preached that it was the system of government and the lack of public legal protection that was at fault. He said all troubles lay in the lack of a "public or just law." He hated the Confucianists of his day and called them a pack of gabbling fools, which might be fittingly applied to so many of our "long-gown patriots" to-day. He said of the officials of that time that they were encouraged in their corruption because there was no punishment for them. He said in these very words: "Although their national territory is sacrificed, their families have got rich. If they succeed, they will be powerful, and if they fail, they can retire in wealth and comfort"—words that might have been written for a great part of the villadom that is living in retirement in Dairen or the Shanghai Settlements. He said that because of the lack of a system, "people were promoted according to their party connections, and were obliged to divert their attention to social entertainments rather than the fulfilment of the law." How true these words are to-day, only officials and official candidates themselves know.

There was an important passage which contained the very interesting phrase *kungmin* ("public citizen") and which tried to account for the general apathy and indifference of the people toward their national affairs. He said in effect: "Now you send people to fight. They will be killed whether they go forward or turn back. That is dangerous for them. You ask them to forsake their own private pursuits and join the military service, and when they are poor, those above do not pay them any attention. Of course, they remain poor. Now who likes to be in danger and poverty? Naturally, they will try to keep away from you. Therefore they will mind their own business and will be interested in building their own houses and will try to avoid war. By avoiding war, they will have security. But by practising graft and bribery, they can become rich and secure themselves for life. Now who would not like to be wealthy and to live in peace? And how can you prevent them from seeking peace and wealth? *This is the reason why there are so few public citizens and so many private individuals.*"

It is still true to-day that we have too few public citizens and too many private individuals and the reason is to be found in the lack of adequate legal protection. It has nothing to do with morals. The evil lies in the system. When it is too dangerous for a man to be too public-spirited, it is natural that he should take an apathetic attitude toward national affairs, and when there is no punishment for greedy and corrupt officials, it is too much to ask of human nature that they should not be corrupt.

Hence Hanfeitse believed in the establishment of an "inviolable law which should apply to both the ruler and the ruled alike." He believed that the law should be supreme, that all people should be equal before the law, and that this law should be applied in place of personal preferences and connections.

Here we have not only a conception of equality that is almost Western, but we have a type of thinking that strikes me as being most un-Chinese. It is strange that, in contrast to the Confucianist dictum that "courtesy should not be extended to the commoners and punishment should not be served up to the lords," we have here a legalist who says that we should have a "law that does not fawn upon the mighty, and statutes that should be applied rigidly, so that wherever the law applies, the clever will submit and the powerful will not protest, the nobility will not be exempted from punishment and rewards will not go over the heads of the humble." Hanfeitse conceived of a law "before which the high and the low, the clever ones and the stupid ones shall stand equal." He pushed the idea of a mechanistic rule of the law so far that he believed it would not be necessary to have wise and able rulers—a mechanistic notion which is totally un-Chinese.

Hence the Taoistic element in his system that "the king should do nothing." The king should do nothing, because he saw the kings could not do anything anyway, as the average run of kings goes, and there should be a machinery of government running so justly and perfectly that it does not matter whether we have good or bad rulers. The king, therefore, becomes a figurehead, as in the modern constitutional government. The English people have a king to lay foundation stones and christen ships and knight people, but it is entirely unimportant to the nation whether they have a good or bad king, an intelligent king or a comparatively mediocre king. The system should run of itself. That in essence is the theory of do-nothingism concerning the king, as interpreted by Hanfeitse and practised also with great success in England.

It is a queer irony of fate that the good old schoolteacher Confucius should ever be called a political thinker, and that his moral molly-coddle stuff should ever be honoured with the name of a "political" theory. The idea of a government by virtue and by benevolent rulers is so fantastic that it cannot deceive a college sophomore. One might just as well regulate motor traffic on Broadway by trusting to the drivers' spontaneous courtesy, instead of by a system of red and green lights. And any thinking student of Chinese history should have observed that the Chinese government *à la Confucius* with its tremendous moralizing has always been one of the most corrupt the world has ever seen. The reason is not that Chinese officials are any more corrupt than Western ones. The plain, inexorable political and historical truth is that when you treat officials like gentlemen, as we have been doing in China, one-tenth of them will be gentlemen and nine-tenths of them will turn out to be crooks; but when you treat them like crooks, with prisons and threats of prisons, as they do in the West, considerably less than one-tenth succeed in being crooks and fully nine-tenths of them succeed in pretending that they are gentlemen. As a result, you have at least the semblance of a clean government. That semblance is worth having. That is what China should have done long ago, and that was Hanfeitse's advice two thousand years ago, before he was made to quaff poison.

What China needs, then, is not more morals but more prisons for politicians. It is futile to talk of establishing a clean and irreproachable government when unclean and reproachable officials can safely book a first-class berth for Yokohama or Seattle. What China needs is neither benevolence, nor righteousness, nor honour, but simple justice, or the courage to shoot those officials who are neither benevolent, nor righteous, nor honourable. The only way to keep the officials clean is to threaten to shoot them when they are caught. Officials who feel hurt at my legalist view of human nature should reflect a little whether they would be willing to invest money in a stock company run strictly on the Confucian-gentlemanly principle, with no stockholders' meeting, no accounting, no auditing and no possibility of arresting an absconding treasurer or manager. The Chinese government was run strictly on such a gentlemanly basis. What improvements the present government has made are due to the influence of Westerners who have the audacity to ask for accounts from their rulers, without being afraid of implying a slight on their gentlemanly honour. But until that change is complete, the Chinese government will always be like an unbusiness-like company, always profitable for the manager and staff but disheartening for the stockholders who are the common people.

Chapter Seven

LITERARY LIFE

I. A Distinction

THE Chinese make a distinction between literature that instructs and literature that pleases, or literature that is "the vehicle of truth" and literature that is "the expression of emotion." The distinction is easy to see: the former is objective and expository, while the latter is subjective and lyrical. They all pretend that the former is of greater value than the latter, because it improves the people's minds and uplifts society's morals. From this point of view, they look down upon novels and dramas as "little arts, unworthy to enter the Hall of Great Literature." The only exception is poetry, which they not only do not despise but cultivate and honour more intensively and generally than in the West. As a matter of fact, all of them read novels and dramas on the sly, and the official who writes only of benevolence and righteousness in his essays will be found, in private conversations, to be quite familiar with the heroes and heroines of *Chinp'inmei* (*Gold-Vase-Plum*), the pornographic novel *par excellence*, or of *P'inhua Paochien*, an equally porno-graphic homosexual novel.

The reason for this is not far to seek. The "literature that instructs" is on the whole of such low, second-rate quality, so full of moral platitudes and naïve reasoning, and the scope of ideas is so hemmed in by the fear of heresy, that the only Chinese literature that is readable is literature in the Western sense, including the novels, dramas and poetry, *i.e.*, literature of the imagination rather than literature of ideas. Scholars who were not economists wrote about taxation, literary men who did not know how to handle a sickle wrote about agricul-ture, and politicians who were not engineers wrote about "A Plan for Huangho Conservancy" (an extremely popular topic).

In the sphere of ideas the scholars were, as we say in Chinese, only turning somersaults in the Confucian school and looking for cow's hair in the courts of the Confucian temple. All of them denounced Chuangtse, the greatest writer of libels against Confucianism, and all of them read Chuangtse. Some of them even dared to play with Buddhist classics, but their cult of Buddhism was dilettantish and their vegetarianism half-hearted. The fear of heresy hung over their heads like the sword of Damocles, and the fear of heresy could only mean the fear of originality. Literature which lives only on spontaneity was harnessed with the classical tradition of ideas. The "free-play of the mind" was extremely limited in scope, and the "somersaults in the Confucian school," however skilful they might be, were nothing but somersaults within the Confucian precincts.

After all, a nation of scholars could not discuss benevolence and righteousness for two thousand five hundred years without repeating themselves. Actually, an essay which won the first place in the triennial imperial examinations, when rendered into plain English, would stagger English readers by its puerility and childishness. The gigantic literary feat produced by the gigantic brain-power gives one the impression of the antics of a flea circus. A writer could therefore be original only in the sphere of novels and dramas, where one could be comfortably oneself, and where imagination could be creative.

As a matter of fact, all literature that is worth while, that is the expression of man's soul, is lyrical in origin. This is true even in the literature of ideas: only ideas that come straight from man's heart will survive. Edward Young made this point clear as far back as 1795 in his *Conjectures on Original Composition*. Ch'in Shengt'an, a distinguished critic of the seventeenth century, said repeatedly in his letters: "What is poetry but a voice of the heart? It can be found in women's and children's hearts, and it comes to you by morning and by night." The origin of literature is really as simple as that, in spite of all the rhetorical and compositional technique that professors of literature try to encumber it with. Ch'in Shengt'an also says: "The ancient people were not compelled to say anything, but they suddenly said something purely of their own accord. They spoke sometimes of events, and sometimes of their own feelings, and having finished what they had to say, they took leave and departed." The difference between literature and mere writing is only that some say it beautifully and others do not, and they who say it more beautifully than others survive.

The lyrical origin of literature makes it possible for us to regard literature as a reflection of man's soul, and to regard a nation's literature as the reflection of man's spirit in that nation. For if life may be compared to a large city, a man's writing may be regarded as the window in his garret from which he views the city. In reading a man's writing we but wish to look at life from his garret window and obtain a view of life as the writer sees it. The stars, the clouds, the mountain peaks lining the horizon, and the alleyways and housetops in the city are all the same, but that garret view of the city is individualistic and peculiarly his own. In reviewing a nation's literature we are therefore but trying to get a glimpse of life as the best minds of that nation see it and as they express it through their own peculiar medium.

II. LANGUAGE AND THOUGHT

The accident of the Chinese literary medium, or the Chinese language, has largely determined the peculiar development of Chinese literature. By comparison with the European languages it is possible to trace how much of the peculiarities of Chinese thought and literature are due simply to their possession of a so-called monosyllabic language. The fact that the Chinese spoke in syllables like *ching, chong, chang* was appalling in consequences. This monosyllabism determined the character of the Chinese writing, and the character of the Chinese writing brought about the continuity of the literary heritage and therefore even influenced the conservatism of Chinese thought. It was further responsible for the development of a literary language quite distinct from the spoken language. This, in turn, made learning difficult and necessarily the privilege of a limited class. Finally, the monosyllabism directly

P

influenced the development of certain peculiarities of Chinese literary style.

Every nation has developed a writing most suitable to its language. Europe did not develop a writing on pictorial principles because the phonetic structure of Indo-Germanic words, with its comparative profusion of consonants and infinitely variable combinations, required an analytic alphabet, and would make the representation of these words by pictographs hopelessly inadequate. For no system of ideographs could be used alone, and it was found, as in the case of Chinese, necessary to supplement the pictorial principle by the phonetic principle before it could have any important development. These elementary pictographs were then used in combinations purely for their phonetic value, and actually nine-tenths of the over forty thousand characters in Chinese dictionaries are built on the principle of phonetic combination, with about thirteen hundred ideographs as phonetic signs. With a mono-syllabic language, such as the Chinese, which has only about four hundred syllabic combinations (not counting the tones) like *ching, chong, chang*, this could suffice. But with a Germanic language the invention of a new symbol for every new sound-combination like *Schlacht* and *Kraft* in German or *scratched, scraped, splash* and *scalpel* in English would be obviously an impossible task. The Chinese language failed to develop a phonetic script in the Western sense because the phonetic use of ideographic symbols could suffice. Had the Chinese been speaking a language with words like the German *Schlacht* and *Kraft* or the English *scratched* and *scalpel*, they would have, by sheer necessity, invented a phonetic script long ago.

The perfect adjustment between the Chinese monosyllabic language and the written characters can be easily made plain. The language is characterized by a great scarcity of syllabic forms and consequently a great number of homonyms or words of the same sound. The sound *pao* can mean over a dozen things: "a package," "to carry," "well-filled in stomach," "a bubble," etc. Since the pictorial principle was limited in application to concrete things or actions, and was even then necessarily complicated, the original word for "package" was used for its purely phonetic value and "borrowed" to denote other words of the same sound. What happened then was that there was a great deal of confusion, and before the script was more or less fixed in the Han Dynasty, we had a great number of such "borrowed" words indicating different things. Necessity forced the Chinese to add a sign (called "radical") to indicate the class of ideas which this particular *pao* was intended to refer to.

The use of phonetic symbols was not too exact, and hence we have the following words, pronounced *pao* or *p'ao* in different tones in modern Chinese, all written with the original "package"-sign (包), but each taking a class-sign or radical, as in: 抱 跑 袍 飽 泡 炮 鮑 胞 砲 咆 刨 苞 雹
Thus *pao* plus a "hand" radical means *to carry*, plus a "foot" means *to run*, plus "clothes" means *a gown*, plus an "eat" means *well-filled in stomach*, plus "water" means a *bubble*, plus "fire" means *firecrackers*, plus a "fish" means the name of *a fish*, plus "flesh" means *the womb*, plus "stone" means *a cannon*, plus "mouth" means *to roar*, plus "grass" means *a flower bud*, plus "rain" means *hail*, plus a "knife" means *to scrape*. This was the adjustment to solve the problem of homonyms.

But suppose the problem was not homonyms, suppose the Chinese language had words like the English *scraped, scratched*, and *scalpel*, or suppose the English people started out with a basic phonetic picture for *sc-a-p*, they would have been forced equally by necessity to distinguish between the sounds *cape* and *scape*, or between *scape* and *scrape*, or between *scrape* and *scraped*, or between *scrape* and *scratch*, and the result could not have been anything except an alphabet with signs to denote *s, r, ed(t), p, ch*, etc. Had the Chinese done this they too would have had an alphabet, and consequently have had a more widespread literacy.

Given, therefore, the monosyllabic character of the Chinese language, it was almost inevitable that pictorial characters were used. This fact alone has profoundly changed the character and position of learning in China. By their very nature the Chinese characters are not subject to changes in the spoken tongue. The same symbol could be read in different ways in different dialects or even languages, as the sign of the Christian cross could be pronounced *cross* in English and *croix* in French.

This has a very close bearing on the unity of Chinese culture throughout the old empire. More important than that, the use of the characters made the reading of the Confucian classics possible after the lapse of a thousand years. The idea that the Confucian classics could have become unreadable in the sixth century of our era is extremely intriguing, and one is tempted to wonder what would have happened to the tremendous respect for Confucianism had that happened.

Actually, the Chinese characters underwent a great revolution at the time of the burning of books by Ch'in Shihhuang, and to-day Confucian scholars are split into two camps, one believing in the classic texts in "ancient scripts" which are supposed to have escaped destruction in the walls of Confucius's own home, and the other believing in the "modern scripts" which were handed down orally by old scholars who had committed the classic texts to memory, and survived the short-lived Ch'in Dynasty. Nevertheless, from that time onward (213 B.C.), there is a continuity of writing, with a comparatively unimportant evolution of forms, which must largely account for the hypnotic power these classics have exercised over the Chinese minds.

What is true of the early texts of Confucianism is true of the entire literary heritage, especially that coming after the Han days. A Chinese schoolboy who can read an author of a hundred years ago could, by that very training, read works of the thirteenth, tenth or second century, almost in the same sense that a modern artist can appreciate the Venus de Milo with the same ease as he appreciates Rodin. Would the influence of the classic heritage have been so powerful, and would the Chinese mind have been so conservative and worshipful of the past, had that past been less readily understood? One wonders.

Yet in another way the use of the characters helped in the creation of a fairly stable literary language, quite different from the spoken language, and rather too difficult for the average scholar to master. Whereas a phonetic script would follow naturally the changes and idioms of a living language, the language of written symbols, by being less dependent upon sounds, achieved a greater freedom in idiom and grammar. It did not have to obey the laws of any spoken language, and, in time, it had its laws of structure and a store of idioms which accumulated by literary accidents from the works of different dynasties. Thus it came to have an independent reality of its own, subject more or less to literary fashions.

As time went on, this discrepancy between the literary language and the living language of the age became greater and greater, until to-day the study of the ancient language is, in point of psychological difficulties involved, exactly similar to the learning of a foreign tongue for the Chinese people. The laws of ordinary sentence-structure differ between the literary and the spoken language, so that one cannot write in the ancient language by merely substituting certain ancient words for the modern words. A simple phrase like *three ounces silver* should be syntactically changed into *silver three ounces*, and whereas the modern Chinese say *I never saw (it)*, the ancient idiom requires the construction *I never it saw*, the accusative object being regularly placed before the verb in the case of negative verbs. Modern Chinese schoolboys are therefore apt to commit the same idiomatic blunders as when English school-boys say *je vois vous* in learning French. Just as in learning a foreign language a very extensive acquaintance with that language is necessary before one can really master the ordinary idioms, so in the practice of writing ancient Chinese, years of oral repetition and reading of masterpieces (minimum ten years) are required before one can write fairly presentable ancient Chinese. And just as very few people succeed in really mastering a foreign language, so in reality very few Chinese scholars succeed in writing really idiomatic ancient Chinese. Actually, there are only three or four Chinese to-day who can write "idiomatic" Chinese of the classic Chou Dynasty. Most of us have to put up with that bookish sort of language which foreigners command easily enough, but which lacks the true flavour of the mother tongue.

The use of the Chinese characters made this development possible. Moreover, the independence of character from sound greatly accelerated its monosyllabic quality. Actually, bi-syllabic words in the spoken language can be represented by a monosyllabic character, because the character itself by its composition makes the meaning already quite clear. Thus, in the spoken language we require a bisyllabic *lao hu* ("old tiger") to distinguish it aurally from a dozen other *hu*'s, but in writing, the character *hu* alone is sufficient. The literary language is therefore much more monosyllabic than the spoken language, since its basis is visual and not aural.

From this extreme monosyllabism then developed an extreme terseness of style, which cannot be imitated in the spoken language without the risk of unintelligibility, but which is the characteristic beauty of Chinese literature. Thus in China we have a metre of exactly seven syllables to each line as the standard metre, saying probably as much as two lines of English blank verse, a feat which is inconceivable in the English language, or in any spoken language. Whether in prose or in verse, this economy of words produced a style where each word or syllable is carefully weighed to its finest nuance in sound-value and is surcharged, as it were, with meaning. As with meticulous poets, Chinese writers are careful in the use of a syllable. A real mastery of this clean-cut style therefore means extreme mastery in the choice of words. Hence arose a literary tradition for mincing words which later became a social tradition and finally a mental habit of the Chinese.

The consequent difficulty of this literary craft caused the limitation of literacy in China, which needs no elaboration. The limitation of literacy in turn changed the whole organization of Chinese society and the whole complexion of Chinese culture, and one sometimes wonders whether the Chinese people as a whole would be so docile and so respectful to their superiors had they spoken an inflexional language and consequently used an alphabetic language. I sometimes feel that, had the Chinese managed to retain a few more final or initial consonants in their language, not only would they have shaken the authority of Confucius to its foundations, but very possibly would have long ago torn down the political structure and, with the general spread of knowledge and given the millenniums of leisure, would have forged ahead in other lines and given the world a few more inventions like printing and gunpowder which would have likewise affected the history of human civilization on this planet.

III. SCHOLARSHIP

Before we pass on to the non-classical literature, or literature of the imagination, achieved by obscure or unknown writers who broke through the classical tradition and wrote out of the gladness of their hearts and for the sheer delight of creation— in other words, before we pass on to those novels and dramas which constitute literature *par excellence* in the Western sense, it is perhaps proper to examine the content of classical literature, the qualities of Chinese scholarship, and the life and education of that mass of educated men who feed on the people, moralize a lot and create nothing. What do these scholars write and what is their mental occupation?

China is a land of scholars, where scholars are the ruling class, and in times of peace, at least, the worship of scholarship has always been sedulously cultivated. This worship of scholarship has taken the form of a popular superstition that no paper bearing writing should be thrown about or used for indecent purposes, but should be collected and burned at schools or temples. In times of war the story is slightly different, for soldiers used to go into a scholar's house and either burn old rare editions as fuel, or blow their noses with them, or commit them to a general conflagration. Yet so stupendous was the literary activity of the nation that the more books the soldiers burned, the bigger the collections of books became.

In the Sui Dynasty, around the year 600, the imperial dynasty already counted 370,000 volumes. In the T'ang Dynasty the imperial collection numbered 208,000 volumes. In the year 1005, in the Sung Dynasty, the first encyclopædia, consisting of 1,000 volumes, was compiled. The next great imperial collection, the *Yunglo Tatien*, collected under Emperor Yunglo (1403–1424), consisted of 22,877 books, in 11,995 volumes, of selected rare ancient works. In the Manchu Dynasty, the most statesmanlike act of Emperor Ch'ienlung was to make a thorough overhauling of extant books for the ostensible purpose of preserving them, but with the equally important purpose of destroying works that savoured of dissatisfaction with the alien régime, and he succeeded in collecting 36,275 volumes which were preserved originally in seven sets in the well-known *Ssŭk'u Ch'ŭanshu*. But he also succeeded in ordering the complete or partial destruction of about 2,000 books, involving about a score of cases of dismissal from office, imprisonment, flogging or death of the authors, sometimes including the destruction of their ancestral temples and the selling of their family as slaves—all this because of the misuse of a word. The figures of both the *Yunglo Tatien* and the *Ssŭk'u Ch'ŭanshu* represented a selection of works worthy of preservation according to the orthodox standards. There was a slightly higher number of works which received honourable mention, with a brief description in the catalogue, but these were not collected in the *Ssŭk'u Ch'ŭanshu* for perpetuation. These, of course, did not include the truly creative works like *All Men Are Brothers* or the *Red Chamber Dream*, although they included a tremendous amount of *pichi*, or "notebooks," on odds and ends, from historical researches to notes on tea-leaves and famous springs and sketches of foxes, water spirits and chaste widows, which were the delight of the Chinese scholars.

What, then, did these books talk about? A review of the orthodox classification system of Chinese libraries, handed down from the *Ssŭk'u Ch'ŭanshu*, would be of interest. Chinese books are classified into the four big divisions: (*a*) Classics, (*b*) History, (*c*) Philosophy, and (*d*) Collected Works or Literature. The Classics Division includes the classics and classic philology, which waste the greater part of Chinese scholars' time. The History Divison includes dynastic histories, special histories, biography, miscellaneous records, geography (including travel sketches and local history of districts or famous mountains), civil service system, laws and statutes, bibliography, and historical criticism. The Philosophy Division originally borrowed its name from the schools of philosophy of the Chou Dynasty, but was made to include all the special arts and sciences of China (as in the "Faculty of Philosophy" of a Western university), including military science, agriculture, medicine, astronomy, astrology, necromancy, fortune-telling, boxing, calligraphy, painting, music, house decoration, cuisine, botany, biology, Confucianism, Buddhism, Taoism. reference works. and a host of the above-mentioned "notebooks," containing a wilderness of promiscuous, un-shifted, unscrutinized and unclassified data on all phenomena of the universe, with a preference for the weird and the super-natural. In popular bookshops the novels are also included in this division. The Collected Works Division may be called the Literature Division, because it includes the collected works of scholars, literary criticism, and special collections of poetry and drama.

The array of sciences is more imposing than an examination of their contents would show. Actually, there are no special sciences in China, outside the serious sciences of classic philology and history, which are truly branches of exact classified know-ledge, and which provide fields for painstaking research. Astronomy, apart from the works of Jesuit disciples, is very near astrology, and zoology and botany are very near *cuisine*, since so many of the animals and fruits and vegetables are eatable. Medicine usually occupies the same shelf in ordinary book stores as necromancy and fortune-telling. Psychology, sociology, engineering, and political economy are hidden all over among the notebooks, and writers whose books get into the classification of botany and zoology in the Philosophy Division or Miscellaneous Records in the History Division achieve that distinction by the more specialized nature of their notes, but, with the exception of oustanding works, do not essentially depart from the notebooks in the Literature Division in spirit and technique.

Chinese scholars have briefly three lines in which to develop their peculiar genius: real scholarly research, political candi-dacy, and literature in the classical sense, and we may accord-ingly classify Chinese scholars into the three types, scholars, the gentry, and writers. The training for the scholar and the candidate of official examinations is so different that there must be an early choice between the two. There was a *chüjen*, or candidate of the second rank, who had never heard of *Kungyangchüan*, one of the "Thirteen Confucian Classics" and there were many learned scholars who for their life could not have written an "eight-legged essay" to pass the official examinations.

But the spirit of old Chinese scholarship was admirable. The best of the scholars corresponded to the scientist type of Europe, with the same scientific devotion to learning and capacity for drudgery, although often without the scientific technique, and their works lacked the Western lucidity of style and cogent reasoning. For old Chinese scholarship meant immense drudgery, a prodigious learning and an almost superhuman memory, made possible only by a lifelong devotion to learning. There were scholars who could repeat Ssŭma Ch'ien's voluminous *History* from beginning to end, for without an index system man had to trust to his store of memory. In fact, easily located knowledge which could be found in any encyclopædia was rather looked down upon, and good scholars did not need encyclopædias. We had many such walking encyclopædias in flesh and blood. And after all, when it came to digging up original sources, it did not matter in the old scheme of life whether one found them at a moment's notice or after wasting a whole day. The English nobility used to spend a whole day on a fox-hunt, and did not enjoy it the less, and Chinese scholars found the same excitement in "scenting" their game, the same disappointment after finding a red herring and the same joy when they had tracked the fox to its lair. In this spirit, monumental works were produced by individual scholars, like the encyclopædias of Ma Tuanlin or Cheng Ch'iao, or the etymological dictionary of Chu Chünsheng, or the *Shuowen* Commentary of Tuan Yüts'ai. In the beginning of the Manchu Period, the scholar Ku Yenwu, in his research on Chinese cultural geography, used to travel with three carts of books, and whenever he found discrepancies in material evidences or contradicting stories from old people from whom he collected first-hand data, he would check them in his books.

Such quest for knowledge was in spirit no different from the labours of Western scientists. There were certain fields in Chinese learning which offered an opportunity for painstaking and disciplined research. Such fields were, for instance, the evolution of the Chinese script (*shuowen*), the history of Chinese sounds, the emendation of ancient texts, the restoration of lost texts from quotations, the study of ancient rites, customs, ceremonials, architecture and costumes, the verification of names of animals and fishes in the classics, the study of bronze, stone and bone inscriptions, the study of foreign names in the history of the Mongol Dynasty. Others had as their hobbies the ancient non-Confucian philosophers, the Yüan dramas, the *Book of Changes (Yiking)*, Sung philosophy (*lihsüeh*), history of Chinese painting, ancient coins, Chinese Turkestan, the Mongol dialects, etc. So much depended on the teachers with whom they came in contact and on the fashion of academic studies of the period. In the middle of the Manchu régime, when Chinese philologic scholarship had reached its summit, there were collected in the *Huangch'ing Chingchieh* and *Shu Huangch'ing Chingchieh* about four hundred works running to over a thousand volumes, consisting of scholarly treatises on extremely specialized topics, very similar in nature and spirit to the doctorate dissertations of modern universities, only with a maturer scholarship and involving much longer years of labour, one of which I know took the author thirty years.

IV. The College

But true scientists are as rare in China as they are in the West. On the other hand, we have as many political candidates as there are Ph.D.s in America, men who need a rank to earn their own bread and other people's respect. Perhaps the Chinese official candidates are a greater pest to society than the American Ph.D.s. Both of them pass an examination which means no more or less than that the candidate has done a certain amount of drudgery with a mediocre intelligence, both of them want the rank for purely commercial reasons, and both of them have received an education which totally unfits them for anything except the handling of books and the peddling of knowledge.

The Chinese Ph.D.s, however, had a distinctly official favour about them. There were among them real talents, who took these degrees for no earthly reason except the fun and ease of taking them, and who climbed very high, reaching the last stage of imperial examinations, becoming a *chinshih* or *hanlin*. These went out as magistrates or became officials in the capital. The great majority of them sunk in the first or second grades, called *hsiuts'ai* (B.A.) and *chüjen* (M.A.) respectively. Still a greater majority never reached even the first grade, and they were called the "students" or *chusheng*. There were many such "students" (men of mature age) fed by their districts from official or municipal foundations, and these swarmed in the countryside like so many unemployed.

Among the first two grades or those of no grade at all, the better type became schoolmasters, while the worse ones became the "local gentry." They were amateur lawyers who handled lawsuits for a living, working hand in hand with the yamen bureaucrats, or bought out "tax monopolies," working hand in hand with the local rich. They did not know anything about scholarship except that they could repeat the texts of the *Five Classics* by rote, and in most cases also the official commentaries by Chu Hsi, which were for them the one and only correct interpretation of Confucian truths. They could not write good poetry, and their training for the official examinations was so limited in scope and the eight-legged essay style they had learned was so conventional that they could not write either a correct newspaper report of events or a simple business note involving rather vulgar names of commodities, in which experienced business men easily surpassed them. But their power was not to be despised. They had a class consciousness, a class organization, and a class ideology. I quote in part from Ku Yenwu in his Essays on these "Students," written at the beginning of the Manchu régime.

There must be half a million of these students in the three hundred *hsien*. What they learn is writing for the examinations, and not one in several tens can write decently. Not one in a thousand really has mastered the classic learning and could be used by the Emperor. . . . They are excused from official labour, are free from the oppression of the bureaucrats and exempt from the punishment of flogging at court, and may call on magistrates in their scholars' gowns. Hence many people desire to be students, not necessarily for the honour of the title, but for the protection of their persons and their families. Taking seventy per cent as the average, we have then three hundred and fifty thousand students in the country who come for such official protection. . . . It is these students who go in and out of the yamen to interfere with the administration. It is these students who rely on such power and bully the country people. It is these students who make friends with the yamenites or become yamenites themselves. It is these students who, whenever the administration does not follow their wish, bind themselves together in a row. It is these students who know the secrets of the officialdom and trade with them. . . . With the slightest rebuff, they cry out, "You are killing the scholars. You are burying Confucianists." . . . The greatest trouble of a country is made when strangers come together and form a party. These students come from all parts of the land, some from a distance of several hundred *li*, others from a distance of ten thousand *li*. They do not know each other's names or dialects. But once they have passed the examinations . . . they form a solid, unbreakable block. The mails are full of their letters of recommendation, and officialdom is full of their private requests. . . .

Ku wrote in an age when this evil had been especially aggravated, but the parasitic nature of these B.A.s and M.A.s, or educated loafers, is essentially unchanged down to this day, when they have been redubbed "college graduates."

Not all of them, of course, are such blackguards. There are in every town and village good, retiring, thrifty and contented scholars, who belong to the oppressed rather than the oppressing class, because they choose to remain poor. Occasionally there are some sound scholars in a town who purposely avoid the examinations and bury themselves in their own learning. It is often from these people or from the more talented and successful candidates that scholarly works are to be expected.

After all, the old scholar is, on the whole, a sounder product than the modern college graduate. His knowledge of world geography is less reliable, but his training in character and ordinary manners is more thorough. Both the old and modern educational systems suffer from the foolish belief that you can weigh a man's knowledge by a series of examinations, which must by necessity be of a mechanical nature, and which must concentrate on the storing of information rather than on the development of a critical mind. For a critical mind cannot be easily graded or given a marking of 75 or 93, while a question on the dates of the Punic Wars can. Moreover, any college examination must be of such a nature that students can prepare for it at a week's notice, or all of them will flunk, and any knowledge that can be crammed at a week's notice can be forgotten in as short a period. There have not yet been devised any series of examinations which are cram-proof and student-proof, and the victims are only the professors who are led to believe that their students have really understood their subjects.

The old college system, whether in the village school or in the *shuyüan* (college of higher standard), had a distinct advantage over the modern one, for the simple fact that, except for the official examinations which were entirely optional, it did not rely on the counting of "units" and "marks." It was a tutorial system, where the teacher knew exactly what his pupils had or had not read, and where there was a very close and intimate relationship between teacher and student. No one was promoted, and no one ever "graduated," and no one studied for a diploma, because there was none. Above all, no one was obliged to mark time and wait for the last lame sheep to jump over the fence. No one was required to read three pages of economics on a Thursday morning and stop at the second paragraph; he could read to the end of the chapter if he wanted, and he had to if he was truly interested. And last of all, no one believed, or tried to make others believe, that by piling up "units" of psychology, religion and salesmanship and English constitutional history on a person, you can create an educated man out of him. No one believed, or tried to make others believe, that you can "test" a man's appreciation of Shakespeare by either a "paraphrase" of any passage or by asking a question on the date of authorship of *Othello*, or by making him answer questions on Elizabethan idioms. The only thing a college education really does for a man is to instil in him such a permanent distaste for Elizabethan idioms and the De Valorem commentaries that for the remainder of his life he will shun Shakespeare as he shuns poison.

V. PROSE

There was very little good prose in the classical Chinese literature. This statement perhaps sounds extremely unfair and needs clarification. There are many samples of high-flown, rhetorical prose, excellent in their way and possessing great virtuosity; there are also many samples of poetic prose, which by their cadence of vowels are eminently singable. In fact, the regular way of reading prose whether at schools or in private was to *sing* them. There is really no appropriate word for this type of reading in English; the so-called "singing" is to read the lines aloud with a kind of regulated and exaggerated intonation, not according to any particular tune, but following more or less the tonal values of the vowels in a general tune, somewhat similar to the reading of the "lesson" by the dean of an Episcopalian church, but with the syllables a great deal more drawn out.

This type of poetic prose is especially bad in the euphuistic compositions of the fifth and sixth centuries, which developed directly out of the *fu*, or high-flown prose, used in imperial eulogies, as unnatural as any court poetry and as awkward as a Russian ballet. Such euphuistic prose, running in parallel constructions of alternate sentences of four and six syllables—hence called the *ssŭlin* or "four-six style," also called *p'ient'i* or "parallel style"—was possible only in a dead and highly artificial language, entirely cut apart from the living realities of the age. But neither euphuistic prose, nor poetic prose, nor high-flown rhetorical prose is good prose. These may be called good prose only by a wrong literary standard. By good prose I mean prose which has the sweep and rhythm of a good chat by the fireside, such as used by the great story-tellers like Defoe or Swift or Boswell. Now it is clear that such prose is possible only in a living, and not in an artificial, language. Extremely good prose there is in the non-classical literature of novels written in the spoken language, but we are speaking of classical writings.

The use of the literary language, with its peculiarly crisp style, makes this almost impossible. First, good prose must be able to reflect the prosaic facts of life, and for this task the old literary language was unsuited. Secondly, good prose must have the sweep and width of canvas for full display of its powers, and the classical tradition always inclined to extreme economy of words. It believed in concentration, selection, sublimation and reorganization. Good prose must not be dainty, and the aim of classical prose was only to be dainty. Good prose must move along with natural big strides, and classical prose only moved about on bound feet, where every step was an artistic gesture. Good prose requires perhaps ten to thirty thousand words for a full-length portrait of a character, as for instance in Lytton Strachey's or Gamaliel Bradford's portraits, and Chinese biographical sketches always limited themselves to between two hundred and five hundred words. Good prose must not have too well-balanced constructions, and the euphuistic prose was distinctly too well-balanced.

Above all, good prose must be familiar, chatty and a little personal, and the Chinese literary art consisted in concealing one's feelings and putting on an impersonal front. One would expect a biography of at least five thousand words from Hou Ch'aochung, giving an intimate portrait of his lover Li Hsiangchün, and then finds that Hou did his *Biography of Miss Li* in exactly three hundred and seventy-five words, written in a manner as if he were describing the virtues of his neighbour's grandmother. Owing to such a tradition, research on the lives of people of the past must for ever grope among sketches of three or four hundred words, giving the barest beggar's outline of facts.

The true fact is, the literary language was entirely unsuitable to discuss or narrate facts, which was the reason why writers of novels had to resort to the vernacular language. The *Chochüan*, written probably in the third century B.C., still commanded a power for describing battles. Ssŭma Ch'ien (140–80? B.C.), the greatest master of Chinese prose, still kept a close touch with the language of his day, and dared to incorporate words which later scholars would have sneered at as "vulgar," and his language still retained a virility unmatched by any later writer in the classical language. Wang Ch'ung (A.D. 27–107) still wrote good prose, because he wrote more or less as he thought, and was against the *précieux* style of writing. But after that good prose became almost impossible. The terseness and refinement which the literary language had come to may be seen in the following *Life of Mr. Wu Liu (Five Willows)* by T'ao Yüanming (A.D. 327–427), supposed to be a portrait of imself, in exactly one hundred and twenty-five Chinese words, nd held up as a literary model:

Mr. [Wu Liu] is a native of I don't know what place. His name and surname, too, are unknown. There are five willows by his house: hence the title. He is quiet and talks very little. [He] does not care for money or fame. [He] likes to read books, without trying to know their exact meaning. Whenever he appreciates [a passage], he is so happy as to forget about his food. He loves wine, but, being poor, cannot always provide it. His friends and relatives know this fact and they sometimes ask him to come over for a drink. He always finishes the wine, and makes up his mind to be drunk. After he gets drunk, he retires, and does not mind where he finds himself. His walls are bare and do not shelter him from wind or sunshine. He wears a short jacket of flax-cloth in tatters, and his rice-bowl is always empty. But he does not care. He often writes to amuse himself and indicates his ambition in life, and forgets all about the worldly successes or failures. He dies like that.

That is dainty prose, but not good prose, according to our efinition. It is an absolute proof that the language was dead. uppose one were compelled to read only prose of this type, /here the characterization is the vaguest, the facts are the imsiest, and the narration the barest—what would happen to ne's intellectual content?

This leads to a more important consideration of the intellecual content of Chinese prose works. If one picks up any 'Collected Works" of a writer, with which Chinese libraries nd book stores abound (these always forming the largest livision in Chinese catalogues), and examines its contents, one las the feeling of being lost in a desert of essays, sketches, iographies, prefaces, postscripts, ceremonial writings, official

Q

memorandums, and miscellaneous notes on a most promiscuous variety of topics, historical, literary and supernatural. A most characteristic fact is that almost all such works contain fifty per cent of poetry, and all scholars are poets. Remembering the fact that many of these authors have elsewhere written consecutive treatises on special topics, this promiscuity is perhaps pardonable. Against such kind considerations, however, is the fact that these essays and sketches contain the cream of the literary activity of many authors, and the only literary activity of most, and that they represent to the Chinese "literature" *par excellence*. A Chinese schoolboy, in cultivating a prose style, is made to repeat a selection of these essays and sketches as his literary models.

Further consider the fact that these represent the main bulk of the tremendous literary activities of a tremendous number of scholars of all ages of a tremendously literary-inclined nation, and one can feel only resignation or total disappointment. Perhaps we are judging it by a modern standard which is foreign to it. The human element is always there, too, human joys and sorrows, and back of these works there were always men whose personal lives or social surroundings we may be interested in. But being modern, we cannot help judging it by the modern standard. When one reads Kuei Yukuang's biographical sketch of his mother, which is the work of the foremost writer of his time and leader of a literary movement, and remembers that this is the highest product of a lifetime of devotion to learning, and then discovers in it only a purely linguistic *craftsmanship* in imitating the ancients, laid over a paucity of characterization, a vacuity of facts and a baldness of sentiment, one has a right to be disappointed.

Good prose there is in Chinese classical literature, but one will have to find it for oneself, with a new standard of valuation. Whether for liberation of thought and sentiment or for liberation of style, one will have to find it among a class of slightly unorthodox writers, with a slight tinge of heresy in them, who had so much intellectual content that they must have had a natural contempt for the carcass of style. Such writers are, for instance, Su Tungp'o, Yüan Chunglang, Yüan Mei, Li Liweng, Kung Ting-an, all of whom were intellectual rebels, and whose writings were either banned or greatly depreciated by the court critics at one time or another. They had that *personal* style of writing or of thought which orthodox scholars regarded as friendly to radical thought and dangerous to morality.

VI. LITERATURE AND POLITICS

It is natural that the bondage of language has brought with it the bondage of thought. The literary language was dead, so dead that it could not express an exact thought. It always lost itself in vague generalities. Brought up amidst such generalities, with a total lack of discipline in logical reasoning, Chinese scholars often displayed an extreme childishness of argument. This disparity between thought and literature brought about a situation where thought and literature were regarded as having no relation with one another.

This brings us to the relation between literature and politics. In order to understand Chinese politics, one should understand Chinese literature. Perhaps one should here avoid the word literature (*wenhsüeh*) and speak of *belles-lettres* (*wenchang*). This worship of *belles-lettres* as such has become a veritable mania in the nation. This is clearest in modern public statements, whether of a student body, a commercial concern, or a political party. In issuing such public statements, the first thought is how to make them nice-sounding, how to word them beautifully. And the first thought of a newspaper reader is whether such statements read nicely or not. Such statements almost always say nothing, but almost always say it beautifully. A palpable lie is praised if it is told in good form.

This has led to a type of *belles-lettres* which, when translated into English, seems extremely silly. Thus in a comparatively recent statement by an important political party we read: "Whoever violates our national sovereignty and invades our territory, we will drive them out! Whoever endangers the peace of the world, we will stop them! We are determined. . . . We are resolved to exert our utmost. . . . We must unite together. . . ." A modern public would refuse to accept such a statement. They would require a more exact analysis of the foreign and domestic political situation of the moment and a more detailed account of the ways and means by which they are going to "drive out" the invaders and "stop" the breakers of international peace. This literary malpractice is sometimes carried to stupid extremes, as when a commercial advertisement for silk stockings takes the form of a long five-hundred-word essay, beginning with "Since the Manchurian provinces have been lost. . . ."

That does not mean, however, that the Chinese people are simple-minded. Their literature is full of generalities, but it is not simple. Rather on the contrary, from this hedging about the problems and these vague generalities of expression, there has developed, strange to say, the utmost finesse of expression. The Chinese, versed in this literary training, have learned to read between the lines, and it is the foreigners' inability to read between the lines, or the fault of the bad translators in missing the "meaning beyond the words" (as we say in Chinese) that causes the foreign correspondents to curse both China and themselves for their inability to make head or tail of such cleverly-worded and apparently harmless public statements.

For the Chinese have developed an art of mincing words—largely due, as we have seen, to the monosyllabic character of the literary language—and we believe in words. It is words by which we live and words which determine the victory in a political or legal struggle. Chinese civil wars are always preceded by a battle of words in the form of exchange of telegrams. The public assiduously read this exchange of abusiveness or of polite recriminations or even brazen-faced lies, and decide which has a better literary style, while they appreciate fully that an ominous cloud is hanging over the horizon. This is called in Chinese "first politeness, and then weapons." The party about to revolt charges the central government with "corruption" and "selling the country to its enemy," while the central government more adroitly charges the rebelling party to "co-operate for peace" and "for the unity of the nation," "because we are living in a period of national trouble," etc., etc., while both armies move nearer and nearer the clashing line and dig deeper and deeper trenches. The party that finds a better-sounding pretext wins in the eyes of the public. The dead language therefore became a dishonest language. Anything is permissible so long as you call it by the wrong name.

Some instances of the Chinese literary finesse are the following. When a provincial government embarked on a policy of public sale of opium, it found an extremely clever war-cry of four syllables, "Imply banning in taxing," and the discovery of that slogan alone carried the policy through as no other slogan possibly could. When the Chinese government removed its capital from Nanking to Loyang following the Shanghai War, it found another slogan called "long-term resistance." In Szechuen some of the war-lords forced the farmers to plant opium, and had the cleverness to call it "laziness tax," the tax being on those farmers who are lazy enough not to plant opium. Recently, the same province has produced a new tax called "goodwill tax," *i.e.*, an extra tax on top of those which are already thirty times the regular farm tax, which is to bring about goodwill between the people and the soldiers by paying the soldiers and making it unnecessary for the unpaid army further to help themselves. That is why, when we are among ourselves, we laugh at the foreign devils for their "simple-mindedness."

Such literary catastrophes are possible only in a nation believing in a false literary standard, and are in fact merely the result of the wrong method of teaching composition in primary schools. A modern Chinese, seeing the performance of such a literary atrocity, can only do either of two things. First, he can take the traditional view of literature and blandly regard it as pure *belles-lettres*, which need have no correlation with the facts which the writing is supposed to convey—and then read between the lines. Or he must demand a closer approximation between words and thought and a new literary standard, with a language more capable of expressing man's life and thoughts. In other words, he must regard the prevalence of such verbose statements as a malpractice more of a literary than of a political origin. But he must also believe that unless such literary malpractices are weeded out, political malpractices must also follow.

VII. LITERARY REVOLUTION

A literary revolution was in fact necessary, and a literary revolution came in 1917, led by Dr. Hu Shih and Ch'en Tuhsiu, advocating the use of the spoken language as the literary medium. There were other revolutions before this. Han Yü in the T'ang Dynasty had revolted against the euphuistic style of the fifth and sixth centuries, and advocated the use of a simple style, bringing it back to a saner literary standard and giving us a more readable prose. But it was by going back to the early literature of the Chou Dynasty. This was still classical in point of view; it was only trying to imitate the ancients, and it was not easy. After Han Yü, literary fashions fluctuated between imitating the Chou Period and the Ch'in-Han Period, and when Han Yü himself became sufficiently ancient, the T'ang Period also became, at different times, a great period itself for imitation. The Sung people imitated the T'angs, and the Ming and Ch'ing writers imitated the T'angs and Sungs. Literary fashions became then a battle of imitations.

Only as late as the end of the sixteenth century did there rise a man who said that "modern people should write in the modern language," showing throughout a sound historical perspective. This was Yüan Chunglang, together with his two brothers. Yüan dared to incorporate words of ordinary intercourse and even slang words in his prose, and for a time he obtained great literary vogue, with a school of followers known as the Kung-an school (Kung-an being the name of Yüan's district). It was he, too, who advocated the liberation of prose from current formal and stylistic conventions. It was he who said that the way of writing essays was just to take the words down as they flow from your "wrist," *i.e.*, from your pen. It was he who advocated a personal, individualistic style, believing that literature was but the expression of one's personality, *hsingling*, which should not be repressed.

But the use of commonplace and slang words was soon frowned upon by the orthodox court critics, and this author received nothing except epithets like "frivolity," "inelegance," "unorthodoxy," in all histories of literature. Only as late as

1934 was this founder of the personal style of writing rescued from partial or total oblivion. Yüan also never had the courage, or the insight, to advocate the use of *pehhua*, or the vernacular tongue, in writing. It was rather the writers of popular novels who had given up all ambition to literary fame and who were forced to write in the *pehhua* to make their novels intelligible to the public that laid the true foundation of literature in the living tongue. Consequently, when Dr. Hu Shih advocated the use of this medium, he had, as he repeatedly insisted, the groundwork thoroughly prepared for him for nearly a thousand years by these novelists, and people writing in the new medium had ready first-class models before them. Hence its complete overwhelming success in the space of three or four years.

Two important changes followed the literary revolution. First, the cultivation of the personal, familiar style of writing, represented by the Chou brothers, Chou Tsojen and Chou Shujen ("Lusin"). It is noteworthy that Chou Tsojen was greatly influenced by the school of Yüan Chunglang. The second change was the so-called "Europeanization of Chinese" *in syntax as well as in vocabulary*, as silly in the former as it is inevitable in the latter. The introduction of Western terms is only natural, for old terms are not adequate to represent modern concepts. It began with Liang Ch'ich'ao in the eighteen nineties, but was greatly aggravated or accelerated after 1917. With the mania for Western things, this Europeanization of Chinese may well be regarded as an aggravation, but the style introduced is so foreign to the Chinese language that it cannot last. This situation is especially bad in translations of foreign works, which are as preposterous as they are unintelligible to the average Chinese reader.

Actually, such atrocities are perpetrated by translators for no other reason than their insufficient mastery of the foreign language, which forces them to translate word by word without sensing the total concept of the phrase. (*Notre-Dame de Paris* has actually been translated as "My Parisian Wife.") Imagine also the grotesqueness of translating long English relative clauses following their antecedents into Chinese, with the relative clauses (which do not exist in Chinese) changed into a long string of modifiers extending over several lines before coming to the word they modify. Certain changes are evident improvements, like the introduction of the loose construction. Whereas it was impossible to put an *if* clause behind the main clause (*I shan't go, if it rains*), it is now possible to do so. This makes the prose so much more supple and flexible.

Chinese prose has a great future before it. It can in time rival any national language in power and beauty. The best modern English prose is distinguished by a healthy mixture of concrete words of imagery, taken from the homely English language, and words of more exact definition and literary meaning, taken from the Romanic heritage. A written language which considers such expressions as "a *nose* for news," "the *cobwebs* of knowledge," "the *drift* of language," "riding on the *tide* of success" and "Lloyd George's *flirtations* with the Conservative Party" as good, standard English must remain a virile literary medium. A false literary standard which weeds out the words *nose, cobwebs, drift, tide,* etc., and enforces substitutes like *appreciation, accumulations, tendency, forward movement,* must at once lose this virility. The two components, concrete and abstract words, exist in great richness in the Chinese language. Its basic structure is concrete throughout, like the Anglo-Saxon words, and the literary heritage of the classical literature has left behind a vocabulary more stylistic and refined in meaning, which corresponds to the Romanic terminology in English. From the mixture of these two elements in the hands of a true literary craftsman there will yet emerge a prose of the greatest power and beauty.

VIII. Poetry

It seems fair to say that poetry has entered more into the fabric of our life than it has in the West and is not regarded with that amused indifference which seems quite general in a Western society. As I have already mentioned, all Chinese scholars are poets, or pretend to be, and fifty per cent of the contents of a scholar's collected works usually consists of poetry. The Chinese imperial examinations, ever since the T'ang Period, have always included the composition of poems among the important tests of literary ability. Even parents who had talented daughters to give away, and sometimes the talented girls themselves, often chose their bridegrooms on the strength of a few lines of really good poetry. Captives often regained their freedom or received extra courtesy by their ability to write two or three verses which appealed to the men in power. For poetry is regarded as the highest literary accomplishment and the surest and easiest way of testing a man's literary skill. Moreover, Chinese painting is closely connected with Chinese poetry, being akin to it, if not essentially identical with it, in spirit and technique.

To my mind, poetry has taken over the function of religion in China, in so far as religion is taken to mean a cleansing of man's soul, a feeling for the mystery and beauty of the universe, and a feeling of tenderness and compassion for one's fellowmen and the humble creatures of life. Religion cannot be, and should not be, anything except an inspiration and a living emotion. The Chinese have not found this inspiration or living emotion in their religions, which to them are merely decorative patches and frills covering the seamy side of life, having largely to do with sickness and death. But they have found this inspiration and living emotion in poetry.

Poetry has taught the Chinese a view of life which, through the influence of proverbs and scrolls, has permeated into society in general and given them a sense of compassion, an overflowing love of nature, and an attitude of artistic acceptance of life. Through its feeling for nature it has often healed the wounds in their souls, and through its lesson of enjoyment of the simple life it has kept a sane ideal for the Chinese civilization. Sometimes it appeals to their romanticism and gives them a vicarious emotional uplift from the humdrum workaday world, and sometimes it appeals to their feeling of sadness, resignation and restraint, and cleanses the heart through the artistic reflection of sorrow. It teaches them to listen with enjoyment to the sound of raindrops on banana leaves, to admire the chimney smoke of cottages rising and mingling with the evening clouds nestling on a hillside, to be tender toward the white lilies on the country path, and to hear in the song of the cuckoo the longing of a traveller for his mother at home. It gives them a kind thought for the poor tea-picking girl or for the mulberry maiden, for the secluded and forsaken lover, for the mother whose son is far away in army service, and for the common people whose lives are harassed by war. Above all, it teaches them a pantheistic union with nature, to awake and rejoice with spring, to doze off and hear time visibly flying away in the droning of the cicada in summer, to feel sad with the falling autumn leaves, and "to look for lines of poetry in snow" in winter. In this sense, poetry may well be called the Chinaman's religion. I hardly think that, without their poetry—the poetry of living habits as well as the poetry of words—the Chinese people could have survived to this day.

Yet Chinese poetry would not have achieved such an important place in Chinese life without definite reasons for it. First, the Chinese artistic and literary genius, which thinks in emotional concrete imagery and excels in the painting of atmosphere, is especially suitable to the writing of poetry. Their characteristic genius for contraction, suggestion, sublimation and concentration, which unfits them for prose within the classical limits, makes the writing of poetry natural and easy to them. If, as Bertrand Russell says, "in art they aim at being exquisite, and in life as being reasonable," then it is natural for them to excel in poetry. Chinese poetry is dainty. It is never long, and never very powerful. But it is eminently fitted for producing perfect gems of sentiment and for painting with a few strokes a magical scenery, alive with rhythmic beauty and informed with spiritual grace.

The whole tenor of Chinese thought, too, encourages the writing of poetry as the highest crown of the literary art. Chinese education emphasizes the development of the all-round man, and Chinese scholarship emphasizes the unity of knowledge. Very specialized sciences, like archæology, are few, and the Chinese archæologists always remain human, capable of taking an interest in their family or in the pear tree in their courtyard. Poetry is exactly that type of creation which calls for man's faculty of general synthesis; in other words, for man's ability to look at life as a whole. Where they fail in analysis, they achieve in synthesis.

There is yet another important reason. Poetry is essentially

thought coloured with emotion, and the Chinese think always
with emotion, and rarely with their analytical reason. It is no
mere accident that the Chinese regard the belly as the seat of
all their scholarship and learning, as may be seen in such
expressions, "a bellyful of essays" or "of scholarship." Now
Western psychologists have proved the belly to be the seat of
our emotions, and as no one thinks completely without emotion,
I am ready to believe that we think with the belly as well as
with the head. The more emotional the type of thinking, the
more are the intestines responsible for one's thoughts. What
Isadora Duncan said about women's thoughts originating in
the abdomen and travelling upward, while men's thoughts
originate in the head and travel downward, is true of the
Chinese. This corroborates my theory about the femininity of
the Chinese mind (Chapter III). Whereas we say in English
that a man "ransacks his brain" for ideas during a composition,
we say in Chinese that he "ransacks his dry intestines" for a
good line of poetry or prose. The poet Su Tungp'o once asked
his three concubines after dinner what his belly contained.
The cleverest one, Ch'aoyün, replied that he had "a bellyful
of unseasonable thoughts." The Chinese can write good poetry
because they think with their intestines.

Further, there is a relation between Chinese language and
poetry. Poetry should be crisp, and the Chinese language is
crisp. Poetry should work by suggestion, and the Chinese
language is full of contractions which say more than what the
words mean. Poetry should express ideas by concrete imagery,
and the Chinese language revels in word-imagery. Finally,
the Chinese language, with its clear-cut tones and its lack of
final consonants, retains a sonorous singing quality which has
no parallel in non-tonal languages. Chinese prosody is based
on the balance of tonal values, as English poetry is based
on accent. The four tones are divided into two groups: the
"soft" tones (called *p'ing*), long and theoretically even but
really circumflex, and the "hard" tones (called *tseh*), which
consist of acute, grave and abrupt tones, the last theoretically
ending in *p*, *t*, *k*'s, which have disappeared in modern mandarin.
The Chinese ear is trained to sense the rhythm and alternation
of soft and hard tones. This tonal rhythm is observed even in

good prose, which explains the fact that Chinese prose is "singable" (see page 219). For anyone who has ears, this tonal rhythm can be easily sensed in Ruskin's or Walter Pater's prose. Observe the contrast between words ending in "liquids" like *l, m, n, ng* and words ending in "explosives" like *p, t, k* in Ruskin's writings, and this total rhythm can be easily analysed.

In classical T'ang poetry this alternation is quite complex, as in the following "regular" scheme ("o" standing for the soft tones and "●" standing for the hard tones). In reading the following, say "sing" for "o" and "*say*" for "●", to feel the contrasting effect, giving the *says* a final, more or less abrupt tone:

$$
\begin{cases}
1. & \circ \ \circ \ \bullet \ \bullet \ \bullet \ \circ \ \circ \quad \text{(rhyme)} \\
2. & \bullet \ \bullet \ \bullet \ \circ \ \circ \ \bullet \ \bullet \ \circ \quad \text{(rhyme)}
\end{cases}
$$

$$
\begin{cases}
3. & \bullet \ \bullet \ \bullet \ \circ \ \circ \ \circ \ \bullet \ \bullet \\
4. & \circ \ \circ \ \bullet \ \bullet \ \bullet \ \circ \ \circ \quad \text{(rhyme)}
\end{cases}
$$

$$
\begin{cases}
5. & \circ \ \circ \ \bullet \ \bullet \ \circ \ \circ \ \bullet \\
6. & \bullet \ \bullet \ \circ \ \circ \ \bullet \ \bullet \ \circ \quad \text{(rhyme)}
\end{cases}
$$

$$
\begin{cases}
7. & \bullet \ \bullet \ \circ \ \circ \ \circ \ \bullet \ \bullet \\
8. & \circ \ \circ \ \bullet \ \bullet \ \bullet \ \circ \ \circ \quad \text{(rhyme)}
\end{cases}
$$

After the fourth syllable in each line there is a hiatus. Each two lines form a couplet by themselves, and the middle two couplets must be real couplets, *i.e.*, all the words in each line must be balanced against corresponding words in the other line, both in tone and meaning. The easiest way to understand this sense of alternation is to imagine two interlocutors speaking to one another, each speaking a line. Take the first four and the last three syllables of each line as two individual units, and substitute for them two English words, and the result is a pattern as outlined below.

(A) ah, yes?
(B) but, no?

(A) but, yes!
(B) ah, no!
(A) ah, yes?
(B) but, no?
(A) but, yes!
(B) ah, no!

Notice that the second interlocutor always tries to counter the first, while the first always takes up the thread of the second in its first unit (the "ahs" and "buts") but varies the second unit. The exclamation and question marks merely serve to indicate that there are two different kinds of "yeses" and "noes." Notice that with the exception of the second unit of the first couplet all the units are properly balanced in tone.

But we are more interested in the inner technique and spirit of Chinese poetry than in its prosody. By what inner technique did it enter that magic realm of beauty? How did it throw a veil of charm and atmosphere over an ordinary landscape and, with a few words, paint a striking picture of reality, surcharged with the poet's emotion? How did the poet select and eliminate his material and how did he inform it with his own spirit and make it glow with rhythmic vitality? In what way was the technique of Chinese poetry and Chinese painting really one? And why is it that Chinese poets are painters, and painters, poets?

The striking thing about Chinese poetry is its plastic imagination and its kinship in technique with painting. This is most evident in the handling of perspective. Here the analogy between Chinese poetry and painting is almost complete. Let us begin with perspective. Why is it that when we read the lines of Li Po (701–762)—

Above the man's face arise the hills;
Beside the horse's head emerge the clouds,

we are presented with a picture in bold outline of a man travelling on horseback on a high mountain path? The words, short and sharp and meaningless at first sight, will be found, with a moment's use of the imagination, to give us a picture as a painter would paint it on his canvas, and conceal a trick of perspective by using some objects in the foreground ("the man's face" and "the horse's head") to set off the distant view. Entirely apart from the poetic feeling that the man is so high up in the mountains, one realizes that the scenery was looked at by the poet as if it were a piece of painting on a flat surface. The reader would then see, as he actually sees in paintings or snapshots, that hilltops seem to rise from the man's face and the clouds nestling somewhere in the distance form a line broken by the horse's head. This clearly was not possible if the poet was not on horseback and the clouds were not lying on a lower level in the distance. In the end, the reader has to imagine himself on horseback on a high mountain path and view the scene from the same perspective as the poet did.

In this way, and really through this trick of perspective, these pen-pictures gain a bold relief impossible with other methods. It cannot be said that the Chinese poets were conscious of the theory of this technique, but had in any case found the technique itself. Hundreds of examples might be cited. With this technique of perspective, Wang Wei (699–759), probably China's greatest descriptive poet, said:

> In the mountains a night of rain,
> And above the trees a hundred springs.

Of course, it requires a little effort to imagine "springs on tree-tops" (which are the exact words in the original); but exactly because such a perspective is so rare and can only be found when high mountain gorges, forming, after the previous night's rainfall, a series of cascades in the distance, appear above the outline of some trees in the foreground, the reader gains a clear perspective otherwise impossible. As with the former example from Li Po, the art lies in the selection of an object in the foreground to set it off against the objects in the distance, like clouds, cascades, hilltops and the Milky Way, and then painting these together *on a flat surface*. Thus Liu Yühsi (772–842) wrote:

> [For an] autumn scene: several dots of hills
> over the wall.

The picture technique here is perfect: the hilltops appearing as several "dots" over the wall give one a stereoscopic sense of distance from the hills. In this sense, we can understand Li Liweng (seventeenth century), when he says in one of his dramatic works:

> First we look at the hills in the painting,
> Then we look at the painting in the hills.

The poet's eye is the painter's eye, and painting and poetry become one.

This affinity between painting and poetry is all the more natural and apparent when we consider not only their similarity of technique, but also their similarity of themes, and the fact that the title of a painting is often actually a line taken from some verse. In any case, the painter after finishing his painting usually writes a verse at the top in those vacant spaces characteristic of Chinese paintings. Of this, more later on when we discuss painting proper. But this affinity is responsible for another point in Chinese poetry, viz., the impressionistic technique. It is a technique which gives a series of impressions, vivid and unforgettable, and leaves merely a flavour, an indefinable feeling behind, which awakes the reader's senses but does not satisfy his understanding. Chinese poetry is consummate in the art of sublimation, suggestion and artistic restraint. The poet does not try to say all he has to say. His business is but to evoke a picture, making a pen sketch by a few swift, clear strokes.

Hence arose the great school of pastoral poets, specializing in landscape paintings and using the impressionistic technique. Such masters in pastoral poetry are T'ao Yüanming (372–427), Hsieh Lingyün (385-433?), Wang Wei (699–759) and Wei Ingwu (740–c. 830), but the technique is practically universal with Chinese poets. Of Wang Wei (perhaps better known as Wang Mochieh) it is said that "there is poetry in his painting and painting in his poetry," because Wang was a great painter himself. His *Wangch'üanchi* is nothing but a collection of pastoral landscapes. A poem like the following can only be written by one inspired by the spirit of Chinese painting:

> Amidst the mist-like autumn showers,
> Shallow the stony rapids flow;
> Its sprays besprinkle one another,
> Up and down the egrets go.
> —*The Lüanchia Rapids.*

And here we come to the problem of suggestion. Some modern Western painter has attempted the impossible by trying to paint "the sound of sunshine going upstairs," but the problem of artistic limitations has been partly overcome by Chinese painters by the use of suggestion, really developed by the poetic art. One can actually paint sounds and smell by the method of suggestion. A Chinese painter would paint the sound of temple bells without showing the bells at all on the canvas, but possibly by merely showing the top of a temple roof hidden among trees, and the effect of the sound on men's faces. Interesting is the method of Chinese poets in suggesting smell, which lends itself to pictorial handling. Thus a Chinese poet describing the fragrance of the open country would write:

> Coming back over flowers, fragrant are the
> horse's hoofs.

Nothing would be easier than painting a flock of butterflies flitting after the horse's hoofs, which is what a Chinese painter actually did. By the same technique of suggestion, the poet Liu Yühsi wrote about the fragrance of a court lady:

> In her new dress, she comes from her vermilion towers;
> The light of spring floods the palace which Sorrow embowers.
> To the court she comes, and on her carved jade hair-pin
> Alights a dragon-fly, as she is counting the flowers.

The lines suggest to the reader the beauty and fragrance both of the carved jade hair-pin and of the lady herself, a beauty and fragrance which deceived the dragon-fly.

From this impressionistic technique of suggestion arose that method of suggesting thought and sentiments which we call symbolic thinking. The poet suggests ideas, not by verbose

statements but by evoking a mood which puts the reader in
that train of thought. Such thoughts are as indefinable as the
scene which evokes them is clear and vivid. Picturesque
scenery is then used to suggest certain thoughts very much in
the same way as certain chords in the Wagnerian operas are
used to suggest the entrance of certain characters. Logically,
there is little connection between the scenery and the man's
inner thoughts, but symbolically and emotionally, there is a
connection. The method, called *hsing*, or evocation, is as
ancient as the *Book of Poetry*. In T'ang poetry, for instance, the
passing of a fallen dynasty is variously expressed by such
symbolic method, without mentioning the thoughts themselves. Thus Wei Chuang sang of the past glories of Nanking
in the following manner in his poem *On a Painting of Chinling:*

> The rain on the river is mist-like, and the grass on the
>   banks is high.
> The Six Dynasties passed like a dream, and forlorn's the
>   birds' cry.
> Most heartless of all are the willows of the palace walls,
> Even now in a three-mile green, lurid resplendour they lie.

The scene of the three-mile-long willow-overgrown walls was
enough to remind his contemporaries of the past glories of
Ch'en Houchu in his most glorious days, and the mention of
the "heartless willows" strikes a contrast between human
vicissitudes and nature's serenity. By the same technique, Po
Chüyi (772–846) expressed his sadness over the past glories of
T'ang Minghuang and Yang Kweifei by merely drawing a
picture of white-haired, old imperial chambermaids gossiping
in a deserted palace, without of course going into the details of
their discourse:

> Here empty is the country palace, empty like a dream,
> In loneliness and quiet the red imperial flowers gleam.
> Some white-haired, palace chambermaids are chatting.
> Chatting about the dead and gone Hsüanchuang régime.

In the same way Liu Yühsi sang about the decay of the Black-

gown Alley, which once was the home of the great Wang and
Hsieh families:

> Now by the Red-sparrow Bridge wild grasses are growing,
> And on the Blackgown Alley the ev'ning sun is glowing,
> And the swallows which once graced the Wang and
> Hsieh halls,
> Now feed in common people's homes—without their
> knowing.

The last and most important point is the investment of
natural objects with human actions, qualities and emotions,
not by direct personification but by cunning metaphors, like
"idle flowers," "the sad wind," "the chafing sparrow," etc.
The metaphors in themselves are nothing: the poetry consists
in the poet spreading his emotion over the scenery and com-
pelling it by the force of his emotion to live and share his own joys
and sorrows. This is clearest in the above example, where the
three-mile-long gay and green willows are referred to as "heartless" because they did not, as they ought to, remember Ch'en
Houchu and share the poet's feeling of poignant regret.

Once when I was travelling with a poet friend, our bus passed
a small secluded hillside, with just a single cottage, with all
doors closed and a solitary peach tree in full blossom standing
idly in front, apparently wasting its fragrant glory on a deserted
valley. I still remember the last two lines of the quatrain
which my friend sketched in his notebook:

> The farmer couple to the fields have gone,
> And dead-bored are the flowers outside its doors.

What is achieved, then, is a poetic feeling for the peach tree,
supposed to be capable of being "bored" to death, which
borders on pantheism. The same technique, or rather attitude,
is extremely common in all good Chinese poetry. So, for
instance, did Li Po begin one of his best poems:

> Late at twilight I passed the verdant hills,
> And the mountain moon followed me hom

Or, in one of his best-known poems, *Drinking Alone under the Moon:*

> A pot of wine amidst the flowers,
> Alone I drink sans company.
> The moon I invite as drinking friend,
> And with my shadow we are three.
> The moon, I see, she does not drink,
> My shadow only follows me:
> I'll keep them company a while,
> For spring's the time for gayety.
>
> I sing: the moon she swings her head;
> I dance: my shadow swells and sways.
> We sport together while awake,
> While drunk, we all go our own ways.
> An eternal, speechless trio then,
> Till in the clouds we meet again!

This is more than a metaphor: it is a poetic faith of union with nature, which makes life itself pulsate with human emotions.

The expression of this pantheism or fellowship with nature is best illustrated in Tu Fu's *Quatrains on Sundry Moods,* showing successively a humanizing of nature, a tender feeling for its mishaps, a sheer delight in its contact, and finally a complete union with it. So goes the first stanza:

> I see the traveller's unwaking sorrow.
> The vagabond spring's come in a clatter.
> Too profusely rich are the flowers,
> Too garrulous the parrots' chatter.

The words "vagabond," "garrulous," and "chatter" here indirectly invest the spring and the parrots with a human quality. Then he lodges a complaint against the brutal winds of last night, which "bullied" the peach and pear trees in his yard:

> My hand-planted pear trees are not orphans!
> The old man's low walls are like their house!
> But the spring wind thought fit to bully them,
> Last night it broke some of their boughs!

This tender feeling for the trees is repeated in the last stanza:

> Weak and tender is the willow next door,
> Like a fifteen-year-old maiden's waist.
> Who would have thought this morning that it happened,
> The wind did break its longest bough, its best!

Once more, the willows dancing gaily before the wind are referred to as *abandonnée*, and the peach blossoms which carelessly drop and float on the water wherever it might carry them are regarded as women of fickle character in the fifth stanza:

> I deeply rue the passing of spring,
> And on a cane I pace the scented isle.
> Before the winds dance the wanton willows,
> And on the water the petulous petals smile.

This pantheistic outlook sometimes loses itself in a sheer delight in contact with worms and flying insects as in the third stanza. But we may take an example from a Sung poet, Yeh Li, who wrote on *A Scene in Late Spring:*

> Pair by pair, little swallows on the bookshelves hop.
> Dot by dot, little petals on the ink-slab drop.
> Reading the *Book of Changes* I sit near a window,
> Forgetful how much longer spring will with us stop.

This subjectivity of outlook, coupled with an infinitely tender feeling for the birds and animals, enables Tu Fu to speak of the "clenching fists" of white egrets resting on the sand-bank, and of the "striking fins" of jumping fish near his boat. And here we see the most interesting point in Chinese poetry—the *Einfühlung*. The use of the word "fists" for the egrets' claws is then not merely a literary metaphor, for the poet has so identified himself with them that he probably feels the clenching himself and wishes his readers to share this emotional insight with him. Here we do not see the scientist's minute observation of details, but rather the poet's keenness

which comes from love, as sharp as a lover's eyes, and as un-
failing and correct as a mother's intuition. This *Einfühlung*,
this sharing of human emotions with the universe, this poetic
transformation of dead objects which makes the moss "mount"
one's doorstep and the colour of grass "enter" one's window-
screen, this poetic illusion, for illusion it is, is felt so intuitively
and so constantly that it seems to constitute the very essence of
Chinese poetry. An analogy ceases to be an analogy, but
becomes a poetic truth. A man must be indeed more or less
intoxicated with nature to write the following lines (by Ch'en
Ngo) about the lotus flower, suggestive of Heine:

> Lightly dips her green bonnet,
> When a zephyr past her has blown;
> Red and naked she shows herself,
> When she is sure of being alone.

This review of the two sides of the poetic technique, regarding its treatment of scenery (*ching*) and emotion (*ch'ing*), enables us to understand the spirit of Chinese poetry and its
cultural value to the nation. This cultural value is twofold,
corresponding to the broad classification of Chinese poetry
into the two types: (1) *haofang* poetry, or poetry of romantic
abandonment, carefree, given to a life of emotion, and expressing a revolt against the restraints of society and teaching a
profound love of nature, and (2) *wanyüeh* poetry, or poetry of
artistic restraint, tender, resigned, sad and yet without anger,
teaching a lesson of contentment and the love of one's fellow-
men, especially the poor and down-trodden, and inculcating a
hatred of war.

Among the first type may be classified Ch'ü Yüan (343-290
B.C.), the pastoral poets like T'ao Yüanming, Hsieh Lingyün,
Wang Wei, Meng Haojan (689-740), the crazy monk Hanshan
(around the year 900), while nearer Tu Fu are Tu Mu (803-
852), Po Chüyi, Yüan Chen (779-831) and the greatest
poetess of China, Li Ch'ingchao (1081-1141?). No strict
classification is, of course, possible, but there was a third group
of sentimental poets, like Li Ho (Li Ch'angchi, 790-816), Li
Shangyin (813-858) and his contemporary Wen T'ingyün,

Ch'en Houchu (ruler of Ch'en, 553–604) and Nalan Hsingteh (a Manchu, 1655–1685), most distinguished for their love lyrics.

The first type is best represented by Li Po, of whom Tu Fu says:

> With a jar of wine, Li makes a hundred poems,
> He sleeps in an inn of Ch'angan city.
> The Emperor sent for him and he'd not move,
> Saying, "I'm the God of Wine, Your Majesty!"

Li Po is China's prince of vagabond poets, with his drink, his dread of officialdom, his companionship with the moon, his love of high mountain scenery, and his constant aspiration:

> Oh, could I but hold a celestial sword
> And stab a whale across the seas!

Li Po's romanticism ended finally in his death from reaching for the shadow of the moon in the water in a drunken fit and falling overboard. Good, infinitely good, that the staid and apparently unfeeling Chinese could sometimes reach for the shadow of the moon and die such a poetic death!

Well it is that the Chinese had this love of nature which constituted the poetry of their existence, and which overflowed from the fullness of their hearts into literature. It taught the Chinese a more widespread love of birds and flowers than is usual among the common folk of other nations. I have seen a Chinese crowd get excited at the sight of a bird in a cage, which made them childish and good-humoured again, made them share a common feeling of gay irresponsibility and broke down the barriers of hostility among strangers, as only an object of common delight could. The worship of the pastoral life has coloured the whole Chinese culture, and to-day officials or scholars speak of "going back to the farm" as the most elegant, the most refined and most sophisticated ambition in life they can think of. The vogue is so great that even the deepest-dyed scoundrel of a politician will pretend that he has something of Li Po's romanticism in his nature. Actually I suspect even he is capable of such feelings, because after all he is a Chinese. As a Chinese, he knows how much life is worth, and at midnight, gazing through his window at the stars, the lines he learned at childhood come back to him:

> I was drunk, half asleep, through the whole livelong day.
> Hearing spring'd soon be gone, I hurried on my way.
> In a bamboo courtyard I chatted with a monk,
> And so leisurely passed one more half-day away.

To him, it is a prayer.

The second type is best represented by Tu Fu, with his quiet humour, his restraint, his tenderness toward the poor and oppressed, and his unconcealed hatred of war.

Well it is, too, that the Chinese have poets like Tu Fu and Po Chüyi, who portray our sorrows in beauty and beget in us a sense of compassion for mankind. Tu Fu lived in times of political chaos and banditry and soldiery and famine like our own, and wrote:

> Meats and wines are rotting in the mansions,
> And human bones are rotting outside their doors.

A similar note was struck in the *Song of the Mulberry Maiden* by Hsieh Fangteh:

> When cuckoos cried fourth watch in the dead of the night,
> Then I rose, lest the worms, short of leaves, hunger might.
> Who'd think that those dames weren't yet through with
>   their dance?
> The pale moon shone through willows o'er their windows
>   bright.

Note the peculiarly Chinese ending, where instead of driving home a socialistic thought, the poet contents himself with drawing a picture. Even then, this poem is a little too rebellious for the average Chinese poetry. The usual note is one of sadness and resignation, as in so many of Tu Fu's poems, describing the harassing effects of war, of which the following, *The Bailiff of Shihhao*, is a good example:

> I came to Shihhao village and stayed that eve.
> A bailiff came for press-gang in the night.
> The old man, hearing this, climbed o'er the wall,
> And the old woman saw the bailiff at the door.
> Oh, why was the bailiff's voice so terrible,
> And why the woman's plaint so soft and low?
> "I have three sons all at the Niehch'eng post.
> And one just wrote a letter home to say
> The other two had in the battle died.
> Let those who live live on as best they can,
> For those who've died are dead for evermore.
> Now in the house there's only grandson left;
> For him his mother still remains—without
> A decent patticoat to go about.
> Although my strength is ebbing weak and low,
> I'll go with you, bailiff, in the front to serve.
> For I can cook congee for the army, and
> To-morrow I'll march and hurry to the Hoyang front."
>
> —So spake the woman, and in the night, the voice
> Became so low it broke into a whimper.
> And in the morning with the army she went;
> Alone she said good-bye to her old man.

That is characteristic of the art of restraint and the feeling of sadness in Chinese poetry. It gives a picture, expresses a sentiment, and leaves the rest to the reader's imagination.

IX. DRAMA

The Chinese drama occupies a mean position between classical literature and that body of literature which is nearer what the Western people mean by the term, namely, literature of the imagination. The latter, including the dramas and novels, was written in the *pehhua* or vernacular language, and consequently was least ridden with classical standards, and constantly grew and profited from that freedom. Because Chinese dramatic composition happened to be largely poetry, it was accepted as literature on a higher level than the novels, and almost on a par with the T'ang lyrics. Scholars were less ashamed to be known as writing dramatic works than writing novels. On the whole, the authorship of dramas was not anonymous or subject to debate like the authorship of novels.

From now on we shall see how that body of imaginative literature constantly grew in beauty and importance until it compelled recognition in modern times on its own merits, and exerted an influence over the people as no classical literature ever succeeded in doing.

This hybrid character of the Chinese drama accounts for its peculiar composition and also for its great popular influence. The Chinese drama is a combination of dialogues in the spoken language, which on the whole is readily intelligible to the populace, and songs which are sung and often partake of a high poetic quality. Its nature is therefore entirely different from that of the conventional English play. The songs come in at short intervals and are more in prominence than the spoken parts. As is natural, the comic plays are more in dialogue, while the tragedies or dramas of human loves and sorrows more often burst out into songs. Actually, the theatre is attended, from the point of view of the Chinese theatre-goer, more for its singing than for its acting. One speaks of going to "listen" to a play, rather than to "see" it. It would seem, therefore, that the translation of the Chinese word *hsi* as "drama" is misleading, and it would be more proper to speak of it as Chinese "opera."

Only by understanding the Chinese *hsi* as a form of opera will its wide appeal to the people, as well as the peculiarities of its composition, be truly understood. For the appeal of the drama—especially of the modern English drama—is largely an appeal to the understanding, while the opera makes a combined appeal to the senses of colour, voice, atmosphere and emotion. The medium of the drama is the spoken language, but that of the opera is music and the song. A theatre-goer who attends a play expects to follow a story which pleases him

by its conflicts of character and its surprises and novelty of
action, and an opera-goer is prepared to spend an evening
during which his intellect is appropriately benumbed and his
senses soothed by music and colour and song.

This accounts for the fact that most dramatic performances
are not worth attending a second time, although people go to
the same operas for the fiftieth time without losing the edge of
their keen enjoyment. Thus it is with the Chinese theatre.
The so-called *chinghsi* ("Peking plays") has a general repertoire
of less than a hundred pieces which are played over and over
again without losing their popularity. And the people applaud
by shouting "*Hao!*" invariably at the arias which have the
most intense or intricate musical appeal. Music is therefore
the soul of the Chinese drama, and acting is merely an accessory
to the technique of the opera-singer, and remains on essentially
the same level as that of Western prima donnas.

The Chinese opera-goer, therefore, appraises the Chinese
actor under the two categories of his "singing" (*ch'ang*) and his
"acting" (*chuo*). But this so-called "acting" is often purely
technical and consists of certain conventional ways of expressing
emotions—in the West, what is to us the shockingly inartistic
heaving and swelling of the prima donna's chest, and in the
East, what is to Occidentals the ludicrous wiping of a tearless
eye by a long sleeve. If the actor has personal charm and beauty
and a good voice, this modicum of acting is always enough to
satisfy the audience. But when well done, every gesture may
be beautiful and every pose a perfect tableau. In this sense,
the popular appreciation of Mei Lanfang by Americans is
essentially correct, although how much of his singing is
appreciated *as* singing may be questioned. One marvels at
his beautiful poses and gestures, his graceful, white fingers, his
long black eyebrows, his feminine gait, his flirtatious side
glances and the whole outfit of his fake sex-appeal—the same
fake sex-appeal which ingratiates him with the Chinese
audience and is at the back of his tremendous popularity in
China. When done by so great an artist, this appeal is universal,
for it speaks the language of gestures, which is international as
music and dancing are international. So far as real acting in
the modern sense of the word is concerned, Mei Lanfang may

appropriately learn the A B Cs from Norma Shearer or Ruth Chatterton. When he holds a whip and pretends to be riding on horseback or when he plays at paddling a boat, his acting is neither better nor worse than that of my five-year-old daughter who plays at horse-riding by trailing a bamboo stick between her thighs.

If we study the construction of the Yüan and subsequent dramas, we shall find that the plot, as with Western operas, is often of the flimsiest character, the dialogue unimportant, while the songs occupy the centre of the play. In actual performances, very often popular selections from the operas, rather than the entire plays, are given, in the same manner that operatic selections are rendered in Western musical concerts. The audience knows the stories by heart, and the characters are recognized by their conventional masks and costumes rather than by the contents of the dialogue. The first Yüan dramas, as we see them in extant works of the masters, consisted, with a few exceptions, of four acts. The songs in each act were sung to a definite set of tunes in a well-known musical suite. The dialogues were unimportant, and in many existing copies they are left out, which is probably because the dialogue part was largely spoken extempore.

In the so-called "northern dramas" the songs in each act were sung by the same person, although many actors took part in the acting and the spoken dialogue (a limitation probably due to the scarcity of singing talent). In the "southern dramas" the limitations of dramatic technique were much less rigid; there was a great deal more freedom, and from these dramas were evolved the longer plays which in the Ming Dynasty were known as *ch'üanchi*. The number of acts (corresponding in length to the "scenes" in English plays) was no longer limited to four, different rhymes could be used in songs of the same act, several singers could sing in alternation or in unison in the same act, and the tunes themselves were different from those used in the northern dramas, being of the type which gives long modulations over single syllables.

Of such dramas, the *Western Chamber* (*Hsihsiang*) and *Autumn in the Han Palace* (*Hankungch'iu*, portraying the story of the exiled imperial concubine Chao Chün), may be taken as representative of the northern dramas, while the *Moon Pavilion* (*Paiyüeht'ing*) and the *Romance of the Guitar* (*P'ip'achi*) may be taken as representative of the southern dramas. The *Western Chamber*, although consisting of twenty acts, was strictly in the nature of a dramatic sequence of five plays, with four acts in each.

There is one difference between Chinese and Western opera. While in the West the opera is the privilege of the classes, very often attended for its social glitter and out of an "opera complex" rather than for real musical appreciation, so far as the occupants of the "golden horseshoe" are concerned, the Chinese operas are the mental food of the poor. Deeper than any other literary art, the operas have gone down to the hearts of the people. Imagine a people whose masses know the airs of *Tannhäuser* and *Tristan und Isolde* and *Pinafore* by heart, gaily singing them in the streets and at all odd moments, and you have a picture of the relation between Chinese operas and the Chinese masses. There is a type of mania in China, unknown in the West, called *hsimi* or "opera mania," and one may often see a maniac of the lower class, with dishevelled hair and clad in tatters, singing the airs of *K'ungch'engchi* and acting the part of the great Chuko Liang in the streets of old Peking.

Foreign visitors at Chinese theatres are often struck by the excruciating noise emanating from the gongs and drums in military plays and the equally nerve-racking falsetto of male singers, while the Chinese evidently cannot live without them. This must, on the whole, be credited to Chinese nerves, although the theory seems to be counter-evidenced by the apparent comfort with which Americans tolerate squeaks from the saxophone and other sound-madness from the jazz band which set any Chinese gentleman's nerves on end. It is possibly all a question of adaptation. But the origin of the drums and gongs and the falsetto can only be understood in the light of Chinese theatre surroundings.

The Chinese theatre of the better type was built in a yard like the Elizabethan theatre. In most cases, however, the stages consisted of temporary wooden racks, built high above the ground in the open, or sometimes right across a thoroughfare, to be taken down immediately after the occasion. The theatre was therefore in the open and the actors had to compete with the peddlers' cries, the barbers' tuning forks, the malt-sugar sellers' small gongs, the shouting of men, women and children and the barking of dogs. Above such a din, only a thin falsetto keyed in a high pitch could have been heard, as anybody may verify for himself. The gongs and drums were also used as a means of attracting attention; they always preceded the plays and could be heard a mile away, thus serving the purpose of street posters for the movies. When staged in a modern theatre building, the volume of noise thus produced is truly terrific, but somehow the Chinese have adapted themselves to it, as the Americans have adapted themselves to jazz. They want noise and they want life to get a "kick" out of it. Time will erase all this, and Chinese theatrical shows will eventually be tamed and "civilized" when they are housed in modern theatre buildings.

From a purely literary point of view, Chinese dramatic works contain a type of poetry which far surpasses the T'ang lyrics in power and beauty. It is my firm belief that, lovely as the T'ang poetry is, we have to go to the dramas and the odd dramatic songs (hsiaotiao) to find some of China's greatest poetry. For classical poetry moves more or less along certain traditional patterns of thought and style. It has a cultivated, super-refined technique, but it lacks grandeur and power and richness. The feeling one gets on turning from classical poetry to poetry in the dramas (and Chinese dramas are essentially regarded, as has been pointed out, as a collection of poems) is like turning from an exquisite plum branch in a vase to one's ontside garden, so much superior in freshness, richness and variety.

Chinese lyrics are dainty, but never long and never very powerful. By their very terseness, narrative and descriptive passages are necessarily limited in character. In the dramas the scope and style of poetry are different. Words are used which would have been scoffed at by the court critics as vulgar. Images arise, and dramatic situations are presented which call for a wider range of literary power and which clearly would lie outside the province of the lyric. Human emotions reach a height unattainable by the exquisite quatrains or eight lines. The language itself, which is the *pehhua*, being free from the classical bondage, achieves a freedom, naturalness and virility entirely undreamed of before. It is a language taken raw from the people's mouths, and shaped into beauty by writers who felt themselves free of the classical standards and who relied solely on their artistic sense of sound and rhythm. Some masters of the Yüan drama used a raw *patois* with an inimitable beauty of its own, which defies all translation either into modern Chinese or into any foreign language. It can only be suggested in the following:

> Muzzy, dizzy, lackadaisical, I'm squatting smug-smugly on an earthen divan.
> Clatter, patter, the old *p'op'o* is shaking her coarse-great-big grain-pan.
> Lousy, slouchy lies the donkey under the willow, his legs sprawling,
> Lapping, patting, that coolie's hand on the donkey's neck is pawing.
> Oh, wake up a while!
> Oh, wake up a while!
> Time like a bullet past a window is flying!
> —*Ma Chihyüan: Huangliangmeng.*

Writers of dramatic poetry had to conform to the exigencies of the operatic airs, but the lines were longer, the insertion of extra syllables was allowed and the rhythm was broader and more suitable to the vernacular language in which it was written. The liberation of metre achieved in the Sung *tz'ŭ* originating in songs and set to these airs, already provided for a metre of irregular lengths, obeying the rhythm of the spoken rather than the written language. This metre was still more emancipated in the dramas. As an approximate example of this irregular metre, I give here an English rendering of passages in the *Western Chamber* (a masterpiece of the first order in Chinese literature), which describe the beauty of Inging, the heroine:

Before she spoke, she had reddened,
   Like a cherry ripe-broken,
   Like a statue white, molten;
   In a moment,
   She'd have spoken
A string of notes sweet and golden.

When she turned sideways, her beauty was described in the following manner:

Sideways inclining,
Her jade hair-pin declining,
Brows à la palace like the new moon reclining,
Into her black velvet temples resigning.

When she moved it was described:

Now she moves her steps, cunning, pretty,
Her waist soft like a southern ditty,
   So gracefully slender,
   So helplessly tender,
Like weeping willows before a zephyr giddy.

It is interesting to note here that rhythm as understood in Chinese dramatic poetry and in Chinese music is different from the regular rhythm in Western poetry and music. There is no reason why the two fundamental metres of twos and threes should not be used in some kind of regular combination in English poetry. This has been done with great success in the Sung *tz'ŭ* and Yüan dramas, producing a more modulated rhythm than the straight use of twos or threes throughout the line. The idea is worth experiment by some qualified English poets.

Through its immense popularity the theatre has achieved a place in the national Chinese life very nearly corresponding to its logical place in an ideal republic. Apart from teaching the people an intense love of music, it has taught the Chinese people, over ninety per cent of whom are illiterate, a knowledge of history truly amazing, crystallizing, as it were, the folklore

and entire historical and literary tradition in plays of characters·
that have captured the heart and imagination of the common
men and women. Thus any amah has a livelier conception than
I have of many historical heroes like Kuan Yü, Liu Pei,
Ts'ao Ts'ao, Hsüeh Jenkwei, Hsüeh Tingshan and Yang
Kweifei from her intimate knowledge of Chinese plays, as I was
prevented from attending the theatres in my childhood through
my missionary education, and had to learn it all piecemeal from
the cold pages of history books. Before my teens I knew
Joshua's trumpets blew down the walls of Jericho, but I did
not know until I was about thirty that when Mengchiangnü
cried over the bones of her husband who had died building the
Great Wall in conscript labour, the torrent of her tears washed
away a section of the Great Wall. This is a type of ignorance
that cannot be found among the illiterate Chinese.

But the theatre, besides popularizing history and music
among the people, has an equally important cultural function
in providing the people with all their moral notions of good and
evil. Practically all the standardized Chinese notions of loyal
ministers and filial sons and brave warriors and faithful wives
and chaste maidens and intriguing maid-servants are reflected
in the current Chinese plays. Represented in the form of
stories with human characters, whom they hate or love as the
case may be, they sink deep into their moral consciousness.
Ts'ao Ts'ao's hypocrisy, Min Tzŭ's filial piety, Wenchün's
romance, Inging's passion, Yang Kweifei's pampered tastes,
Ch'in Kwei's treason, Yen Sung's greed and cruelty, Chuko
Liang's strategy, Chang Fei's quick temper, and Mulien's
religious sanctity—they all become associated in the Chinese
minds with their ethical tradition and become their concrete
conceptions of good and evil conduct.

The story of the *Romance of the Guitar* (*P'ip'achi*) is given here
to show the type of moral influence of the theatre in general on
the Chinese public and as an example of the kind of story, with
a direct appeal to domestic loyalty, that has captured the
popular fancy. It is distinguished neither for dramatic unity
in the modern sense, being composed of forty-two acts and the
action extending over years, nor for delicacy of imagination
which is better shown in *The Peony Pavilion* (*Moutant'ing*),

nor for poetic beauty which is better shown in the *Western Chamber (Hsihsiang)*, nor for grandeur of passion as in *The Hall of Longevity (Ch'angshengtien)*. But the *Romance of the Guitar* nevertheless holds its own in popularity by its sheer appeal to the beauty of domestic love and loyalty, which always finds a warm place in the Chinese heart. Its influence is more truly typical.

There was a talented scholar of the Han Dynasty whose name was Ts'ai Yung. Because his parents were old, he forsook all ambitions for a political career and was content to stay with his parents at home. He had just married a girl, Chao Wuniang, and the play opens with a scene of their happy family feast in their garden in spring. There was, however, an imperial edict calling for literary talents in the country, and the magistrate had reported Ts'ai's name to the court. This meant a trip to the capital and long years of absence, and there was a struggle between loyalty to the Emperor and filial piety and wedded love. His old father, in a spirit of self-sacrifice, urged him to go, while his mother, with her sounder common sense, opposed. Ts'ai finally had to go, leaving his aged parents in the care of his young bride and a good friend by the name of Chang.

Ts'ai was successful in his examinations, coming out as the first scholar of the land. Then trouble began. For the prime minister Niu had an only daughter, a beautiful and talented girl, whom he loved more than anything else on earth. Ts'ai was forced into marriage with her against his wish, and on their wedding night, with all worldly glory before him, his happiness was marred by the thought of Chao Wuniang. The minister's daughter found out the truth and planned with her husband to ask permission to go home and see their parents, but her father was greatly angered and would not hear of it.

In the meanwhile the conditions at home were going from bad to worse. Chao Wuniang was the only one supporting the family by her handiwork, and there came a famine. Luckily there was famine relief from the public grainage, and Chao received her share. On her way home, however, she was robbed of her rice, and was going to jump into an old well when she thought of her responsibility toward the old people and desisted. Then she went to see Chang, Ts'ai's friend, to borrow a handful of rice to feed her parents with, while she herself ate the husks in secret. The passage where she sings about the husks, comparing them to herself, parted from the rice which was compared to her husband, is by consensus of opinion the most moving part of the whole story.

Soon, however, the parents found this out and asked her forgiveness for past complaints against the thin meals. But old Mrs. Ts'ai soon died, and old Ts'ai himself fell ill. She nursed him through his illness, and when he, too, died, she cut off her hair and sold it to defray part of the funeral expenses. With the help of her good friend Chang, she built her father-in-law's grave with her own hands. Tired and hungry, she lay down on the ground beside the grave, and in her dream she saw that the God of the Earth had taken pity on her and sent two spirits, the White Monkey and the Black Tiger, to help her in the work. When she awoke she found, to her great joy and surprise, that the grave had been finished, and she told the story to Chang.

Chang then advised her to set out to the capital in search of her husband. So she painted a portrait of her husband, and disguising herself as a nun, she begged her way to the capital, carrying a guitar. Going through all kinds of hardships, she finally arrived at Loyang, and it happened there was a Buddhist celebration at a temple, where she therefore went and hung her husband's picture in public. Ts'ai, the bridegroom, happened to come to the temple to pray for his parents, and recognizing his own picture had it taken home. Chao Wuniang appeared the next day at Ts'ai's home as a nun, begging for alms. She was accepted by the prime minister's daughter, who sweetly conspired with her to test her husband's heart. They were then happily reunited, and the play ends with the two wives officially honoured by the Emperor himself.

Such are the elements which make a popular play in China. The story has that element of nobility which makes it popular with the Chinese as the society's doings are popular with English newspaper readers. It has an official examination, which plays such an important part in the changes of fortune in all Chinese stories. But more than that it shows a faithful wife and devoted daughter, a pair of aged parents in need of care, a true friend in trouble, a model madame who was not jealous of her rival, and finally a high official somewhat in love with his own power and glory. These are some of the elements in the Chinese drama on which the public are fed, the same elements that make moving pictures like *Way Down East* and *Over the Hill* great popular hits in China. They also show the Chinese as a profoundly emotional people, with a weakness for sentimental plots.

X. THE NOVEL

Chinese novelists were afraid to let people know that they could condescend to such a thing as the writing of novels. Take the case of a comparatively recent work, *Yehsao Paoyen*, written by Hsia Erhming in the eighteenth century. He wrote very original essays and beautiful poetry, and many travel and biographical sketches like all conventional scholars, now collected in *Huanyühsienchi*. But he also wrote the *Yehsao Paoyen*, and his authorship of this novel can be proved beyond a doubt through poems and essays in his collected works. However, as late as the autumn of 1890 his dutiful great-grandson reprinted the *Huanyühsienchi* in order to perpetuate Hsia's name, but he dared not or would not, anyway did not, include the novel, incontrovertibly Hsia's best work, in the list of his literary works. Only as late as 1917 did Dr. Hu Shih definitely establish and clarify the authorship of the *Red Chamber Dream* as written by Ts'ao Hsüehch'in, undoubtedly one of the greatest, if not the greatest master of Chinese prose (in *pehhua*). We still do not know who was the true author of *Chinp'inmei* (*Gold-Vase-Plum*), and we are still in doubt as to which of the two alleged authors, Shih Nai-an or Lo Kuanchung, was the author of *All Men Are Brothers*.

Characteristic of this attitude toward the novel are the beginning and ending of the *Red Chamber Dream*. A Taoist monk found the story inscribed on a huge rock, which was the extra one left behind by the legendary goddess Nüwo when she was using 36,500 rocks to mend a huge crack in the sky, caused by a terrific fight of "Olympian" giants. This rock was one hundred and twenty feet high and two hundred and forty feet wide. The Taoist monk copied the story from the rock inscriptions, and when it came to Ts'ao Hsüehch'in's hands he worked at it for ten years and revised it five times, dividing it into chapters, and he wrote a verse on it:

These pages tell of babbling nonsense,
A string of sad tears they conceal.
They all laugh at the author's folly;
But who could know its magic appeal?

At the end of the story, when one of the most tragic and deeply human dramas was enacted, and the hero had become a monk and the soul which had given him intelligence and capacity for love and suffering had returned to the rock as Nüwo left it thousands of years ago, the same Taoist monk reappeared. This monk is said to have copied the story again and one day he came to the author's study and put the manuscripts in his care. Ts'ao Hsüehch'in replied, laughingly: "This is only babbling nonsense. It is good for killing time with a few good friends after a wine-feast or while chatting under the lamp-light. If you ask me how I happen to know the hero of the story, and want all the details, you are taking it too seriously." Hearing what he said, the monk threw the manuscripts down on his table and went away laughing, tossing his head and mumbling as he went: "Really it contains only babbling nonsense. Both the author himself and the man who copies it, as well as its readers, do not know what is behind it all. This is only a literary pastime, written for pleasure and self-satisfaction." And it is said that, later on, someone wrote the following verse on it:

When the story is sad and touching,
Then sadder is its tomfoolery.
But we are all in the same dream,
Do not sneer at its buffoonery.

But the tomfoolery, sad and touching as it was, was extremely good. Because such literature was written for pleasure and self-satisfaction, its creation was determined by a true creative impulse and not by love of money or fame. And because it was ostracized literature in respectable circles, it escaped the banal influence of all classical, conventional standards. So far from giving the author money or fame, the authorship of a novel could endanger a scholar's personal safety.

At Kiangyin, the home of Shih Nai-an, the author of *All Men Are Brothers*, there is still a legend about what Shih did in order to get himself out of trouble. In this legend, Shih was credited with the gift of foreknowledge of events. He had written this novel, and was living in retirement, having refused to serve the new Ming Dynasty. One day the Emperor came with Liu Powen, Shih's classmate and now the Emperor's right-hand man. Liu saw the manuscripts of this novel on his table, and recognizing Shih's superior talent, Liu plotted for his ruin. It was a time when the security of the new dynasty was not yet ensured, and Shih's novel, advocating as it did the common "brotherhood of all men," including the robbers, contained rather dangerous thoughts. So one day, on this basis, Liu petitioned the Emperor to have Shih summoned to the capital for trial. When the warrant came, Shih knew that his manuscripts had been stolen and realized that it would mean his death, so he borrowed five hundred taels from a friend with which to bribe the boatman and asked the latter to make the voyage as slowly as possible. Therefore on the way to Nanking he hurriedly composed a fantastic supernatural novel, the *Fengshenpang*,[1] in order to convince the Emperor of his insanity. Under this cover of insanity, Shih saved his own life.

Thus surreptitiously the novel grew, like a wayward flower, casting its glance on the lonely wayfarer in a sheer effort to please. Like the wayward flower, too, impressively growing on the surface of a barren rock, it grew without cultivation, and it gave without expecting return, from a sheer inner creative impulse. Sometimes such a flower gives only a single blossom in a quarter of a century, but how that blossom shines! That blossom seems to be the justification for its existence; it has drained its life-blood and having blossomed, the flower dies. Such is the origin of all good tales and all good novels. So did

[1] The authorship of this novel is really unknown.

Cervantes write, and so did Boccaccio, out of the sheer delight of creation. Money had nothing to do with it. Even in modern times, where there are royalties and copyright protection, money is purely an accident. No amount of money can make an uncreative mind tell a good story. A secure living made the writing by our creative minds possible, but a secure living never created anything. Money sent Charles Dickens on his American tour, but money could not produce a *David Copperfield*. Our great story-tellers, like Defoe and Fielding and Shih Nai-an and Ts'ao Hsüehch'in, wrote because they had a story to tell and because they were born story-tellers. Nature seemed to have placed Ts'ao Hsüehch'in in a fabulously luxurious home surrounding and then blasted this life all into nothingness, so that in his old age, as a bankrupt scholar and in his decrepit hut, he could recall it all like an awakened dreamer, and having relived that dream in his imagination, he felt compelled to put it down as he relived it, and we call it literature.

I regard the *Red Chamber Dream* as one of the world's masterpieces. Its character-drawing, its deep and rich humanity, its perfect finish of style and its story entitle it to that. Its characters live, more real and more familiar to us than our living friends, and each speaks an accent which we can recognize. Above all, it has what we call a great story:

A fabulously beautiful Chinese house-garden; a great official family, with four daughters and a son growing up and some beautiful female cousins of the same age, living a life of continual raillery and bantering laughter; a number of extremely charming and clever maid-servants, some of the plotting, intriguing type and some quick-tempered but true, and some secretly in love with the master; a few faithless servants' wives involved in little family jealousies and scandals; a father for ever absent from home on official service and two or three daughters-in-law managing the complicated routine of the whole household with order and precision, the ablest, most gifted, most garrulous and most beloved of all, Fengchieh, being entirely illiterate; the "hero," Paoyü, a boy in puberty, with a fair intelligence and a great love of female company, sent, as we are made to understand, by God to go through this phantasmagoria of love and suffering, overprotected like the sole heir of all great families in China, doted on by his grand-mother, the highest authority of the household, but extremely afraid of his father, completely admired by all his female cousins and catered for by his maid-servants, who attended to his bath and sat in watch over him at night; his love for Taiyü, his orphan cousin staying in their house, who was suffering from consumption and was fed on birds'-nest soup, easily outshining the rest in beauty and poetry, but a little too clever to be happy like the more stupid ones, opening her love to Paoyü with the purity and intensity of a young maiden's heart; another female cousin, Paots'a, also in love with Paoyü, but plumper and more practical-minded and considered a better wife by the elders; the final deception, arrangements for the wedding to Paots'a by the mothers without Paoyü's or Taiyü's knowledge, Taiyü not hearing of it until shortly before the wedding, which made her laugh hysterically and sent her to her death, and Paoyü not hearing of it till the wedding night; Paoyü's discovery of the deception by his own parents, his becoming half-idiotic and losing his mind, and finally his becoming a monk.

All of this is depicted against the rise and fall of a great family, the crescendo of piling family misfortunes extending over the last third of the story, taking one's breath away like the *Fall of the House of Usher*. Its heyday of pleasure was passed; bankruptcy hung in the air; instead of a wine-feast under the mid-autumn moon, we hear ghosts wailing in the silent courtyard; the beautiful girls grew up and married off into different homes with different luck; Paoyü's personal maid-servants were sent away and married, and the most devoted one, Ch'ingwen, died chaste and true. The phantas-magoria vanished.

If, as some Chinese critics say, the *Red Chamber Dream* could ruin a country, it should have ruined China long ago. Taiyü and Paots'a have become the nation's sweethearts, and a num-ber of other types are there, too: the impetuous Ch'ingwen, the feminine Hsijen, the romantic Hsiangyün, the womanly T'anch'un, the garrulous Fengchieh, the talented Miaoyü, all there for one to settle one's choice upon, each representing a different type. The easiest way to find out a Chinaman's temperament is to ask him whether he likes Taiyü more or

Paots'a more. If he prefers Taiyü, he is an idealist, and if he prefers Paots'a, he is a realist. If he likes Ch'ingwen, he will probably become a good writer, and if he likes Hsiangyün, he should equally admire Li Po's poetry. I like T'anch'un, who has the combination of Taiyü's and Paots'a's qualities, and who was happily married and became a good wife. The character of Paoyü is decidedly weak, and far from desirable as a "hero" to be worshipped by young men, but whether desirable or not, the Chinese, men and women, have most of them read the novel seven or eight times over, and a science has developed which is called "redology" (*hunghsüeh*, from *Red Chamber Dream*), comparable in dignity and volume to the Shakespeare or Goethe commentaries.

The *Red Chamber Dream* represents probably the height of the art of writing novels in China, all things considered, but it represents also only one type of novel. Briefly, Chinese novels may be classified into the following types, according to their contents. Their best-known representative works are given below:

1. The novel of adventure: *Shuihu Chuan* (*All Men Are Brothers*).
2. The supernatural novel or tale of wonder: *Hsiyuchi.*
3. The historical novel: *Three Kingdoms.*
4. The love romance: *Red Chamber Dream.*
5. The pornographic novel: *Chinp'inmei* (*Gold-Vase-Plum*).
6. The novel of social satire: *Julinwaishih.*
7. The novel of ideas: *Chinghuayüan.*
8. The novel of social manners: *Strange Things of the Last Twenty Years.*

A strict classification is, of course, difficult. The *Gold-Vase-Plum*, for instance, although four-fifths pornographic, is probably the best novel of social manners in its ruthless and vivid portrayal of common characters, the gentry and the "local rich," and particularly of the position of women in Chinese society of the Ming Period. To these novels proper we should have to add tales and short stories in the broad sense, which have a very long tradition, best represented by *Liaotsai* (*Strange Stories from a Chinese Studio*) and *Chinku Ch'ikuan* (*Madame Chuang's Incon-stancy and Other Tales*), the last representing the best collection of old popular stories that have come down through the ages.

I have grouped these more or less in the order of their popular influence. A catalogue of common novels in "cir-culating libraries" on the street would show that novels of adventure, in Chinese called "novels of chivalry," easily top the list. A strange phenomenon this, of course, in a society where chivalric, dare-devil deeds are so often discouraged by teachers and parents. Yet psychologically it is most easy to explain. In China chivalric sons, who are likely to involve their families in trouble with the police or the magistrate, have been driven out of the home into the gutter, and chivalric citizens who are too public-spirited and who must meddle in other people's affairs, when they see injustice done to the poor or the helpless, have been driven out of society into the "green forests" (a term for bandits). For if the parents do not "break" them, they are likely to break their families, owing to the absence of constitutional protection. A man who insists on seeing justice done to the poor and oppressed in a society with-out constitutional protection must indeed be a hero of the "unbreakable" sort. It is obvious that those who remain in the home and in respectable society are the type that is not worth the trouble of "breaking" at all. These "good citizens" of China therefore admire the sons of the forest very much as helpless women admire the he-man with a swarthy face, an unshaven beard and a hairy chest. What is more easy and more exciting than for a consumptive lying in bed to read *All Men Are Brothers* and admire the prowess and exploits of Li Kuei? And it should be remembered that Chinese novels are always read in bed.

The tale of wonder or novel of supernatural beings, involving fights of giants and fairies, covers a large store of folk tradition that lies very close to the Chinese heart. In the chapter on the "Chinese Mind" it has been pointed out how, in the Chinese mind, the supernatural is always mixed with the real. The *Hsiyuchi*, translated in outline by Dr. Timothy Richards in *A Mission to Heaven*, describes the exploits and adventures of the monk Hsüantsang in his pilgrimage to India, in the company of three extremely lovable semi-human beings, Sun the Monkey, Chu the Pig, and the Monk Sand. It is not an original creation, but is based on a religious folk legend. The most lovable and popular character is of course Sun the Monkey, who represents the mischievous human spirit, eternally aiming at the impossible. He ate the forbidden peach in heaven as Eve ate the forbidden apple in Eden, and he was finally chained under a rock for five hundred years as Prometheus was chained. By the time the decreed period was over, Hsüantsang came and released him, and he was to undertake the journey, fighting all the devils and strange creatures on the way, as an atonement for his sins, but his mischievous spirit always remained, and his development represents a struggle between the unruly human spirit and the holy way. He had on his head an iron crown, and whenever he committed a transgression, Hsüantsang's incantation would cause the crown to press on his head until his head was ready to burst with pain. At the same time Chu the Pig represents the animal desires of men, which are gradually chastened by religious experience. The conflict of such desires and temptations in a highly strange journey undertaken by a company of such imperfect and highly human characters produces a continual series of comical situations and exciting battles, aided by supernatural weapons and magic powers. Sun the Monkey had stuck away in his ear a wand which could at will be transformed into any length he desired, and, moreover, he had the ability to pull out hairs on his monkey legs and transform them into any number of small monkeys to harass his enemies, and he could change himself into a cormorant or a sparrow or a fish or a temple, with the windows for his eyes, the door for his mouth and the idol for his tongue, ready to gobble up the hostile monster in case he should cross the threshold of the temple. Such a fight between Sun the Monkey and a supernatural spirit, both capable of changing themselves, chasing each other in the air, on earth, and in the water, should not fail to interest any children or grown-ups who are not too old to enjoy Mickey Mouse.

This love of the supernatural is not confined to the tale of wonder, but finds its way to all types of novels, invalidating in parts even such a first-class novel as the *Yehsao Paoyen*, which is a novel of adventure and home love combined. It has invalidated Chinese tales of mystery, as in the *Paokung An* (*Cases of Paokung*), and makes the development of the detective story impossible, which is due also to such causes as the lack of scientific reasoning and the cheapness of Chinese lives. For when a Chinese dies the general conclusion is that he is dead, and that is final. The Chinese detective, Paokung, who is, by the way, a magistrate himself, solves his mysteries and murders always by visions in dreams instead of by Sherlock Holmes's reasoning.

In looseness of plot, the Chinese novel is like the novels of D. H. Lawrence, and in length like the Russian novels of Tolstoy and Dostoievsky. The similarity between Chinese and Russian novels is quite apparent. Both have an extremely realistic technique, both revel in details, both content themselves with telling the story without the subjectivity characteristic of the novels of Western Europe. Fine psychological portrayal there is, but there is very little room for the author to expand over his psychological knowledge. The story is told primarily as a story. In unmitigated delineation of stark depravity, too, the *Gold-Vase-Plum* has nothing to lose by comparison with *The Brothers Karamazov*. The plot is generally best in the class described as love romances, but in the novel of social manners, which has been in vogue in the last three decades, the plot wanders and disperses into a series of badly connected anecdotes and short stories interesting in themselves. The short story itself did not even come into being until the very last decade, when modern writers are trying to create something similar to what they have read in Western literature in the original or in translation.

On the whole, the tempo of the Chinese novel reflects very well the tempo of Chinese life. It is enormous, big and variegated and is never in a hurry. The novel is avowedly created to kill time, and when there is plenty of time to kill and the reader in no hurry to catch a train, there is no reason why he must hurry to the end. A Chinese novel should be read slowly and with good temper. When there are flowers on the way, who is going to forbid the traveller from stopping to cull them?

XI. Influence of Western Literature

When two cultures meet, it is natural and logical that the richer one should give and the other should take. It is true, but it is sometimes hard to believe that it is more blessed to give than to take. China has apparently gained much in the last thirty years in literature and thought which must be entirely credited to Western influence. This acknowledgement of the general superiority of Western literature in richness came as something of a bad shock to the self-styled "literary nation" that is China. Some fifty years ago the Chinese were impressed only by European gun-boats; some thirty years ago they were impressed by the Western political system; about twenty years ago they discovered that the West even had a very good literature, and now some people are making the slow discovery that the West has even a better social consciousness and better social manners.

That is a rather large morsel for an old and proud nation to swallow, but perhaps China is big enough to swallow it. Anyway, in literature the change has come. Chinese literature has undergone a more profound change in style and content than it ever went through in the past two thousand years. Directly due to the foreign influence, the spoken language has come into its own as a literary medium: the emancipation of the language has come from a man imbued with the Western spirit. Its vocabulary has been greatly enriched, which means the increase of new concepts, scientific, philosophical, artistic and literary, generally more exact and more well-defined than the old material of our thinking. With this enrichment of the raw material of our thought has come a change in style, which has been so modernized beyond recognition that old scholars find great difficulty in following the new pattern and would be at a complete loss to write a magazine article that could be accepted regarding either style or content. New forms of literature, like the *vers libre*, poems in prose, the short story and the modern drama have come into being, and the technique of writing novels has been greatly modified. Above all, the old standards of criticism, on the whole rather similar to those of

the French neo-classical school that made the appreciation of
Shakespeare impossible for a century and a half in Europe, have
been abandoned, and in their place we have a fresher, richer
and broader literary ideal, which in the end must bring about
a closer harmony between literature and life, a greater accuracy
of thinking and a greater sincerity of living.

Of course it is more blessed to give than to take. For with this
change there has come chaos. Progress is fun, but progress is
painful. More than that, progress is always ugly. With the
profound intellectual upheaval that is going on in Young
China's minds, we have lost a centre of gravity in thought and
we have lost a cheerful common sense. The task of adjustment
between the old and the new is usually too much for the
ordinary man, and modern Chinese thought is characterized
by an extreme immaturity of thinking, fickleness of temper and
shallowness of ideas. To understand the old is difficult, and
to understand the new is not too easy. A little bit of romanticism, a tinge of libertinism, a lack of critical and mental
ballast, extreme impatience with anything old and Chinese,
extreme gullibility in accepting the yearly "new models" of
thought, a perpetual hunt for the latest poet from Jugoslavia
or the newest novelist from Bulgaria, great sensitiveness toward
foreigners in revealing anything Chinese, which simply means
a lack of self-confidence, an eighteenth-century rationalism,
fits of melancholia and hyper-enthusiasm, the chase of slogans
from year to year like a dog biting its own tail—these characterize the writings of modern China.

We have lost the gift of seeing life steadily and seeing life
whole. To-day literature is clouded by politics, and writers are
divided into two camps, one offering Fascism and the other
offering Communism as a panacea for all social ills, and there is
probably as little real independence of thinking as there ever
was in old China. With all the apparent emancipation of ideas,
the old psychosis of the Grand Inquisition is still there, under
the cloak of modern terms. For, after all, the Chinese love
liberty as they love a foreign cocotte, for whom they have no
real affection. These are the ugly features of the period of
transition, and they in time will wear off, when China becomes
politically better organized, and its soul has less sensitive spots.

All these changes have come through the influence of European literature. This influence is, of course, not confined to literature, for China has reaped in one harvest the fruits of Western scholarship in philosophy, psychology, science, technology, economics and all those things contained in the modern critical culture. Even foreign children's games and songs and dances are now being introduced. The net positive result of its progress in literature has been summarized in the discussion on the literary revolution. This influence comes as a direct result of translations of European literature. A glance at the range and content of these translations would show the extent and, incidentally, the type of this influence.

The *1934 Yearbook of Chinese Publications* (in Chinese) gives a list of these translations of poems, short stories and novels made in the last twenty-three years, covering twenty-six countries. This list is by no means complete, but will serve for our present purpose. Given in the order of the number of authors represented, they are as follows: England 47, France 38, Russia 36, Germany 30, Japan 30, United States 18, Italy 7, Norway 6, Poland 5, Spain 4, Hungary 3, Greece 3, Africa 2, Jews 2, and the rest, Sweden, Belgium, Finland, Czechoslovakia, Austria, Latvia, Bulgaria, Jugoslavia, Syria, Persia, India and Siam, represented by one author each.

An examination of the translations from English authors shows that the novelists are represented by George Eliot, Fielding, Defoe (including *Moll Flanders*), Kingsley, Swift, Goldsmith, the Brontë sisters (*Wuthering Heights* and *Villette*), Scott, Conrad, Mrs. Gaskell and Dickens (*Old Curiosity Shop, David Copperfield, Oliver Twist, Dombey and Son, Nicholas Nickleby, A Tale of Two Cities, Christmas Carol, Hard Times*). Rider Haggard, through the influence of Lin Shu's translations, has obtained a popularity entirely out of proportion with his standing. The poets are represented by Spenser (*Faerie Queene*), Browning, Burns, Byron, Shelley, Wordsworth, Ernest Dowson. Five of Shakespeare's plays (*Merchant of Venice, As You Like It, Twelfth Night, Henry VI* and *Romeo and Juliet*—rather haphazard, as one can see) have been translated by separate translators. The drama is represented by Galsworthy (seven of his plays), Pinero, Jones, Sheridan (*School for Scandal*) and

Shaw (*Mrs. Warren's Profession, Widowers' Houses, The Philanderer, Arms and the Man, Man and Superman* and *Pygmalion*). The Irish school is represented by Synge and Dunsany. Essayists are represented by Lamb, Arnold Bennett and Max Beerbohm. James Barrie and Oscar Wilde have received a large share of attention; there are two translations of *Lady Windermere's Fan* and three translations of *Salome;* also Wilde's *Picture of Dorian Gray* and *De Profundis* have been translated. H. G. Wells is known through his *Time Machine, Mr. Britling Sees It Through, The First Man in the Moon,* and especially through his *Short History of the World*. Thomas Hardy is only known through his short stories and poems, although his name is very familiar. Katherine Mansfield, through the influence of the late Hsu Tzŭmo, is rather well known. This list covers only authors whose translated works have appeared in book form and, of course, does not cover authors in other fields like Bertrand Russell, whose influence is very great.

In the French section one comes across names like Balzac, Molière, Maupassant (complete works), France (nine of his works; *Thaïs* twice translated), Gide, Voltaire (*Candide*), Rousseau (*Confessions* and *Émile*), Zola (poorly represented), Gautier, Flaubert (*Madame Bovary* thrice translated, *Salammbô* and *Un Cœur Simple*). Dumas *père et fils* have long been popular, especially *La Dame aux Camélias,* which has become common property among the Chinese. Hugo is well represented by *Les Travailleurs de la mer, Les Misérables, Notre-Dame de Paris, Quatre-vingt-treize, Hernani, Ruy Blas,* and *Lucrèce Borgia*. The early romanticists are represented by Chateaubriand (*Atala* and *René*) and Bernardine de Saint-Pierre. Daudet's *Sappho* and Prévost's *Manon Lescaut* are, of course, favourites. Baudelaire is well known, and Rostand's *Cyrano* has its devotees. Barbusse has two translations of his novels *Le Feu* and *Clarté,* and even the long *Jean Christophe* of Rolland is now available in Chinese, besides his *Le Montespan, Pierre et Luce* and *Le Jeu de l'amour et de la mort*.

Classical German literature is represented, of course, by Goethe, among whose works *Faust, Werther* (two translations), *Egmont, Clavigo, Stella* and part of *Wilhelm Meister* have been translated, and Schiller (*Die Jungfrau von Orleans, Wilhelm Tell,*

Wallenstein and *Die Räuber*). Represented also are Lessing (*Minna von Barnhelm*), Freytag (*Die Journalisten*), Heine (*Buch der Lieder*, selected, and *Die Harzreise*) . . . . De la Motte-Fouqué's *Undine* and Storm's *Immensee* (three translations) are extremely popular. Hauptmann is known through his *Die Weber*, *Der rote Hahn*, *Der Biberpelz*, *Einsame Menschen* and his recent novel *Der Ketzer von Soana* (two translations), while his *Die Versunkene Glocke* was once the name of a magazine. Among others are Sudermann's *Frau Sorge* and more modern works like Wedekind's *Frühlings Erwachen* and Leonhard Frank's *Karl und Anna*.

Apart from a few translations from Hawthorne, Mrs. Stowe, Irving, Mark Twain and Jack London, the interest in American literature centres around more modern works. The best known is Upton Sinclair, whose popularity came with the tide of Russian communist literature. Thirteen of his works have been translated, and in this category may also be mentioned Michael Gold's short stories and his novel, *Jews Without Money*. Sinclair Lewis is represented only by *Main Street*, and Theodore Dreiser by a volume of short stories, although both are well known. Two of Eugene O'Neill's plays (*Beyond the Horizon* and *The Moon of the Caribbees*) have been translated. Pearl S. Buck's *The Good Earth* exists in two Chinese translations, while her *Sons* and short stories have also been translated.

The tide of Russian literature came in or about 1927 with the establishment of the Nanking Government and the suppression of the communist movement. For, like literary Jacobitism in England, which grew with the defeat of political Jacobitism, literary Bolshevism inundated China after the success of the Nationalist revolution. The tremendous young enthusiasm, which helped very largely to make the Nationalist revolution in 1926–7 a reality, was denied fields of expression with the official suppression of the Youth Movement by the Kuomintang, and a process of introversion took place. A strong undercurrent was set on its way which grew from a general dissatisfaction with the things as they are.

And so the tide turned. The trumpet call for a "revolutionary literature" (synonymous with "proletariat literature") was sounded and at once found a large following. Leaders of

Renaissance of 1917 became out of date overnight, and were generously labelled as "old men." Young China was disgusted and rebelled. Most intellectual leaders had learned to keep quiet and started collecting curios and old seals. Hu Shih continued to thunder and to roar, but his words fell on a comparatively apathetic audience, which wanted something very much more radical. Chou Tsojen, Yu Tafu and writers of the Yüssü school were too much individualists to join the throng. Lusin fought, resisted the tide for a year and then went over.

In the short space of hardly two years (1928–9), over a hundred Russian literary works, long and short, were put on the market with hectic speed, before the Government could quite wake up to the situation. These include works by the following authors: Lunacharsky, Liebediensky, Michels, Fadeev, Gladhov, Kollontay, Shishkov, Romanov, Pilniak, Ognyov, Sosnovsky, Shaginian, Yakovlev, Alexei Tolstoy, Demidov, Erenburg, Arosev, Babel, Kasatkin, Ivanov, Iva, Luuts, Sannikoff, Seyfullina, Bakhmetev, Fedin, Serafimovitch, Prishvin, Semenov, Sholokhov, NVNV, Vessely, Zoschenko, Tretiakev, Sobole, Kolosov, Formanov, and Figner. We have omitted to mention, of course, the "great Russians" of prerevolutionary days, like Pushkin, Tchekov, Tolstoy and Turgeniev, who had before this time been familiar to the reading public. Tchekov's complete works have been translated; Tolstoy is known through twenty of his works, including the long *War and Peace* (translated in part only), *Anna Karenina* and *The Resurrection;* Dostoievsky is a great favourite (seven of his works, including *Crime and Punishment*); Turgeniev had long been known (twenty-one of his works translated). Gorky, bridging across the two periods, is, of course, popular. Eroshenko, Andreyev and Artzybashev are also popular, due to Lusin's influence. As a sign of the feverish demand for things Russian may be mentioned the curious fact that twenty-three out of the barely over hundred post-revolutionary works had double translations published by rival companies at about the same time, including four which appeared in three simultaneous translations. Among the more popular works may be mentioned Madame Kollontay's *Red Love* (two translations)

Gladhov's *Cement* (three translations), Ognyov's *Diary of a Communist Schoolboy* (three translations), Artzybashev's *Sanine* (three translations), the various works of Serafimovitch and Pilniak, the plays of Shishkov, Ivanov and the critical works of Lunacharsky.

This seems a very large meal for Young China to devour, and if digestion is not perfect, Young China cannot be blamed. No wonder that Hawthorne and Anatole France are hopelessly out of date. The authorities are rubbing their eyes now and doing something about it. What they can do and what will be the outcome no one can foretell. Censorship is easy and has been applied lately. What is not so easy is to give people a sense of satisfaction with the state of things. This can be done in three ways. The first is to give many of these writers good jobs, which proves sometimes effective. The second is to forbid them to say that they are dissatisfied, which is, of course, foolish. And the third is to make the things really satisfactory for the nation, which censorship alone cannot do. The nation is divided between optimists and pessimists, with the latter in the majority. But unless there is a great deal of constructive work and honest thinking and critical balance, the mere worship of slogans and pompous verbosity will not give China a new state, whether communist or fascist. The older generation who want to shunt China back to the old track of Confucianism, including the seclusion of women and the worship of "chaste widowhood," will only estrange the sympathies of Young China. At the same time, the communist idealist, with a volume of Karl Marx under his arm and unkempt hair on his head and smoking a Russian cigarette and perpetually fulminating against somebody, will not bring China into salvation. Literature, I suspect, is still a pastime of the *literati*, old and new.

Chapter Eight

THE ARTISTIC LIFE

I. The Artist

I THINK of all phases of the Chinese civilization, Chinese art alone will make any lasting contribution to the culture of the world. This point, I think, will not be seriously contested. Chinese science, in any case, does not make any pretensions, although the Chinese empirical medicine provides a rich field for medical research and discoveries. Chinese philosophy will never make any lasting impression on the West, because Chinese philosophy, with its moderation, restraint and pacifism, which are all physically conditioned by the decrease of bodily energy, can never suit the Western temperament, with its aggressive exuberance and vitality.

For the same reason, the Chinese social organization will never fit the West. Confucianism is too matter of fact, Taoism too nonchalant, and Buddhism too negative to suit the Western positive outlook on life. No people that are daily sending men to explore the North Pole or conquer the air or break speed records can become good Buddhists. I have seen a few examples of European Buddhist monks, who talk altogether too loudly and too vehemently to conceal the tumultuous passions in their souls. In particular, I have seen one who, in his energetic denunciation of the West, is willing to call down fire and brimstone from heaven to burn up all Europe. When Europeans put on Buddhist gowns and try to look calm and passive, they merely look ridiculous.

Moreover, it would be unfair to judge the Chinese as a nation without an understanding of their art. There are certain hidden innermost recesses of the Chinese soul that can be known only through its reflection in Chinese art, for, like Cyrano de Bergerac, the extreme sensitiveness and fine feeling of the

Chinese soul are hidden behind a somewhat unprepossessing exterior. Behind the Chinese flat, unemotional face is concealed a deep emotionalism, and behind his sullen, decorous appearance resides a carefree, vagabond soul. Those rough yellow fingers mould and fashion objects of pleasing design and harmony, and from the almond eyes behind the high cheekbones shines a tender light that dwells fondly on forms of exquisite beauty. From the Temple of Heaven to the scholar's letter-paper and other products of artcraft, Chinese art shows a taste and finesse and understanding of tone and harmony that distinguish the best products of the human spirit.

Calm and harmony distinguish Chinese art, and calm and harmony come from the soul of the Chinese artist. The Chinese artist is a man who is at peace with nature, who is free from the shackles of society and from the temptations of gold, and whose spirit is deeply immersed in mountains and rivers and other manifestations of nature. Above all, his breast must brood no ill passions, for a good artist, we strongly believe, must be a good man. He must first of all "chasten his heart" or "broaden his spirit," chiefly by travel and by contemplation. This is the severe training we impose on the Chinese painter. It would be only too easy to give testimonies from Chinese painters to illustrate this point. Thus Wen Chenming said: "If one's moral character is not high, his art will also lack style." A Chinese artist must absorb in himself the best of human culture and nature's spirit. Tung Ch'ich'ang (1555–1636), one of the greatest of China's calligraphists and painters, once said of another painter: "How can one be the father of painting without reading ten thousand books and travelling ten thousand *li*?" The Chinese artist does not learn painting by going into a room and stripping a woman naked in order to study her anatomy, nor does he make copies of plaster figures of ancient Greece and Rome, as some backward art schools in the West still do. The Chinese artist travels and visits the famous mountains like Huangshan in Anhui or the Omei mountains in Szechuen.

This escape to the mountains is important for several reasons. First of all, the artist must absorb impressions from the myriad forms of nature, its insects and trees and clouds and waterfalls.

In order to paint them, he must love them, and his spirit must commune with them. He must know and be familiar with their ways, and he must know how the same tree changes its shade and colour between morning and night or between a clear day and a misty morning, and he must see with his own eyes how the mountain clouds "entwine the rocks and encircle the trees." But more important than cold, objective observations is the spiritual baptism in nature. So did Li Jihhua (1565–1635) describe the spiritual baptism of a great painter:

Huang Tzŭchiu often sits the whole day in the company of bamboos, trees, brushwood and piles of rocks in the wild mountains, and seems to have lost himself in his surroundings, in a manner puzzling to others. Sometimes he goes to the place where the river joins the sea to look at the currents and the waves, and he remains there, oblivious of wind and rain and the howling water-spirits. This is the work of the Great Absent-Minded [name of the painter], and that is why it is surcharged with moods and feelings, ever-changing and wonderful like nature itself.

Secondly, Chinese paintings are always painted from mountain tops and specialize in those awesome grand aspects of mountain peaks or rocks, which only those who have seen them can believe. The retreat to the mountains is a search for grandeur in nature. A Chinese artist in America would first of all take for his subject the Grand Canyon or the mountains around Banff. And having come to such a grand surrounding, it is inevitable that he should obtain an elevation of the spirit as well as a physical elevation. It is strange that spiritual elevation always goes with physical elevation on this planet, and life always looks different from an altitude of five thousand feet. People fond of horseback-riding always say that the moment one goes up on horseback one obtains a different view of the world, which I imagine must be true. The retreat to the mountains means, therefore, also a search for moral elevation, which is the last and most important reason for travel. Thus from his god-like height the artist surveys the world with a calm expansion of the spirit, and this spirit goes into his painting. Then, chastened in spirit, he comes back to city life and tries to communicate it to those who are less fortunate. His subjects may alter, but his spirit of mountain calm remains, and when he feels he has lost or exhausted this spirit, he travels again and rebaptizes himself in the mountain air.

It is this spirit of calm and harmony, this flavour of the mountain air (*shanlin ch'i*) always tinged a little with the recluse's passion for leisure and solitude, which characterizes all forms of Chinese art. Consequently, its characteristic is not supremacy over nature, but harmony with nature.

II. Chinese Calligraphy

All problems of art are problems of rhythm. Hence, in trying to understand Chinese art, we must begin with Chinese rhythm and the source of artistic inspiration. Allowing that rhythm is universal and that the Chinese do not own a monopoly of nature's rhythms, it is still possible to trace a difference of emphasis. It has already been pointed out, in the discussion on the ideal of womanhood in China, that the Western artist invariably goes to the feminine form as inspiration for the highest ideal of perfect rhythm, while the Chinese artist and art-lover usually rest supremely happy in contemplating a dragon-fly, a frog, a grasshopper or a piece of jagged rock. From my observation, it seems therefore that the spirit of Western art is more sensual, more passionate, more full of the artist's own ego, while the spirit of Chinese art is more chastened, more restrained, and more in harmony with nature. We may express this difference by using the Nietzschean language and saying that Chinese art is Apollonian art, while Western art is Dionysian art. This enormous difference is possible only through a different understanding and appreciation of rhythm as such. While it is true that all problems of art are problems of rhythm in whatever country, it is also true that until recently in the West, rhythm has not played the dominant role which it has always enjoyed in Chinese paintings.

Curiously enough, this cult of rhythm in the abstract arose

from the development of Chinese calligraphy as an art. The strange pleasure derived from contemplating a picture of barren rocks done in a few strokes and hung on the wall to be looked at day in and day out—this strange pleasure will become understandable to the West when the West has understood the artistic principles of Chinese calligraphy. So fundamental is the place of calligraphy in Chinese art *as a study of form and rhythm in the abstract* that we may say it has provided the Chinese people with a basic æsthetics, and it is through calligraphy that the Chinese have learned their basic notions of line and form. It is therefore impossible to talk about Chinese art without understanding Chinese calligraphy and its artistic inspiration. There is, for instance, not one type of Chinese architecture, whether it be the *pailou*, the pavilion or the temple, whose sense of harmony and form is not directly derived from certain types of Chinese calligraphy.

The position of Chinese calligraphy in the history of the world's art is thus truly unique. Owing to the use in writing of the brush, which is more subtle and more responsive than the pen, calligraphy has been elevated to the true level of an art on a par with Chinese painting. The Chinese are fully aware of this when they regard painting and calligraphy as sister arts, *shu-hua*, "calligraphy and painting," forming almost an individual concept and always being mentioned in the same breath. Should there be a question as to which has a wider appeal, the answer would undoubtedly be in favour of calligraphy. It has thus become an art cultivated with the same passion and devotion, dignified by as worthy a tradition, and held in as high esteem as painting itself. Its standards are just as exacting, and its masters have reached heights as unattainable by the common run of men as the masters in other lines. The great Chinese painters, like Tung Ch'ich'ang and Chao Mengfu, are usually great calligraphists also. Chao Mengfu (1254–1322), one of the best known of Chinese painters, said of his own painting: "Rocks are like the *feipo* style of writing [with hollow lines in the strokes], and the trees are like the *chuan* style of writing [with relatively even and twisted strokes]. The method of painting lies yet in the 'eight fundamental strokes' of writing. If there is one who can understand this, he will realize that the secret of calligraphy is really the same."

It seems to me that calligraphy, as representing the purest principles of rhythm and composition, stands in relation to painting as pure mathematics stands in relation to engineering or astronomy. In appreciating Chinese calligraphy, the meaning is entirely forgotten, and the lines and forms are appreciated in and for themselves. In this cultivation and appreciation of pure witchery of line and beauty of composition, therefore, the Chinese have an absolute freedom and entire devotion to pure form as such, as apart from content. A painting has to convey an object, but a well-written character conveys only its own beauty of line and structure. In this absolutely free field, every variety of rhythm has been experimented upon and every type of structure has been explored. The Chinese brush makes the conveyance of every type of rhythmic movement possible, and the Chinese characters, which are theoretically square but are composed from the oddest elements, present an infinite variety of structural problems which every writer must solve for himself. Thus, through calligraphy, the Chinese scholar is trained to appreciate, as regards line, qualities like force, suppleness, reserved strength, exquisite tenderness, swiftness, neatness, massiveness, ruggedness, and restraint or freedom; and as regards form, he is taught to appreciate harmony, proportion, contrast, balance, lengthiness, compactness, and sometimes even beauty in slouchiness or irregularity. Thus the art of calligraphy provides a whole set of terms of æsthetic appreciation which we may consider as the bases of Chinese notions of beauty.

As this art has a history of well-nigh two thousand years, and as every writer tried to distinguish himself by a new type of rhythm or structure, therefore, in calligraphy, if in anything, we are entitled to see the last refinement of the Chinese artistic mind. Certain types, such as the worship of beauty of irregularity or of a forever toppling structure that yet keeps its balance, will surprise the Westerners by their finesse, all the more so because such types are not easily seen in other fields of Chinese art.

What is of significance to the West is the fact that, not only has it provided the æsthetic basis for Chinese art, but it represents an animistic principle which may be most fruitful of results when properly understood and applied. As stated, Chinese calligraphy has explored every possible style of rhythm and form, and it has done so by deriving its artistic inspiration from nature, especially from plants and animals—the branches of the plum flower, a dried vine with a few hanging leaves, the springing body of the leopard, the massive paws of the tiger, the swift legs of the deer, the sinewy strength of the horse, the bushiness of the bear, the slimness of the stork, or the ruggedness of the pine branch. There is thus not one type of rhythm in nature which has not been copied in Chinese writing and formed directly or indirectly the inspiration for a particular "style." If a Chinese scholar sees a certain beauty in a dry vine with its careless grace and elastic strength, the tip of the end curling upward and a few leaves still hanging on it haphazardly and yet most appropriately, he tries to incorporate that into his writing. If another scholar sees a pine tree that twists its trunk and bends its branches downward instead of upward, which shows a wonderful tenacity and force, he also tries to incorporate that into his style of writing. We have therefore the "dry-vine" style and the "pine-branch" style of writing.

A famous monk and calligraphist had practised writing for years without result, and one day walking on a mountain path he chanced upon two fighting snakes, each straining its neck, which showed strength in apparent gentleness. From this inspiration he developed a most individualistic type of writing, called the "fighting-snakes" style, suggesting the tension and wriggling movement of the snakes' necks. Thus Wang Hsichih (321–379), China's "prince of calligraphists," spoke about the art of calligraphy in terms of imagery from nature:

Every horizontal stroke is like a mass of clouds in battle formation, every hook like a bent bow of the greatest strength, every dot like a falling rock from a high peak, every turning of the stroke like a brass hook, every drawn-out line like a dry vine of great old age, and every swift and free stroke like a runner on his start.

One can understand Chinese calligraphy only when one's

eyes have been opened to the form and rhythm inherent in every animal's body and limbs. Every animal body has a harmony and beauty of its own, a harmony which grows directly from its vital functions, especially the functions of movement. The hairy legs and tall body of the draught-horse are as much a form of beauty as the more neatly formed outline of the racing-horse. That harmony exists in the outline of the swift, springing greyhound, as it exists also in that of the hairy Irish terrier, whose head and limbs end almost in square formations—strikingly represented in Chinese calligraphy by the blunt *li-shu* style (current in the Han Dynasty and elevated into an art by Teng Shih-ju of the Ch'ing Dynasty).

The important thing to observe is that these plant and animal forms are beautiful because of their suggestion of movement. Consider a sprig of plum blossoms. How carelessly beautiful and artfully irregular it is! To understand the beauty of that sprig fully, artistically, is to understand the underlying principle of Animism and of Chinese art. The sprig, even when deprived of its blossoms, is beautiful because it lives, because it expresses a living impulse to grow. The outline of every tree expresses a rhythm resulting from certain organic impulses, the impulse to grow and reach out toward the sunshine, the impulse to maintain its equilibrium, and the necessity of resisting the movement of the wind. Every tree is beautiful because it suggests these impulses, and particularly because it suggests a movement toward somewhere, a stretching toward something. It has not tried to be beautiful. It has only wanted to live. Yet the result is something perfectly harmonious and immensely satisfying.

Nor does nature artificially invest the greyhound with an abstract beauty apart from its functions: the high arch of the greyhound's body and the connecting line between its body and its hind legs are built for swiftness, and they are beautiful because they suggest swiftness. Yet from this harmonious function emerges a harmonious form. The softness of the cat's movements results in the softness of its contour, and even the dogged squatting outline of a bulldog has a beauty of force all its own. This is the explanation of nature's infinite richness of patterns, which are always harmonious, always rhythmic,

ANIMISM AS A PRINCIPLE OF CHINESE ART

The rhythm of a cypress as seen by a Chinese artist.
Painting by Hsiao Chihch'üan, a contemporary.

The writing of Lin Changmin, a distinguished scholar who died a decade ago. This writing is nearer the "pointer" style, being muscular and smooth in its rhythm. Note that every character and every stroke is made rapidly in a controlling rhythm, with no possibility of corrections.

and infinitely variable without ever exhausting its forms. In other words, nature's beauty is a dynamic, and not a static, beauty.

It is exactly this beauty of movement which is the key to Chinese calligraphy. Its beauty is dynamic and not static, and because it expresses a dynamic beauty, *a beauty of momentum*, it lives, and it, too, is infinitely variable without exhaustion. A swift, sure stroke is appreciated because it is made swiftly and powerfully at one stroke, thus possessing a unity of movement, defying imitation or correction, for any correction is immediately detected as disharmonious. Incidentally, that is why calligraphy as an art is so difficult.

That the ascribing of beauty in Chinese calligraphy to the animistic principle is not my own fancy can be proved from Chinese references to the "meat," "bones" and "tendons" of strokes, although their philosophic import has never been consciously laid bare until one comes to think of ways and means by which calligraphy can be made intelligible to the West. Thus Madame Wei, the talented aunt of Wang Hsichih, said:

> In the writing of those who are skilful in giving strength of stroke, the characters are "bony"; in the writing of those who are not skilful in giving strength of strokes, the characters are "fleshy." Writing that has a great deal of bone and very little meat is called "sinewy writing," and writing that is full of flesh and weak bones is called "piggy writing." A writing that is powerful and sinewy is divine; a writing that has neither power nor sinews is like an invalid.

The dynamic principle of movement results in a principle of structure which is essential to an understanding of Chinese calligraphy. The mere beauty of balance and symmetry is never regarded as the highest form. One of the principles of Chinese writing is that a square should never be a perfect square, but should be higher on one side than the other, and that two symmetrical parts should never be exactly similar in size and position. This principle is called *shih*, or "posture," which represents a beauty of momentum. The result is that, in the highest examples of this art, we have structural forms which are seemingly unbalanced and yet somehow maintain the balance. The difference between this beauty of momentum and beauty of merely static proportions is the difference between the picture of a man standing or sitting in a resting position and the snapshot of a man swinging his golf-stick, or of a football player who has just sent the ball soaring through the air. Just as the picture of a lady tossing her head is more suggestive of movement than one with her head on a straight level, so the Chinese characters written with their tops tilted to one side are preferred artistically to those with a symmetrical head. The best examples of this type of structure are contained in the tomb-inscription of Chang Menglung, whose characters give the effect of being always on the point of toppling over, and yet always remain in balance. The best modern example of this style is to be seen in the writings of Yü Yüjen, Chairman of the Control Yüan, who owes his present position very largely to his renown as a calligraphist of high order.

Modern art is in search of rhythms and experimenting on new forms of structure and patterns. It has not found them yet. It has succeeded only in giving us the impression of trying to escape from reality. Its most apparent characteristic is the effort, not to soothe us but to jar on our senses. For this reason, a study of Chinese calligraphy and its animistic principle, and ultimately a restudy of the rhythms of the natural world in the light of this animistic principle or rhythmic vitality, gives promise of great possibilities. The profuse use of straight lines, planes, and cones striking one another at different angles can only excite us, but they can never be alive with beauty. These planes, cones, straight lines and wavy lines seem to have exhausted the modern artist's ingenuity. Why not go back to nature? It remains yet for some Western artist to strike a pioneer path by practising English calligraphy with the brush for ten years, and then, if he is talented and really understands the animistic principle, he will be able to write for signboards on Times Square, in lines and forms truly worthy of the name of an art.

The full significance of Chinese calligraphy as the basis of Chinese æsthetics will be seen in a study of Chinese painting and architecture. In the lines and composition of Chinese painting and in the forms and structures of Chinese architecture, we shall be able to recognize the principles developed from Chinese calligraphy. These basic ideas of rhythm, form and atmosphere give the different lines of Chinese art, like poetry, painting, architecture, porcelain and house decorations, an essential unity of spirit.

III. Painting

Chinese painting, the flower of Chinese culture, is distinguished by a spirit and an atmosphere all its own, entirely different from Western painting. It is as different from Western painting as Chinese poetry is different from Western poetry. That difference is hard to grasp and express. It has a certain tone and atmosphere, visible in Western painting, but essentially different and achieved by different means. It shows a certain economy of material, marked by the many blank spaces, an idea of composition determined by its own harmony and marked by a certain "rhythmic vitality," and a boldness and freedom of the brush which impress the onlooker in an unforgettable manner. Somehow the picture before us has undergone an inner process of transformation in the artist's mind, shorn of its irrelevancies, its disharmonies, and giving us only a completely satisfying whole, so true to life and yet so different from it. The design is more obvious, the elimination of material more rigidly carried out, the points of contrast and concentration easier to trace, and we decidedly feel that the artist has interfered with the material reality and presented it to us only as it appears to him, without losing its essential likeness or intelligibility to others. It is subjective without the violent assertions of the artist's ego in the modern Western painting, and without the latter's unintelligibility to us common men. It manages to achieve a decidedly subjective appearance of things without making contortions. It does not try to paint all before one's eyes, and it leaves a great deal to the onlooker's imagination, without degenerating into a geometric puzzle. Sometimes the concentration on the immediate object is so intensive that only the tip of a plum branch is given in the whole picture and left there as perfect. And yet, with all this subjective interference with the material reality, the effect is not a jarring assertion of the artist's ego, but a complete harmony with nature. How was this achieved, and how did this peculiar tradition grow up?

This artistic tradition did not come by chance or by an accidental discovery. Its characteristics may be most conveniently summed up, I think, in the word *lyricism*, and this lyricism came from a certain type of human spirit and culture. For we must remember that Chinese painting is closely related, in spirit and technique, to Chinese calligraphy and Chinese poetry. Calligraphy gave it its technique, the initial twist which determined its future development, and Chinese poetry lent it its spirit. For poetry, painting and calligraphy are closely related arts in China. The best way of understanding Chinese painting is to study these influences which went into the building of that peculiar tradition.

Briefly stated, this peculiar tradition, which we have called its lyricism, is the result of two revolts which modern Western painting is going through, but which came to the history of Chinese painting in the eighth century. They are the revolt against the subjection of the artist's lines to the painted objects, and the revolt against a photographic reproduction of the material reality. Chinese calligraphy helped it to solve the first problem, and Chinese poetry helped it over the second. A study of these revolts and of the genesis of this artistic tradition will enable us to see why Chinese painting came to have its present character.

The first problem of Chinese painting, and of all painting, is: What shall be done with the lines or strokes as paint is put on the canvas or ink on the silk? It is a purely technical problem, the problem of "touch." But no artist can escape it, and the touch used will determine the whole style of his work. If the line is mechanically used to trace the lines of the painted objects, it can have no freedom of its own. Sooner or later, we shall get tired of it.

It is the same rebellion which we see in modern art, a rebellion which came up in China with Wu Taotzŭ (c. 700–760),

"A HORSE," BY PʼON JU, A CONTEMPORARY CHINESE PAINTER, SHOWING HOW THE RHYTHMIC STROKES AND MASTERY OF THE BRUSH ARE DEVELOPED FROM THE CULTIVATION OF CALLIGRAPHY AND STILL REMAIN AKIN TO IT IN TECHNIQUE.

and Wu Taotzŭ solved it by his mastery of the brush, distinguished by its boldness and freedom. Instead of concealing the line, the artist glorified it. (We shall see the same principle in Chinese architecture.) Thus in place of the dead and servile lines of Ku K'aichih (346–407) which were more or less even as if drawn by a steel pen, Wu started the so-called "orchid-petal line," curling and constantly changing in width, due to the natural rhythm of a stroke laid with the sensitive brush. In fact, it was from Wu Taotzŭ's strokes that his pupil Chang Hsü created the extremely swift style of entwining ropes in calligraphy. Wang Wei (Mochieh, 699–759) further developed and modified the stroke in painting, sometimes abolishing the traditional method of "tracing outlines," and consequently is generally credited with having founded the "southern school." Its far-reaching consequences we shall soon see.

The second problem is: How shall the artist's personality be projected into the work and make it worthy of the name of an art, transcending mere efforts at verisimilitude, yet without sacrificing truth, harmony or reality? This revolt against mere physical accuracy is also back of all the new tendencies in modern art, which may be described as searching for an escape from the material reality and for methods of indicating the artist's own ego in the work. The same revolt came in the history of Chinese art in the eighth century with the new school. People felt tired or dissatisfied with photographic reproductions of the material reality.

Here was the same old problem: How could the artist invest the objects with his own emotions or reactions without producing a grotesque caricature? The problem had already been solved in Chinese poetry. The revolt was a revolt against mere accuracy and minute craftsmanship. The contrast between the new and the old school is interestingly shown in the story of two paintings of Szechuen landscapes on palace walls, done by Li Ssŭhsün (651–716) and Wu Taotzŭ during the reign of T'ang Minghuang. It is said that Li, the master of the "northern school," did his landscape in about a month, with all its tracery work and golden colours, while Wu did his grand landscape of the entire Chingling river in a day's time in splashes of ink, and the Emperor said, "Li Ssŭhsün did it in

a month, and Wu Taotzŭ did it in a day, and each is perfect
in its own way."

When this revolt against minute artistry came, there was
Wang Wei, a first-class landscape painter himself, and he
introduced into it the spirit and technique of Chinese poetry,
with its impressionism, its lyricism, its emphasis on atmosphere
and its pantheism. Thus the "father of the southern school,"
which makes Chinese painting deservedly famous, was a man
nurtured in the Chinese poetic spirit.

Chronologically, the development was as follows: It seem
that the Chinese artistic genius first became conscious of itsel
in the fourth, fifth and sixth centuries. It was in this perio
that art criticism and literary criticism were developed. An
it was Wang Hsichih (321–379), belonging to one of the mos
aristocratic families of this time, who became known as "th
prince of calligraphists." During the following centuries th
influence of Buddhism was at work, giving us the famou
sculptures of Tat'ung and Lungmen. The style of writin
which developed in Northern Wei, now preserved in the so
called "Wei rubbings" from inscriptions of this period, set th
high watermark for Chinese calligraphy, in my opinion stil
the best in its whole history. The Wei style was the great style
it was not merely beautiful but had beauty and power an
finesse combined. Hsieh Ho in this period first enunciated th
principle of "rhythmic vitality" which became the centra
principle of all Chinese painting in the last fourteen hundre
years.

Then came the great eighth century, which, for some reasor
or other which I cannot quite explain, became the mos
creative period of Chinese history, in painting, poetry an
prose. The cause was at least partially to be found in th
infusion of new blood which took place during the chao
of the preceding centuries. Li Po and Wang Wei were bot
born in the north-west, where race mixture was most active
but we lack more adequate genealogical data. Anyway, th
human spirit became free and creative. This century gav
us Li Po and Tu Fu and a good number of other first-clas
poets: Li Ssŭhsün, Wang Wei and Wu Taotzŭ in painting
Chang Hsü in the "running style" and Yen Chench'ing in th

formal style of calligraphy, and Han Yü in prose. Wang Wei was born in 699, Wu Taotzŭ about 700, Li Po in 701, Yen Chench'ing in 708, Tu Fu in 712, Han Yü in 768, Po Chüyi in 772, and Liu Chungyüan in 773—all first-class names in Chinese history. And in this century, too, a beauty of beauties, Yang Kweifei, was born to keep the Emperor company and grace the court with the poet Li Po. Nor was this period distinguished by peace, either.

However that may be, the "southern school" came into being, and it is the southern school that we are primarily interested in, as being most peculiarly Chinese. This type of painting became known as the "scholars' painting," and later on in the eleventh century, under the influence of Sung scholars like Su Tungp'o (1035–1101), Mi Fei (1050–1107) and his son Mi Yüjen (1086–1165), it reached still greater simplicity and subjectivity. It was also known as "literary men's painting." Su Tungp'o even painted a bamboo tree without its joints, and when someone protested, he replied by asking, "Did the bamboo grow by adding one joint to another?" Su, who was a great writer and poet, specialized in painting bamboos, and he was so fond of them that he once said, "I would rather go without meat in my meals than go without bamboos in my house." His bamboo was, like his "drunken style" of "running script," a splash of ink without colours; and his manner of painting was to get drunk and, after dinner, under the stimulation of alcohol when his spirit was heightened, dip his brush in the ink and write characters, or bamboos, or poetry as the inspiration came—it did not matter which. Once, in such a state, he scribbled a poem on his host's wall, which is hardly translatable: "Sprouts come from my dry intestines, moistened by wine, and from my lungs and liver grow bamboos and rocks. So full of life they grow that they cannot be restrained, and so I am writing them on your snow-white wall." For now painting was no longer "painted," but "written" like characters. Wu Taotzŭ, too, often did his paintings under the inspiration of wine or of his friend's sword-dance, whose rhythm he incorporated into his work. It is evident that work done under such momentary stimulation could have been accomplished only in a few strokes or a few minutes, after which the alcoholic effect would have already vanished.

Back of all this drunkenness, however, there was a very fine philosophy of painting. The Chinese painter-scholars, who left behind a tremendous amount of very profound art criticism, distinguished between *hsing*, or the objects' physical forms, *li*, or the inner law or spirit, and *yi*, or the artist's own conception. The "scholars' painting" was a protest against slavish verisimilitude, of which it would be easy to give quotations, from the earliest to modern times. The Sung scholars emphasized especially *li*—the inner spirit of things. Mere accuracy of detail was the work of commercial artists, whereas painting worthy of the name of an art should aim at catching the spirit. It was not just mere drunkenness.

But the fact that such painting was the work, not of professional artists but of scholars at play, was of profound significance. It was their spirit of amateurism which enabled them to deal with painting in a light and pleasant spirit. For during the eleventh century, when there was a brief outburst of the spirit of "scholars' painting," such painting was referred to as *mohsi*, or "play with ink." It was a pastime of the scholars when they were in the playing mood, like calligraphy and like poetry. There was no heaviness of spirit. It seemed as if the scholar, after having obtained mastery of the brush in calligraphy, had an exuberance of energy which he applied to art as a pleasant and interesting change. The material equipment was the same: the same scrolls, the same brushes and the same ink and water, and they were all there before his desk. For no palette was necessary. Mi Fei, one of the greatest of scholar-painters, sometimes used even a roll of paper for his brush, or the pulp of sugar-cane, or the stalk of a lotus flower. When the inspiration came and there was magic in the scholar's "wrist," there was nothing which seemed impossible to these artists. For they had mastered the art of conveying fundamental rhythms, and everything else was secondary. There are to-day painters who make sketches with their bare fingers, and one even with his mobile tongue, dipped in ink and licking the paper as he draws along. Painting was, and still is, the scholar's recreation.

This playing mood accounts for a certain quality of Chinese painting, called *yi*. The nearest word for this in translation is "fugitiveness," if this word may be used to denote at the same time "romanticism" and "the spirit of the recluse." It is this quality of light-hearted and carefree romanticism which distinguishes Li Po's poetry. This *yi* or "fugitive" or "recluse" quality is prized as the highest quality of the scholar's paintings, and it comes from the playing spirit. Like Taoism, it is the effort of the human spirit to get away from the workaday humdrum world, and achieve a light-hearted freedom.

This desire is understandable when we realize how much the scholar's spirit was restrained in the moral and political spheres, and in painting at least, it did its best to recover that freedom. Ni Yünlin (1301–1374), a great Yüan painter most distinguished for this quality, said: "My bamboo paintings are not intended merely to paint the fugitive spirit in my breast. What do I care whether they are exact or not, whether the leaves are thick or thin, or whether the branches are straight or crooked?" Again, he said: "What I call painting is only a few swiftly-made strokes of the romantic brush, not intended to copy reality, but *merely to please myself*."

One should recognize, therefore, in Chinese ink-drawings of human figures and landscapes of the southern school, certain influences of calligraphy. First, one sees the swift, powerful and always highly rhythmic strokes. In the twisting lines of the pine tree one sees the same principle of twisting used in Chinese writings. Tung Ch'ich'ang said about painting trees that every line should twist all along, and Wang Hsichih said of calligraphy that every slanting line should have three twists. Tung Ch'ich'ang also said that "when scholars paint, they should apply the laws of the running script, the *lishu*, and the archaic script." One sees also in the hollow wavy lines of the rocks a type of script called *feipo*, which is written with a relatively dry brush, leaving many hollow lines in the centre of the strokes, and sees in the entwining branches of the trees the wriggling lines of the seal character. For this is a secret left us by Chao Mengfu himself. Further, the artistic use of blank space is an important calligraphic principle, for proper spacing is the very first law of calligraphy, as stated by Pao Shenpo. If the spacing is correct, even mere symmetry of form may be sacrificed, as may be seen in Yü Yüjen's writing to-day. It does not matter in Chinese writing if the contour of the character is unsymmetrical, but incorrect spacing is an unforgivable offence, which is the surest sign of immature craftsmanship.

And one recognizes further in the simple unity of design of Chinese paintings the controlling rhythm of the brush, called *piyi*. *Yi* means the "conception" in the artist's mind. To make a Chinese drawing is but to "write out a conception," *hsiehyi*. Before one puts the brush on the paper, the artist has a definite conception in his mind; then as he draws along, he is only writing out that conception through certain strokes; he brooks no interference of irrelevancies, and adds a twig here or a blade there to preserve the organic rhythm; and when he has expressed the essential conception in his mind, he leaves off. For that reason, the picture lives because the conception behind it lives. It is like reading a good epigram; the words end, but the flavour remains. The Chinese artists express this technique by saying that "the conception precedes the brush, and when the brush has done its work, the conception still remains." For the Chinese are consummate masters in suggestion and "leaving off at the right moment." They like good tea and olives which give a "back-flavour," *hweiwei*, which is not felt until a few minutes after eating the olive or drinking the good tea. The total effect of this technique in painting is a quality called *k'ungling*, "empty-and-alive," which means extreme vitality coupled with economy of design.

Chinese poetry gives Chinese painting its spirit. As stated already in the discussion on poetry, it more often happens in China than in the West that the poet is a painter, and the painter, poet. Poetry and painting come from the same human spirit, and it is natural that the spirit and inner technique of both should be the same. We have seen how painting influenced poetry in perspective, because the poet's eye is the painter's eye. But we shall also see how the painter's spirit is the poet's spirit, how the painter shows the same impression, the same method of suggestion, the same emphasis on an indefinable atmosphere, and the same pantheistic union with nature, which characterize Chinese poetry. For the poetic mood and the picturesque moment are often the same, and the artist mind which can seize the one and give it form in poetry can also, with a little cultivation, express the other in painting.

First, we can dismiss the question of perspective, which puzzles Westerners, by explaining once again that Chinese pictures are supposed to be painted from a very high mountain. The perspective one obtains of the world of objects from a high altitude, say, from an aeroplane flying six thousand feet above the earth, must be different from the perspective on the ordinary level. The higher the vantage point, the less, of course, the lines converge toward a point. This is also visibly influenced by the oblong shape of Chinese scrolls, which requires a long distance from the foreground at the bottom of the scroll to the line of the horizon at the top of the scroll.

Like the modern Western painters, the Chinese artists wish to portray, not reality but their own impressions of reality, and hence their impressionistic method. The trouble with Western impressionists is that they are a little too clever and a little too logical. With all their ingenuity, the Chinese artists are not able to produce artistic freaks to startle the layman. The basis of their impressionism is, as has been explained, the theory that "the conception must precede the using of the brush." Not the material reality, therefore, but the artist's conception of the reality is the purport of the painting. They remember that they are painting for fellow human beings and the conceptions must be humanly intelligible to others. They are restrained by the Doctrine of the Golden Mean. Their impressionism is therefore a human impressionism. In painting a picture, their object is to convey a unified conception, which determines what to include and what to leave out, resulting in the *k'ungling* quality.

Since the conception is of primary importance, the greatest pains must be taken to conceive a poetic conception. In the Sung Dynasty, when scholars had competitive examinations in painting under the Imperial Bureau of Painting, we see how this consideration of the poetic conception overruled every other standard. Invariably it was the painting which showed the best conception that won. Now it is characteristic that the best conceptions always depended on the method of suggestion. The themes were poetic enough in themselves, since they were always a line taken from a poem. But the ingenuity lies in the most suggestive interpretation of that poetic line. A few examples will suffice. In the reign of Huichung, once the subject for examinations was a line:

Bamboos cover a wine-shop by the bridge.

Many competitors tried to concentrate on the wine-shop as the centre of the picture. There was one man, however, who painted only a bridge, a bamboo grove by its side, and hidden in that grove, only a shop-sign bearing the character "wine," but no wine-shop at all. And this picture won because the wine-shop was hidden in the imagination.

Another subject given was a line from Wei Ingwu's poem:

At the deserted ferry, a boat drifts across by itself.

The poet had already used the method of suggestion in conveying the atmosphere of silence and desolation by showing that the boat, left alone, drifted across by the force of the current, but the painter carried the method of suggestion further. The winning picture was one which conveyed this feeling of silence and desolation by drawing a bird resting on the boat, and another one about to perch on it. The presence of the birds near the boat suggests that the boat was deserted and no human beings were about.

There was another painting, which was intended to portray the atmosphere of luxury in the rich man's mansion. A modern painter, sick of painting reality, would also try to suggest. But he would probably paint a jumble of a saxophone that magically penetrates through a champagne glass that rests on a woman's breast that hides underneath three-quarters of a motor-car wheel that grazes over the funnels of a Cunard liner, etc., etc. The Chinese impressionist painted, however, only a rich mansion in the background, with its gate standing half-open and a maid peeping out and pouring out a basketful of rich men's delicacies, like ducks' feet, *lichi*, walnuts, hazelnuts, etc. which were delineated with the greatest realism of detail. The sumptuous feast inside was not seen, but only suggested by these left-overs to be thrown into the refuse heap. The conception is therefore everything, on which depends very largely the poetic quality of the work. It is shy of straight portrayal and it always tries to suggest. The constant care of the Chinese artists is: *Leave something for the imagination!*

Had Chinese painting remained content, however, with the emphasis on "conception," which is more a matter of the head than of the heart, it would have struck a blind alley, for art, which ought to appeal primarily to our feelings and our senses, would have degenerated into a mathematical puzzle or a logical problem. No amount of technical skill or cleverness of intellectual conception can give us great art, if it fails to achieve an atmosphere and evoke in us a sympathetic state of emotion. We see this in all great paintings, whether Chinese or European. The mood is therefore everything. The drawing of two birds alighting on a boat serves merely to suggest the absence of any boatman near by, and that absence can mean nothing to us unless, at the same time, it evokes in us a mood of solitude and desolation. Why should not the boat drift across by the force of the current if it wants to? The picture becomes alive and full of meaning to us only when we feel that the boat would not have drifted across like that if it had not been left alone, and this leads to a reflection on the desolation of the scene which could touch our emotions. Of what avail is it to paint the sign of a wine-shop hidden in a bamboo grove by the bridge unless we are led to imagine the people who might be gathered in that wine-shop, where time hangs heavy and life is at peace, and men can spend whole afternoons gossiping about the fisherman's rheumatism and the queen's girlhood romance? The evocation of the mood is therefore everything, in painting as in poetry. This leads us to a consideration of "atmosphere," otherwise called "rhythmic vitality," which has been the highest ideal of Chinese painting for the last fourteen hundred years, since Hsieh Ho first enunciated it and other painters elaborated and discussed and quarrelled over it.

For we must remember that the Chinese painters did not want mere accuracy of detail. Su Tungp'o said: "If one criticizes painting by its verisimilitude, one's understanding is similar to that of a child." But taking away mere verisimilitude, what has the painter to offer us? What, after all, is the purpose of painting? The answer is that the artist should convey to us the spirit of the scenery and evoke in us a sympathetic mood in response. That is the highest object and ideal of Chinese art. We remember how the artist makes periodic visits to the high mountains to refresh his spirit in the mountain air and clean his breast of the accumulated dust of urban thoughts and suburban passions. He climbs to the highest peaks to obtain a moral and spiritual elevation, and he braves the winds and soaks himself in rain to listen to the thundering waves of the sea. He sits among piles of wild rocks and brushwood and hides himself in bamboo groves for days in order to absorb the spirit of life and nature. He should convey to us the benefit of that communion of nature, and communicate to us some of the spirit of the things as it is instilled into his soul, and re-create for us a picture, "surcharged with moods and feelings, ever-changing and wonderful like nature itself." He might, like Mi Yüjen, give us a landscape of nestling clouds and enveloping mists which entwine the rocks and encircle the trees, in which all details are submerged in the general moistness of the atmosphere, or, like Ni Yünlin, he might give us a picture of autumn desolation, with the country a stretch of blank whiteness and the trees so sparse of foliage that only a few dangling leaves affect us by their loneliness and their shivering cold. In the power of this atmosphere and this general rhythm, all details will be forgotten and only the central mood remains. That is "rhythmic vitality," *ch'iyün shengtung*, the highest ideal of Chinese art. Thus poetry and painting meet again.

This is the message of Chinese art, that it teaches us a profound love of nature, for the Chinese painting which really excels by its unique accomplishments is painting of landscape and of nature. The best of Western landscapes, like Corot's, give us the same atmosphere and the same feeling for nature.

But in the portrayal of human forms, the Chinese are

deplorably backward. For the human form is made sub-
servient to the forms of nature. If there is any appreciation of
the female human form as such, we see no traces of it in painting. Ku K'aichih's and Ch'iu Shihchou's female forms suggest,
not the beauties of their bodies but the lines of the winds and
the waves. For this worship of the human body, especially of
the female body, seems to me to be the most singular characteristic of Western art. The most singular contrast between
Chinese and Western art is the difference in the source of
inspiration, which is nature itself for the East and the female
form for the West. Nothing strikes a Chinese mind as being
more grotesque than that a female figure should be labelled
"Contemplation" or that a nude bathing girl should be made
to represent "September Morn." To-day many Chinese are
still unable to reconcile themselves to the fact that Western
civilization requires actual living "models," stripped and
placed before one's eyes, to be stared at daily for two hours at
a time, before one can learn even the first essentials of painting.
Of course there are also many Westerners who are willing only
to hang Whistler's "My Mother" above their mantelpiece,
and who do not dare so much as contemplate a female figure
called "Contemplation." There is still to-day a large proportion of English and American society who apologize for
French pictures in their flats by saying that the room is rented
furnished, and who do not know what to do with a Viennese
porcelain doll that some of their friends have presented them
for Christmas. They generally banish the whole topic from a
conversation by calling these things "art," and the ones who
made then "crazy artists." Nevertheless, the fact remains that
orthodox Western painting is Dionysian in its origin and
inspiration, and that the Western painter seems unable to see
anything without a naked, or nearly naked, human body in
it. Whereas the Chinese painter symbolizes spring by a fat and
well-shaped partridge, the Western painter symbolizes it by
a dancing nymph with a faun chasing after her. And whereas
the Chinese painter can delight in the fine lines of a cicada's
wings and in the full limbs of the cricket, the grasshopper and
the frog, and the Chinese scholar can daily contemplate such
pictures on his wall with continual delight, the Western painter

cannot be satisfied with anything less than Henner's *Liseuse* or *Madeleine*.

This discovery of the human body is, to-day, one of the most potent influences of Western civilization in China, for it changes the whole outlook of life by changing the source of artistic inspiration. In the final analysis this must be called a Greek influence. The Renaissance revival of learning came with the Renaissance worship of the human body and its hearty avowal that life is beautiful. A great part of the Chinese tradition is humanistic enough without any Greek influence, but the proclamation that the human body is beautiful has been strangely lacking in China. Once, however, our eyes are opened to the beauty of the human body, we are not likely to forget it. This discovery of the human body and worship of the female form is bound to be a most potent influence because it is linked up with one of the strongest of human instincts, that of sex. In this sense, we may say that Apollonian art is being replaced by Dionysian art in China, inasmuch as Chinese art is not being taught in most of the Chinese schools, not even in most of the art schools. They are all copying female anatomy from human models or from plaster figures of classical (Greek and Roman) sculpture. It is useless to plead Platonic æstheticism in the worship of the nude, for only effete artists can regard the human body with a passionless admiration, and only effete artists will stoop to make the plea at all. The worship of the human body is sensual, and necessarily so. Real European artists do not deny the fact, but proclaim it. The same accusation cannot be made against Chinese art. But whether we will it or not, the trend has set in and is not likely to be stopped.

IV. ARCHITECTURE

Nature is always beautiful, but human architecture usually is not. For unlike painting, architecture is not even an attempt to copy nature. Architecture was originally a matter of stones and bricks and mortar, piled together to give man shelter from wind and rain. Its first principle was utility, and is often purely so even to this day. Hence the unmitigated ugliness of the best modern factory buildings, school-houses, theatres, post offices, railway stations, and rectilinear streets, whose oppressiveness accounts for the fact that we constantly feel the need to escape to the country. For the greatest difference between nature and these products of the human mind is the infinite richness of nature and the extreme limitations of our ingenuity. The best human mind cannot invent anything besides block houses, with a few conventional mouldings, a rotunda here and a triangular gable there. The most impressive mausoleum or memorial cannot compare with the inventiveness of the trees, even the mutilated and disinfected trees that line the avenues of our main streets, when we remember to put them there. Yet how nature dares! If these trees with their rough surface and irregular shapes had been the products of a human architect, we would have consigned the architect to an insane asylum. Nature even dares to paint the trees green. We are afraid of irregularity. We are afraid even of colour. And we have therefore invented the word "drab" to describe our own existence.

Why is it that, with all the fertility of the human mind, we have not succeeded in producing anything less oppressive than terrace houses and modern pavements and rectilinear streets, from which we have to seek perennial escape by going to summer resorts? Utility is the answer. But utility is not art. The modern industrial age has aggravated the situation, especially with the invention of reinforced concrete. This is a symbol of the industrial age, and it will live as long as the modern industrial civilization lasts. Most of the concrete buildings have forgotten even to put on a roof, because, we are told, the roof is useless. Some have even professed to see an inspiring beauty in the New York skyscrapers. If so, I have not seen any. Their beauty is the beauty of gold: they are beautiful because they suggest the power of millions. They express the spirit of the industrial age.

Yet because we have to look at the houses we build for ourselves every day and have to spend most of our days in them, and because bad architecture can cramp the style of our living, there is a very human demand to make it beautiful. Very subtly the houses change the face of our towns and cities. A roof is not just a roof to shelter us from sun and rain, but something that affects our conception of a home. A door is not just an opening to get inside, but should be the "open sesame" that leads us into the mysteries of people's domestic lives. After all, it makes some difference whether we knock at a drab-coloured house-door or at a vermilion-painted gate with golden hobs on it.

The problem is how to make the bricks and mortar alive and speak the language of beauty. How can we inform it with a spirit and make it say something to us, as European cathedrals are informed with a spirit and speak a silent language of the greatest beauty and sublimity to us? Let us see how the best of Chinese architecture tried to solve this problem.

Chinese architecture seems to have developed along a line different from that of the West. Its main tendency is to seek harmony with nature. In many cases it has succeeded in so doing. It has succeeded because it took its inspiration from the sprig of plum blossoms—translated first into the moving, living lines of calligraphy and secondarily into the lines and forms of architecture. It has supplemented this by the constant use of symbolic motives. And it has, through the prevalent superstition of geomancy, introduced the element of pantheism, which compels regard for the surrounding landscape. Its essential spirit is the spirit of peace and contentment, with its best product in the private home and garden. Its spirit does not, like the Gothic spires, aspire to heaven, but broods over the earth and is contented with its lot. While Gothic cathedrals suggest the spirit of sublimity, Chinese temples and palaces suggest the spirit of serenity.

Unbelievable as it seems, the influence of calligraphy comes in even in Chinese architecture. This influence is seen in the bold use of skeleton structures, like pillars and roofs, in the hatred of straight, dead lines, notably in the evolution of the sagging roof, and in the general sense of form and proportion and grace and severity of temples and palaces.

The problem of revealing or concealing skeleton structures is exactly similar to the problem of "touch" in painting. Just as in Chinese painting the outlining strokes, instead of serving merely to indicate the contour of shapes of things, acquire a bold freedom of their own, so in Chinese architecture the pillars in walls, or rafters and beams in roofs, instead of being hidden in shame, are frankly glorified and become important elements in giving structural form to the buildings. In Chinese buildings the whole structural framework is, as it were, purposefully revealed in full to us. We simply like to see these structural lines, as indicating the basic pattern of the building, as we like to see the rhythmic sketches of outline in painting which stand for the substance of objects for us. For that reason, the wooden framework is usually revealed in house-walls, and the rafters and beams are left visible both inside and outside the house.

This arises from a well-known principle in calligraphy, the principle of "framework," or *chienchia*. Among the various strokes of a character, we usually choose a horizontal or a vertical stroke, or sometimes an enveloping square, which is regarded as giving support to the rest, and this stroke we must make powerfully and make longer, more obvious than the others. Having obtained support in this main stroke, the other strokes will cluster round it or take their point of departure from it. Even in the design of a group of buildings, there is a principle of *axis*, as there is an axis in most Chinese characters. The whole city-planning of Peiping, old Peking, one of the most beautiful cities of the world, is due very largely to an invisible axis of several miles running north and south from the outermost front gate, right across the Emperor's throne, to the Coal Hill central pavilion and the Drum Tower behind. This axis is clearly visible in the character for "middle" or *chung*, 中 , and in other characters, like 東 柬 棗 律 乘.

Perhaps more important than the principle of a straight axis is the use of curves, wavy lines, or irregular rhythmic lines to contrast with the straight lines. This is most clearly seen in the Chinese roofs. Every Chinese temple or palace building or mansion is based, in its essence, upon the combination or contrast of the straight vertical lines of the pillars and the curved lines of the roof. The roof itself contains a contrast between the straight line at the ridge and the sagging line below. This is due to our training in calligraphy in which we are taught that when we have a straight main line, which may be horizontal, vertical or slanting, we must contrast it with curved or soft broken lines around it. The ridge of the roof is furthermore broken by only a few decorative motives. Only by the contrast of these lines are the straight lines of the pillars and the walls endurable. If one sees the best examples of Chinese temples and dwelling-houses, one notices that the roof forms the decorative point of emphasis rather than the pillars or the walls (which often do not exist in front)—the latter being proportionately small compared with the roof itself.

A   B   C

THREE CHARACTERS BY CHENG HSIAOHSU, PREMIER OF "MANCHUKUO," AND FAMOUS CALLIGRAPHIST.

The origin of the famous roof-line traced to calligraphy.

The top of the characters "A" and "B" is a component of Chinese writing, signifying the "roof." Note the sag in the middle and the sweeping effect given by Chinese roofs. The top of character "C" signifies "man," but resembles the upper lines of a roof. Note also the sweeping gesture and the upward curling at the lower ends.

Note further the principle of structure involved and applied to Chinese architecture. Note the rigid vertical line (the pillar) in "A," contrasted with the curve in the "roof" and with other horizontal strokes attached to it. Note in "B" the central vertical curve, with the other strokes clustering around a point at its top and strangely balancing one another.

The origin of the sagging roof, probably the most unique and obvious characteristic of Chinese architecture, has never been properly understood. Some imagine a connection with the primitive tents of our nomadic days. And yet the reason for it is obvious in calligraphy. No one who knows the elements of Chinese calligraphy can fail to see the principle of gracefully sweeping lines. In Chinese calligraphy the greatest difficulty is to bring about strength of stroke, as it is always difficult to give strength to a perfectly straight stroke. On the other hand, a slight bent on either side will give it immediately a feeling of tension. It is only necessary to point to the graceful sag in the "radical" signifying a roof in Chinese characters to see that this is no mere imagination of the author.

Our love for rhythmic or wavy lines or broken lines and our hatred of straight, dead lines become obvious when it is remembered that we have never perpetrated anything quite as ugly as the Cleopatra's Needle. Some modern Chinese architect has perpetrated a Western-styled lighthouse-shaped thing called the West Lake Exhibition Memorial, and it stands there amidst the beauties of West Lake like a sore on a beauty's face, causing all sorts of eye troubles when one looks at it too long.

It would be easy to give examples of our devices to break straight, dead lines. The best classic example is perhaps the balustraded round bridge. The round bridge harmonizes with nature, because it is in a curve and because it is balustraded. Its spans are not as long and its balustrades not as useful as the steel trusses of the Brooklyn Bridge, but no one can deny that it suggests less human cleverness and more beauty. Consider also the pagoda, and how its entire beauty derives from the fact that its outline is broken by a succession of projecting roofs, especially those end-lines that curl upward like the slanting strokes of Chinese writing. Consider also the peculiar pair of stone pillars outside the Tienanmen at Peiping. Nothing is more striking than the wavy-lined symbol of clouds placed horizontally across the top on each pillar, resulting in a form unparalleled in audacity even in Chinese art. The pillars themselves have a wavy surface, whatever the pretext may be. It happens that the waves represent clouds, but this is an artistic pretext to introduce rhythm into the surface. The stone pillars of the Temple of Confucius bear, too, the wavy lines of the entwining dragons. Because the wavy lines of the dragon's body help to break the straight lines, we find the dragon constantly used as a useful decorative motive, apart from its symbolic value.

Everywhere we try to catch and incorporate the natural rhythm of nature and imitate its irregularity. The spirit underlying it all is still the spirit of animism in calligraphy. We break the lines of window bars by using green-glazed tiles of the bamboo pattern. We dare to use round and oblong and vase-shaped doors to break the monotony of the straight walls. Our windows are of as many shapes as the small cakes of Western pastry, imitating a banana leaf, or a peach, or a double-curved melon or a fan. Li Liweng, poet, dramatist and epicure, was responsible for introducing the branch-inlaid windows and partitions. The outline of the window is usually straight. Along this outline, however, he introduced a branch-shaped carving, to give the effect of a living branch stretched across the window. The device is applied to partitions, bed-posts and other types of lattice-work. And lastly, the use of rockery is probably the clearest example of our efforts to introduce into human architecture the natural irregular lines of nature.

In other words, we see everywhere in Chinese architecture an effort to seek relief from straight lines through some form of irregularity suggestive of animal and plant forms. This leads to a consideration of the use of symbolism. The bat, for instance, is very much used as a decorative motive, because its curved wings are capable of so many variations in design, but also because it is a homonym for "good luck." The symbol is the language of the primitive and the child-mind. It is something that every Chinese woman and child can understand.

But symbolism has, further, the virtue of containing within a few conventional lines the thought of the ages and the dreams of the race. It kindles our imagination and leads us into a realm of wordless thought, like the Christian cross or the Soviet hammer and sickle. For such racial thoughts are so big and so enormous that we cannot convey them in words. A Chinese pillar goes up in perfect simplicity and then when it reaches the top and loses itself in a riot of brackets and cornices and bars, we like to see there, as we look up, a pair of mandarin ducks or a grasshopper or an ink-slab and a brush. As we look up at the mandarin ducks which always go in pairs in wedded bliss, our thoughts are turned to woman's love, and as we look at the ink-slab and the brush, we think of the quiet scholar in his study. There, painted in green and blue and gold are the grasshoppers and the crickets and the mandarin ducks, and it is as much happiness as we dare to dream of in this earthly life.

Sometimes we paint landscapes, and sometimes we paint the pleasures of home life, for these are the two eternal themes of Chinese painting.

The dragon is the most honoured animal in China, being a symbol of the Emperor, who always had the best of everything. It is most used in art as a decorative motive, partly because the twining body of the dragon contains in itself such a perfect rhythm, combining grace with power. I daresay we would have used the snake also, had it not been for the fact that the dragon, as a decorative motive, had a profounder meaning, besides having those beautiful claws and horns and beards which are always so useful in breaking monotony. The dragon represents other-worldliness, the "fugitive" or *yi* principle we have mentioned before, and it represents great Taoist wisdom, for it often hides itself among clouds and seldom reveals its whole self. For so is the great Chinaman. Perfect in wisdom and in power, he yet often chooses to conceal himself. He could descend to the depths of mountain ponds as he could rise to the clouds. Beneath the dark waters of the deep pond we cannot see any trace of his existence, but when he rises, like Chuko Liang, he convulses the whole world. For floods in China are always caused by the movements of the dragon, and sometimes we can see him swooping up to heaven in a column of clouds, amidst thunder and lightning, tearing up house-roofs and uprooting old banyan trees. Why, then, should we not worship the dragon, the embodiment of power and wisdom?

But, then, the dragon is not a purely mythological or ante-diluvian entity. To the Chinese, the mountains and rivers are alive, and in many of the winding ridges of mountains we see the dragon's back, and where the mountains gradually descend and merge into the plain or the sea we see the dragon's tail. That is Chinese pantheism, the basis of Chinese geomancy. Thus, although geomancy is undeniably a superstition, it has a great spiritual and architectural value. Its superstition consists in the belief that by placing one's ancestors' tombs in a beautiful scenery, overlooking those dragon mountains and lion hills, one can bring good luck and prosperity to the dead man's descendants. If the location and the landscape scenery are truly unique, if, for instance, five dragons and five tigers unite in

w

making homage to the tomb, it is almost inevitable that one descendant of the line should found an imperial dynasty, or at least become a premier.

But the basis of the superstition is a pantheistic enjoyment of landscape, and geomancy sharpens our eyes to beauty. We then try to see in the lines of mountains and general topography the same rhythm we see in animal forms. Everywhere we turn, nature is alive. Its rhythmic lines sweep east and west and converge toward a certain point. Again in the beauties of the mountains and rivers and general topography, we see not a beauty of static proportions but a beauty of movement. A curve is appreciated less because it is a curve than because it is a sweeping gesture, and a hyperbola is more appreciated than a perfect circle.

The æsthetics of Chinese geomancy has therefore a very close bearing on Chinese architecture in the broad sense of the word. It compels discrimination of the setting and the landscape. By the side of an ancestral grave of one of my friends there was a little pool. The pool was regarded as propitious because it was interpreted as a dragon's eye. And when the pool was dried up, the family lost its fortune. As a matter of fact, the pool, set at one side a distance below the grave, was æsthetically an important element in the general setting of the grave, balancing a line on the other side in a subtly beautiful manner. It was, indeed, like the last dot put on the picture of a dragon, representing its eye and making the whole picture alive. In spite of the superstition and occasional bitter family feuds or clan wars caused by it, as when someone builds a structure to obstruct the perfect sweep and rhythm of line enjoyed from the point of the grave or the ancestral hall, or someone digs a ditch somewhere and therefore breaks the neck of the dragon and dispels all hopes of the family's rise to power—in spite of all this, I wonder very much whether geomancy has not contributed more to the richness of our æsthetic life than it has hindered our knowledge of geology.

For the last and most important element of Chinese archi-tecture always remains its essential harmony with nature. In a way, the setting is more important than the jewel. Architecture that is perfect in itself but does not fit into the landscape can only jar us by its disharmony and by its violent self-assertion, which we call bad taste. The best architecture is that which loses itself in the natural landscape and becomes one with it, belongs to it. This principle has guided all forms of Chinese architecture, from the camel-back bridge to the pagoda, the temple and the little open pavilion on the edge of a pond. Its lines should soothe but not obtrude. Its roofs should nestle quietly beneath the kind shade of trees and soft boughs should gently brush its brow. The Chinese roof does not shout out loud and does not point its fingers at heaven. It only shows peace and bows in modesty before the firmament. It is a sign of the place where we humans live, and it suggests a certain amount of decency by covering up our human habitations. For we always remember to put a roof on *all* our houses, and do not allow them to stare at heaven in their unashamed nakedness like modern concrete buildings.

The best architecture is that in which we are not made to feel where nature ends and where art begins. For this, the use of colour is of supreme importance. The terra-cotta walls of the Chinese temple merge harmoniously into the purple of the mountain sides, and its glazed roofs, laid in green, Prussian blue, purple or golden yellow, mingle with the red autumn leaves and the blue sky to give us a harmonious whole. And we stand and look at it from a distance and call it beautiful.

Chapter Nine

THE ART OF LIVING

I. The Pleasures of Life

WE do not know a nation until we know its pleasures of life, just as we do not know a man until we know how he spends his leisure. It is when a man ceases to do the things he has to do, and does the things he likes to do, that his character is revealed. It is when the repressions of society and business are gone and when the goads of money and fame and ambition are lifted, and man's spirit wanders where it listeth, that we see the inner man, his real self. Life is harsh and politics is dirty and commerce is sordid, so that it would often be unfair to judge a man by his public life. For this reason, I find so many of our political scoundrels are such lovable human beings, and so many of our futile bombastic college presidents extremely good fellows at home. In the same way, I think the Chinese at play are much more lovable than the Chinese in business. Whereas the Chinese in politics are ridiculous and in society are childish, at leisure they are at their best. They have so much leisure and so much leisurely joviality. This chapter of their life is an open book for anyone who cares to come near them and live with them to read. There the Chinese are truly themselves and at their best, because there they show their best characteristic, geniality.

Given extensive leisure, what do not the Chinese do? They eat crabs, drink tea, taste spring water, sing operatic airs, fly kites, play shuttle-cock, match grass blades, make paper boxes, solve complicated wire puzzles, play *mahjong*, gamble and pawn clothing, stew *ginseng*, watch cock-fights, romp with their children, water flowers, plant vegetables, graft fruits, play chess, take baths, hold conversations, keep cage-birds, take afternoon naps, have three meals in one, guess fingers, play at palmistry, gossip about fox spirits, go to operas, beat drums and gongs, play the flute, practise on calligraphy, munch duck-gizzards, salt carrots, fondle walnuts, fly eagles, feed carrier-pigeons, quarrel with their tailors, go on pilgrimages, visit temples, climb mountains, watch boatraces, hold bullfights, take aphrodisiacs, smoke opium, gather at street corners, shout at aeroplanes, fulminate against the Japanese, wonder at the white people, criticize their politicians, read Buddhist classics, practise deep-breathing, hold Buddhist séances, consult fortune-tellers, catch crickets, eat melon seeds, gamble for moon-cakes, hold lantern competitions, burn rare incense, eat noodles, solve literary riddles, train pot-flowers, send one another birth-day presents, kow-tow to one another, produce children, and sleep.

For the Chinese have always had geniality, joviality, taste and finesse. The great majority still keep their geniality and their joviality, although the educated ones in modern China are usually bad-tempered and pessimistic, having lost all their sense of values. Few of them still show any taste and finesse, and this is natural, for taste comes with tradition. Man is taught to admire beautiful things, not by books but by social example, and by living in a society of good taste. The spirit of man in the industrial age is ugly, anyway, and the spirit of man in China, throwing overboard all that is best and finest in their social tradition in a mad rush for things Western without the Western tradition, is uglier still to look at. In the whole villadom of Shanghai, with all its millionaires, there is only one decent Chinese garden and it is owned by a Jew. All of the Chinese have gone in for the tennis lawn and geometric flower-beds and trimmed hedges, and tailored trees trained to look a perfect circle or a perfect cone, and flowers planted to represent letters of the English alphabet. Shanghai is not China, but Shanghai is an ominous indication of what modern China may come to. It leaves a bad flavour in our mouths like those Chinese-made Western cream-cakes made with pigs' lard. And it jars on our senses like those Chinese brass bands playing "Onward, Christian Soldiers!" in a funeral march. Tradition and taste must take time to grow up.

There was taste in ancient China, and we can see what is left of it in beautiful old bookbindings, in exquisite letter-

papers, in old porcelain, in great paintings, and in all the old
knick-knacks not yet touched by the modern influence. One
cannot fondle the beautiful old books or see the scholars'
letter-papers without seeing that man's spirit in old China had
an understanding of tone and harmony and mellow colours.
Only two or three decades ago there was still a time when men
wore gowns of the ducks'-egg green, and women wore mauve,
and when *crêpe de Chine* was really *crêpe de Chine*, and good red
ink-pad for the seal still had a market. Now the whole silk
industry has collapsed recently because artificial silk is so much
cheaper, and it washes so well, and good red ink-pad, costing
thirty-two dollars an ounce, has no market because it has given
place to purple ink for rubber stamps.

This ancient geniality is best reflected in the Chinese familiar
essay, *hsiaop'inwen*, which is the product of the Chinese spirit
at play. The pleasures of a leisurely life are its eternal themes.
Its subject-matter covers the art of drinking tea, the carving of
seals and the appreciation of the cuts and the quality of the
stones, the training of pot-flowers and the caring for orchids,
boating on the lake, climbing historically famous mountains,
visiting ancient beauties' tombs, composing poetry under the
moon and looking at a storm on a high mountain—all written
in a style leisurely and chatty and suave, as disarmingly hos-
pitable as a friend's chat by the fireside and as poetically
disorderly as the recluse's dress, a style trenchant and yet
mellow, like good old wine. And through it all pervades the
spirit of man happy with himself and the universe, poor in
possessions but rich in sentiments and discriminating in taste,
experienced and full of worldly wisdom and yet simple-
hearted, a bottle of emotions and yet apparently indifferent
to all the outside world, cynically contented and wisely idle,
loving simplicity and good material living. This spirit of geniality
is best seen in the Preface to *All Men Are Brothers*, attributed to
the author, but really forged by the great seventeenth-century
critic, Ch'in Shengt'an. This Preface, in itself an excellent example of the Chinese familiar essay regarding both manner and
matter, reads like an essay on Leisure, and the amazing thing
is that it was intended by its author as a preface to a novel.[1]

[1] See translation by Pearl S. Buck in *All Men Are Brothers*, John Day, 1933.

In China, man knows a great deal about the art of all arts, viz., the art of living. A younger civilization may be keen on making progress, but an old civilization, having seen naturally a great deal of life, is keen only on living. In the case of China, with the spirit of humanism, which makes man the centre of all things and human happiness the end of all knowledge, this emphasis on the art of living is all the more natural. But even without humanism, an old civilization must have a different standard of values, for it alone knows "the durable pleasures of life," which are merely matters of the senses, food, drink, house, garden, women, and friendship. That is what life comes to in its essence. That is why in old cities like Paris and Vienna we have good chefs, good wine, beautiful women and beautiful music. After a certain point human intelligence struck a blind alley, and, tired of asking questions, took again the vine for its spouse in the Khayyám manner. Any nation, therefore, that does not know how to eat and enjoy living like the Chinese is uncouth and uncivilized in our eyes.

In the works of Li Liweng (seventeenth century), there is an important section devoted to the pleasures of life, which is a vade-mecum of the Chinese art of living, from the house and garden, interior decorations, partitions, to women's toilet, coiffures, the art of applying powder and rouge, on to the art of cooking and directions for the *gourmet*, and finally to the ways of securing pleasure for the rich man and the poor man, and in all the four seasons, the methods of banning worry, regulating sex-life, preventing and curing illness, ending in the unique division of medicine into the very sensible three categories: "medicine that one likes by temperament," "medicine that is needed by the moment," and "medicine that one loves and longs for." This chapter alone contains more wisdom regarding medical advice than a whole college course of medicine. This epicure dramatist, for he was a great comic poet, spoke of what he knew. Some instances of his thorough understanding of the art of living are given here, as showing the essential Chinese spirit.

Thus Li Liweng wrote about "Willows" in his intensely human study of different flowers and trees and the art of enjoying them:

The important thing about willows is that their branches hang down, for if they did not hang down, they would not be willows. It is important that the branches be long, for otherwise they cannot sway gracefully in the wind. What then would be the use of their hanging down? This tree is a place where the cicadas love to rest, as well as the birds. It is to the credit of this tree that we often hear music in the air and do not feel lonely in summer. Especially is this the case with tall willow trees. In short, the planting of trees is not only to please the eye, but also to please the ear as well. The pleasure of the eye is sometimes limited because we are lying down on a bed. On the other hand, the ear can take its pleasure all the time. The most lovely notes of the birds are not heard when we are sitting but when we are lying down. Everyone knows that the birds' songs should be heard at dawn, but does not know why they should be heard at dawn, as people do not think about it. The birds are continually afraid of the shooting gun, and after seven o'clock in the morning all the people are up and the birds no longer feel at ease. Once they are on their guard they can never sing whole-heartedly, and even if they sing their song cannot be beautiful. That is why daytime is not the proper time for listening to the birds. At dawn the people are not up yet, with the exception of a few early risers. Since the birds are then free from worry, naturally they can finish their song at ease. Besides, their tongues have been lying idle for the whole night, and are now itching to try their skill. Consequently, when they sing they sing with the full gladness of their hearts. Chuangtse was not a fish and could understand the happiness of the fish; Liweng is not a bird and can understand the happiness of the birds. All singing birds should regard me as their bosom friend. . . . There are many points about the planting of trees, but there is one point which is an annoyance to the cultivated. When the tree-leaves are too thick they shut out the moonlight, like shutting off a beauty from our view. The trees cannot be held guilty of this, because it is the men who are at fault. If we could spend a thought on this point at the time of planting trees, and allow a corner of the sky to be shown behind them in order to wait for the rising and setting of the moon, we could then receive its benefits both at night and day.

Again, we see some very good sense in his advice on women's dress:

The important thing about women's dress is not fineness of material but neatness, not gorgeous beauty but elegance, not that it agrees with her family standing but that it agrees with her face. . . . If you take a dress and let several women try it on in succession, you will see that it agrees with some and not with others, because the complexion must harmonize with the dress. If a wealthy lady's face does not agree with rich patterns but agrees with simple colours, and she should insist on having rich patterns, would not her dress be the enemy of her face? . . . Generally, one whose complexion is white and soft and whose figure is light and round will be shown to advantage in any dress. Light colours will show her whiteness but deep colours will still better show her whiteness. Dresses of fine material will show her delicacy but dresses of coarse material will still better show her delicacy. . . . But how few women are of this type? The average woman must choose her dress, and must not take any kind of material. . . .

When I was young, I remember the young girls used to wear shades of pink, and the older women used to wear mauve, and later scarlet was changed for pink, and blue was substituted for mauve, and still later scarlet gave place to purple and blue gave place to green. After the change of the dynasty [beginning of Manchu régime], both green and purple disappeared, and both young and old women changed into black.

Then Li Liweng went on to discuss the great virtue of black, his favourite colour: how it fitted all complexions and all ages, and how among the poor it enabled them to wear a dress longer without showing dirt, and how among the rich they could wear beautiful colours underneath, so that when the wind blew, the beautiful colours would be revealed underneath, leaving a great deal to the imagination.

Again, in the essay on "Sleep," there is a beautiful section on the art of taking afternoon naps:

> The pleasure of an afternoon nap is double that of sleep at night. This is especially to be recommended for summer, but not for the other three seasons. This is not because I am favouring summer, but because a summer day is twice as long as a winter day, and a summer night is not equal to half a winter night. If a man rests only at night in summer, that means he is spending one-quarter of his time in recuperating and three-quarters in working. How can a man's energy last under this arrangement? Besides, the summer heat is intensive and naturally brings about fatigue. It is as natural to go to sleep in fatigue as to eat when hungry, or to drink when thirsty. This is the soundest of all hygiene. After the midday meal, he should wait a while until the food is digested and then pace near the bed gradually. He should not have the idea of being determined to sleep, for if one sleeps with that idea the sleep is not sweet. He should first attend to something, and before the thing is done, a drowsiness comes over him, and the people of the dreamland come to beckon him, and he arrives at the fairy place without any effort or consciousness of his own. I like a line from an old verse: "My hands when weary throw the book away and the afternoon nap is long." When you hold a book in your hand, you have no idea of going to sleep, and when you throw it away, you have no idea of doing any reading. That is why you do it without any consciousness and without any effort. This is the alpha and omega of the art of sleeping. . . .

When mankind knows the art of sleeping as Li Liweng describes it, then mankind may truly call itself civilized.

II. HOUSE AND GARDEN

Some of the principles of Chinese architecture have already been explained in the discussion on this subject. The Chinese house and garden, however, present a more intricate aspect that deserves special attention. The principle of harmony with nature is carried further, for in the Chinese conception the house and garden are not separate, but are parts of an organic whole, as evidenced in the phrase *yüancheh*, or "garden-home." A house and a garden can never become an organic whole so long as we have a square building, surrounded by a mown tennis lawn. The word for "garden" here does not suggest a lawn and geometric flower-beds, but a patch of earth where one can plant vegetables and fruits and sit under the shade of trees. The Chinese conception of the home requires that the home, with a well, a poultry yard, and a few date trees, must be able to arrange itself commodiously in space. And given commodious space, in ancient China as in all rural civilizations, the house itself dwindles to a comparatively less important position in the general scheme of the home garden.

Human civilization has changed so much that space is something that the average man cannot own and cannot have. We have gone so far that a man is entirely complacent when he owns a *mow* of civilized lawn, in the midst of which he succeeds in digging a five-foot pond to keep his goldfish and making a mound that would not take ants five minutes to crawl to the top. This has changed entirely our conception of the home. There is no more poultry yard, no well and no place where one's children can catch crickets and get comfortably dirty. Instead, our home becomes physically like a pigeon's house called an "apartment," with a combination of buttons, switches, cabinets, rubber mats, keyholes, wires and burglar-alarms which we call a home. There are no attics, no dirt and no spiders. Our perversion of the idea of a home has gone so far that some Western people are even proud of the fact that they sleep on a bed which is the back of a daytime sofa. They show it to their friends and marvel at modern technological civilization. The modern spiritual home is broken up because the physical home has disappeared, as Edward Sapir pointed out. People move into a three-room flat and then wonder why they can never keep their children at home.

The average poor Chinese in the country has more space of his own than a New York professor. But there are Chinese living in cities as well, and not all of them own huge gardens.

Art consists in doing with what one has on hand and still allowing for human fancies to come in and break the monotony of
blank walls and cramped backyards. Shen Fu (middle
eighteenth century), author of the *Fousheng Liuchi*, outlines in
this tender little book, which reflects the best spirit of Chinese
culture, how even a poor scholar can manage to have a beautiful house. From the principle of irregularity in Chinese architecture we develop, with intricate human fancies, the principle
of concealment and surprise, as capable of infinite development
in the designing of the rich man's country villa as in that of the
poor scholar's dwelling house. In *Fousheng Liuchi* (*Six Chapters of
a Floating Life*) we find an important statement of this principle.
With this formula we can, according to the author, make even
a poor scholar's house artistically satisfying. This principle
is stated in the formula that we should "show the large in the
mall and the small in the large, provide for the real in the
nreal and for the unreal in the real." Shen Fu ssays:

> As to the planning of garden pavilions and towers, of
> winding corridors and outhouses, and in the designing of
> rockery or the training of flower-trees, one should try to show
> the small in the large and the large in the small, and provide
> for the real in the unreal and for the unreal in the real. One
> reveals and conceals alternately, making it sometimes
> apparent and sometimes hidden. This is not just "rhythmic
> irregularity," nor does it depend on having a wide space and
> a great expenditure of labour and material. Pile up a mound
> with earth dug from the ground and decorate it with rocks,
> mixed with flowers; use live plum branches for your fence,
> and plant creepers over the walls. Thus there will be a hill
> in a place which is without hills. In the big open spaces,
> plant bamboos that grow quickly and train plum trees with
> thick branches to cover them. This is to show the small in
> the large. When the courtyard is small, the wall should be
> a combination of convex and concave shapes, decorated with
> green, covered with ivy, and inlaid with big slabs of stone
> with inscriptions on them. Thus when you open your window
> you seem to face a rocky hillside, alive with rugged beauty.
> This is to show the large in the small. Contrive so that an

apparently blind alley leads suddenly into an open space and the kitchen leads through a backdoor into an unexpected courtyard. This is to provide for the real in the unreal. Let a door lead into a blind courtyard and conceal the view by placing a few bamboo trees and a few rocks. Thus you suggest something which is not there. Place low balustrades along the top of a wall so as to suggest a roof garden which does not exist. This is to provide for the unreal in the real. Poor scholars who live in crowded houses should follow the method of the boatmen in our native district who make clever arrangements with their limited space on the bows of their boats, making certain modifications. . . . When my wife and I were staying at Yangchow, we lived in a house of only two rooms, but (by such arrangements) the two bedrooms, the kitchen and the parlour were all arranged with an exquisite effect, and we did not feel the cramping of space. Yün once said laughingly to me, "The arrangements are exquisite enough, but, after all, it lacks the atmosphere of a rich man's house." It was so indeed.

Let us follow for a while these two guileless creatures, a poor Chinese scholar and his artistic wife, and see how they try to squeeze the last drop of happiness from a poor and sorrow-laden life, always fearful of the jealousy of the gods and afraid that their happiness may not last.

Once I visited my ancestral tombs on a hill and found some pebbles of great beauty with faint tracings on them. On coming back I talked it over with Yün, and said: "People mix putty with Hsüanchow stones in white stone basins because the colours of the two elements blend. The yellow pebbles of this hill, however, are different, and although they are very elegant, they will not blend in colour with putty. What can we do?" "Take some of the worse quality," said she, "and pound them into small pieces and mix them in the putty before it is dry, and perhaps when it is dry it will be of the same colour." So we did as she suggested, and used a rectangular Yihsing earthen pot, over which we piled up a mountain peak on the left, coming down in undulations to the right. On its back we made rugged square lines like those in the painting of Ni Yünlin, so that the whole looked like a rocky precipice overhanging a river. On one side we made a hollow place which we filled with mud and on which we planted multi-leaf white duckweed. On the rocks we planted dodder. This took us quite a few days to finish. In late autumn the dodder grew all over the hill, like wistarias hanging down from a rock. The red dodder flowers made a striking contrast to the white duckweed, which had grown luxuriantly, too, from the pond underneath. Looking at it, one could imagine oneself transported to some fairy region. We put this under the eaves, and discussed between ourselves where we should put a pavilion, where we should put a farmer's hut, and where we should put a stone inscription, "Where petals drop and waters flow." And Yün further discussed with me where we could build our home, where we could fish, and where we would have to jump across, all so absorbed as if we were moving into the little imaginary universe to live. One night two cats were fighting for food and it fell down from the eaves, broken into pieces, basin and all. I sighed and said, "The gods seem to be jealous even of such a little effort of our own." And we both shed tears.

What distinguishes a home from a public building is the personal touch that we give it, and the time and thought we spend on it. Home designs and interior decorations are not something that we can buy outright from an architect or a first-class firm, and it is only when this spirit of leisure and tender loving care exists that living at home can become an art and a pleasure. Both Shen Fu and Li Liweng show this tender love for the small things of life, and give ingenious advice on the training of flowers, the arrangement of flowers in vases, the use of courtyards, the art of perfuming, the art of making windows look out on a superb view that could go into a painting, the hanging of scrolls, the arrangement of chairs, including Li Liweng's invention of a heated desk with charcoal burning underneath so as to keep the feet warm in winter. It would be manifestly impossible to go into all these details of interior decoration. Suffice it to say that in the arrangement of courtyards and the scholars' studios, and in the arrangement of vases, the essential idea is the beauty of simplicity. Many of the scholars' studies are made to look out on a small clean courtyard, which is the very embodiment of quietude itself. In the middle of that courtyard stand just two or three of those rhythmic and perforated rocks, bearing the mark of sea-waves, or some rare specimens of fossilized barks, and a small bush of bamboos which are so loved because of the fineness of their lines. Perhaps in the wall is a fan-shaped window with glazed tiles in bamboo pattern as bars, giving just the merest suggestion of the existence of a world of wheat fields and farmers' houses outside.

The principle of surprise which Shen Fu outlined for the poor scholar's small residence holds good in a rich man's home garden. The English word "garden" gives an entirely erroneous idea of the Chinese *yüan*, for "garden" suggests a lawn and an infinite variety of flowers, altogether too prim and tidy to suit Chinese taste. The Chinese *yüan* suggests first of all a wild landscape, perhaps better arranged and more artistically planned than nature, but still a bit of nature itself, with trees, mounds, creeks, bridges, a rowing boat, a patch of vegetable fields, fruit trees and some flowers. Dotted in this natural landscape are the human structures, the bridges, pavilions, long winding corridors, irregular rockeries, and sweeping roofs, so perfectly belonging to the scenery as to become a whole with it. There are no even-cut hedges, no perfectly conical or circular trees, no symmetric rows lining avenues as if in battle formation, and no straight pavements—none of all those elements that contribute to make Versailles so ugly in Chinese eyes. Everywhere we see curves, irregularity, concealment and suggestion.

No Chinese mansion allows an outsider to look through the iron gates at a long drive, for that would be against the principle of concealment. Facing the gate, we see perhaps a small courtyard or a mound giving no idea whatsoever of the expansiveness of space inside, and leading one step by step into newer and bigger views, in a continual series of surprises and astonishments. For we wish to show the small in the large, and show the large in the small. There is little possibility of gaining a bird's-eye view of the whole at a glance, and if there were, there would be nothing left for the imagination. The Chinese garden is characterized by studied disorderliness, which alone can give the feeling of the infinite and make one imagine the garden to be larger than it is.

There is something amounting to religious fervour and sacred devotion when a cultivated rich Chinese scholar begins planning for his garden. The account of Ch'i Piauchia (1602–1645) is interesting as showing this spirit.

In the beginning, I wanted to build only four or five rooms, and some friends told me where I should build a pavilion and where I should build a summer-house. I did not think seriously of these suggestions, but after a while these ideas would not let me alone, and it seemed indeed I should have a pavilion here and a summer-house there. Before I had finished the first stage, new ideas forced themselves upon me, and they chased after me in all out-of-the-way places, and sometimes they came to me in my dreams, and a new vista opened before my imagination. Hence my interest grew more and more intense every day and I would go to the garden early in the morning and come back late at night, and leave any domestic business to be attended to under the lamplight.   Early in the morning, while resting on my pillow, I saw the first rays of the morn and got up and asked my servant to go with me on a boat, and although it was only a mile off, I was impatient to get to the place. This continued through winter and summer, rain or shine, and neither the biting cold nor the scorching sun could restrain ne from it, for there was not a single day when I was not out ɔn the spot. Then I felt under my pillow, and knew my money was gone, and felt annoyed over it. But when I arrived at the spot, I wanted always more and more stones and material. Hence for the last two years my purse is always empty, and I have been ill and got well again, and fallen ill again. . . . There are two halls, three pavilions, four corridors, two towers and three embankments. . . . In general, where there is too much space I put in a thing; where it is too crowded I take away a thing; where things cluster together I spread them out; where the arrangement too diffuse I tighten it a bit; where it is difficult to walk upon I level it; and where it is level I introduce a little unevenness. It is like a good doctor curing a patient, using both nourishing and excitative medicines, or like a good general in the field, using both normal and surprise tactics. Again it is like a master painter at his work, not allowing a single dead stroke, or like a great writer writing essays, not permitting a single unharmonious sentence. . . .

Harmony, irregularity, surprise, concealment and suggestion —these are some of the principles of Chinese garden-planting, as they are of other forms of Chinese art.

III. EATING AND DRINKING

The question has often been asked as to what we eat. The answer is that we eat all the edible things on this earth. We eat crabs by preference, and often eat barks by necessity. Economic necessity is the mother of our inventions in food. We are too over-populated and famine is too common for us not to eat everything we can lay our hands on. And it stands to reason that in this positively exhaustive experiment on edibles, we should have stumbled upon important discoveries, as most scientific or medical discoveries have been stumbled upon. For one thing, we have discovered the magic tonic and building qualities of *ginseng*, for which I am willing to give personal testimony as to its being the most enduring and most energy-giving tonic known to mankind, distinguished by the slowness and gentleness of its action. But apart from such accidental discoveries of medical or culinary importance, we are undoubtedly the only truly omnivorous animals on earth, and so long as our teeth last, we should continue to occupy that position. Some day a dentist will yet discover that we have the best teeth as a nation. Gifted with these teeth and driven by famine, there is no reason why we should not at some particular time of our national life suddenly discover that roasted beetles and fried bees' chrysalis are great delicacies. The only thing

x

we have not discovered and will not eat is cheese. The Mongols could not persuade us to eat cheese, and the Europeans do not have a greater chance of doing so.

It is useless to use logical reasoning in the matter of our food, which is determined by prejudices. On both sides of the Atlantic Ocean two shellfish are common, the soft-shelled clam, *Mya arenaria*, and the edible mussel, *Mytilus edulis*. The species of these two molluscs are the same on both sides of the water. In Europe, mussels are eaten freely, but not clams, while the reverse is the case on the American side, according to the authority of Dr. Charles W. Townsend (*Scientific Monthly*, July, 1928). Dr. Townsend also mentions the fact that flounders fetch high prices in England and in Boston but are considered "not fit to eat" by Newfoundland villagers. We eat mussels with the Europeans and eat clams with the Americans, but we don't eat oysters raw as the Americans do. It is useless, for instance, for anybody to convince me that snake's meat tastes like chicken. I have lived in China forty years without eating a snake, or seeing any of my relatives do so. Tales of eating snakes travel faster than tales of eating chicken, but actually we eat more chickens and better chickens than the white people, and snake-eating is as much a curiosity to the Chinese as it is to the foreigners.

All one can say is that we are very catholic in our tastes, and that any rational man can take anything off a Chinese table without any qualm of conscience. What famine dictates is not for us human mortals to choose. There is nothing that a man will not eat when hard pressed by hunger. And no one is entitled to condemn until he knows what famine means. Some of us have been forced in times of famine to eat babies—and even this must be humanly rare—but, thank God, we do not eat them raw as the English eat their beef!

If there is anything we are serious about, it is neither religion nor learning, but food. We openly acclaim eating as one of the few joys of this human life. This question of attitude is very important, for unless we are honest about it we will never be able to lift eating and cooking into an art. The difference of attitude regarding the problem of food is represented in Europe by the French and the English. The French eat enthusiastically, while the English eat apologetically. The Chinese national genius decidedly leans toward the French in the matter of feeding ourselves.

The danger of not taking food seriously and allowing it to degenerate into a slipshod business may be studied in the English national life. If they had known any taste for food their language would reveal it. The English language does not provide a word for *cuisine:* they call it just "cooking." They have no proper word for *chef:* they just call him a cook. They do not speak about their *menu*, but know only what are called "dishes." And they have no word for *gourmet:* they just call him "Greedy Gut" in their nursery rhymes. The truth is, the English do not admit that they have a stomach. No stomach is fit for conversation unless it happens to be "sick" or "aching." The result is that while the Frenchman will talk about the *cuisine* of his *chef* with—what seems to the English mind—immodest gestures, the Englishman can hardly venture to talk about the "food" of his "cook" without impairing the beauty of his language. When hard pressed by his French host he might be willing to mutter between his teeth that "that pudding is awfully good" and there let the matter rest. Now if a pudding is good it is good for some definite reasons, and about these problems the Englishman does not bother himself. All the English are interested in is how to strengthen themselves against influenza, as with Bovril, and save the doctor's bills.

Now you cannot develop a national culinary art unless you are willing to discuss it and exchange your opinions on it. The first condition of learning how to eat is to talk about it. Only in a society wherein people of culture and refinement inquire after their cooks' health, instead of talking about the weather, can the art of *cuisine* be developed. No food is really enjoyed unless it is keenly anticipated, discussed, eaten and then commented upon. Preachers should not be afraid to condemn a bad steak from their pulpits and scholars should write essays on the culinary art as the Chinese scholars do. Long before we have any special food, we think about it, rotate it in our minds, anticipate it as a secret pleasure to be shared with some of our closest friends, and write notes about it in our invitation letters, like the following: "My nephew has just brought some special vinegar from Chinkiang and a real Nanking salted duck from Laoyuchai," or this, "This is the end of June, and if you don't come, you won't taste another shad till next May." Long before the autumn moon rises, a real scholar, like Li Liweng as he himself confesses, would plan and save money for the crabs, decide upon an historical place where he could have the crab dinner with his friends under the mid-autumn moon or in a wilderness of chrysanthemums, negotiate with some of his friends to bring wine from Governor Tuan Fang's cellar, and meditate upon it as the English meditate upon their champion sweepstakes number. Only in this spirit can the matter of feeding ourselves be elevated into the level of an art.

We are unashamed of our eating. We have "Su Tungp'o pork" and "Kiang bean-curd." In England, a Wordsworth steak or Galsworthy cutlet would be unimaginable. Wordsworth sang about "simple living and high thinking," but he failed to note that good food, especially fresh-cut bamboo-shoots and mushrooms, counts among the real joys of a simple rural life. The Chinese poets, with a more utilitarian philosophy, have frankly sung about the "minced perch and *shun*-vegetable soup" of their native home. This thought is regarded as so poetic that officials in their petition for resignation will say that they are "thinking of *shun*-vegetable" as a most elegant expression. Actually our love of fatherland is largely a matter of recollection of the keen sensual pleasures of our childhood. The loyalty to Uncle Sam is the loyalty to American dough-nuts, and the loyalty to the *Vaterland* is the loyalty to *Pfann-kuchen* and *Stollen*, but the Americans and the Germans will not admit it. Many Americans, while abroad, sigh for their ham and sweet potatoes at home, but they will not admit that this makes them think of home, nor will they put it in their poetry.[1]

The seriousness with which we regard eating can be shown in many ways. Anyone who opens the pages of the *Red Chamber Dream* or of any Chinese novel will be struck by the detailed and constant descriptions of the entire *menu* of what Taiyü

[1] A striking fact is the frequency of words like "intestines" and "belly" in Chinese poetry: *e.g.*, "The bamboo-shoots are fresh and my rice-bowl is too small; the fish is delicious, and my wine-intestines widen."

had for breakfast or what Paoyü had at midnight. Cheng Panch'iao apotheosized rice congee in his letter to his brother:

> On cold days, when poor relatives or friends arrive, first hand them a bowl of fried rice in boiling water, with a small dish of ginger or pickles. It is the most effective means of warming up old people and the poor. In your days of leisure, swallow cakes made of broken rice, or cook "slip-slop congee," and hold the bowl between your two hands and eat it with shrugged shoulders. On a cold frosty morning, this will make your whole body warm. Alas! Alas! I think I'll become a farmer for the remainder of my days!

The Chinese accept food as they accept sex, women and life in general. No great English poet or writer would condescend to write a Cook Book, which they regard as belonging outside the realms of literature and worthy of the efforts of Aunt Susan only. But the great poet-dramatist Li Liweng did not consider it beneath his dignity to write about the cooking of mushrooms and all kinds of vegetarian and non-vegetarian foods. Another great poet and scholar, Yüan Mei, wrote a whole book on cooking, besides writing a most wonderful essay on his cook. He described his cook as Henry James described the English butler, as a man carrying himself with dignity and understanding in his profession. But H. G. Wells, who of all English minds is the one most likely to write about English food, evidently cannot write it, and no hope is to be expected from the less encyclopædic minds. Anatole France was the type that might have left us some wonderful recipe for frying calf's liver or cooking mushrooms, possibly in his intimate letters, but I doubt very much whether he has left it as part of his literary heritage.

Two principles distinguish Chinese from European cooking. One is that we eat food for its *texture*, the elastic or crisp effect it has on our teeth, as well for fragrance, flavour and colour. Li Liweng said that he was a slave to crabs, because they had the combination of fragrance, flavour and colour. The idea of texture is seldom understood, but a great part of the popularity of bamboo-shoots is due to the fine resistance the young shoots give to our teeth The appreciation of bamboo-shoots is probably the most typical example of our taste. Being not oily, it has a certain fairy-like "fugitive" quality about it. But the most important principle is that it lends flavour to meat (especially pork) cooked with it, and, on the other hand, it receives the flavour of the pork itself. This is the second principle, that of mixing of flavours. The whole culinary airt of China depends on the art of mixture. While the Chinese recognize that many things, like fresh fish, must be cooked in their own juice, in general they mix flavours a great deal more than Western cooks do. No one, for instance, knows how cabbage tastes until he has tasted it when properly cooked with chicken, and the chicken flavour has gone into the cabbage and the cabbage flavour has gone into the chicken. From this principle of mixture, any number of fine and delicate combinations can be developed. Celery, for instance, may be eaten raw and alone, but when Chinese see, in a foreign dinner, vegetables like spinach or carrots cooked separately and then served on the same plate with pork or roast goose, they smile at the barbarians.

The Chinese, whose sense of proportion is so wonderfully acute in painting and architecture, seem to have completely lost it in the matter of food, to which they give themselves whole-heartedly when they seat themselves around a dinner-table. Any big course, like the fat duck, coming after twelve or thirteen other courses, should be a sufficient meal in itself for any human being. This is due to a false standard of courtesy, and to the fact that as course after course is served during dinners, the people are supposed to be occupied in different wine-games or contests of poetry during the intervals, which naturally lengthens the time required and gives more time for the stomach to assimilate the food. Most probably the relatively lower efficiency of Chinese government officials is due directly to the fact that all of them are subjected to an inhuman routine of three or four dinners a night. One-fourth of their food goes to nourish them and three-fourths to kill them. That accounts for the prevalence of rich men's ailments, like diseases of the liver and the kidneys, which are periodically announced in the newspapers when these officials see fit to retire from the political arena for reasons of convenience.

Although the Chinese may learn from the West a great d about a sense of proportion in arranging for feasts, they have, in this field as in medicine, many famous and wonderful recipes to teach the Westerners. In the cooking of ordinary things like vegetables and chickens, the Chinese have a rich store to hand to the West, when the West is ready and humble enough to learn it. This seems unlikely until China has built a few good gun-boats and can punch the West in the jaw, when it will be admitted that we are unquestionably better cooks as a nation. But until that time comes, there is no use talking about it. There are thousands of Englishmen in the Shanghai Settlement who have never stepped inside a Chinese restaurant, and the Chinese are bad evangelists. We never force salvation on anybody who does not come to ask for it. We have no gun-boats, anyway, and even if we had, we would never care to go up the Thames or the Mississippi and shoot the English or the Americans into heaven against their will.

As to drinks, we are naturally moderate except as regarding tea. Owing to the comparative absence of distilled liquor, one very seldom sees drunkards in the streets. But tea-drinking is an art in itself. It amounts with some persons almost to a cult. There are special books about tea-drinking as there are special books about incense and wine and rocks for house decoration. More than any other human invention of this nature, the drinking of tea has coloured our daily life as a nation, and gives rise to the institution of tea-houses which are approximate equivalents of Western cafés for the common people. People drink tea in their homes and in the tea-houses, alone and in company, at committee meetings and at the settling of disputes. They drink tea before breakfast and at midnight. With a teapot, a Chinese is happy wherever he is. It is a universal habit, and it has no deleterious effect whatsoever, except in very rare cases, as in my native district where according to tradition some people have drunk themselves bankrupt. This is only possible with extremely costly tea, but the average tea is cheap, and the average tea in China is good enough for a prince. The best tea is mild and gives a "back-flavour" which comes after a minute or two, when its chemical action has set in on the salivary glands. Such good tea puts everybody in good humour.

I have no doubt that it prolongs Chinese lives by aiding their digestion and maintaining their equanimity of temper.

The selection of tea and spring water is an art in itself. I give here an example of a scholar in the beginning of the seventeenth century, Chang Tai, who wrote thus about his art of tasting tea and spring water, in which he was a great connoisseur with very few rivals in his time:

Chou Molung often spoke to me in enthusiastic terms about the tea of Min Wenshui. In September of a certain year, I came to his town, and when I arrived, I called on him at Peach Leaves Ferry. It was already afternoon, and Wenshui was not at home. He came back late and I found him to be an old man. We had just opened our conversation when he rose suddenly and said that he had left his stick somewhere and went out again. I was determined not to miss this chance of having a talk with him, so I waited. After a long while, Wenshui came back, when it was already night, and he stared at me, saying, "Are you still here? What do you want to see me for?" I said, "I have heard about your name so long, and am determined to have a drink with you to-day before I go!" Wenshui was pleased, and then he rose to prepare the tea himself. In a wonderfully short time it was ready. Then he led me into a room, where everything was neat and tidy, and I saw over ten kinds of Chingch'i pots and Hsüanyao and Ch'engyao teacups, which were all very rare and precious. Under the lamplight, I saw that the colour of the tea was not distinguishable from that of the cups, but a wonderful fragrance assailed my nostrils, and I felt ever so happy. "What is this tea?" I asked. "Langwan," Wenshui replied. I tasted it again and said, "Now don't deceive me. The method of preparation is Langwan, but the tea-leaves are not Langwan." "What is it then?" asked Wenshui smilingly. I tasted it again and said, "Why is it so much like Lochieh tea?" Wenshui was quite struck by my answer and said, "Marvellous! Marvellous!" "What water is it?" I asked. "Huich'üan," he said. "Don't try to make fun of me," I said again. "How can Huich'üan water be carried here over a long distance,

and after the shaking on the way still retain its keenness?" So Wenshui said, "I shan't try to deceive you any
longer. When I take Huich'üan water, I dig a well, and wait
at night until the new current comes, and then take it up. I
put a lot of mountain rocks at the bottom of the jar, and
during the voyage I permit only sailing with the wind, but
no rowing. Hence the water still keeps its edge. This
water is therefore better even than ordinary Huich'üan
water, not to speak of water from other springs." Again he
said, "Marvellous! Marvellous!" and before he had finished
his sentence, he went out again. Soon he came back with
another pot, and asked me to taste it. I said, "Its fragrance
is strong, and its flavour is very mild. This must be spring
tea, while the one we just had must be autumn tea." Then
Wenshui burst into laughter and said, "I am a man of
seventy, and yet have never met a tea connoisseur like you."
After that, we remained fast friends.

That art is now almost gone, except among a few old art-
lovers and connoisseurs. It used to be very difficult to get good
tea on the Chinese national railways, even in the first-class
carriages, where Lipton's tea, probably the most unpalatable
to my taste, was served *with milk and sugar*. When Lord Lytton
visited Shanghai he was entertained at the home of a prominent
rich Chinese. He asked for a cup of Chinese tea, and he could
not get it. He was served Lipton's, with milk and sugar.

But enough has been said to show that the Chinese, in their
moments of sanity, know essentially how to live. The art of
living is with them a second instinct and a religion. Whoever
said that the Chinese civilization is a spiritual civilization is a
liar.

EPILOGUE

I. THE END OF LIFE

IN the general survey of Chinese art and Chinese life, the conviction must have been forced upon us that the Chinese are past masters in the art of living. There is a certain whole-hearted concentration on the material life, a certain zest in living, which is mellower, perhaps deeper, anyway just as intense as in the West. In China the spiritual values have not been separated from the material values, but rather help man in a keener enjoyment of life as it falls to our lot. This accounts for our joviality and our incorrigible humour. A heathen can have a heathenish devotion to the life of the present and envelop both spiritual and material values in one outlook, which it is difficult for a Christian to imagine. We live the life of the senses and the life of the spirit at the same moment, and see no necessary conflict. For the human spirit is used to beautify life, to extract its essence, perhaps to help it overcome ugliness and pain inevitable in the world of our senses, but never to escape from it and find its meaning in a life hereafter. When Confucius said, in reply to a question by a disciple on death, "Don't know life—how know death?" he expressed there a somewhat bourgeois, unmetaphysical and practical attitude toward the problems of life and knowledge which has characterized our national life and thinking.

This standpoint establishes for us a certain scale of values. In every aspect of knowledge and of living, the test of life holds. It accounts for our pleasures and our antipathies. The test of life was with us a racial thought, wordless and needing no definition or giving of reasons. It was that test of life which, instinctively I think, guided us to distrust civic civilization and uphold the rural ideal in art, life and letters, to dislike religion in our rational moments, to play with Buddhism but never quite accept its logical conclusions, and to hate mechanical ingenuity. It was that instinctive trust in life that gave us a robust common sense in looking at life's kaleidoscopic changes and the myriad vexatious problems of the intellect which we rudely ignored. It enabled us to see life steadily and see life whole, with no great distortions of values. It taught us some simple wisdom, like respect for old age and the joys of domestic life, acceptance of life, of sex and of sorrow. It made us lay emphasis on certain common virtues, like endurance, industry, thrift, moderation and pacificism. It prevented the development of freakish extreme theories and the enslaving of man by the products of his own intelligence. It gave us a sense of values, and taught us to accept the material as well as the spiritual goods of life. It taught us that, after all is said and done, human happiness is the end of all knowledge. And we arrange ourselves to make our lives happy on this planet, under whatever vicissitudes of fortune.

We are an old nation. The eyes of an old people see in its past and in this changing modern life much that is superficial and much that is of true meaning to our lives. We are a little cynical about progress, and we are a little bit indolent, as are all old people. We do not want to race about in a field for a ball; we prefer to saunter along willow banks to listen to the bird's song and the children's laughter. Life is so precarious that when we know something truly satisfies us, we hold on to it tight, as a mother hugs her baby close to her breast in a dark, stormy night. We have really no desire for exploring the South Pole or scaling the Himalayas. When Westerners do that, we ask, "What do you do that for? Do you have to go to the South Pole to be happy?" We go to the movies and theatres, but in the heart of our hearts we feel that a real child's laughter gives us as much real joy and happiness as an imaginary child's laughter on the screen. We compare the two and we stay at home. We do not believe that kissing one's own wife is necessarily insipid, and that other people's wives are necessarily more beautiful because they are other people's wives. We do not ache to reach the foot of the mountain when we are in the middle of the lake, and we do not ache to be at the top of the hill when we are at its foot. We drink what wine there is in the pot and enjoy what scenery there is before our eyes.

So much of life is merely a farce. It is sometimes just as well to stand by and look at it and smile, better perhaps than to take part in it. Like a dreamer awakened, we see life, not with the romantic colouring of yesternight's dream but with a saner vision. We are more ready to give up the dubious, the glamorous and the unattainable, but at the same time to hold on to the few things that we know will give us happiness. We always go back to nature as an eternal source of beauty and of true and deep and lasting happiness. Deprived of progress and of national power, we yet throw open our windows and listen to cicadas or to falling autumn leaves and inhale the fragrance of chrysanthemums, and over the top there shines the autumn moon, and we are content.

For we are now in the autumn of our national life. There comes a time in our lives, as nations and as individuals, when we are pervaded by the spirit of early autumn, in which green is mixed with gold and sadness is mixed with joy, and hope is mixed with reminiscence. There comes a time in our lives when the innocence of spring is a memory and the exuberance of summer a song whose echoes faintly remain in the air, when, as we look out on life, the problem is not how to grow but how to live truly, not how to strive and labour but how to enjoy the precious moments we have, not how to squander our energy but how to conserve it in preparation for the coming winter. A sense of having arrived somewhere, of having settled and found out what we want. A sense of having achieved something also, precious little compared with its past exuberance, but still something, like an autumn forest shorn of its summer glory but retaining such of it as will endure.

I like spring, but it is too young. I like summer, but it is too proud. So I like best of all autumn, because its leaves are a little yellow, its tone mellower, its colours richer, and it is tinged a little with sorrow and a premonition of death. Its golden richness speaks not of the innocence of spring, nor of the power of summer, but of the mellowness and kindly wisdom of approaching age. It knows the limitations of life and is content. From a knowledge of those limitations and its richness of experience emerges a symphony of colours, richer than all, its green speaking of life and strength, its orange speaking of golden content and its purple of resignation and death. And the moon shines over it, and its brow seems white with reflections, but when the setting sun touches it with an evening glow, it can still laugh cheerily. An early mountain breeze brushes by and sends its shivering leaves dancing gaily to the ground, and you do not know whether the song of the falling leaves is the song of laughter or of parting tears. For it is the Song of the Spirit of Early Autumn, the spirit of calm and wisdom and maturity, which smiles at sorrow itself and praises the exhilarating, keen, cool air—the Spirit of Autumn so well expressed by Hsin Ch'ichi:

> In my young days,
>   I had tasted only gladness,
> But loved to mount the top floor,
> But loved to mount the top floor,
>   To write a song pretending sadness.
>
> And now I've tasted
>   Sorrow's flavours, bitter and sour,
> And can't find a word,
> And can't find a word,
>   But merely say, "What a gold autumn hour!"

II. REAL CHINA

[*The following must not be taken as reflecting on the National Government, but rather on the immensity of the task which the Government is faced with in its gigantic work of evolving order out of chaos.*]

But let us be honest. It would be easy for a sinologue to paint a picture of idealized China, the China of blue porcelain bowls and the exquisite figures on the blue porcelain bowls, and the China of silk scrolls and the happy scholars sitting under pine trees on the scrolls. It would be easy to say with the sinologue: Even if Japan should conquer China for a few centuries, what of it? A Chinese cannot say: What of it? For we are living in a real China, not the China of blue porcelain bowls and exquisite silk scrolls, but a China in the midst of pangs and throes of labour, a China facing the collapse of an empire and a civilization, a China of living millions of toiling humanity, with a desire to work and to live, struggling against floods and famines and bandit-soldiers and a bandit-gentry, and living in a state of chaos without meaning, turmoil without direction, unrest without change, verbiage without conviction, action without purpose, and misery without hope. And if one is a Chinese, one feels like saying with Hamlet that the time is sadly out of joint and cursed are we born to set it right, or crying out with the Hebrews, "O Lord! How long?" and it is a cry of despair which is not mere petulance, but a despair based on an intimate knowledge of present-day China as no foreigners know it.

Paint as one will a glorious picture of dream-China, the China of her classics and philosophy and art, sooner or later one will have to face the puzzle of a real China, and perhaps through a process of long and painful thought, demand of the past an answer to the present, and demand of the present a meaning for the future. To glorify the past and paint the future is easy, to survey the present and emerge with some light and understanding is difficult. For between the glorious past and the possibly glorious future there lies a valley, and one has to descend in order to ascend. There is need for a robust realism more than for innocent faith, and more for an open-eyed wisdom than for patriotic ardour; for patriotic ardour is a cheap commodity and can be had at so many cents a catty in the form of printer's ink for the newspapers and blue paint for the yamen walls.

There is a Chinese saying that it is better to be a dog in peaceful times than be a man in times of unrest. All Chinese are wishing they were dogs in peaceful times, but they have not that luck. For we are living in a period of complete and unmitigated disillusionment, in a period of lack of faith, not only in the present revolution but in all revolutions. Mencius has said that the greatest sorrow is the death of the heart, and now truly the heart is dead. The optimism and cheerful idealism of 1926 have given place to the cynicism and disillusionment of 1934, a rumbling cynicism visible in all newspaper articles and private talks.

Slowly and laboriously has come the realization that the

more we change, the more we remain the same; that underlying the superficial changes of government system, the essential state of things, the essential corruption, futility and incompetence remain, and the essential hopelessness. To Western admirers of Marco Polo's Cathay, with its magnificence and grandeur, real China comes as a bad shock, and to the Chinese it comes as an admission of defeat. Slowly and painfully one realizes that we are still being ruled in the provinces by feudal chieftains with vulgar names and by their illiterate wives with sing-song names, and that the province is lucky which sees the type of enlightened despotism of General Han Fuchü, despite his woeful mediævalism. Acting as governor, magistrate, judge, jury and lawyer at the same time, he flogs the one and sends the other away with a hundred dollars according to his intuition and knowledge of physiognomy, and gives the people some sort of a rough justice and security. Then, all of a sudden, one realizes that we have but substituted a dozen disguised monarchies for a genuine one, and that the Revolution of 1911 was a success only in the sense of a racial revolution, that it only blew an empire into powder and left some ruins and débris and choking dust behind. Sometimes one wishes that China had remained a monarchy, and wonders with regret why Tseng Kuofan did not march his soldiers on Peking after suppressing the Taiping Rebellion, and found a Chinese dynasty, as he could very well have done, and as someone had advised him to do. But Tseng Kuofan was a Confucianist scholar with moral scruples, and it took an unscrupulous imperial brigand to found an imperial dynasty. So much the worse for the people of China!

Vain regrets. But how can one be blamed for these vain regrets, when one was brought up in a China before her complete disintegration? I can still recall the China of my childhood days, a China none too well ruled, it is true, but nevertheless a peaceful China. The greed and corruption and incompetence of the Manchu Government were the same, and some officials squeezed more than the others, but the worst ones were impeached and deposed or sent to jail, for there was a system. There were good governors and bad governors, but they were educated mandarins, and not onion-eating, oath-swearing, and hell-breathing war-lords, masters unto themselves and ruling by the grace of their illiterate fists. There were good magistrates and bad magistrates, some whom the people loved and some whom the people feared, but those who overstepped their limits encountered "town strikes," and their case was reported to the governor or the Emperor, and they were dismissed, transferred or punished. Thus was there a system, however imperfect, and some sort of justice, however qualified, and where there was justice, there was peace. There were no civil wars, bandits were yet rare, and one could travel from one part of the province to another with security.

For old China was not the topsy-turvydom it is to-day. If taxation was not based on the consent of the people, it was based on custom and usage, which was the real law of the land, and the farmers knew what they had to pay in spring and what they had to pay in autumn. One had not yet heard of the coffin tax, the wedding-sedan-chair tax[1] and the pig-intercourse tax, the pig-birth tax, the young-pig tax, the pig-trough tax, the pig-weighing tax, the pig-butchery tax, and the pork-in-the-restaurant tax and finally the pork-after-the-digestion-and-in-the-toilet tax.[2]   One had not yet heard of the righteousness tax and the benevolence tax and the civic welfare tax and the red-hot patriotism tax, and the house-number tax, and there was no "laziness tax" to punish the farmers who failed to plant opium. The farmers of China did not have to sell their wives and daughters to pay the tax, as some farmers of Kiangpei are doing; they were not forbidden by soldiers to reap their harvest as a reprisal for failure to pay a new tax, as the farmers of Fanyu *hsien* in Kwangtung were forbidden by their magistrate in the autumn of 1934. People were not taxed thirty years ahead, as the people of Szechuen now are;[3]   they were not subjected to farm surtaxes thirty times the regular farm tax, as is being done in Kiangsi.[4]   The farmers were not compelled

[1] In southern Fukien.

[2] These various taxes are known in Swatow and Hankow.

[3] See the various numbers of the *Szechuen Monthly*, 1934.

[4] Wang Chingwei, speaking on the ninth anniversary of Dr. Sun's death, March 12, 1934, said: "Investigation conducted by the Rural Rehabilitation Commission last year showed that the farm surtax collected in different provinces sometimes amounted to from 25 to 31 times the regular farm tax." (*China Press*, March 13, 1934.)

to pay taxes above their means and then taken to prison for failure to turn in the money and flogged so that you could hear their cries and moans all night, as you can hear the farmers of Shensi being flogged and crying and moaning in jail at night now.[1] The poor people of China, the most misruled nation on earth, who are caught in a whirl of forces they cannot understand, but who abide it all with an indomitable industry and patience and real goodness which must eventually triumph. Let them turn bandits, when their last cow is sold. Let them turn beggars, when their last chattel has been taken away from them. The urge to work and to live rises indomitable, and they still keep their good humour, and for their goodness and their good humour, God will still love them.

Surely there has been a dislodgement, a dislocation of national life and thought somewhere in a country which has known national greatness, but which is to-day ashamed of itself. Some maladjustment, or maladjustments, of a profound order, which disturb the mental balance and produce a temporary delirium, as if the spirit had left the body and the body made only futile, meaningless gestures. A madness and a loss of restraint and all decency, produced by a loss of national self-confidence, as if there were a common foreboding of evil, and man's follies and evil passions are let loose in an each-man-for-himself and scramble-as-one-scramble-can fight, the goal of which is the buying of a house and a car to live in security in the foreign settlements, and the holding of a large account in the Hongkong and Shanghai Banking Corporation. For surely a country is mad when some high officials and guardians of the Peiping National Museum cannot take their eyes off those national treasures until they have sold them to the highest bidders and converted them into cash in their private pockets, and when these officials can safely reside somewhere and defy the law court when they are publicly prosecuted. Surely a country is mad when a general, who lost the whole Jehol territory without putting up the pretence of a fight, but used two hundred military trucks to cart off his concubines and his treasures, is pardoned by the National Government; when

[1] According to a report by Professor Hsü Pingch'ang, published in a 1933 number of the *Independent Review*, edited by Dr. Hu Shih.

so many generals leave their arms and ammunition behind during a defeat, but take care to cart away their store of opium, for with opium they can get gold, and with gold they can buy themselves back into power; when the farmers are compelled to plant opium rather than rice in order to maintain a rabble and never-paid army; and when a famed agricultural country is compelled to import millions of *taels* of rice and wheat from abroad every year, and when in the midst of all this insanity the people, whose interests are immediately affected, cannot say "no" to their rulers and oppressors. Surely something is wrong with the body politic, and the nation, as a nation, must have lost all its moral values and its sense of right and wrong.

For it is apparent that a system of ideas has collapsed, ideas moral and ideas political. Old China had a system of government and a system of moral ideas which were adequate to maintain the national life, but which to-day are thrown out of their bearings and perhaps do more harm than good. Who would buy patience? Let them come to China, for patience in this country can be had for the asking. And who would buy meekness and humility and all those nice Christian herd virtues that Christendom has not learned after two millenniums of praying and psalm-singing and sermonizing? Let them come to China, for in pagan China these Christian virtues are as abundant as sands in the desert and as crocodiles in the Ganges. For a change of tempo has come over the national life, and instead of the primitive, patriarchal heyday of peace and leisure and courtesy, we are living in an age of haste and gold and self-assertion, and all the patience and meekness and humility that adorned the ancient pattern of life cannot retard, but rather must hasten, its collapse.

It seems the race cannot adjust itself to a new world, with healthier, more aggressive people all around and demanding a new ethics to suit the new tempo of life; and, fearful and angry with itself, has lost its calm and poise and good sense for which it was so renowned. It has, it seems only so recently, lost its ethos and its national self-confidence, and from this loss of self-confidence it has become freakish, bad-tempered, oversensitive, and does and says many foolish things, like an unhappy husband or an old man suffering from hardened veins. The nation frisks and frets, and alternates between megalomania and melancholia, and easily becomes hysterical. This is especially observable in the more articulate, I dare not say more intelligent, class, who are wont to get into fits of excitability, quite natural because they are fits of an overwhelming sense of helplessness, and then settle down to a permanent depression of spirits. Some of these scholars are ashamed of our own country, of our farmers and coolies, and of our own customs and language and arts and literature, and would like to cover China up with a huge shroud as if it were a stinking carcass, and allow foreigners to see only white-collared, English-speaking Chinese like themselves, whereas the common people merely suffer and carry on.

Then once in a while the subconscious leaps to the fore, and the ruling classes know that someone, not themselves of course, is running the country to perdition, and they turn moralists, and panaceas for "saving the country" are offered. Some advocate salvation by learning the use of machine-guns, another by frugality and the wearing of sandals, another by dancing and wholesale introduction of Western life, another by selling and buying national goods, another by physical culture through good old boxing, another by learning Esperanto, another by saying Buddhist masses, another by reintroducing the Confucian classics in school, and another by "throwing the classics into the toilet for thirty years." To hear them discussing the salvation of the country would be like listening to a council of quack doctors at a patient's deathbed. It would be humorous if it were not so pathetic. Since a fundamental reform of the political life would mean the abolition of militarism and militarist interference with politics, and the weeding out of political corruption would mean the abolition of the privileges of the ruling class and sending ninety-five per cent of them to jail, both of which are obnoxious to themselves, they have turned themselves into moral uplifters and preached old morality which can injure and give offence to nobody. One sees everywhere a tumult and chaos, a tumult and chaos of the spirit more than of the body, a madness without method in its sham progressiveness as well as in its sham nationalism. The highest officials of the Government alternate between initiating lama prayers for the salvation of the country and suppressing the traditional boatrace of the Dragon Festival by branding it as a superstition. The provincial governments, who find it so difficult to make any real achievements in reconstruction, find themselves very busy regulating the costumes of men and women, for the girls' sleeves are too short in Kwangsi, and the men's gowns are too long in Szechuen ("because in this period of national crisis, we must save more cloth"), and the women's hair should not be curled in Shantung, and the boys' heads must be shaved close in certain schools in Hunan, and the girls' breasts should not be bound in Chekiang, and high-collared dress and high-heeled shoes should not be worn by the prostitutes in Nanking, and women should not keep male dogs and lead them through the streets in Peiping.[1]

All this confusion, this busy triviality, this madness and hypocrisy, and these exaggerations of pride and solicitude seem to indicate the existence of a wish unfulfilled, and a conflict of will and character. Custom and convention, which are the mainstay of any society, are no longer held in honour; the old can no longer command the respect of the young, and the young grow over-critical of the old; a deep chasm exists between the growing generation and mature age. Culture, which is the fruit of a continuity of life and thought, is no longer possible, and criticism, which is the sole guardian of modern culture, and which should keep a watchful eye over the flux of life, lies prostrate before a task too big for itself, while cheerful, robust good sense, for which China was so distinguished, buries its head in shame. Man has something undernourished and neurasthenic, something partial and incomplete and eternally frustrated about him.

III. A QUEST FOR LEADERSHIP

When I ponder over all this confusion, this meanness and insincerity, I feel like Gabriel asking Lot: Where are the good

[1] See the various 1933 numbers of the *Analects Fortnightly*.

men of China, and how many are they? Are there a hundred? Are there fifty? Are there ten? Are there five? Or rather I wonder how I would answer Gabriel myself. Are these mutilated examples of undernourished neurasthenic half-men, so much in evidence with their busy triviality, all we have left of man in modern China, so that a nation of four hundred million souls is condemned to carry on like a flock without a shepherd? Where have the good men hidden themselves, as if in shame? But I am reminded that the good men in China have always hidden themselves, have in fact always wanted to hide themselves in wine and women and song, or for the less emotional souls, in going back to the farm and living a simple life of nature. I am led then to ponder over the lack of constitutional protection in China, how much this tremendous fact alone has altered profoundly the general outlook on life of the nation, has influenced its very philosophy of life, so that the philosophy of life is an outcome of the social and political environment rather than vice versa, and, through that change in philosophy of life from activity to passivity, how much goodness and constructive endeavour have been lost to the nation, and real progress thereby retarded.

Man, it seems, has been more sinned against than sinning in China. For I remember Sung Chiang and the host of good souls who turned bandits in the end of the Northern Sung Dynasty. For these were brave glorious bandits, men who could afford to be good and chivalrous because physically they did not need any constitutional protection. And I remember how every great poet expressed his contempt for society by taking to wine and nature, how Ch'ü Yüan in a rage jumped into the Hsiang River, and Li Po fell overboard in attempting to reach for the reflection of the moon, how T'ao Yüanming satisfied himself that his door was seldom opened to visitors and grass grew over his garden paths; how even great and upright Confucianists who retained a sense of right and wrong always ended in official banishment, how Su Tungp'o was exiled to Huangchow, Han Yü was exiled to Ch'aochow and Liu Chungyüan was exiled to Liuchow. I remember how another class of truly great souls grew impatient of the small official burden and retired to their poetry and their simple

village home; how Yüan Chunglang, Yüan Mei and Cheng
Panch'iao, one and all, avoided politics like poison and learned
to live at peace with their bowl of hot congee on a winter
morning and their bed-bugs and mosquitoes at night. I remember how in times of national misrule and disorder the good
scholars were hounded and their wives and children and
distant relatives were murdered *en masse*, as during the beginning of the Manchu Dynasty, and I begin to see how they
needed Buddhism, which some of them espoused, and the
negative philosophy of life, which all of them espoused.

Then I look over the modern times and see how the good
men, as in all countries, have abstained from politics; how
Wang Kuowei jumped into the lake of the Summer Palace,
and K'ang Yuwei spent the last years of his life in lonely
pride, and how Lusin shut himself up in dark and unmitigated
despair until the call for the literary revolution came, and how
Chang T'aiyen is to-day shutting himself up in Soochow, and
how Hu Shih, the student of Dewey and influenced by a more
progressive outlook, is pragmatizing and patching up the sores
of the people, without great enthusiasm, but still unwilling to
give up and turn China to the dogs—Hu Shih who, in a
moment of prophetic fury, cried out, "If China does not perish,
God is blind!" These are the good men of China who cannot
help the country, for man has sinned against man, and the
bad men have sinned against the good men, and the good men
need a simple cotton gown for disguise. Yet there are other
good men, not only five, not only fifty, but millions of them
suffering and carrying on, unsung and unheard of. The thought
wrings pity from the onlooker that there should be so many
good men and not a leader half the size of a Gandhi, that in
China individually men are more mature, but politically and
nationally we are as mere children. And I begin to seek for
the causes and ask for the way out.

I push the question further and ask: Why are we individually
mature but politically and nationally mere children? And
why, out of the millions of good men, are there so few great
leaders to lead the nation out of chaos? Have these potential
leaders been assassinated, caught the flu, or otherwise died an
untimely death? Or have they grown old and feeble at forty;

have they run against a social background too powerful and all-pervading for human reform, temporized, become frustrated and given themselves up for lost, unhappy souls, like the beauty in Po Chüyi's song who became a shopkeeper's wife in middle age? Then I realize that perhaps the other minority were lucky, that they were indeed those God loved who died young and left a good name. Yet history seems to deny this acceptance: history reveals and the Confucian theory of imitation affirms that in times of national crisis it is the great men who change the destiny of a nation. But then I remember that in the Chinese wheel of success, many great men have been ground small. It would be easy to blame the system or the collapse of a system, and not the men. It would be easy to expound with a materialistic dialectic the logical outcome of militarism. It would be easy to demonstrate that the militarists are all good men, made victims of an unhappy environment, forced by the logic of their position to tax the people and strengthen themselves against their rivals, and exposed to a temptation too much for any human being to resist. Yet I remember how Japan passed through the same phase of militarism, triumphantly led by a great man, Prince Ito. But then, you may say, Japan is small, and one can lay the blame to the size of our nation. Then I remember the example of Russia, with the size of half a continent, and peopled with a peasantry just as poor and illiterate as the Chinese people, and a bourgeoisie just as indifferent and a gentry just as corrupt. Yet there was vigour in those old bones, and Old Russia shook off its old carcass and emerged the youngest child of the family of nations, radiant with hope and energy. And I say, Bah! with the materialistic dialectic! For if the times have sinned against the great men in China, the great men have sinned more against the times.

The search for causes always leads back to a search for leadership, for courageous and honest leadership, for with Confucius I believe that great men, by their example, can change the whole morale of a nation, as Prince Ito did in Japan. I remember how in 1926 the whole nation was set on fire by faith in the memory of a great leader, when a young party seemed to have emerged to lead the nation out of chaos and despondency, how young men climbed over school walls and travelled a thousand miles to join a revolutionary army and gladly laid down their lives for the cause of a regenerated China; how only recently, in 1931, the guns of the Nineteenth Route Army set the whole nation on fire once more, and the young and old gave unto their last penny and showed a mettle that no one had dreamed existed in the nation. Old China seemed in a moment to have found her soul again. Then the fire was dampened: it flickered, went out and left a darkness behind, for want of someone to tend and nourish it. If there were one, the smouldering ashes could be kindled into a glowing flame again, even now.

IV. THE WAY OUT

I turn my thoughts to other lines. It seems, then, that our steps are indeed caught in a hopeless tangle of dark realities, but it also seems to be otherwise. For here is a nation whose potential possibilities are yet unexplored, but lacking in something to let loose these potential powers. Here is a nation of fine soldiers but bad captains, fine business men but bad business policies, fine friends but bad clubhouses, fine citizens but bad statesmen, and fine democratic men but a bad republic. It only needs a system to put the nation in running order, a something which the nation woefully lacks. What is that thing? Big words with capital letters shoot across my mind, like Democracy, Morality, Grit, Spunk, Efficiency, A Good Executioner. . . . But what is Democracy? The Chinese people are, and always have been, the most democratic, the most casteless, the most self-respecting on earth. And what is even Socialism? Have we not had the most advanced form of Anarchism, a Village Socialism, automatic, self-ruling, and a central government on top only to collect taxes and render justice? "The heaven is high and the Emperor is far away." It was even so always. Replace the word "guild" with the word "village," and there you have the most advanced type of Socialism you want. But that, too, I give up, for aeroplanes are making Village Socialism impossible, and the family solidarity and the village solidarity have been broken up. I cannot accept democracy in the sense of parliamentarism, for I know full well that a Chinese M.P. is not an M.P.; he cannot be if he is a Chinese, for an M.P. in China is an "official," too, in the most pathetic sense of the word, and we have too many of them, so why bother to elect them at the cost of five thousand dollars a ticket, for which we will eventually have to pay?

Nor can I accept, for that matter, any *ism*, for I have seen how foreign *isms*, even the most fast-dyed and fadeless kind, lose colour in a Chinese laundry, and give off only a stinking laundry steam odour. Nor can I accept another revolution, for I have heard the familiar boom of guns and the racket of fusillades, and they have ceased to scare me now, for the boom of guns soon ceased and the racket that sounded like a fusillade seemed more and more like firecrackers in the next street, and I learned that it was only Mr. Yang celebrating his assumption of a new post. Nor can I accept Moral Upliftism, for I have had enough of it and it has ceased to amuse me. This nation of moral uplifters, with their eternal pagan sermonizing for two thousand years, has not yet rescued itself from rampant official corruption and heartless oppression of the people. Besides, the moral uplifter, as I have pointed out, is a selfish man, not only because he wants to uplift other people's morality but because he is avoiding going to jail himself. He would have to go to jail if he stopped preaching moral uplift and began talking a government by law. The moral uplifter erects a *pailou* in honour of other moral uplifters after their death, if they turn out to be gentlemen, but inevitably fails to send other moral uplifters to prison if they turn out, as most of them do, to be thieves. And what he does not do unto others he does not want done unto himself. Therein lie the gaiety and pleasantness of Moral Upliftism.

Meanwhile the country must live; it cannot be allowed to sink lower and lower under foreign domination. A temporary national extinction, even with eventual restoration to independence, is cold comfort and no real consolation. The people are being bled white and rendered homeless, and a ruthless, artificial process of moral and financial ruination of the Chinese countryside is going on at a gallop. Some way out must be found. If this great and fine people, with their indomitable industry and good humour, who only want peace and security, could only be let alone, free from the grip of the octopus Militarism, they would know how to save themselves. But who would free them from the octopus? Who would bell the cat? I asked myself this and turned back in despair. . . .

At last I thought of the Great Executioner, and the moment I saw him in my vision I knew he would save China. Here comes the Saviour, he with the great sword that would only obey Dame Justice's command, and that no one else could pull out of its place without her bidding, the sword that was drowned in a lake centuries ago. That lake where so many of the officials' heads should peacefully lie in, but where the sword is sunk now. The Great Executioner comes, and pulls that sword out of the deep, and he is preceded by drum-boys in blue uniform. *Dum—Dum—Dum!* the procession comes, and the trumpeters in yellow uniform proclaim the rule of the law. *Dum—Dum—Dum!* the procession comes from the country, approaching the town and down the main streets, and at the distant rumble of the drums and the sight of the banner, with Dame Justice sitting in state, and the Great Executioner with the gleaming sword by her side, the people cheer, but the mayor and the town councillors run away higgledy-piggledy and hide themselves. For behold, here the Saviour comes! The Great Executioner nails the banner of Justice on the city wall, and makes every one of them bow before it as they pass. And a notice is posted all over the city that whosoever says he is above the law and refuses to bow before the banner will be beheaded and his head will be thrown into the lake where the sword was sunk for so many hundreds of years. And he goes into the city temple and throws out their goddesses, whose names are Face, Fate and Favour, and converts it into a House of Justice. To this place he herds together the priests and councillors who ruled the city under their goddesses' names, and with the great sword he chops off their heads and commands that they be thrown, together with their goddesses, into the lake. For Face, Fate and Favour have plotted against Justice, and she hates them with the jealousy of a woman. And of those whose heads the Great Executioner chops off great is the number, many of them from distinguished families, and the lake is dyed red with their blood of iniquity. And, strange to say, in three days the relatives of the distinguished families who have robbed and betrayed the people behave like noble gentlemen, and the people are at last let alone to live in peace and security and the city prospers.

So, in my mind, I pictured the Saviour of China. I would believe in a revolution, any revolution, and in a party, any party, that would replace the present government by Face, Fate and Favour by a government by law. These three have made the rule of Justice and the weeding out of official corruption impossible. The only reason why official corruption remains is that we have never shot the officials, not one of them. We couldn't so long as these three goddesses still remain. The only way to deal with corruption in the officials is just to shoot them. The matter is really as simple as that. And democracy is an easy thing when we can impeach an official for breaking the law with a chance of winning the case. The people do not have to be trained for democracy, they will fall into it. When the officials are democratic enough to appear before a law court and answer an impeachment, the people can be made democratic enough overnight to impeach them. Take off from the people the incubus of official privilege and corruption and the people of China will take care of themselves. For greater than all the other virtues is the virtue of Justice, and this is what China wants. This is my faith and this is my conviction, won from long and weary thoughts.

That time will come, but it requires a change of ideology; the family-minded Chinese must be changed into social-minded Chinese, and the pet ideas, age-old, of face, favour and privilege and official success and robbing the nation to glorify the family must be overthrown. The process will be slow and laborious, how slow and laborious the preceding study of the whole mentality and cultural tradition of the race has shown. But that process is already at work, invisible, penetrating the upper and lower social strata, and as inevitable as dawn. For a time yet there will still be ugliness and pain, but after a while there will be calm and beauty and simplicity, the calm and beauty and simplicity which distinguished old China. But more than that, there will be justice, too. To that people of the Land of Justice, we of the present generation shall seem but like children of the twilight. I ask for patience from the friends of China, not from my countrymen, for they have too much of it. And I ask for hope from my countrymen, for to hope is to live.

APPENDICES

CHINESE DYNASTIES

Name	Dates	Centuries (approximate)	Remarks
(Mythical)	2697-2206 B.C.	XXVII-XXIII	Legendary
Hsia ..	2205-1784 B.C.	XXII-XIX	Together with Chou, called "Santai" or "Three Dynasties"
Shang (Yin)	1783-1123 B.C.	XVIII-XII	
Chou	1122-222 B.C.	XI-III	Classic period; Ch'unch'iu period 722-481; Chankuo period 403-221
Ch'in	221-207 B.C.	end of III	Reunified China
Han	206 B.C.-A.D. 219	II B.C.-A.D. II	"Eastern Han" from A.D. 25
Wei	220-264	middle III	Wei, Wu and Shu forming the "Three Kingdoms" from about A.D. 200
Ch'in	265-419	mid. III-IV	"Eastern Ch'in" from 317. Barbarians' kingdoms in North China 304-439
"N. & S." { Sung	420-478	} V-VI	These are called "North and South" Dynasties for distinction. Together with preceding Wu and Eastern Ch'in, called "Six Dynasties," a term referring to southern culture
Ch'i	479-510		
Liang	502-556		
Ch'en	557-588		
Sui	589-617	round A.D. 600	Reunified China
T'ang	618-906	VII-IX	
Liang	907-922	} first half X	These are called "Wutai," or "Five Dynasties" for distinction from other dynasties of the same name
T'ang	923-935		
Ch'in	936-946		
Han	947-950		
Chou	951-959		
Sung	960-1276	latter half X-XIII	"Southern Sung" from 1127 onward, with Northern China under Manchus and Mongols
Yüan (Mongol)	1277-1367	end of XIII-mid. XIV	Foreign rule
Ming	1368-1643	mid. XIV-mid. XVII	Restored to Chinese rule
Ch'ing (Manchu)	1644-1911	mid. XVII-XIX	Foreign rule
Republic	1911-	XX	

APPENDIX II

A Note on the Spelling and Pronunciation of Chinese Names.

A GREAT deal of confusion with regard to Chinese names has been caused by the lack of a consistent method of spelling, owing to the fact that some Chinese spell their surnames first and their personal names last (the Chinese way), and o hers spell their surnames last in the English fashion. Thus no one can tell whether one should address Chu Chin Chow as Mr. Chu or Mr. Chow.

This difficulty can be easily obviated, first, by consistently spelling the surname first and the personal name last, and secondly, by spelling the personal name, which usually consists of two syllables, as one bisyllabic word. There is no warrant for writing these two syllables separately any more than there is for spelling *Shanghai* as *Shang Hai*, or *Kuomintang* as *Kuo Min Tang*. In this book, all such personal names are consistently spelt as one bisyllabic word without hyphen, as *Wu Peifu, Su Tungp'o*. This method of spelling will help to make the names more easily recognizable. Try to spell *Mussolini, Nicaragua, Rabindranath* as *Mus So Li Ni, Ni Ca Ra Gua, Ra Bin Dra Nath*, and see the immediate loss in word-individuality. The mystification of Chinese names is entirely due to our own making.

In the pronunciation of Chinese names, the vowels *a, e, i, o, u* have their Latin values. The vowel *ŭ* in *tzŭ* and *ssŭ* is pronounced with the tongue held in essentially the same position as that for the consonants *tz* and *s*. The vowel *ih* in *shih, chih* is pronounced with the tongue held in essentially the same position as that for *ch* or *sh*. *Hs* comes before *i* and *ü*, but for all practical purposes may be pronounced just as an ordinary *sh*.

Aspiration is an important distinction in many pairs of Chinese consonants, as *p* and *p'*, *k* and *k'*. Pronounce the aspirated *p'* as the *p* in English *pan*, and the unaspirated *p* as the *p* in English *span*. Likewise contrast the *k* in *kin* and *skin*.

INDEX

CPSIA information can be obtained
at www.ICGtesting.com
Printed in the USA
BVHW031726010619
549899BV00001B/35/P